Oman
EXPLORER

EXPLORER
www.Explorer-Publishing.com

Passionately Publishing...

Oman Explorer 2005/2ⁿᵈ Edition

First Published 1999
Second Edition 2005   ISBN 976-8182-07-5

Copyright © Explorer Group Ltd, 1999, 2005
All rights reserved.

Front Cover Photograph — Pamela Grist

Printed and bound by Emirates Printing Press, Dubai, United Arab Emirates.

Explorer Publishing & Distribution
PO Box 34275, Zomorrodah Bldg, Za'abeel Rd, Dubai
United Arab Emirates
Phone   (+971 4) 335 3520
Fax   (+971 4) 335 3529
Email   Info@Explorer-Publishing.com
Web   www.Explorer-Publishing.com

Publishing
Publisher
Alistair MacKenzie
— *Alistair@Explorer-Publishing.com*

Editorial
Editors
Claire England
— *Claire@Explorer-Publishing.com*
Jane Roberts
Jane@Explorer-Publishing.com

Writer
David Quinn
— *David@Explorer-Publishing.com*

Authors
Lucie Cruickshank
Grace Todino-Gonguet
Elisendra Verges Vidal
Jacqueline Veen
Fiona Rowand
Marie Henning

Proofreader
Jo Holden-MacDonald

Research Manager
Tim Binks
— *Tim@Explorer-Publishing.com*

Researchers
Helga Becker
— *Helga@Explorer-Publishing.com*
Yolanda Singh
Yolanda@Explorer-Publishing.com

Design
Creative Manager
Pete Maloney
— *Pete@Explorer-Publishing.com*

Graphic Designers
Jayde Fernandes
— *Jayde@Explorer-Publishing.com*
Zainudheen Madathil
Zain@Explorer-Publishing.com
Sayed Muhsin
Muhsin@Explorer-Publishing.com
Jay Pillai
Jay@Explorer-Publishing.com

Photography
Pamela Grist
— *Pamela@Explorer-Publishing.com*

Sales & Advertising
Media Sales Manager
Alena Hykes
— *Alena@Explorer-Publishing.com*

Media Sales Executive
Laura Zuffa
— *Laura@Explorer-Publishing.com*

Sales/PR Administrator
Janice Menezes
— *Janice@Explorer-Publishing.com*

Distribution
Distribution Manager
Ivan Rodrigues
— *Ivan@Explorer-Publishing.com*

Distribution Supervisor
Abdul Gafoor
— *Gafoor@Explorer-Publishing.com*

Distribution Executives
Mannie Lugtu
— *Mannie@Explorer-Publishing.com*
Stephen Drilon
Stephen@Explorer-Publishing.com
Rafi Jamal
Rafi@Explorer-Publishing.com

Administration
Office Manager
Andrea Fust
— *Andrea@Explorer-Publishing.com*

Administrators
Enrico Maullon
— *Enrico@Explorer-Publishing.com*
Swati Sagar
Swati@Explorer-Publishing.com

Accounts Manager
Kamal Basha
— *Kamal@Explorer-Publishing.com*

Accounts Assistant
Sohail Anwar
— *Sohail@Explorer-Publishing.com*

IT & Web Manager
Joe Nellary
— *Joe@Explorer-Publishing.com*

Programmer
Smitha Sadanand
— *Smitha@Explorer-Publishing.com*

You Lucky People!

Like Dhofar's summer rain, the all-new Oman Explorer was a long time coming – but boy was it worth the wait. This mighty volume that you now hold is no mere guidebook, it's your lifestyle support system and worth its weight in frankincense and gold.

We assembled a motley crew of modern-day missionaries, resident in Oman since before they could remember, and released them into the wild armed with nothing more than a freshly sharpened pencil, a bloodhound's nose for sniffing out facts and bags of halwa and enthusiasm. Their brief was simple – go forth and explore, enquire and investigate, and don't stop until you've discovered everything there is to know about Oman. The result is this book, the ultimate insider's guide to getting things done and living life to the full in this beautiful and beguiling country.

So you'll find a General Info chapter giving a quick geography and history lesson, lots of fascinating facts and figures and details of where to stay if you're just passing through. The New Residents chapter is for those who plan to stay a little longer, with advice on visas and vital documents, housing, healthcare, education and work. The Exploring chapter travels the length and breadth of the country lifting the lid on all there is to see and do, while Activities leaves you with absolutely no excuse for staying in and watching telly all weekend. The Shopping chapter takes you by the purse and leads you through the souks (and malls) of Oman, while Going Out reviews all manner of eateries, drinkeries and danceries!

Consider this book as your very own tour guide, your bureaucracy battler, your personal shopper, your partner in pastimes, and your gourmet guru.

In fact, the Oman Explorer is your new best friend - treat it well and it'll never let you down.

Enjoy!

The Explorer Team

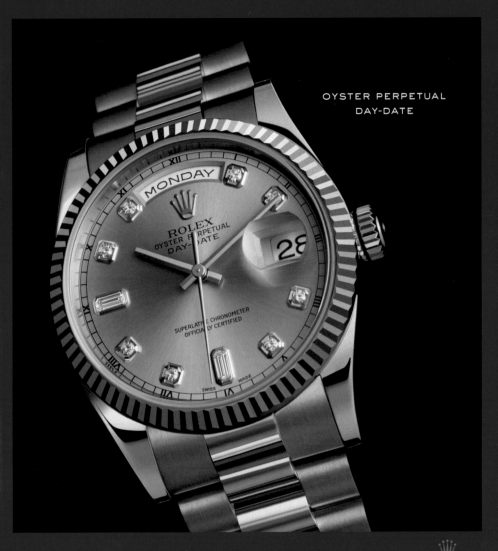

OYSTER PERPETUAL
DAY-DATE

WWW.ROLEX.COM **ROLEX**

From Oman to Germany four times a week.
Over 120,000 people touching down daily.
And that very first unforgettable time.
All for this one moment.

Flying has always been fascinating. And with impeccable standards onboard and on the ground, you can rely on us to keep it that way. After all, your trust is our greatest reward. Thank you for flying with Lufthansa! For further information and reservations, please call your nearest Travel Agent, Lufthansa on +968 24796692 or visit **www.oman.lufthansa.com**

There's no better way to fly.

A STAR ALLIANCE MEMBER

BE THE FIRST
TO EXPLORE THE BEST

Be the first to share the latest and the best entertainment with the whole family.

Cleopatra's Palace
on The Discovery Civilization Channel

CSI
new season on TV Land

Kill Bill
on Home Cinema in July

Everybody Loves Raymond
on Paramount

WWE Smackdown
on TV Land

Save with one of our great offers. Call now for more information.

Call now for the best entertainment

- Mustafa Sultan Secom **607 277**
- Oman Computer Engineers **708 000**
- Shanfari & Partners, Salala **292 480**
- Oman International Electronics & Trading Co. L.L.C **694 906**

SHOWTIME.
Brings you the Best in entertainment

www.showtimearabia.com

Bringing more to life

In everything we do we strive to bring our customers that little bit extra which ends up making a big difference. So whether you're booking a business trip or a holiday, visiting our retail shops or having a night out in Uptown, you're guaranteed world-class products, service and value.

oua

bringing more to life

CONSUMER 24786368 | TRAVEL 24700363 | RETAIL 24798235 | UPTOWN 24706020

THE EXPLORER FAMILY

Alistair MacKenzie
Media Mogul

If only Alistair could take the paperless office one step further and achieve the officeless office he would be the happiest publisher alive. Remote access from a remote spot within the Hajar mountains would suit this intrepid explorer. The only problem could be staffing – unless he can persuade Midnight Cafeteria to deliver!

Claire England
Poached Ed

No longer able to freeload off the fact that she once appeared in a Robbie Williams video, Claire now puts her creative skills to better use – looking up rude words in the dictionary! A child of English nobility, Claire is quite the lady – unless she's down at Jimmy Dix.

David Quinn
Sharp Shooter

After a short stint as a children's TV presenter was robbed from David because he developed an allergy to sticky back plastic, he made his way to sandier pastures. Now that he's thinking outside the box, nothing gets past the man with the sharpest pencil in town.

Alena Hykes
Sales Supergirl

A former bond girl, Alena speaks more languages than we've had hot dinners and she's not afraid to be heard. She dresses to kill and has a sales pitch to die for with everything she touches turning to gold – must be that Goldfinger!

Pete Maloney
Graphic Guru

Image conscious he may be, but when Pete has his designs on something you can bet he's gonna get it! He's the king of chat up lines, ladies – if he ever opens a conversation with 'D'you come here often?' then brace yourself for the Maloney magic.

Zainudheen Madathil
Map Captain

Often confused with football star Zinedine Zidane because of the equally confusing name, Zain tackles design with the mouse skills of a star striker. Maps are his goal and despite getting red-penned a few times, when he shoots, he scores!

But we couldn't have done it without....
Caroline Dempsey, Darren Murphy, Elaine Peckover Jones, Elisendra Verges Vidal, Grace Todino-Gonguet, Jane Bickmore, Lucie Cruickshank,

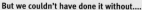

Sayed Muhsin

Design Drummer

They say it's the quiet ones that you want to watch and Mushin is no exception. Laying low behind his layouts, what many of you don't know is that he used to be the drummer for Led Zepellin. Now he drums up designs that are music to our eyes.

Yolanda Singh

Fast Talker

With an iron will and a heart of gold, Yoyo manages to bounce back from every hurdle and still finds time for a good gossip. If you want to get a memo around she's far quicker than email.

Jayde Fernandes

Pop Idol

When he isn't secretly listening to Britney Spears or writing to Blue to become their fifth member, Jayde actually manages to get a bit of designing done (but not before he has got through his well practised list of 'the dog ate my homework' excuses). He's The Man, and all because the ladies love his in-tray!

Janice Menezes

Materials Girl

How does Janice manage to whiz round the office so efficiently chasing ads and artwork and generally keeping on top of the books? Rollerskates of course! When she's not practising her toe-stops, she spreads the Explorer message to over a thousand people a day.

Jane Roberts

Word Wizard

meticulous is her middle name and after creatively shrivelling in a dingy government office, Jane thankfully found her way to the Explorer offices with her red pen in tow. She's learning by other people's mistakes and teaching the rest of us that quantity and quality can live in harmony.

Helga Becker

Fantasy Foodist

From alfresco eateries to burger joints, and cocktail bars to nightclubs, Helga has been around the Dubai block a few times (in the culinary sense of course). A walking restaurant and bar guide, Helga is the goddess of going out and makes Explorer look good enough to eat.

Marie Henning, Michael Nicholls, Miki Binks, Namrata Sardar, Paul Francis, Peter D'Onghia, Rania Adwan, Teresa Vallancey

Tim Binks

Cookie Monster

After flying the Explorer nest at the beginning of the Millennium in search of sushi, Tim eventually tired of egg rolls and flew back with the promise of a more calorific career. When the cookie crumbles Tim is the man to gather the pieces – as long as it's chocolate chip of course! Thankyou please.

Sohail Butt

Abacus Ace

By day he may be cooking the books but by night Sohail cooks up a storm at the local Karaoke bar – while his routine includes the entire back catalogue of Abba hits, it's his heartfelt rendition of 'Money Money Money' that really brings the house down.

Nadia D'Souza

Mother Hen

Poor Nadia has the displeasure of sitting opposite the toilet, but like the Explorer adopted mother that she is she soon takes charge of any sticky toilet situations – humorous or not. When she isn't giving the boys a telling off, Nadia can be found navigating new recruits through telephonic technology.

Mannie Lugtu

Distribution Demon

When the travelling circus rode into town their master juggler, Mannie, decided to leave the Big Top and explore Dubai instead. He may have swapped his balls for our books but his juggling skills still come in handy.

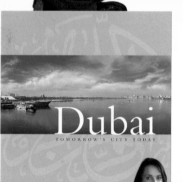

Pamela Grist

Happy Snapper

If a picture can speak a thousand words then Pam's photos say a lot about her – through her lens she manages to find the beauty in everything – even this motley crew. And when the camera never lies, thankfully Photoshop can.

Laura Zuffa

Travelling Salesgirl

Laura's passport is covered in more stamps than Kofi Annan's, and there isn't a city, country or continent that she won't travel to. With a smile that makes grown men weep, our girl on the frontlines always brings home the beef bacon!

Kamal Basha

Chief Calculator

Kamal has the best bottom line in Dubai and makes many an accountant jealous with his mean index finger. In fact, he's been the UAE calculator champion in the Mathematic Games for the last three years, and now has the world title in his sights. Go Kamal!

Ivan Rodrigues

Head Honcho

After making a mint in the clip board market, Ivan came to Explorer out of the goodness of his heart. Distributing joy across the office he is the man with the master plan – if only we could understand his spreadsheets.

Abdul Gafoor

Ace Circulator

After a successful stint on Ferrari's Formula One team Gafoor made a pitstop at our office and decided to stay. As Explorer's most cheerful employee, he's the only driver in Dubai yet to succumb to road rage.

Rafi Jamal

Soap Star

After a walk on part in The Bold and the Beautiful, Rafi swapped the Hollywood Hills for the Hajar Mountains. Although he left the glitz behind, he is frequently spotted practising his pensive to-camera pose in the office's bathroom mirror.

We like to think that our team is like no other. Many media and publishing companies may sell you an image of dedication and efficiency when in fact it is all work and no play with an unhealthy dose of office politics. We, on the other hand just work hard... then play hard! Our hearts and souls are laid bare on the plentiful pages that follow. The end result is books that we're proud of and that you will hopefully put in pride of place!

Stephen Drilon

Record Breaker

Not to be outdone by the Burj tower, Stephen sits alongside Nakheel in the record books for successfully stacking the highest book tower ever constructed, even if it did only stand for 0.03 seconds. He has now moved his sights on to calendar castles.

Joe Nellary

Head Hacker

While we once blamed the system for all our technical hiccups we can now turn to Joe for much needed support. And if he doesn't have the answer a bit of techno jargon fools us into thinking he does.

Explorer Insiders' City & Country Guides

These are no ordinary guidebooks. They are your lifestyle support system, medicine for boredom, ointment for obstacles, available over the counter and prescribed by those in the know. An essential resource for residents, tourists and business people, they cover the what, the how, the why, the where and the when. All you have to do is read!

Abu Dhabi Explorer

The ultimate guide to the UAE's capital just got bigger and better. Now covering Al Ain, you'll wonder how you ever managed without it.

Bahrain Explorer

The inside track on where and how to experience everything this fascinating gulf state has to offer.

Dubai Explorer

The original, and still the best by far. Now in its 9th year, this is the only guide you'll ever need for exploring this fascinating city.

Geneva Explorer

Your very own personal guide giving the low-down on everything to do and see in this European gem of a city and its surroundings.

Oman Explorer

All the insider info you'll ever need to make the most of this beautiful, beguiling country.

Explorer Photography Books

Where words fail, a picture speaks volumes. These award-winning photography books take you across landscapes and seascapes, through bold architecture, the past and the present, introducing a wonderland of diversity. They're an optical indulgence as well as stimulating additions to bookshelves and coffee tables everywhere.

Dubai: Tomorrow's City Today

A photography book showcasing the sheer splendour and architectural audacity of this stunning city.

Images of Geneva

From snow-capped mountains and azure waters to historic cobbled streets and contemporary architecture, the beauty of Geneva and its surroundings is captured in a stunning collection of photographs.

Sharjah's Architectural Splendour

Magnificent photographs show how modern-day Sharjah has remained true to its cultural heritage.

Images of Dubai & the UAE

Breathtaking images from this land of contrasts - from unspoilt desert, to the truly 21st century city of Dubai.

Images of Abu Dhabi & the UAE

Awe inspiring images of exquisite natural beauty and ancient cultures juxtaposed with the modern metropolis of Abu Dhabi.

Explorer Activity Guides

Why not visit stunning marine life and mysterious wrecks, or stand poised on the edge of a natural wadi or pool in the mountains? Get a tan and a life with our activity guidebooks.

Off-Road Explorer (UAE)

Let's go off-road! Over 20 adventurous routes covered in minute detail. Go off the beaten track and discover another side to the UAE.

Underwater Explorer

Dive dive dive! Detailed info on all the underwater action, from reefs to wrecks, all around the UAE.

Family Explorer (Dubai & Abu Dhabi)

The only family-friendly guide of its kind for the UAE – just add kids.

Trekking Guide (Oman)

A booklet and individual cards detailing amazing walks through spectacular scenery. The maps correspond to waypoints that are actually painted on the ground to aid navigation.

Street Map Explorer (Dubai)

Never get lost again. A first of its kind for Dubai, this handy map book lists every highway and byway in crystal clear detail.

Explorer Other Products

With such an incredible array of insiders' guides and photography and activity books you'd think we wouldn't have the time or energy to produce anything else. Well think again! Here are some of our other products – no home should be without them.

2005 Calendar (Abu Dhabi)

Spend a whole year in the company of stunning images of the capital of the Emirates.

2005 Calendar (Dubai)

A 12-month visual feast, featuring award-winning images of Dubai's finest sights.

Starter Kit (Dubai)

Three great books - the Dubai Explorer, Zappy Explorer and Street Map - everything you need to get started and sorted.

Images Collection (UAE)

A combination of award-winning excellence, containing both the Images of Dubai and Images of Abu Dhabi photography books (limited edition).

Zappy Explorer (Dubai)

Page after page of fuss-free advice on getting things done in Dubai. All the info you'll ever need to get yourself sorted.

General Information

New Residents

Exploring

Introduction

Table of Contents

Shopping

Activities

Going Out

Maps

Commonly Regarded As The Most Perfect Design

Until now…

General
Information

EXPLORER

General Information

Highlights...

Places to stay
p.24

Oman is extending an increasingly warm welcome to tourists and visitors, with the result that accommodation options for the weary traveller are on the up. From simple rest houses to luxurious five-star pampering, in this section you'll find details on where you can doss down while visiting this fascinating country.

Omani Cuisine
p.16

A visit to a foreign country is all the more rewarding when you sample the local culture and cuisine, so it's worth hunting around to find outlets serving traditional Omani fare. Grilled meats, seafood and rice feature heavily, as do delicious fresh salads. An encounter with a local family will almost certainly result in an offer of 'kahwa', the strong black Arabic coffee - particularly good when taken with is the local sweet delicacy 'Halwa.'

Geography

Situated in the south-eastern quarter of the Arabian Peninsula, the Sultanate of Oman is bordered by the Kingdom of Saudi Arabia to the west, Yemen to the south-west and the United Arab Emirates (UAE) to the north-west. Estimates of its total land area vary but the official figure is 309,500 square kilometres, making it the third largest country in the peninsula. Mountain ranges (15% of the land) and a narrow strip of coastal plains (3%) break up a topography that is predominantly made up of valleys and desert (82%). Oman's coastline, which is about 1,700 km long, extends to the Gulf of Oman and the Arabian Sea as well as the Indian Ocean. The geographic coordinates for Oman are 21 00N, 57 00E.

The country is divided into eight administrative regions: three governorates (Muscat, Dhofar and Mussandam) and five regions (A' Dakhliyah, A' Dhahirah, Al Batinah, Al Wusta and A' Sharqiyah). Each region is further divided into smaller 'wilayats' (districts) headed by a 'wali' (district governor). The capital of the country is Muscat.

Mussandam, known as the Norway of Arabia because of its majestic fjords, lies at the furthest east point of the Arabian peninsula and is separated from the rest of the country by the United Arab Emirates (UAE). This is an area of great strategic importance, lying south of Iran and controlling the main navigable stretch of the Strait of Hormuz, through which 90% of the world's crude oil passes. An Omani enclave also lies in the small village of Al Madha in the UAE.

Off the coast there are several islands, the largest of which is Masirah Island in the south-east. It is a strategic entry point from the Arabian Sea to the Gulf of Oman, and houses military facilities used by the United States.

Oman's countryside is among the most stunning and varied in the Gulf region. It features 'sabka' (salt flats), 'khwars' (lagoons), oases, and stretches of sand and gravel plains dominated by stark mountains of rock and brownish-green ranges of ophiolites. The Hajar Mountains are the largest range, stretching from Mussandam, through the UAE, to northern Oman, and rising to 3,000 metres at Jebel Shams, the highest peak in the country. The countryside is crossed by 'wadis' (riverbeds), which are formed by the force of torrential water during the rainy season.

Oman is home to a large part of the seemingly endless Rub Al Khali (Empty Quarter) desert, which continues into Saudi Arabia and the UAE. The other main desert is the Ramlat Al Wahaybah (Wahiba Sands), home to nomadic Bedouin tribes, where dunes can rise to a spectacular 200 metres.

In contrast, the Dhofar region in the south is renowned for its green, tropical appearance and monsoon season with relatively high rainfall. It is one of the few places in the world where the frankincense tree grows; ancient trade in this resin features prominently in Oman's history.

Most of the population lives along the coast, on the Al Batinah plains and in the Muscat metropolitan area. You can discover more about Oman's landscapes in the Exploring section of this book [p.97].

History

Archaeological evidence suggests that an early form of civilisation existed in Oman at least 5,000 years ago. The name 'Oman' is said to come from the Arab tribes that migrated to the area from a place in Yemen called Uman. The Omanis were among the first Arabs to embrace Islam, in 630 AD, and Oman became an Ibadhi state ruled by an elected religious leader, the Imam.

Oman's geographical position on some of the world's most important trade routes between Africa and Asia has given it a unique dimension. From the first to third centuries, the southern part of the country was one of the wealthiest regions in the world due to the ancient trade in Arabian horses and the world's purest frankincense. Oman became a prosperous seafaring nation, sending dhows to Africa, India and the Far East.

The Portuguese arrived by force in 1507 with a view to protecting supply lines to the east and constraining Oman's trading power. They were driven out of their main bases, first from Hormuz in 1622, and eventually from Muscat in 1650, by Sultan bin Saif Al-Ya'arubi. This event marked the

> ### Maps
>
> *For a good overview of Oman, refer to the excellent maps at the back of this book to orientate yourself. Alternatively, see the Tourist Map of Oman, a handy, foldout map that includes essential visitor information. For in-depth directions, try the A-Z Muscat Street Atlas and the Salalah A-Z Street Atlas and Gazetteer. They are available from all good bookshops in Muscat and Salalah.*

start of full Omani independence, making the country the oldest independent state in Arabia.

From the 1600s to the 1800s Oman vied with both Portugal and Britain for trade in the Gulf and the Indian Ocean. During the Ya'aruba Dynasty (1624 – 1744), Oman entered an era of prosperity and many of its great buildings and forts were built. But tribal warfare over the election of a new Imam halted this expansion and Persian forces invaded the coastal areas.

The history of Oman has always been a struggle for economic and political power between the interior (ruled by an Imam), and the coastal areas and Muscat (ruled by a Sultan). In 1744, Omani tribes elected Imam Ahmed bin Said, founder of the present Al Busaidi Dynasty. He expelled the Persian invaders, united the country, restored Oman's fortunes and moved the capital from the interior to Muscat. He also adopted the title of Sultan, which continues to this day.

Government treaties in 1798 and 1800 furthered links with Britain. These gave Oman British protection while maintaining Omani independence. In return, Britain could maintain the supply route further east.

The Omani empire reached the height of its power in the mid-19th century under Sayyid Said bin Sultan. He extended control all the way to Zanzibar and Mombassa in Africa, and to parts of Persia, Pakistan and India. (Oman only withdrew from Gwadar in 1958 when Sultan Said bin Taimur, father of the current ruler, allowed it to be reintegrated into Pakistan in exchange for £3 million). Sayyid Said established political links with France, Britain and the United States, making Oman the first Arab state to establish relations with the USA. When Sultan Said died the empire was split between his two sons. One became the Sultan of Zanzibar and the other, the Sultan of Muscat and Oman. Zanzibar became the nation's capital until it was declared an independent sultanate in 1861.

Sultan Said Bin Taimur came to power in 1932. He was able to enforce his rule over the interior, partly with the backing and encouragement of the British who needed stability in order to search the interior for oil. However, after establishing his rule, the Sultan became progressively more isolated, closing the nation's borders and shielding his country from the influences of the outside world. Eventually the only contacts were through the Sultan's mainly British advisors and certain well established trading families. Although Oman began commercialising oil in the late 1960s, the people spent much of the 20th century living as they had for centuries, under great restrictions.

In the 1960s a serious new threat arose from Dhofar. By 1965, the Dhofar rebellion was underway, led by the Dhofar Libération Front and aided by South Yemen. The escalating rebellion and the Sultan's refusal to spend any of the oil revenue eventually triggered a bloodless coup led by his son, the present Sultan.

On 23 July 1970, a day henceforth celebrated as Renaissance Day, His Majesty Sultan Qaboos Bin Said assumed power after a bloodless coup. He was only 30 years old at the time but already had a strong vision for his country. Born in Salalah on 18 November 1940, he is the only son of the late Sultan Said bin Taimur and is eighth in the direct line of the Al Busaidi Dynasty. He spent his youth in Salalah, where he was educated until he was sent, at the age of 16, to a private school in England. In 1960, Sultan Qaboos entered the Royal Military Academy at Sandhurst as an officer cadet, where he reputedly discovered a love for classical music. After military service in Germany he studied local government administration in England and went on a world tour. He returned to Salalah where he spent the next six years, some say, under virtual house arrest imposed by his father. He devoted this time to studying Islam and Omani history. The Sultan married in 1976 but later divorced; there are no children from the marriage.

Using the new oil wealth he immediately set about transforming Oman and modernising the infrastructure. However, he continued to face problems in Dhofar and it was not until 1982, when Oman and South Yemen established diplomatic ties, that assistance to the few remaining rebel groups was cut off. Many of the Sultan's advisors and army officers were British and Britain, along with Iran and Jordan, helped him to finally end the rebellion.

Said bin Taimur

Said bin Taimur came to power in 1932 at the age of 22. After an assassination attempt in 1966, his policies became more erratic – eyeglasses, football and music were disallowed, city gates were shut at night, people who appeared in his dreams were punished, etc. Unfortunately, he is remembered more for his xenophobic policies that kept Oman in the Middle Ages than for his success in effectively curbing Oman's growing debt at that time. Weary of internal troubles, he spent the last 12 years of his reign in Salalah and governed from there. After a palace coup d'etat in 1970 led by his son, Sultan Qaboos bin Said, he lived in exile in London until his death in 1972.

In 1970, Oman had only three primary schools, ten kilometres of paved roads, two health centres, no infrastructure to speak of and a per capita income of less than $50 a year. Nowadays it is peaceful, stable and relatively prosperous. The Sultan has been a strong yet benign leader, drawing his people into the modern world but at the same time preserving much of the character and heritage of his country, thus making Oman a unique place to visit.

Economy

Overview

The Sultanate's economic strategy is based on a series of five-year plans. In 'Vision 2020', Oman aims to become a 'Newly Industrialised Economy' and to double gross domestic product (GDP) per capita (currently $8,593).

At around 40%, oil remains the largest contributor to GDP. The GDP for 2003 was approximately RO 8.3 billion. Petroleum Development Oman (PDO) – a consortium between the government (60%), Royal Dutch Shell (34%), Total-Fina-Elf (4%) and Partex (2%) – contributes more than 90% of total oil revenues and accounts for nearly 95% of oil production. Most of Oman's estimated recoverable oil reserves (5.5 billion barrels) are located in the northern and central regions. At current production levels of about 760,000 barrels per day there should be enough for another 20 years. Oman's only oil refinery and terminal is at Mina Al Fahal, near Muscat.

Endowed with modest oil reserves, Oman aims to create a viable non-oil economy by shifting economic emphasis to tourism, agriculture, fisheries, mining and light industry, while continuing aggressive development of natural gas to offset depleting oil production. Oman's main export partners are Japan, South Korea, China, Thailand, Taiwan, Singapore and USA. The main import partners are the UAE, Japan, UK, USA and Germany.

Gross Domestic Product

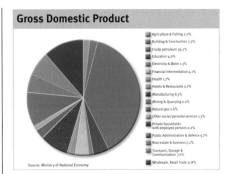

- Agriculture & Fishing 2.0%
- Building & Construction 2.3%
- Crude petroleum 39.2%
- Education 4.6%
- Electricity & Water 1.3%
- Financial intermediation 4.1%
- Health 1.7%
- Hotels & Restaurants 0.7%
- Manufacturing 8.3%
- Mining & Quarrying 0.2%
- Natural gas 2.6%
- Other social/personal services 1.3%
- Private households with employed persons 0.2%
- Public Administration & defence 9.7%
- Real estate & business 5.2%
- Transport, Storage & Communication 7.0%
- Wholesale, Retail Trade 11.8%

Source: Ministry of National Economy

Efforts to diversify the economy also include 'Omanisation', or a gradual replacement of the expatriate workforce with Omani nationals. This means that all companies must employ a certain percentage of Omanis. By 2005, a rather utopian goal is to nationalise jobs in the public sector to 95% and in the private sector to 75%. Government training schemes aim to give nationals the necessary skills.

Oman belongs to the World Trade Organisation, the International Monetary Fund and various pan-Arab economic groups, like the Arab Gulf Cooperation Council (AGCC) and the Indian Ocean Rim Association (IORARC) – both of which Oman is a founding member. It is not a member of the Organisation of Petroleum Exporting Countries (OPEC) – although its pricing policy tends to follow that of OPEC fairly closely.

The situation in the Sultanate is radically different from that of 34 years ago when Oman was an economically backward nation. It is now a middle-income developing country with the 18th most liberal economy in the world, free universal welfare services and impressive infrastructure. Real GDP growth has been averaging 5% annually over the past 20 years. In recent years Oman has experienced deflation thanks to government subsidies and lower import prices in local currency terms.

Tourism Developments

Other options → Oman Annual Events [p.40]

Oman has much to offer tourists – stunning and unspoiled landscapes, rich marine life, a stable political climate, a low crime rate, an ancient culture, and most importantly, genuinely hospitable people.

After years of seclusion from the world, Oman started welcoming tourists in the mid 80s. There were 1.3 million tourists in 2003, mostly coming from the UAE, UK, Germany and France. Many come to visit family and friends or to enjoy the country's rugged landscape. Expatriates and nationals of surrounding Arab countries also see Oman as an alternative to foreign travel, particularly in today's geo-political climate.

In 2003 the government earned RO 58.1 million from tourism (a mere 0.7% of GDP). The aim is to double this rate by 2010 and further increase it to 5% by 2020. With about 50% of the population under the age of 18, the tourist sector is expected to absorb the wave of young Omanis that enter the job market annually.

In contrast to neighbour, Dubai, that encourages visitors of any background, Oman has repeatedly stressed its desire to develop this sector only to the extent that it does not conflict with the values of a traditionally conservative society. It is keen to promote upmarket tourism, focusing resources on adventure tourism, eco-tourism, cultural and heritage attractions, and coastal resorts. Backpackers will remain a rare sight for the foreseeable future!

Shangri-La Barr Al Jissah Resort

The slow growth in this sector has given more time to expand services and hotels to meet the demands of the modern traveller. To realise its full potential, the government engaged International Development Ireland (IDI) in July 2002 to perform the same miracles it did for Ireland's tourism sector. A marketing budget of $30 million up to the end of 2005 will further promote Oman on the tourist map.

A new Ministry of Tourism was created in June 2004, underscoring tourism's importance in the new economy. Primary target markets have been identified – UK, France, German-speaking Europe and the GCC states. Travel restrictions have been eased; visitors from 75 countries may now get a visa, valid for one month, on arrival at Oman's air, land or sea entry points. Oman has a joint visa facility with Dubai and a cross-border agreement with Qatar. The government undoubtedly hopes to attract some of Dubai's 4.7 million visitors, particularly during the summer months when the cooling mists of the Dhofar region provide a refreshing respite from the searing heat that blankets the region.

Seeb International Airport is set to undergo major redevelopment, including construction of a new terminal which will increase current capacity to 6.5 million passengers per year. The international airport in Salalah will be upgraded to handle more inbound charter flights. Oman Air, the National airline, has acquired new aeroplanes and expanded its list of destinations.

Almost all well-known hotel chains are present. There are currently over 60,000 rooms, but this is set to increase to 100,000 by 2010. Hotels are continually upgrading their offerings to better attract business travellers. In the face of stiff competition in the Gulf, Oman's showcase property, the Al Bustan Palace Hotel, has undergone extensive renovation of its rooms and facilities. Two new hotels are the five-star The Chedi in Muscat and the four-star Golden Tulip Khasab Hotel and Resort in Mussandam.

The Shangri-La Barr Al Jissah Resort, a massive 730 room resort set in spectacular mountain and sea surroundings, is scheduled to open in late 2005. One of the most talked about development projects on the cards in Oman is The Wave, a multi-million dollar venture that will see the staggered completion of four zones of entertainment, leisure and residential facilities. The development will involve land reclamation and will eventually spread for over seven kilometres along Oman's coastline near Muscat. Zone 1A will feature an 18 hole, international standard golf course, a five-star hotel and spa, conference facilities and an exclusive tower of 24 condos. Zone 1B will house a yacht club and marina, a hotel and two residential blocks, as well as a village of 850 apartments and a shopping and dining centre. Zone 1C will be a public beach, and Zone 2 will be a beachfront residential complex with over 200 villas, a sports resort and a shopping centre. It will be the first chance for foreigners to own property in Oman. Once completed, The Wave is set to be the ultimate destination for upmarket living in Oman, catapulting the Sultanate into the investment and tourism spotlight.

Oman's landscape is dotted with over 500 castles, forts and towers, of which about 70 are restored. These have become popular tourist attractions, along with the traditional souks. The Forts and Castles Restoration Project is now focusing on Mussandam Fort, Al Hazm Fort and Nizwa Fort.

To increase its global presence Oman hosts international dune rallies, yacht races, and annual festivals like the Muscat Festival and the Khareef Festival in Salalah. For the business traveller, a new convention centre north-west of Muscat, near Sultan Qaboos University, is under construction.

Other development projects are in the pipeline, although completion dates have not been finalised. The Muscat Golf and Country Club will be Oman's first green golf course but its completion depends on the finalisation of the Muscat Wastewater Project. This project will improve Muscat's water system, adding pipelines, pumping stations, sewage treatment plants and wastewater systems. It will also provide the irrigation water necessary to develop projects such as the country's first green golf course.

Oman is a successful example of how modernisation can be achieved without giving up a country's cultural identity. Muscat is one of the region's most attractive capital cities: clean and unexpectedly green, modern yet architecturally traditional. To visit Oman is, to use today's tourism slogan, to experience 'the Essence of Arabia'.

International Relations

In its foreign relations Oman maintains a stance of non-alignment and non-interference in other countries' affairs, but is committed to Arab unity. Since taking power in 1970, Sultan Qaboos has managed the extremely tricky task of maintaining friendly relations with just about everyone. In 1993

he became the first Gulf leader to welcome an Israeli Prime Minister to his country and was one of only two Arab leaders who did not break off diplomatic ties with Egypt after it signed the peace agreement with Israel in 1979. In recent years Oman has developed into a backroom mediator in solving the more politically volatile issues of the region. It was testimony to the Sultan's unique position on the world's stage when, in October 1998, he was presented with the International Peace Award by former US president Jimmy Carter, and in 2001, the Peace Prize from the Jewish-American Committee.

Oman is a member of the main international organisations, including the United Nations, IMF, WTO, Interpol, Arab League and the Arab Gulf Cooperation Council (GCC).

Most of the major embassies/consulates are located in the Shati Al Qurm area and the Al Khuwayr diplomatic area. A few are in Ruwi commercial business district (CBD).

For a list of embassies and consulates, see [p.22].

Government & Ruling Family

Oman's system of government is an absolute monarchy and hereditary through the male line of Sayyid Turki bin Said bin Sultan of the Al Busaidi Dynasty, the great great-grandfather of the present ruler, His Majesty Sultan Qaboos bin Said. He is the Head of State and Supreme Commander of the Armed Forces. He is also Prime Minister, Defence Minister and Foreign Minister, although the day to day running of these and various other ministries is performed by a Council of Ministers. The political and economic capital and seat of government is Muscat.

Hear Them Roar!

In contrast to many Gulf societies, women play a very visible and vocal role in Oman's development. In 1988, Oman appointed its first female under-secretary in a ministry, the first in any Gulf state. In 1999, Oman appointed its first female ambassador to The Hague, and in 2003, its first female minister. Women in the Muscat region have been candidates for the Majlis A'Shura since 1994, a parliamentary step unheard of in the region. Others have emerged as prominent figures in the oil sector, banking and commerce, education and medical services. Omani women are generally not self-effacing and are willing to talk to strangers, but they are deeply Muslim and should be treated with respect.

General Info

Facts & Figures

Given Oman's history of warring factions, it would have been difficult to put in place any kind of long-lasting economic, social and political reforms without some form of constitution. In November 1996, His Majesty passed the Basic Laws of the State. More importantly, it defines the rules of succession, as the Sultan has no children.

The Basic Law provides for a bicameral legislature presided over by the 'Majlis Oman' (Council of Oman). It consists of the 'Majlis A'Shura' (Consultative Council) whose members are elected by Omani citizens to represent the various wilayats, and the 'Majlis Al Dawla' (State Council) whose members are appointed by the Sultan.

Oman's legal system is based on Islamic Shariah law and English common law, with ultimate appeal to the Sultan. Capital punishment is rare and subject to review by judicial and religious authorities.

The Sultan has reportedly said that his country is not yet ready for full parliamentary democracy, implying that he considers this as the way forward. Nothing has been publicly finalised, although in November 2002 every Omani citizen over 21 years was granted the right to vote.

In his 34 years of rule, the Sultan has proven to be an extremely capable, far-sighted and benign leader, held in high regard by his people. This is most apparent in their reactions when he travels around the various wilayats on his annual 'Meet the People' tour.

His Majesty Sultan Qaboos bin Said

Facts & Figures

Population

A national census is taken every ten years and the last one was held in December 2003. The Ministry of National Economy put the population of Oman at 2,340,815, of which 76.1% are Omanis and 23.9% are expatriates. The population growth rate is 1.84%, comparing favourably with the rate of 3.5% in developing countries. There are 1.02 Omani males to every female, an indication of a demographically stable community. However, in respect of the total population, due to the dominance of male expatriates who outnumber female expatriates by three to one, there are 1.28 males to every female.

Rugged Good Book

Many of Oman's most beautiful spots can only be reached in a 4 WD. So load up your vehicle with tents and supplies and head off into the rocky mountains, desolate dunes and winding wadis. Oh, and don't forget to take the Oman Off-Road Explorer – it's the essential guide to roughing it like a pro! Available late 2005.

In 1970, the life expectancy was 40 years. Today Omani males have a life expectancy of 72.2 years and females of 75.4 years. These compare favourably to the global life expectancy of 68 years for males and 72 years for females.

Muscat Governorate has seen much progress in education the last ten years. Illiteracy among Omanis (ten years and above) has dropped from 22.8% in 1993 to 11.6% in 2003. The average size of an Omani household in Muscat is 7.3 members. As the results of Census 2003 have yet to be completely processed, official figures for expatriate household size and illiteracy rate for the rest of Oman are not available at this time.

National Flag

The flag of Oman comprises three equal horizontal bands of white (top), red (middle) and green (bottom) with a thicker vertical red band on the hoist side. White stands for peace and prosperity, red for the battles fought against foreign invaders, and green for the fertility and greenery of the land. Centred at the top of the

Population by Region

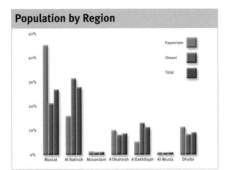

Legend: Expatriate, Omani, Total

Population Age Breakdown

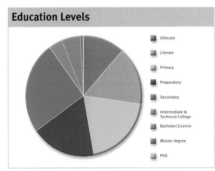

Education Levels

Legend: Illiterate, Literate, Primary, Preparatory, Secondary, Intermediate & Technical College, Bachelor/License, Master degree, PhD

Source: Ministry of National Economy

vertical band is the nation's emblem, an Omani 'khanjar' (dagger) and belt superimposed on two crossed swords, in white.

Local Time

The Sultanate of Oman is four hours ahead of UCT (Universal Co-ordinated Time, formerly known as GMT), and there is no summer time saving. Hence, when it is 12:00 midday in Muscat it is 08:00 in London, 13:30 in Delhi and 17:00 in Tokyo, (not allowing for any summer time saving in those countries).

Social & Business Hours

Social hours vary in Oman – some people get up early, some stay up late, and some do both! The attitude is often very different to the 'time is money' approach in other parts of the world; for most social situations, the 'Inshallah' (God willing) mindset still prevails. Business appointments, however, are generally on time.

The weekend is traditionally Thursday afternoon and Friday (the holy day), but a few organisations close all day Thursday and Friday.

Government offices are open from 07:30 to 14:30, Saturday to Wednesday. Bank hours are usually 08:00 - 12:30, Saturday to Wednesday, and some remain open from 08:00 to 11:30 on Thursdays.

Private sector office hours are mainly split-shift days – 08:00 - 13:00 and 16:00 - 19:00; or straight-shift, usually 09:00 - 18:00, with an hour for lunch.

Shop opening times are mainly based on split-shift hours, 09:00 - 13:00 and 16:30 - 20:00, Saturday to Thursday, and 16:30 - 20:00 on Fridays. Market hours are usually 08:00 - 13:00 and 16:00 - 21:00, except the Mutrah Souk which closes at 19:30. On Fridays shops and souks tend to open in the afternoon at around 16:30 or 17:00. Most big supermarkets remain open throughout the day, seven days a week.

Working hours at embassies and consulates vary but are generally 08:00 - 13:00 or 14:00, with some open in the afternoons. They are closed on Fridays and generally all day Thursday but most leave a contact number on their answering machines in case of emergencies.

During Ramadan work hours in most public and private organisations are reduced by two to three hours per day, and business meetings may be difficult to arrange. Muslims in the private sector may work only six hours per day and government offices close at 14:00. Many private offices start work an hour or so later and shops are open until 22:00 or 24:00. Most restaurants are closed during the day. The Ruwi district in Muscat and more popular shopping malls are usually crowded, even at night, and parking can be hard to find!

Public Holidays

Other options → Oman Annual Events [p.40]

The Islamic calendar starts from the year 622 AD, the year of the Prophet Mohammed's (Peace Be

Upon Him) migration (Hijra) from Mecca to Al-Madinah. Hence the Islamic year is called the Hijra year and dates are followed by AH – After Hijra.

There are 354 or 355 days in the Hijri year, which is divided into 12 lunar months. The Hijri year is 11 days shorter than the Gregorian year.

As some holidays are based on the sighting of the moon, rather than being fixed dates on the Hijri calendar, the dates of Islamic holidays are imprecise, with holidays frequently being confirmed less than 24 hours in advance. Some non-religious holidays are fixed according to the Gregorian calendar.

In addition to Eid Al Adha and Eid Al Fitr, another day of importance for Muslims is the Ascension of the Prophet (PBUH), which is a public holiday.

National Day and the Birthday of HM Sultan Qaboos holidays are sometimes given a week later to make a long weekend and ensure that as many people as possible are in the country during the celebrations.

Public Holidays – 2005

New Year's Day	Jan 1
Eid Al Adha (3)	Jan 21
Muharram (Islamic New Year) (1)	Feb 10
Mouloud (Prophet's Birthday) (1)	Apr 21
Ascension of the Prophet (1)	Sep 1
Eid Al Fitr (3)	Nov 3 - 5
National Day (1)	Nov 18
Birthday of HM Sultan Qaboos (1)	Nov 19

Electricity & Water

Other options → Electricity & Water [p.74]

Electricity and water services are provided by the Omani government although there are plans to privatise them. The electricity supply is 220/240 volts and 50 cycles and there are few shortages or stoppages. The socket type is the three-pin British system.

The mains tap water is purified eight times and is fine to drink but can taste chlorinated. Locally bottled mineral or desalinated water is a cheap alternative and there are many brands available. Bottled water is usually served in hotels and restaurants – make sure the seal on the bottle is unbroken.

Photography

Tourist photography is allowed, but as with everywhere else in the world, ask permission first, particularly when planning to take pictures of local Omanis. Say 'Mumkin shura, min fadlak'

(may I take your picture, please?). Children and males usually oblige but women may not especially if the photographer is male. Photographs of government buildings, military installations, ports and airports should not be taken, since Oman authorities are especially sensitive about security considerations.

There are a wide choice of films available and processing is usually fast, although the quality of reproduction can vary. Ultraviolet filters for your camera are advisable because of the strong sun. Digital, APS, 35mm negative and slide film can all be processed in medium or large format, by the major photo labs like Photocentre or Foto Magic.

Environment

Climate

Oman's climate varies considerably with the different regions, but sunny blue skies and warm temperatures can be expected most of the year. The best time to visit Oman is in winter, between October to April, when temperatures average between 25°C and 35°C during the day and about 18°C at night.

The north is hot and humid during the summer, with June/July temperatures reaching 48°C during the day and averaging about 32°C at night. Humidity can rise to an uncomfortable 90%. The mean summer temperature in Muscat is 33°C, but the 'gharbi' (western) wind from the Rub Al Khali can raise coastal town temperatures by another 6°C to 10°C.

The interior is usually hotter than the coastal area, often reaching 50°C in the shade. In the mountains, night temperatures can fall to -1°C with a light dusting of snow!

Rainfall is infrequent and irregular, falling mainly between November and March. Average annual rainfall in the Muscat area is 75 mm, while rainfall in the mountains can be as high as 700 mm.

The southern Dhofar region usually has high humidity, even in winter. Between June and September the area receives light monsoon rains from the Indian Ocean called the 'khareef'. The area around Salalah is lush and green and at certain times of the year is swathed in a cooling mist – it's hard for visitors to reconcile this image with the usual Arabian landscapes of forbidding deserts and rocky, inhospitable mountains.

Temperature & Humidity

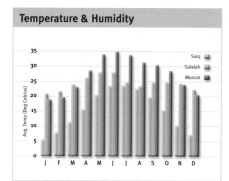

Average Number of Days With Rain

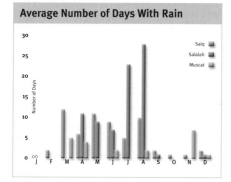

Information on local weather and meteorological conditions is available by dialling 1102 (Arabic) or 1103 (English).

Flora & Fauna

Oman has around 1,200 native plant species, including trees, shrubs and herbs. Of the indigenous flora, date palms provide oases of green covering about 49% of Oman's cultivated area. Heading towards the mountains, flat topped acacia trees give the feeling of an African savannah. The deserts are often surprisingly dotted with wildflowers after a bout of rain but it takes an experienced botanist to get the most out of the area during the dry summer months. Coconut trees, banana trees and other tropical fruit trees thrive amazingly well in the subtropical climate of Salalah.

Oman is home to the frankincense tree, 'Boswelia sacra', which grows only in Dhofar, the Wadi Hadhramaut in Yemen, and Somalia. They are short trees with a gnarled trunk and silvery-green leaves. Incisions are made on the bark to collect the aromatic resin. For hundreds of years, frankincense was more valuable than gold and that from Dhofar was said to be the finest and purest in the world. It was used not only as a fragrance, but also to embalm corpses and as a medicine. The frankincense trade brought immense wealth and importance to southern Arabia – even Alexander the Great had plans to invade the area in order to control the trade at its point of origin.

Mangrove trees (species Avicennia marina), known in Arabic as 'qurm,' used to cover large stretches of Oman's coast but have been threatened with extinction in many areas. Some of the most beautiful and dense mangrove forests today are found in the Qurum Nature Reserve in the heart of Muscat, and at Mahawt Island, 400 km south of the capital. The Qurum reserve contains an important site where prehistoric fishermen exploited mangrove resources, and a nursery that produces seedlings for replanting. Thanks to urgent conservation measures, mangrove forests now cover about 1,088 hectares of Oman's coastline.

Oman has a wide variety of indigenous wildlife which includes many endangered species such as the Arabian oryx, Arabian leopard, Arabian tahr (a mountain goat now found only in Oman), Nubian ibex and humpback whale. Realistically though the only large animals you are likely to see are camels, donkeys and goats, often roaming dangerously close to the road!

Some 460 species of birds (of which 80 are resident) are found at different times of the year – an impressive number considering that Oman has vast areas of desert and no real forests. Millions of birds wintering in East Africa pass over Oman on their spring or autumn migration to Central Asia.

Have goat, will travel

Several new varieties of seashells have been discovered on Oman's beaches. Around 150 species of commercial shell and non-shell fish, 21 species of whales and dolphins and other assorted marine creatures are found in Omani seas. The humpback whale feeds and breeds in the rich waters of central and southern Oman.

There are four breeds of sea turtle that come ashore to lay their eggs. The huge Leatherback turtle is known to swim in the waters offshore but there are no records of it nesting in Oman. The more popular nesting sites are Ras Al Hadd for Green turtles, Masirah Island for the world's largest population of nesting Loggerheads and the Daymaniyat Islands Nature Reserve – Oman's only marine reserve – for Hawksbill turtles.

Be aware that collecting live shells, turtle eggs and shellfish is forbidden in Oman.

Protection

Oman is one of the world's top ten environmentally committed countries and is party to international agreements on biodiversity, climate change, desertification, endangered species, hazardous wastes, marine dumping, Law of the Sea, whaling and ozone layer protection. In 1984, it became the first Arab state to create a ministry dedicated to environmental issues; environmental protection laws have been in place since 1974. At the Earth Summit in 1989, Sultan Qaboos established the biannual Award for Environmental Conservation, the first Arab prize to be awarded in this area. In 1990, a new hybrid of rose was named in the Sultan's honour, in recognition of his commitment to the environment and his support for human rights.

Various organisations have been formed to protect the environment, as well as to educate the people on the importance of environmental issues and the protection of human health. 2001 and 2002 were declared Years of the Environment. The 2003 Law on Nature Reserves and Wild Life Conservation reinforced Oman's policies on biodiversity and environmental management.

The Sultan has always been committed to an extensive 'greening' programme of his cities. Highways are lined with colourful bougainvillaea, grassed areas, palm trees and flowers, all maintained by an army of workers who also pick up the litter on the roadside. It's no surprise then that Muscat Municipality received the UN Public Services Award for cleanliness in June 2003.

The Sultanate aims to protect endangered wildlife species by establishing nature reserves, while working together with local communities to ensure their success. The turtle breeding beaches at Ras Al Hadd and Ras Al Jinz are protected sites, as are the Daymaniyat islands, which are a bird sanctuary to which entry is restricted during the breeding season. The Arabian Oryx Sanctuary on the Jiddat Al-Harasis is a Unesco World Heritage Site. Wadi Al Sarin, one of Oman's oldest reserves, is home to the Arabian tahr, while Jebel Samhan in Dhofar is a refuge for the Arabian leopard. Saleel Park is a new nature reserve inhabited by gazelles and rare trees. Hunting and killing of any wildlife is strictly prohibited and carries stiff penalties.

Despite these efforts there are still some serious threats to the environment facing the Sultanate, such groundwater pollution, rising soil and water salinity, desertification and beach pollution from oil spills.

Culture & Lifestyle

Culture

Oman's culture is firmly rooted in the Islamic traditions of Arabia. Islam is more than just a religion, it is a way of life that governs the minutiae of everyday events, from what to wear to what to eat. It is unfortunate that in parts of the world Islamic fundamentalism has given non-Muslims an extreme, blanket view of the religion, and Muslim countries and culture in general. However, the reality behind this image is very different.

Exposure to different cultures due to Oman's position on ancient trade routes has led to Omanis being tolerant and welcoming people. Foreigners are free to practice their own religion, alcohol is served in hotels and the dress code is relatively liberal. Women face little discrimination and, contrary to the policies of some neighbouring countries, are able to drive and walk around unescorted. Among the most highly prized virtues are courtesy and hospitality, and visitors are sure to be charmed by the genuine warmth and friendliness of the people.

Visitors are, on the whole, able to roam freely in the souks and villages, and may be pleasantly surprised by genuine offers of coffee. Perhaps the only exceptions are mosques and the Lewara quarter, adjacent to the Mutrah Souk in Muscat, where many Shi'a Muslims live.

Omanis greet profusely on meeting and parting, and it would be polite to return the gesture with a friendly remark (master those greetings!) or a handshake. Unlike the firm Western handshake (a sign of aggressiveness), the handclasp is light and may be followed by placing the hand over the heart to show sincerity. Men and women do not shake hands unless offered first by the man. Light cheek-to-cheek kissing between men is also common, but reserved for family and close friends.

Avoid bad and forceful language and discussing local politics with casual acquaintances. It is considered impolite to ask the origin or birthplace of Omanis.

As you travel deeper into the interior the people become more conservative but no less hospitable. The forbidding mountains and formidable deserts have kept them isolated from external influences so a foreign face becomes a welcome diversion!

To get a quick overview of Oman, its traditions and its people, spend some time in one of the many excellent museums in the Muscat area.

Language

Other options → Learning Arabic [p.86]

The official language of the country is Arabic, but English is widely spoken. Other commonly heard languages include Urdu, Baluchi, Swahili, Hindi and other Indian dialects. Most road and shop signs, restaurant menus etc, are in both Arabic and English. The further into the interior you go, the more Arabic you will find, both spoken and on street signs. See overleaf for a quick list of useful Arabic phrases to get you around the country.

Arabic isn't the easiest language to pick up (or to pronounce) but if you learn the usual greetings, you're more likely to receive a warmer welcome. Most Omanis appreciate the effort and will help you with your pronunciation. Just give it a try – it certainly won't hurt and it definitely helps when dealing with officials of any sort.

Religion

Other options → Oman Annual Events [p.40]

Islam is the official religion of Oman, with most Omanis following the Ibadhi sect, named after its founder Abdullah bin Abadha. Ibadhism is regarded as 'moderately conservative' and a distinguishing feature is the choice of a ruler by

communal consensus and consent. Nearly a quarter of Omanis are Sunni Muslims and live primarily in Sur and the surrounding areas, and in Dhofar. The Shi'a minority live in the Muscat-Mutrah area. Today's brand of Islamic fundamentalism has made very little impact here.

The basis of Islam is the belief that there is only one God and that the Prophet Mohammed (Peace Be Upon Him) is his messenger. There are five pillars of the faith (the 'hadith'), which all Muslims must follow – the Profession of Faith (a statement of the belief, as above), Prayer, Charity (giving of alms), Fasting (during the holy month of Ramadan) and Pilgrimage. Every Muslim, if possible, is required at least once in their lifetime to make the pilgrimage or 'Hajj' to the holy city of Mecca (or Makkah) in Saudi Arabia.

Additionally, a Muslim is required to pray five times a day, facing Mecca, the times vary according to the position of the sun. Most people pray at a mosque, although it is not unusual to see them kneeling by the side of the road if one is not near. It is not considered polite to stare at people praying or to walk over prayer mats.

The modern day call to prayer, through loudspeakers on the minarets of each mosque, ensures that everyone knows it's time to pray. The timings are also published in local newspapers. Friday is the holy day.

There are prescribed washing rituals for both Muslim men and women that must be completed before entering a mosque. Non-Muslims with cameras and an intent to gawk are generally not allowed in mosques and signs prohibiting entry may be posted at the entrance. The exception to this is the majestic and architecturally pleasing Sultan Qaboos Grand Mosque in Al Ghubrah (Muscat area). It is open to visitors Saturdays to Wednesdays from 08:00 - 14:00 and 16:00 - 21:00, and Thursdays from 09:00 - 13:00. It is closed on Fridays and public holidays. Ladies' night is on Mondays from 16:00 - 21:00. During Ramadan, timings are Saturday to Wednesday from 08:30 - 13:30 and 20:00 - 23:00, and 09:00 - 12:00 on Thursdays. Women must wear loose fitting, long sleeved shirts, long trousers or skirts (an abaya will be perfect), and headscarves. Men should not wear shorts. Children under the age of ten are not allowed to enter. Photography is allowed.

There is also a prayer hall for ladies, a public library and an information centre. Talks about Islam are given in English every other Sunday in the lecture hall.

Basic Arabic

General

Yes	na'am
No	la
Please	min fadlak [(m)] / min fadliki [(f)]
Thank you	shukran
Please (in offering)	tafaddal [(m)] / tafaddali [(f)]
Praise be to God	al-hamdu l-illah
God willing	in shaa'a l-laah

Greetings

Greeting (peace be upon you)	as-salaamu alaykom
Greeting (in reply)	wa alaykom is salaam
Good morning	sabah il-khayr
Good morning (in reply)	sabah in-nuwr
Good evening	masa il-khayr
Good evening (in reply)	masa in-nuwr
Hello	marhaba
Hello (in reply)	marhabtayn
How are you?	kayf haalak [(m)] / kayf haalik [(f)]
Fine, thank you	zayn, shukran [(m)] / zayna, shukran [(f)]
Welcome	ahlan wa sahlan
Welcome (in reply)	ahlan fiyk [(m)] / ahlan fiyki [(f)]
Goodbye	ma is-salaama

Introduction

My name is	ismiy ...
What is your name?	shuw ismak [(m)] / shuw ismik [(f)]
Where are you from?	min wayn inta [(m)] / min wayn inti [(f)]
I am from ...	anaa min
America	ameriki
Britain	braitani
Europe	oropi
India	al hindi

Questions

How many / much?	kam?
Where?	wayn?
When?	mata?
Which?	ayy?
How?	kayf?
What?	shuw?
Why?	laysh?
Who?	miyn?
To/ for	ila
In/ at	fee
From	min
And	wa
Also	kamaan
There isn't	maa fee

Taxi / Car Related

Is this the road to ...	hadaa al tariyq ila
Stop	kuf
Right	yamiyn
Left	yassar
Straight ahead	siydaa
North	shamaal
South	januwb
East	sharq
West	garb
Turning	mafraq
First	awwal
Second	thaaniy
Road	tariyq
Street	shaaria
Roundabout	duwwaar
Signals	ishaara
Close to	qarib min
Petrol station	mahattat betrol
Sea/ beach	il bahar
Mountain/s	jebel / jibaal
Desert	al sahraa
Airport	mataar
Hotel	funduq
Restaurant	mata'am
Slow Down	schway schway

Accidents

Police	al shurtaa
Permit/ licence	rukhsaa
Accident	Haadith
Papers	waraq
Insurance	ta'miyn
Sorry	aasif (m) / aasifa (f)

Numbers

Zero	sifr
One	waahad
Two	ithnayn
Three	thalatha
Four	araba'a
Five	khamsa
Six	sitta
Seven	saba'a
Eight	thamaanya
Nine	tiss'a
Ten	ashara
Hundred	miya
Thousand	alf

Other religions are recognised and respected, and followers are free to practice their faith. Muscat has four main Christian churches – Good Shepherd Protestant Church (Ghala), Ruwi Protestant Church, Holy Spirit Catholic Church (Ghala) and Catholic Church of Sts Peter and Paul (Ruwi). Other non-Muslim places of worship include the Tamil Full Gospel Church, Shiva and Bajrangbali Temple, Shree Govindrayji Temple, and Shree Ganesh and Devi Kalaka Temple. The Salalah Christian Centre hosts Catholic masses.

Ramadan

Ramadan is the holy month in which Muslims commemorate the revelation of the Holy Quran, the holy book of Islam (also spelt Koran). It is a time of fasting when Muslims abstain from all food, drinks, cigarettes and unclean thoughts between dawn and dusk. In the evening, the fast is broken with what is known as the 'iftar' feast. Iftar timings are listed in the daily newspapers.

The timing of Ramadan is not fixed in terms of the Western calendar, but each year it occurs approximately 11 days earlier than the previous year. For most Muslim countries the start of Ramadan depends on an actual sighting of the moon. Out of respect non-Muslims should not eat, drink or smoke in public places, even in their cars, between sunrise and sunset. Office business hours are usually cut short, while shops and parks open and close later. Small restaurants may be closed during the day and hotels provide screened rooms for those not fasting. Bars are closed and the sale of alcohol is banned. Cinemas limit daytime screenings of films.

Ramadan ends with a three day celebration and holiday called Eid Al Fitr, or 'Feast of the Breaking of the Fast' and 70 days later is Eid Al Adha, or 'Feast of the Sacrifice' and this marks the end of the pilgrimage season to Mecca. For Muslims, Eid has similar connotations as Diwali for Hindus or Christmas for Christians.

National Dress

On the whole, Omanis still choose to wear their traditional dress during working and social hours. For men, this consists of an ankle-length, collarless gown with long sleeves – the 'dishdasha'. It is usually white in colour, although pale brown, blue, lilac and black are also worn. The neckline is adorned with a 'furakha' (tassel) which can be scented with perfume. A plain cloth called a 'wuzar' is worn underneath, from the waist down. On their heads men usually wear a brimless embroidered hat or 'kumah'. Over this a square of finely woven cotton or wool cloth is sometimes wound around the head to make a turban, known as a 'muzzar'. On formal occasions the dishdasha may be covered with a 'bisht' – a black or beige cloak edged in silver or gold thread. At semi-formal events, a 'khanjar' (traditional dagger) hangs from the waist, secured by a belt of leather and silver ('sapta') or a strip of cloth ('shal') made from the same material as the muzzar. Some men also carry a stick ('assa' or 'baakora') as an accessory. Omani men wear sandals, even on formal occasions.

Traditional women's costumes are very colourful and vary from region to region. The main components are a pair of loose trousers ('sirwal'), a long sleeved tunic and a headdress called the 'lihaf'. The tunics are often extremely colourful, with bright greens, reds, purples, and oranges, intricately woven together in embroidered patterns. The lihaf covers the head and shoulders and is black or the same fabric as the tunic. In northern and coastal Oman, women tend to wear a full-length 'khandoura', which is embroidered in different patterns.

In public, women cover their normal clothes with a full length, black 'abaya'. The abaya is usually

Arabic Family Names

Arabic names have a formal structure that traditionally indicates the family and tribe of a person. Names usually start with that of an important person from the Quran or someone from the tribe. This is followed by the word bin (son of) for a boy and bint (daughter of) for a girl, and then the name of the child's father. The last name indicates the person's tribe or family. For prominent families Al, the Arabic word for 'the', comes immediately before it. For instance, the ruler of Oman is Sultan Qaboos bin (Al) Said. When women get married, they do not change their name. Family names are very important here and extremely helpful when it comes to differentiating between the thousands of Mohammeds, Ibrahims and Fatimas!

Made in Oman?

Oman has a long tradition of crafts that include silverwork, pottery, weaving and textiles, indigo dyeing, fragrances, copper work and the making of sweets. Of particular interest is the intricately worked 'khanjar' (curved Omani dagger), attached to an ornate belt. Artisans still produce excellent handicrafts and the souks are the best places to hunt for authentic Omani souvenirs. But be on guard for new 'Omani' silver products that are actually made in 'antique' factories in India!

made of sheer, flowing fabric, sometimes open at the front. Modern women will often wear trousers or a long skirt underneath.

You can still see women, usually in the interior but also in Muscat, wearing the 'burkha' (mask) which covers the brow, cheekbones and nose. It is often dyed gold or indigo. Some older women also pierce their noses on both sides and wear a carnelian stone or a gold flower stud. In Dhofar, indigo is sometimes rubbed on the face to give a bluish tint that complements the robes.

Food & Drink

Visitors will find that as well as Omani food and Arabic cuisine in all its variations they can eat virtually any other style they wish. The cheapest meals can often be found at Indian restaurants or from shawarma stands (best described as the Middle Eastern equivalent of western fast food). Refer to the Going Out section for details on anything and everything that is available to quench both hunger and thirst.

Arabic Cuisine

Arabic cuisine is similar in some respects to Omani cuisine, using many of the same ingredients and styles of cooking. It is basically a blend of many types of cooking, such as Moroccan, Tunisian, Iranian, Egyptian and Afghani, although in general terms modern 'Arabic cuisine' invariably means Lebanese food. The cuisine is excellent for meat eaters and vegetarians alike.

Shawarma (lamb or chicken carved from a rotating spit, then rolled in flat bread with salad) are sold in small shops throughout Oman. These are delicious, inexpensive and filling. You can also have 'foul' (a paste made from fava beans) and 'falafel' (or ta'amiya), which are a small, deep-fried balls of mashed chickpeas.

Arabic sweets are delicious, although very sweet. The most widely known are 'baklava' (filo pastry layered with honey and nuts) and 'Umm Ali' ('Mother of Ali' in English), a dessert with layers of milk, bread, raisins and nuts.

Omani Cuisine

Traditional Omani cuisine is fairly simple, with rice as the main ingredient cooked together with beef, mutton, goat, chicken or fish. The meat is roasted, grilled or baked after marinating in a variety of spices, including cardamom, cinnamon, cumin, ginger, pepper, turmeric and saffron. This is not

surprising considering Oman's position on the ancient trade routes. However, the food is rarely 'hot and spicy' since the flavours are used in a subtle manner.

Traditional Omani meals are eaten with the right hand. The main meal is usually eaten at midday, while the evening meal is lighter. Salads are quite simple – lettuce, cucumber and tomatoes served with a slice of lime for dressing. 'Maqbous' is a saffron coloured rice dish cooked over spicy meat. Skewered meats (kebabs) are often served with flat 'khoubz' bread. 'Harees' is a staple wheat-based dish with chicken, tomato, seasoning and onion. Fish and shellfish are used widely in dishes such as 'mashuai' – whole spit-roasted kingfish served with lemon rice.

Favourite local drinks are 'laban' (heavy, salty buttermilk) and yoghurt, which is often flavoured with cardamom and ground pistachios. Fresh juices, made on the spot from fresh fruits (mango, banana, pineapple, pomegranate, etc), are delicious and very cheap. In particular, the mixed fruit cocktail should not be missed.

Omani 'halwa' is a popular dessert made of eggs, palm honey sugars, water, ghee and almonds flavoured with cardamom and rosewater. These ingredients are blended and cooked to form a sweet, dense block with a delicious flavour and consistency. Traditionally, the making of halwa is very much a male preserve, with recipes being handed down from generation to generation.

It is during Ramadan that one can sample Omani food at its best. Dishes, such as 'shuwa', 'arsia' (lamb with rice) and 'mishkak' (similar to kebabs), are mainly served during Eid celebrations. Shuwa is elaborately prepared by seasoning a large piece of meat (often lamb) and wrapping it in banana leaves, sacking and then burying it in a pit on top of red-hot coals. The meat is left to cook slowly over a couple of days in the embers and when unwrapped, is tender and succulent.

To enjoy a 'genuine' Omani feast, most hotels will set up a Bedouin tent outdoors in the winter months when alfresco dining is a pleasure. However, the Bedouins themselves have a far more limited diet, depending on where they are travelling. This would often be based on meats (usually dried or boiled camel) with large amounts of rice.

A visit to an Omani home is incomplete without an offer of 'kahwa' (coffee) – strong, black, and brewed with water and cardamom. It is drunk in small quantities, generally out of a small hand-

Oman's future generation

crafted kahwa cup. Only half a cup is served every time; always take or give with the right hand and shake the cup when you have had enough. Kahwa is served with dates, fruits or halwa, whose sweetness perfectly complement the bitterness of the brew.

Pork

Pork is not included on the Arabic menu. Do not underestimate how taboo this meat is to a Muslim. To prepare and serve pork, restaurants need a licence, separate fridge, preparation and cooking areas etc, and supermarkets must have a separate pork area and storage facilities. Images of pigs can also cause offence.

In Islam, it is forbidden to consume the blood or meat of any animal that has not been slaughtered in the correct manner. The meat of animals killed in accordance with the Islamic code is known as 'halaal'.

Alcohol

In Oman the attitude to alcohol is far more relaxed than in some other parts of the Middle East. The government grants alcohol licences to hotel outlets and independent restaurants, plus a few clubs.

Alcohol cannot currently be purchased in local supermarkets. Permanent residents who are non-Muslims can easily obtain liquor supplies under a permit system from their embassy. However, it is illegal to carry alcohol around, the only exception being when you are taking your purchases home directly from the liquor store or airport duty free. Keep your receipt as this gives you the right to transport alcohol. It is also illegal to resell alcohol to others. If you have an accident whilst driving under the influence of alcohol, the penalties are high and in addition, your vehicle insurance may well be invalidated.

Alcohol is not served during Ramadan, even in hotels.

Shisha

Throughout the Middle East, smoking the traditional 'shisha' or 'nargile' (water pipe) is a popular and relaxing pastime, usually savoured in a local café while chatting with friends. Shisha pipes can be smoked with a variety of aromatic flavours, such as strawberry and apple. Unlike normal cigarette smoking, the smoke is not inhaled into the lungs and is also smoothed by the water, creating a much more soothing effect.

A few restaurants in Muscat offer shisha smoking (see Going Out [p.229]).

Anyone for shisha?

Entering Oman

Visas

Other options → Entry Visa [p.48]
Residence Visa [p.48]

A passport (valid for at least six months and with enough blank pages) is required for all visitors, except nationals of Bahrain, Kuwait, Qatar and the United Arab Emirates who hold national identity cards; and holders of a Macau (SAR) Travel Permit.

Visa requirements have been greatly simplified as the country welcomes increased tourism. However, regulations should always be checked with your Oman Embassy or Consulate before travelling, especially if you plan to get a visa on arrival. Refer to the website of the Royal Oman Police, (www.rop.gov.om) to get the latest information on visitor visas, residence permits and all other types of visas (employment, investor, student, etc).

A joint visa facility between Qatar and Oman has recently been announced, under which citizens of 33 countries can apply online for a one-month visa that allows free travel between the two countries. After paying with credit card, you print the confirmation and receipt, and present these papers to the entry port in either country. Visit www.e.gov.qa for more information.

If you have sponsorship from an Omani entity, make sure they fax you a copy of the visa before the flight.

Social Visits

When travelling in Oman, the opportunity to visit a local home for some traditional Arabic coffee may arise. You should drink about two cups of coffee (no more!) – to show you've had enough, shake the cup lightly next time the coffee pot comes around.

When entering a local house, you should remove your shoes. Men may gather in a different area to women. Seating may be on carpets or low cushions – another good reason to dress modestly! Make sure the soles of your feet (or shoes) are not facing anyone.

The original should be lodged at As Seeb International Airport for you to collect at the Pre Booked Visa Collection counter before passport control, (assuming you haven't already received the original).

Tourists wishing to enter Oman are grouped, depending on their nationality, under either List No. (1) or (2), for which different procedures and terms of the visa apply. There are four types of visa that are of interest to visitors – single entry, multiple entry, express and common visa facility with Dubai.

Visa application forms are available before passport control, and there is a Travelex counter to ease visa fee payments. Verify the expiration date on your visa before you leave the Immigration counter.

For all visas, there is a stiff penalty of RO 10 per day if you overstay your welcome. This will be charged at the control point when you leave the country. In extreme cases you may not even be allowed to leave Oman until you have applied for an extension.

Single Entry Visa

Nationals in List No (1) may obtain this visa upon arrival at all air, land or sea entry points or through an Omani diplomatic mission, after filling in an application form and payment of RO 6 or its equivalent. The passport must be valid for at least six months. The visa is valid for one month and can be used within six months from date of issue. It can be extended for another month by personally applying to the Directorate General of Passport and Residency (DGPR) and paying a fee of RO 6.

Nationals in List No (2) should be part of a tour package from a government approved tour operator. The package should include accommodation and air tickets on Oman Air or Gulf Air. Visitors must apply for the visa at least two days before arrival; the tour operator usually helps to arrange visas. The completed form is sent to the DGPR who will process the application within two days from date of receipt. The visa is valid for one month and can be used within six months from date

of issue. It can be extended for another month by personally applying to the DGPR and paying a fee of RO 6. This visa is valid for entry at the airport only.

Do you need a Visa?

List No. (1)

Europe: Andorra, Austria, Belgium, Croatia, Czech Republic, Cyprus, Denmark, Estonia, Finland, France, Germany, Greece, Hungary, Iceland, Ireland, Italy, Latvia, Liechtenstein, Luxembourg, Macedonia, Malta, Maco, Netherlands, Norway, Portugal, San Marino, Slovakia, Spain, Switzerland, Sweden, Turkey, United Kingdom, Vatican

South America: Argentina, Bolivia, Brazil, Chile, Colombia, Ecuador, French Guyana, Paraguay, Peru, Suriname, Uruguay, Venezuela

Other Countries: Australia, Brunei Dar as-Salaam, Canada, Hong Kong, Indonesia, Japan, Lebanon, Malaysia, Maldives, New Zealand, Seychelles, Singapore, South Africa, South Korea, Taiwan, Thailand, Tunisia, United States

List No (2)

Albania, Belarus, Bosnia-Herzegovina, Bulgaria, China, Egypt, India, Iran, Jordan, Morocco, Poland, Romania, Russian Federation, Syria, Ukraine

Multiple Entry Visa

Nationals in List No (1) may obtain this visa on arrival at all land, sea or air entry points or through a diplomatic mission, after filling in an application form and payment of RO 10 or its equivalent. The passport must be valid for not less than one year at the time of applying. This visa is valid for one year. The holder can stay for three weeks at a time, but a minimum of three weeks must elapse between each visit. This visa cannot be extended but you may reapply for another multiple entry visa following the same procedure. For nationals in List No (2) the same conditions and procedures as for single entry visa apply. The visa fee is RO 10.

Express Visa

This visa is for nationals that are not in List Nos (1) and (2). It is issued within 24 hours through the Directorate General of Passport and Residency by applying directly at an Omani diplomatic mission abroad or through an Omani commercial or tourist establishment on your behalf. The processing fee is RO 7 or its equivalent. The passport should be valid for at least six months. The visa is valid for two weeks and cannot be extended.

Common Visa Facility

Nationals on List No 1 who are arriving from Dubai, with a Dubai tourist visa or entry stamp, do not need a separate visa to Oman if a joint facility form is completed. Forms are available at airports, sea ports and at the Hatta Hotel for those arriving from the Al Wajaja terminal. Visitors are allowed to stay for the period specified in the Dubai visa or up to a maximum of three weeks. This visa may not be extended. They may return to Dubai via the same route without needing a second UAE visa. A reciprocal visa agreement also exists with Qatar.

Road Permits

Many expatriates in Oman travel to Dubai by road and for this you need a road permit. There are three types: single trip, multiple trips within three to six months and multiple trips within six to 12 months. You will need an application form from the Royal Oman Police, two photos per travelling member, a copy of your labour card and passport, a copy of the sponsor's identity card if the sponsor is an individual, and a letter from the sponsor requesting the permit.

Meet & Greet

The Al Ahlan Lounge, based at As Seeb International Airport, provides a 'Meet & Greet' service. Staff will greet and assist new arrivals and then clear all visa formalities for them, while passengers wait in the comfort of the lounge, with Omani coffee and videos. They will guide clients through a separate Immigration counter (no waiting in line!) and facilitate baggage collection in around 20 minutes or less. They also give general information, will hold visas for collection and can arrange welcome bouquets of flowers and hotel transport. This extremely useful service is perfect for unaccompanied minors or those who require special assistance when travelling.

'Smart Residence Cards'

Beginning in 2004, Oman became the first Arab country to introduce machine-readable residence cards. To be used as a multipurpose identification document, the card stores address, thumbprint, photo, signature, civil status, passport details, and driving licence number for all residents aged 15 years and above. Future versions will also serve as medical record and electronic purse. It is issued at National Registration centres upon submission of a photograph and an application form. The card costs RO 10 for the two year validity period – a small price to pay for breezing through passport controls and for a considerably lighter purse!

The cost varies according to the service required, but the basic Meet & Greet service costs RO 6 per person. Holding a visa for collection costs an additional RO 2. A chauffeured limousine service is also offered from the airport to your hotel (costing between RO 17 and RO 22).

For more information or to book the service, ask your travel agent or call 24 601 758 (09:00 – 13:00 and 16:00 – 19:00, Saturday to Thursday) or the 24 hour As Seeb hotline (24 519 026).

As Seeb International Airport

Customs

No customs duty is levied on personal effects brought into Oman. It is against the law to import narcotics, mind-altering drugs, firearms (including toys and replicas) and pornography. There is no restriction on the import or export of any type of currency.

If you enter the country by air, your bags are X-rayed before you leave the airport and opened if there are suspect items. Up to five videos can be brought into the country and they may be temporarily confiscated for the material to be checked. You will be given a receipt to collect them at a later date and anything offensive will be erased (unless it's the whole thing, in which case you won't get it back!).

If you enter Oman by land, which means driving in from the United Arab Emirates, your bags may be searched at the Omani customs post. It is illegal to bring any alcohol into the country by road.

It is not advisable to bring your pets on holiday with you, as there are strict quarantine rules - various vaccinations and health certificates from the Department of Health and from your own vet may be required. Your pet may be subject to a six-month quarantine period although, strictly speaking, this is not required when coming in from a rabies-free country.

Duty Free Allowances:

- Two bottles of alcohol per non-Muslim adult (maximum two litres)
- 100 ml of perfume
- 400 cigarettes

Travellers' Info

Health Requirements

No health certificates are required for visitors to Oman, except for people who have recently been in a yellow fever infected area. However, it is always wise to check with an Omani diplomatic mission or your travel agent before departure as health restrictions may change. If you are travelling from a yellow fever area, you will need a certified vaccination at least ten days before arriving in Oman. Travellers from Africa may be tested for malaria on arrival.

Malarial mosquitoes are rarely a problem in the cities but they do exist, mainly around the wadis and pools in the mountains but they are not found in the desert or at altitudes above 2,000 metres. Long term residents do not usually take malaria tablets. As of 2001 the World Health Organisation declared Oman malaria-free and prophylaxis is no longer required, however, short-term visitors are advised to take them. Malaria resistance to chloroquine has been reported. Check requirements a month or so before leaving your home country.

Rabies has not been eradicated in Oman, so if you are bitten, seek medical attention immediately. Vaccinations for Hepatitis A and B, and typhoid are recommended.

The Airport

If you're lucky enough to have friends, family or the hotel shuttle to collect you from the airport, you'll avoid the hassles of bargaining for the taxi fare, most probably in broken English, with the driver. You can approach the 'Airport Taxi' desk to get an idea of a reasonable fare.

Need cash? There are Travelex counters in both the departures and arrivals area.

The Omani climate can be harsh, particularly in the summer months. Drink plenty of water and cover up when out in the sun. Try to avoid too much exposure to the sun between 10:00 and 15:00 and use the appropriate factor of sunscreen – sunburn, heat stroke and heat exhaustion can be very unpleasant and in some cases, dangerous.

Health Care

Other options → General Medical Care [p.78]

The quality of medical care in Oman is quite high and visitors should have little trouble obtaining appropriate treatment, whether privately or from government run hospitals. Towns in the interior have at least one health centre. Tourists are strongly encouraged to arrange private medical insurance before travelling since private medical care is fairly costly.

If you need medical assistance you may have to rely on friends, family or even a taxi to get you to a hospital since ambulance services are limited. In the case of life-threatening emergencies you can dial 999 throughout Oman and the Royal Oman Police will arrange appropriate transport.

There are many pharmacies and opticians in Muscat. Check the local newspapers, the English evening news (on TV) or 90.4 FM (Muscat and Salalah) on the radio for information about pharmacies on rotational 24 hour duty.

Public hospital

Travel Insurance

All visitors to Oman should have travel insurance – just in case. Choose a reputable insurer with a plan that suits your needs as well as the activities you plan to do while in Oman.

Embassies and Consulates

Embassies & Consulates

Austrian Embassy	24 793 135
Bahraini Embassy	24 605 075
Canadian Consulate	24 791 738
Chinese Embassy	24 696 698
Danish, Consulate Royal	24 708 304
French Embassy	24 681 800
German Embassy	24 832 482
Indian Embassy	24 810 536
Iranian Embassy	24 696 944
Italian Embassy	24 695 223
Japanese Embassy	24 601 028
Jordanian Embassy	24 692 760
Korean (South) Embassy	24 691 490
Kuwaiti Embassy	24 699 627
Lebanese Embassy	24 695 844
Malaysian Embassy	24 698 329
Netherlands, Embassy of	24 603 719
New Zealand Consulate	24 794 932
Norwegian Embassy	24 703 289
Pakistani Embassy	24 603 439
Qatar, Embassy of	24 691 152
Russian Federation	24 602 894
Saudi Arabian Embassy	24 601 744
South African Embassy	24 694 793
Sri Lankan Embassy	24 697 841
Switzerland, Consulate of	24 568 202
Thai Embassy	24 602 684
United Arab Emirates, Embassy of	24 600 988
UK Embassy	24 693 077
USA Embassy	24 698 989

Female Visitors

Women should face few, if any, problems while travelling in Oman. It is generally safe to walk unescorted in well-lit and well-populated areas in Muscat and Salalah. Travelling alone in the interior or taking a public taxi on your own is not recommended.

Single female travellers who don't want extra attention should dress modestly and avoid lower end hotels. When travelling to the interior, always keep on hand a long-sleeved shirt and long skirt or an abaya, in case you have to cover up quickly. No matter what, most foreign females receive some unwanted stares at some time or another, particularly on the public beaches. If you can ignore it you'll save yourself some aggravation!

Travelling with Children

Oman is a very family friendly place and kids of all ages will have a great time. Although there are few parks and amusement centres, there are endless activities, particularly in the winter, for those who love nature and adventure. Many families go out at weekends to camp and explore Oman's many wadis, beaches and mountains. The Muscat Festival also offers all sorts of fun filled activities for the whole family. The Activities and Exploring sections of this book will give a better idea of what there is to do for kids.

Hotels and shopping malls are generally well geared up for children, offering everything from babysitting services to kids' activities and small play centres. Restaurants, on the other hand, have children's menus but tend not to have many high chairs; it's best to ask when making reservations. Discounted rates for children are common – just ask.

Children are welcome!

Physically Challenged Visitors

Most of Oman's five and four star hotels have wheelchair access and toilet facilities for the physically challenged. However, wheelchair ramps are often really nothing more than delivery ramps, hence the steep angles. Reserved parking spaces for the physically challenged are available, and drivers generally respect them as the police often inspect.

Dress Code

As in all countries, a healthy amount of respect for the local customs and sensibilities is recommended. Short, revealing or tight clothing can be worn, but it will attract attention – most of it unwelcome. Attitudes in the rural areas are more conservative than in the cities.

Lightweight summer clothing is suitable for most of the year, but something slightly warmer may be needed in the evening for the winter months. In winter and summer, be sure to take some sort of jacket or sweater when visiting hotels or the cinema, as the air conditioning can be pretty fierce! In the evenings, restaurants and clubs usually have a mixture of styles – Arabic, Asian or Western – and anything goes. During the day, good quality sunglasses, hats and buckets of sunscreen are needed to avoid the lobster look!

Dos and Don'ts

Do make the most of your stay in Oman – have fun! But don't break the law. It's a simple and easy rule, and common sense will keep you out of trouble. In Oman, drugs are illegal and carry fines and normally a lengthy jail sentence. If you are caught bringing even a small amount of drugs into the country, you can be charged with trafficking. This can result in a life sentence or even the death penalty. Pornography of any sort is also illegal and will be confiscated immediately. Alcohol can be consumed in licensed outlets only, and not in public places such as wadis, beaches, or even your car.

The best rule of thumb is to respect the local laws, culture and religious sensibilities of Oman. Remember that you are a visitor here. Treat the local population with the same respect you'd expect back home.

Safety

While street crimes are uncommon in Oman and violent crimes rare, a healthy degree of caution should still be exercised. Keep your valuables and travel documents locked in your hotel room or in the hotel safe. Don't leave valuables or tempting items like mobile phones or portable computers in plain sight in a parked car, particularly in hotel parking lots. When in crowded areas, be discreet with your money and wallet. As with anywhere in the world (no matter how safe), just remain vigilant and know what's going on around you.

With a variety of driving styles converging on Oman's roads, navigating the streets either on foot or in a vehicle can be challenging. There are very few pedestrian crossings and overpasses but don't be tempted to make a run for it, particularly across the main Sultan Qaboos highway (and while driving, be on the lookout for those who do!).

Omanis are generally polite and will stop to let you cross, but do make eye contact and make sure their vehicle has completely stopped. Learn the rules of the road before getting behind the wheel, and drive defensively. Make sure you have insurance!

Police

The Royal Oman Police (ROP) maintain law and order in Oman. The ROP covers all aspects of public law and order, including crime, traffic and customs.

The ROP website (www.rop.gov.om) is extremely comprehensive and contains information on police services and procedures, as well as the locations of all police stations in Oman. The police headquarters are located on Death Valley Road in Muscat, and the telephone number is 24 560 021. 999 is the number for emergencies only.

Lost/Stolen Property

To avoid a great deal of hassle if your personal documents go missing, make sure you keep one copy with friends or family back home, and one copy in a secure place such as your hotel room safe.

If your valuables do go missing, first check with your hotel. If they can't help you, call the ROP Public Relations number (24 569 270) to report the loss or theft; they may be able to tell you what to do next. If you have lost your passport, your next stop will be your embassy or consulate. Refer to [p.22] for a list of all embassies and consulates in Oman.

Oman Tourist Info Abroad

There are currently no offices which promote Oman to travellers and businesses. Oman participates regularly in major tourism fairs and is believed to have recently obtained sufficient finance to open representative offices in the UK, Germany, Spain, Switzerland, the United States and Hong Kong.

Places to Stay

Visitors to Oman can be assured of a reasonable choice of places to stay, from hotels to hotel apartments, rest houses, officially approved campsites and even desert camps for tourists. The range of good quality, cheap hotels is limited, but there are some youth hostels that have opened recently.

With new emphasis on tourism as an income generator for the country, the number of hotels and resorts is expected to increase, and the facilities and services to get better and more competitive. Visitors can expect attractive promotions during the summer months as hotels strive to fill unused capacity.

Five Star Hotels

Other options → Weekend Breaks [p.146]

The hotels in Muscat are found mainly in the newer areas. Most of the beach hotels are located in Qurm Heights and Shati Al Qurm, except for one in the suburb of Al Ghubbrah, and another to the east of Muscat Old Town at Al Bustan. There are a few good hotels and a number of small, basic ones in Ruwi, the bustling commercial district. In Mutrah there are some less fancy hotels near the Corniche. There are also hotels of international standard in Salalah, Nizwa, Sur, Sohar and Khasab.

It takes around 15-25 minutes from the airport to reach the hotels in Al Qurm, while Al Bustan is a further 20 minutes or so. Ruwi is about 30-40 minutes from the airport. The larger hotels offer an airport shuttle service.

A hotel classification system, which gives an internationally recognised star rating system to hotels and hotel apartments, was recently put in place. This allows visitors to judge more easily the standard of accommodation they will receive.

As with anywhere else in the world, you can usually negotiate for discount on the rack rate or published rate. Check the Internet for discounted rates on the major hotels.

Hotel Apartments

A cheaper alternative to staying in a hotel is to rent furnished accommodation. This can be done on a daily/weekly/monthly or yearly basis. While it may not be as luxurious as a five star hotel room, a hotel apartment can feel more like home. Usually the apartments come fully furnished, from bed linen to cutlery, plus maid service. Additionally, there may be sports facilities, such as a gym and a swimming pool, in the building.

Rest Houses/Motels

Visitors who travel to Salalah and the interior can break their journey at one of the Arab Oryx rest houses on the highways out of Muscat. These are located at Ghaba (319 km from Muscat), Ghaftain (626 km) and Qitbit (765 km) on the Muscat-Salalah highway, and at Al Qabil (172 km from Muscat) on the road to Sur. The rest houses each have about ten simple, clean, air-conditioned rooms and a basic restaurant, with a filling station and fast food outlets. Ghaba Rest House has an indoor pool, but call ahead to make sure it is in use. The Al Qabil Rest House is perfect for visiting the Wahiba Sands or the Turtle Beach in Ras Al Hadd.

Rest Houses	
Al Ghaftain Rest House	99 485 881
Al Noorah Gardens Guest Houses	99 322 247
Al Qabil Rest House	25 581 243
Ghaba Rest House	99 358 639
Majan Guest House	25 431 910
Qitbit Rest House	99 085 686

Hostels

Three youth hostels have recently been built in Al Kamil town and the Al Wusta and Dhofar regions. Another hostel is planned in Al Dakhiliya. However, these hostels are primarily aimed at encouraging

Hotels

	Five Star	Beach	Phone	Map	Double	Email
Muscat	Al Bustan Palace Hotel P.233	✔	24 799 666	14-A1	129	albustan@interconti.com
	Chedi Muscat, The	✔	24 524 400	6-D2	85	reservation@chedimuscat.com
	Grand Hyatt Muscat	✔	24 641 243	6-D1	98	hyattmct@omantel.net.om
	Muscat InterContinental P.237	✔	24 600 500	7-A4	75	muscat@interconti.cpm
	Sheraton Oman Hotel	–	24 799 899	11-E2	52	sheraton@omantel.net.om
	Barr Al Jissah Resort & Spa		na		na	www.shangri-la.com
Salalah	Crowne Plaza Resort	✔	23 235 333	1-E3	40	hinnsl@omantel.net.om
	Hilton Salalah	✔	23 211 234	1-E2	80	sllbc@omantel.net.om

	Four Star	Beach	Phone	Map	Double	Email
Barka	Al Sawadi Beach Resort	✔	26 795 545	1-B2	32	alsawadi@alsawadibeach.com
Buraimi	Al Buraimi Hotel	–	25 652 010	1-B3	26.5	alburaimi@alburaimi.com
Khasab	Khasab Golden Tulip Resort	✔	26 730 777	1-A2	48	info@goldentulipkhasab.com
Muscat	Crowne Plaza Hotel P.231	✔	24 560 100	7-C3	58	cpmuscat@cpmuscat.com
	Golden Tulip Seeb	–	24 510 300	4-E4	43	novoseeb@omantel.net.om
	Haffa House Hotel	–	24 707 207	11-C2	25**	hhh@shanfari.com
	Holiday Inn Muscat	–	24 487 123	6-A2	69	mcthinn@omantel.net.om
	Mercure Al Falaj Hotel	–	24 702 311	11-C1	50	sales@omanhotels.com
	Radisson SAS Muscat P.241	✔	24 487 777	6-B2	43	Sales@radissonsas.com
	Ramada Qurum Beach Hotel	–	24 603 555	6-D1	48	ramadaom@omantel.net.om
Nizwa	Falaj Daris Hotel	–	25 410 500	1-B2	29.5	fdhnizwa@omantel.net.om
	Nizwa Hotel	–	25 431 616	1-B2	38	nizhotel@omantel.net.om
Sohar	Al Wadi Hotel	–	26 840 058	1-B2	31.5	gmalwadi@omanhotels.com
	Sohar Beach Hotel	✔	26 841 111	1-B2	35	soharhtl@omantel.net.om
Sur	Sur Plaza Hotel	–	25 543 777	1-B1	29**	gmsur@omanhotels.com

	Three Star	Beach	Phone	Map	Double	Email
Ibra	Al Sharqiya Sands	–	99 205 113	1-B1	18	na
Ibri	Ibri Oasis	–	25 689 955	1-B2	21.4	na
Khasab	Khasab Hotel	–	26 730 271	1-A2	30	na
Muscat	Al Burj International Hotel	–	24 798 008	9-D3	15	na
	Beach Hotel P.226	–	24 696 601	8-A4	25	beachhtl@omantel.net.om
	Best Western	–	24 692 121	1-B1	30	bwmuscat@omantel.net.om
	Holiday Inn Al Madinah	–	24 596 400	6-B4	50	mcthinn@omantel.net.om
	Holiday Villa Hotel	–	24 564 443	8-C2	25**	bahjahtl@omantel.net.om
	Ruwi Hotel	–	24 704 244	11-D2	28	reservationruwi@omanhotels.com
Salalah	Dhofar Hotel	–	23 292 300	1-E3	23	dhfhotel@omantel.net.om
	Hamilton Plaza Hotel	–	23 211 025	1-E3	25	hamilton@omantel.net.om
Sur	Sur Beach Hotel	✔	25 542 031	1-B1	25	surbhtl@omantel.net.om

	Two Star	Beach	Phone	Map	Double	Email
Muscat	Al Mina	–	24 711 828	10-A3	12	minahotl@omantel.net.om
	Marina Hotel	–	24 714 343	10-A3	16	na
	Mutrah Hotel	–	24 798 401	10-A3	16	na
	Qurum Beach Hotel	–	24 564 070	7-C3	22	qbhotel@omantel.net.om
	Seeb International Hotel	–	24 543 800	2-B3	12**	sihotel@omantel.net.om
Nizwa	Al Jabal Al Akhdar	–	25 429 223	1-B2	29.5	jakhotel@omantel.net.om

	One Star	Beach	Phone	Map	Double	Email
Buraimi	Abha Hotel	–	25 654 700	1-B3	25	na
Muscat	Al Raha	–	24 701 655	12-D3	12	na
	Corniche Hotel	–	24 714 707	10-A3	10	na
Nizwa	Al Diyar	–	25 412 402	1-B2	15	na
Salalah	Al Hanna Hotel	–	23 290 274	1-E3	14	msarawas@omantel.net.om
Sur	Ras Al Hadd Beach Hotel	✔	9937 6989	1-C1	23	na

Note: Rates are for peak season published rack rates and are inclusive of tax and service charges.

**Only 3 b/room duplex available

Al Bustan Palace InterCont. Htl
Map Ref → 14-A1

This award-winning hotel of palatial proportions nestles in a coastal oasis of 200 acres fronting rugged mountains. The elegant Arabic theme of the imposing lobby carries over to its 250 suites, all with private balconies. There are four international restaurants, including one of the best Chinese restaurants in Oman. The Al Khiran Terrace is extremely romantic and dinner, followed by a tour of the grounds and the private beach, is a must.

Barr Al Jissah Resort & Spa
Map Ref → na

A 45-minute drive from As Seeb International Airport, the new Barr Al Jissah resort is actually home to three separate hotels (a six-star and two five-star) offering 680 luxury rooms with a sea view and 19 food and beverage outlets. The resort has half a kilometre of private beach, plus three swimming pools, tennis courts, a fitness centre, diving and watersports facilities and the well-equipped spa. (Resort scheduled to open late 2005)

Crowne Plaza Hotel
Map Ref → 7-C3

Located on a cliff overlooking Al Qurm town and beach, this hotel has one of the best viewpoints in Muscat. The outdoor pool seems to spill onto the beachfront below, which can be accessed by steps from the hotel gardens. Its location makes dining alfresco in any of its three international restaurants, including the excellent Iranian restaurant Shiraz, a real pleasure. A lively African band at Duke's Bar keeps the dancefloor hopping.

Grand Hyatt Muscat
Map Ref → 6-D1

Its beachfront location in Al Qurm, a lazy river and the sumptuous Friday buffet lunch at the Mokha Café more than make up for the rather amusing décor of Arabian kitsch with a touch of Disneyland. Most of the Hyatt's 280 rooms have sea views. It has four international restaurants; the fun pub, Club Safari, and nightclub, Copacabana, are where the young and wealthy hang out.

Muscat InterContinental
Map Ref → 7-A4

This is an older hotel that has recently undergone a major facelift. The InterCon continues to be popular for its outdoor facilities, international restaurants, Al Ghazal Pub and regular entertainment in the form of dinner theatres and visiting bands. Some of its 265 rooms have views of Qurm Beach. A workout in the high tech fitness centre, or lap pool, is a must after the coffee lounge's pastries (the best in Muscat).

Radisson SAS Hotel
Map Ref → 6-B2

Just 15 minutes from the airport, this medium-sized hotel stands out in the Al Khuwar business district, where local and Middle Eastern restaurants abound. Some of its 142 rooms have views of the stark mountains behind. The Al Tajin Grill, Muscat's legendary steakhouse, is guaranteed to satisfy any serious cravings for perfectly grilled meat or seafood and serious desserts. The health club is well-equipped and there is a complimentary shuttle to Qurm Beach.

Sheraton Oman Hotel
Map Ref → 11-E2

One of the first and still the tallest building in Muscat, it dominates the Ruwi skyline and is perfect for the business traveller or serious shopper. It offers all the comforts of a standard Sheraton hotel, plus internet access in every room. The culinary theme nights, particularly Seafood Night on Wednesdays, make it an enduring favourite among expatriates and locals. There are four restaurants and three entertainment outlets, including a popular bowling alley.

The Chedi Muscat
Map Ref → 6-D2

This is the trendiest place to be in Muscat. Designed in traditional Omani architecture, its clean Zen-like lines are a welcome counterpoint to the increasingly opulent Gulf hotels. Guests have the choice of 119 rooms or 32 private villas to contemplate the azure waters and mountain ranges of Muscat. There are spa facilities, two pools, poolside cabanas and a private beach. The eponymous The Restaurant offers contemporary Asian/Mediterranean food.

Crowne Plaza Resort Salalah   Map Ref → 1-E3

Previously the Holiday Inn, this hotel underwent comprehensive renovation in 2004. It is set in a private garden beside the sea, and features 119 rooms and nine suites. There are three pools, kids' facilities, health and fitness facilities and a miniature golf course. Guests have three restaurants to choose from, including the new Dolphin Beach Restaurant offering alfresco dining with stunning views of the white sands and Indian Ocean.

Al Sawadi Beach Resort   Map Ref → 1-B2

Visitors to the Al Sawadi Beach Resort have the option of staying in one of the chalet-style rooms, or bringing a tent and camping on the private beach with access to the resort's facilities. Facilities include a pool, gym, tennis, squash and mini-golf. Available watersports include windsurfing, water-skiing, jet-skiing and kayaking. The dive centre offers PADI courses, and organises regular trips to spectacular dive sites at the nearby Daymaniyat Islands.

Golden Tulip Khasab   Map Ref → 1-A2

Opened in 2003, the Golden Tulip Khasab is situated in a small cove at the foot of the imposing mountains. Visitors can choose from guest rooms and suites or independent chalets. Eating and drinking options include a coffee shop, pool terrace, restaurant, the Oriental Café tent and 'Darts' English-style pub. There's a swimming pool and children's play area, and the hotel organises diving, fishing, and dhow cruising trips.

Sohar Beach Hotel   Map Ref → 1-B2

With its whitewashed exterior in the style of a large Omani fort, the Sohar Beach Hotel is something of a landmark. Five kilometres from Sohar town centre, the hotel offers 41 luxury guest rooms, suites and chalets (all with private balconies) and a choice of dining options such as the Sallan offering international cuisine. Leisure facilities include a swimming pool, gym, tennis court and crazy golf course, and of course the pristine sandy beach right on the doorstep.

Sur Plaza Hotel   Map Ref → 1-B1

Located a few kilometres from the centre of Sur, this hotel is a perfect base from which to explore the surrounding area including the turtle nesting sites at Ras Al Hadd and Ras Al Jinz. Formerly the Sur Mercure, the hotel offers 108 well-appointed guest rooms, and has a swimming pool, health club and gym. Dining options include Oysters Restaurant serving international cuisine, and two bars promising live entertainment each evening.

Nizwa Hotel   Map Ref → 1-B2

Located a few kilometres from the centre of Nizwa, on the main road to Muscat, the Nizwa Hotel benefits from a picturesque setting with landscaped gardens and the Hajar Mountains in the distance. There are 40 guest rooms, and way the hotel is arranged means that all have private access to the central swimming pool. The Birkat Al Mawz restaurant serves international cuisine and the hotel has two comfortable bars.

Hilton Salalah   Map Ref → 1-E2

The newest, and only, five star hotel in Dhofar, its simple Omani style exterior hides a luxurious domed lobby and mirror-like marble floors. Its beachfront location, 12 km from Salalah centre, allows guests to truly 'get away from it all' and enjoy the hotel's facilities. There are three international restaurants, two entertainment outlets, a health spa and a doctor on call.

Al Jabal Al Akhdar Hotel   Map Ref → 1-B2

This is the only hotel in the region, and makes an ideal base for those wishing to explore the stunning scenery of the 'green mountain.' The hotel has 24 rooms and a coffee shop/restaurant serving international cuisine. While the facilities in this new hotel are not comprehensive just yet, a swimming pool, and health and fitness facilities are planned for the near future.

General Info

Places to Stay

Hotel Apartments

Deluxe	Phone	Area	One B/room Apts (Weekly)	Two B/room Apts (Weekly)	Email
Al Amir Hotel Apartments	24 478 087	Al Khuwayr	126	147	na
Al Shorouq	24 789 900	Darsayt	105	175	na
Al Waffa Hotel Flats	24 786 522	Ruwi	126	161	alwaffamuscat@hotmail.com
Asas Residence	24 568 555	Qurm Heights	400	350	asasoman@omantel.net.om
Beach Hotel Apartments	23 235 999	Salalah	229	na	na
Haffa House Salalah	23 295 444	Salalah	287	369	house@omantel.net.om
Isra Hotel Apartments	26 730 562	Khasab	300	430	khastour@omantel.net.om
Manam Hotel Apartments	24 571 555	Al Wutayyah	120	150	www.manamhotel.com
Nuzha Hotel Apartments	24 789 199	Darsayt	98	140	na
Safeer Hotel Suites	24 691 200	Al Khuwayr	259	280	safeer@omantel.net.om
Samharam Tourist Village	23 211 420	Salalah	na	614	na

Note: Rates are for peak season published rack rates and are inclusive of tax and service charges.
   **Only 3 b/room duplex available

Omani youth to explore their country and should not be seen as 'backpacker' accommodation. For those travelling on a budget, some of the smaller hotels and the rest houses are good options.

Campsites

Other options → Camping [p.194]

Good weather and beautiful landscapes make camping a good option for accommodation in Oman. In the mountains or desert you can set up camp wherever you find a suitable spot, as long as it isn't on private or cultivated land and not too close to habitation.

If you are not too sure about camping 'in the rough', there are also official camping grounds with full amenities. The Oman Dive Centre is close to Muscat and for a cost of RO 3 per person (including breakfast) and RO 4 per tent you can camp on their site, which has a swimming pool and watersports facilities (www.diveoman.com). If you want to watch the nesting turtles at Ras Al Hadd you can camp inside the Turtle Beach Resort (25 540 068) which provides meals, bathroom facilities and guides. The fees are RO 3 per adult and RO 1 per child. You can also camp outside the grounds, but if you do you are not allowed to cook and toilet facilities are nothing more than a torch and a shovel!

You can camp in the Arabian Oryx Sanctuary in Jaaluni, which is more than six hours from Muscat by car. There are no facilities. It is very important that you contact them in advance, as they are very strict on poachers and you wouldn't want to be mistaken for one. Check their website (www.oryxoman.com) for requirements.

Getting Around

Other options → Exploring [p.97]
Maps [p.268]

A car, either private vehicle or taxi, is the most popular way of getting around Muscat and to the interior cities of Nizwa, Sur, Sohar and other towns on the highway routes. There are many taxis and a reasonable public bus service in Muscat, but due to the heat, very few people walk or cycle, and motorcycles are limited to a few brave souls. There are no trains and trams; Oman Air links Muscat to Salalah and Khasab, cutting down a day's drive to an hour or so.

Oman's highways are excellent and international traffic symbols are used. The major roads are two to four lanes, usually with European-style traffic circles or roundabouts at busy intersections (remember that, in Oman, drivers on the inside lane always have priority over those entering the roundabout). Further into the interior, the quality of roads is reduced to graded tracks that seem to

Desert/Wadi Driving

As you travel out of Muscat, camels and goats wandering out onto the roads are the major hazards, particularly at night when they are hard to see until it's too late. Camels often do not move out of the way, and some are hobbled which slows them down, so do not rely on them moving to let you by. If you hit one you'll do serious damage, not only to the camel but also to yourself and your vehicle.

Some of the roads cross wadi beds (shown by red and white poles). While these are dry for much of the year, more care should be taken in the wetter months as water levels can rise very quickly.

branch out in every direction. For this reason, 4 WDs are very popular.

Exits and roads are signposted in both English and Arabic, as are street and building/house numbers. However, people generally rely on landmarks to give directions or to get their bearings, and these landmarks are usually shops, hotels, petrol stations or notable buildings. To confuse matters further, places may not be referred to by their signposted name. For example, the Wadi Kabir Roundabout is usually known as the 'Incense Roundabout'.

Don't forget to check out the maps at the back of this book – they're easy to use and will help you point yourself in the right direction. You could also get a copy of the *Muscat Street Atlas* and the *Salalah Street Atlas*. If you're taking a taxi, ask someone to write the address for you in Arabic, just in case your driver speaks little English.

Car

Other options → Transportation [p.88]

Considering that in 1970 there were only 10 km of tarmac road in the whole of Oman, the country's present road network of over 10,000 km is excellent and drivers should have few problems while out and about. A dual carriageway links Muscat to Salalah (12 hours), Nizwa (two hours), Sur (three hours) and Sohar (two and a half hours). Driving to Khasab involves exiting Oman, entering the UAE, then exiting the UAE at Tibat and crossing into Mussandam. The whole journey may take as long as a day. Metalled and secondary roads go to virtually every town in the interior, even crossing the Rub Al Khali and the Ramlat Al Wahaybah.

Sign language

Driving Habits & Regulations

If you're ever going to get comfortable with driving on Oman's roads, the golden rule is to drive defensively. The legal driving age is 17, and the driving conditions can be described as 'immature', with lots of young, macho drivers fighting for their space on the tarmac. According to the Royal Oman Police (ROP), there are about 25 deaths per 100,000 people due to traffic-related incidents. While this figure may be low compared to other developing countries, the combination of high speeds, poor driving skills and inexperience on the roads remains lethal. Drivers seem to be completely unaware of other cars on the road, and the usual follies of driving too fast, too close, swerving, pulling out suddenly, not using the indicator lights and lane hopping happen far too regularly. Try to keep a reasonable stopping distance between yourself and the car in front. Ultimately it also helps to have eyes in the back of your head.

Zero Tolerance

The ROP exercise a strict zero tolerance policy on drinking and driving. It is illegal even to transport alcohol around Oman, except from the airport or liquor shop directly to your home. If you have had ANY alcohol to drink you are much better getting a taxi or appointing a non-drinking friend as your designated driver. If you are pulled over and found to have consumed alcohol you are likely to find yourself enjoying the hospitality of the police station overnight - at the very least.

If you are involved in an accident, whether it's your fault or not, and you are found to have been drinking and driving, your insurance is automatically void. Penalties are severe, so the message is simple – if you're going to drink, don't even think about driving.

The Royal Oman Police website (www.rop.gov.om) offers further information relevant to driving, such as traffic violations, road maps, and contact numbers. The number to call for traffic violations is 24 510 227.

The burgundy and white striped cars seen around are for learner drivers, so give them a wide berth. It is also a good idea to keep a lookout for pedestrians who frequently attempt to cheat death by crossing busy roads and major dual carriageways.

Driving is on the right hand side of the road, and it is mandatory to wear seatbelts in the front seats. Children should be in the back, and the use of handheld mobile phones while driving is banned. These rules apply countrywide, even though you'll

Blood Money

If you are driving and cause someone's death, you may be liable to pay a sum of money, known as 'blood money', to the deceased's family. The limit for this has been set at RO 5,000 per victim and your car insurance will cover this cost (hence the higher premiums). However, insurance companies will only pay if they cannot find a way of claiming that the insurance is invalid (such as if the driver was driving without a licence or, for example, under the influence of alcohol). The deceased's family can, however, waive the right to blood money if they feel merciful.

still see people driving with their child on their lap or happily chatting on their phones. The fine for these violations is RO 10. Drivers should pay the fine as directed by the police and not attempt to pay or negotiate a payment at the time of the violation.

The ROP are active in policing the roads and will even stop you to point out if your car is dirty! It is actually illegal to drive a dirty car in Oman, carrying a stiff penalty of RO 50, but if you're lucky you'll get away with a warning. This applies even to rented cars and off road vehicles, so there is invariably a queue at the car wash at the end of weekends. On the whole, the police are courteous and helpful (especially if you break down) and fairly stringent in applying the law. Carry your vehicle documentation card and driving licence at all times.

Speed Limits

The speed limits are clearly marked and are usually 60, 80 or 100 km/h within the Muscat area, and can be 120 km/h on roads to other parts of the Sultanate. When entering a built up area the speed limit can drop suddenly from 120 km/h to 80 km/h, so keep your eyes peeled for signs and speed traps. The roads have both fixed and moveable speed traps which are activated by travelling over 9 km/h above the speed limit. If you go more than 40 km/h over the speed limit the potential penalty is a year's ban from driving and a three-day prison sentence. In most cases you won't even know you've received a speeding fine until you renew your vehicle registration. You can check your traffic offences online at the ROP's website www.rop.gov.om.

Driving Licence

You can drive a rental vehicle for three months with either an international driving licence or a licence from your country of origin. If you wish to drive a private vehicle, you must first convert your licence

to an Omani licence. Citizens of some countries (see Driving Licence – New Residents [p.50]) can convert their licence directly, after taking a blood test. Unless you have an Omani driving licence you are not insured to drive a private vehicle.

Accidents

If you are involved in a traffic accident, however minor, you must remain with your car at the accident scene, call 999 to report the incident to the ROP, and wait for them to arrive. Under no circumstances should you move your vehicle until instructed by the ROP. Unfortunately, in Oman, when you have an accident you become the star attraction as the passing traffic slows to a crawl with rubberneckers.

In the event of a road accident where medical assistance is required, the ROP will arrange an ambulance to the nearest hospital.

Non-Drivers

In addition to dealing with the speed freaks in cars you will find that pedestrians and cyclists also seem to have a death wish! The few cyclists who do brave the roads will often be cycling towards you on the wrong side of the road, invariably without lights if it is night. Pedestrians often step out dangerously close to oncoming traffic and the lack of convenient, safe crossings makes life for those on foot especially difficult.

Parking

In most cities in Oman parking is readily available and people rarely have to walk too far in the heat. Increasing numbers of pay and display parking metres are appearing around Muscat. These areas are clearly marked with a blue signboard and cost 50 baisas for every half hour. Meters operate between 08:00 – 13:00 and 16:00 – 21:00 Saturday to Thursday. Parking is free of charge on Fridays and public holidays. If you haven't purchased a ticket, do not display it properly or fail to renew an expired one, you may be unlucky enough to receive one from the police for RO 3. Try to have loose change (25 and 50 baisa coins) with you since there are no automatic change machines available.

Petrol/Gas Stations

Petrol stations in Oman are numerous and are run by Shell, Omanoil and Al Maha. Most offer extra services, such as a car wash or a shop selling the usual necessities like bread and milk, cigarettes and newspapers. Most visitors will find petrol far cheaper than in their home countries – prices range from 120 baisas per litre for Super (98 octane), 114 baisas per litre for Regular (95 octane) and 102 baisas per litre for diesel.

Car Hire

You'll find all the main car rental companies, plus many locally owned ones, in Muscat and Salalah. Some have counters open 24 hours at As Seeb International Airport. The larger, more reputable firms generally have more reliable vehicles and a greater capacity to help in an emergency (an important factor when handling the administrative aftermath of a car accident). Depending on the agency, cars can be hired with or without a driver, and the minimum hire period is usually 24 hours. Daily rates range from approximately RO 14 (including insurance) for smaller cars to RO 29 for 4 WDs. Baby/child seats are available on request. Comprehensive insurance is essential (and make sure that it includes personal accident coverage).

Most international and foreign driving licences are accepted. Residents need an Omani driving licence to rent a car.

If using a rental car, tickets for speeding and parking offences may be charged to your credit card, sometimes weeks after your departure!

Car Rental Agencies	
Muscat	
Avis	24 601 224
Budget	24 794 721
Europcar	24 700 190
Hertz	24 566 208
Salalah	
Avis	23 202 581
Budget	23 235 160

Taxi

Apart from cars, taxis are the most common way of getting around and they will often hoot to attract your attention if you are on foot. All taxis have distinctive orange and white stripes. Each taxi is privately owned by an Omani National, who may or may not speak good English. Taxis are not metered so always agree on a price before you get in. The usual fare from As Seeb airport to Muscat is RO 7, but this can be reduced if you have good negotiating skills!

Shared taxis and the small 14-seater mini vans are cheaper and a more popular option, especially for longer journeys. They have set routes and fares and to board one of these, just flag them down at the side of the road. A short ride from Ruwi to Muscat can cost as little as 200 baisas.

Grab a cab

There are two private taxi firms which you can phone for a taxi at any time of the day or night. These are highly recommended for women travelling alone.

Taxi Companies	
Hello Taxi	24 607 011
New Taxi Service	24 501 020

Airport Bus

While there is no official 'airport bus', the ONTC runs a daily bus service (No. 24) from Mutrah Fish Market to As Seeb Souk, with a stop at As Seeb International Airport. The bus leaves Mutrah every hour from 06:00 to 09:00, at 14:00 and then again hourly from 16:00 to 21:00 and takes less than an hour to reach the airport. The return route departs from As Seeb Souk every hour from 06:30 to 10:30, at 15:30, and then again from 17:30 to 19:30, and takes about 15 minutes to the airport.

General Info

Getting Around

Bus

The state-operated Oman National Transport Company runs a national network of buses and coaches all over Oman and to the UAE. Buses operate to all areas of the capital and timetables, destinations and route numbers are found at bus stops (marked with a red bus on a green sign) at the side of the road. Most trips cost a few hundred baisas, making this the cheapest method of getting around. Fares are paid to the driver when you board, so try to have the correct change ready.

Coaches leave from the bus station in Ruwi (just off Al Jaame street, along from the Sheraton Hotel) and Mutrah Fish Market for long distance trips to Salalah, Al Buraimi, Sinaw, Yankul, Ibri, Sur, Fahud-Yibal, Marmul, Dubai and Abu Dhabi. They are comfortable, air-conditioned and generally on time. The daily bus service to Salalah (four times a day) costs RO 16 return and RO 8 one-way and takes a seat-numbing 12 hours. There are also daily buses from Ruwi to Dubai and Abu Dhabi, and from Salalah to Dubai. Tickets from Muscat to Dubai cost RO 10 return and RO 6 single, and the journey takes five hours each way. Check the daily newspapers or the ONTC website (www.ontcoman.com) for coach schedules.

Other contacts: Oman National Transport Company – 24 490 046; Ruwi ticket office – 24 708 522; Head office hot line – 24 492 948; Salalah – 23 292 773.

A private bus company, Comfort Line (24 702 191), offers a twice a day service, although not air-conditioned) from Muscat to Dubai for RO 6 one way and RO 10 return. The ticket office is located behind the Sultan Qaboos mosque in Ruwi.

Air

Other options → Meet & Greet [p.20]

Muscat's location at the crossroads of Europe, Asia and Africa makes it an easily accessible city, with most European cities only seven hours away. Currently, only Gulf Air flies direct to London (eight hours) and Bangkok (six hours). Other international flights to Muscat may stop in other Gulf cities, such as Dubai or Abu Dhabi, which adds another 40 minutes flying time.

Seeb International Airport is located 35 km, or about 20 – 30 minutes, from the main part of Muscat. It is a comfortable, modern airport that also has domestic flights to Salalah and Khasab (Mussandam). The Salalah and Khasab airports handle limited international flights. When leaving the country, there is an airport tax that you will have to pay (RO 3), but this should be included in the cost of your ticket. All flights to and from As Seeb are listed in the daily newspapers.

The country's national carrier is Oman Air, but Oman also has part ownership in Gulf Air along with the UAE, Qatar and Bahrain. Oman Air operates direct flights to various international destinations, including India, Bangladesh, Sri Lanka, Lebanon, Egypt and the UAE. To contact Oman Air, call 24 707 222 for ticket sales, 24 519 223 for flight information, or visit their website at www.oman-air.com.

Flying to Salalah and Khasab (Mussandam) cuts down a full day's journey from Muscat to 90 minutes and is the quickest option if you don't plan to camp or visit the many attractions along the way. Oman Air offers two or three daily flights from Muscat to Salalah. The cost for a return economy

The bus station

class fare from Muscat to Salalah is in the region of RO 68 (for a stay of less than three days), and RO 76 (for a longer stay). Flights to Khasab are on Monday, Wednesday, Friday and Saturday and cost RO 48 return. Oman Air also flies directly to Khasab and Salalah from Dubai.

A duty-free shop is located in the departure area at As Seeb and outbound travellers have a chance to win cash prizes or luxury cars with a raffle ticket. The arrivals hall has two Travelex exchange counters (one before Immigration for visa payments), a smaller duty free shop, a tourist information counter, car rentals and hotel reservations.

Airlines	
Air Canada	24 566 046
Air France	24 704 318
Air India	24 799 801
British Airways	24 568 777
Emirates Airline	24 792 222
KLM Royal Dutch Airline	24 566 737
Lufthansa [P.vi]	24 708 986
Oman Air [P.310]	24 519 495
Swiss Air	24 787 416

Boat

Recently an increasing number of cruise ships have been calling into Muscat as part of their itinerary. However, there are no scheduled passenger services to and from Muscat to other countries. That may change when a planned cruise port terminal at Port Sultan Qaboos in Muscat and a 32 metre quay at Khasab are constructed.

At various places along the coast, it is possible to hire fishing boats or dhows for day trips to hidden bays or, for instance, along the coast of Mussandam. There are no scheduled internal boat services from Muscat to other parts of the country. However, there is a daily ferry from Shanab to Masirah Island, the only way travellers can get to the island. The ferry leaves at high tide (be prepared to wait) and the crossing takes one and a half hours.

Walking

Other options → Hiking [p.205]

Since Muscat is so spread out, walking is not a particularly good way of getting around. However, parts of the city are worth seeing on foot, in particular Qurm Park, Qurm Beach, Ruwi, Muscat Old Town, the Corniche and the souk at Mutrah.

The heat in the summer months, with daytime temperatures of over 40°C, makes it rather a sweaty experience. After sunset, it gets cooler and a walk can be pleasant, even if still a little warm. From October to March the temperatures are perfect for being outside.

Cycling

Other options → Cycling [p.197]

While you won't see many tourists cycling their way around Oman, it can be an enjoyable way to see the country. There are no designated bike lanes, so the busiest parts of Muscat and the highways are best avoided if you're on two wheels. However in the quieter areas there are some good riding spots, and you'll probably see parts of Oman that you might miss in a car.

In the hotter months there is a higher risk of heat exhaustion, dehydration and sunburn, so take the necessary precautions.

Money

Cash is the preferred method of payment in Oman, although credit cards are accepted in larger department stores, restaurants and hotels. Cash and traveller's cheques can be exchanged in licensed exchange offices, banks and international hotels – as usual a passport is required for exchanging traveller's cheques. To avoid additional exchange rate charges, take traveller's cheques in US dollars.

Local cheques are generally accepted in business but not for personal purchases. If you are taking a lease for accommodation, it is likely that you will need to pay by cheque and supply post-dated cheques for the remaining period of the rent. There are no restrictions on the import or export of any currency. Israeli currency is prohibited.

Local Currency

The monetary unit is the Omani rial (RO or OR). It is divided into 1,000 baisas (also spelt 'baiza'). Notes come in denominations of rials 50, 20, 10, 5, 1, 1/2 (i.e. baisa 500), 1/4 (i.e. baisa 250) and baisa 200 and 100. Coin denominations are baisa 50, 25, 10 and 5. Denominations are written in Arabic and English. It is best to take a few minutes to familiarise yourself with the currency, although shopkeepers are generally honest when giving you your change.

The way prices are written can lead to some confusion. An item may be marked 'RO/OR.1,500' – the price could be fifteen hundred rials or one rial and five hundred baisa! The value of the item will usually be obvious.

For clarity in the guidebook we have standardised the way prices are shown. Thus one rial and 500 hundred baisa will be shown as RO 1.500 and fifteen hundred rials as RO 1500, while fifteen rials will be RO 15.

The Omani rial is tied to the US dollar at a mid-rate of approximately US$1 ~ RO 0.385, which has basically remained unchanged for a number of years.

For up to date information on foreign exchange, call 1106 (English) or 1107 (Arabic) 24 hours.

Exchange Rates

Foreign Currency (FC)	1 Unit FC = X RO	RO 1 = X FC
Australia	3.39	0.3
Bahrain	1.02	0.97
Bangladesh	0.006	155.8
Canada	3.18	0.31
Cyprus	0.86	1.16
Denmark	0.06	14.83
Euro	0.5	1.99
Hong Kong	0.49	20.2
India	0.008	113.7
Japan	0.03	268.9
Jordan	0.54	1.83
Kuwait	1.31	0.75
Malaysia	0.1	9.87
New Zealand	0.27	3.65
Pakistan	0.006	153.9
Philippines	0.006	143.5
Qatar	0.1	9.45
Saudi Arabia	0.1	9.74
Singapore	0.23	4.25
South Africa	0.06	15.38
Sri Lanka	0.003	256.3
Sweden	0.05	18.06
Switzerland	0.32	3.08
Thailand	0.01	99.8
UAE	0.1	9.53
UK	0.72	1.38
USA	0.385	2.59

Rates updated — February 2005

Banks

The well structured and ever growing network of local and international banks, strictly controlled by the Central Bank of Oman, offers the full range of commercial and personal banking services.

Transfers can be made without difficulty as there is no exchange control and the Omani Rial is freely convertible to other currencies. Bank headquarters are clustered in the Ruwi business district of Muscat. There are branches all over Muscat and Salalah, and in major towns such as Nizwa, Sur and Sohar.

Banking hours are usually 08:00 - 12:00 (Saturday – Wednesday) and some are also open 08:00 - 11:30 on Thursdays.

Main Banks

Muscat

Bank Banorabe	24 796 896
Bank Dhofar Al Omani Al Fransi	24 790 466
Bank Dhofar Al Omani Al Fransi (Salalah)	23 211 130
Bank Muscat SAOG P.61	24 701 528
HSBC Middle East P.IFC	24 799 920
National Bank of Oman	24 708 894
Oman Arab Bank	24 703 247
Oman Arab Bank (Salalah)	23 292 005
Oman International Bank	24 682 500
Oman International Bank (Salalah)	23 291 512
Standard Chartered Bank	24 703 999

ATMs

Most banks operate Automatic Teller Machines (ATMs) that accept a wide range of cards. Common systems accepted around Muscat include MasterCard, VISA, American Express, Global Access, Plus System and Cirrus. ATMs can be found in shopping malls, at the airport and various street locations in Muscat.

Exchange rates used in the transaction are normally extremely competitive and the process is often faster and less hassle than traditional traveller's cheques.

Money Exchanges

Money exchanges are found all over Muscat and Salalah, offering good service and exchange rates (often better than the banks). Exchange houses are usually open from 08:00 - 13:00 and 16:00 - 19:00 and often operate in the evenings at weekends.

Alternatively, hotels will usually exchange money and traveller's cheques at the standard hotel rate (i.e. poor!). At As Seeb airport, there is a Travelex counter before Immigration to facilitate visa payments.

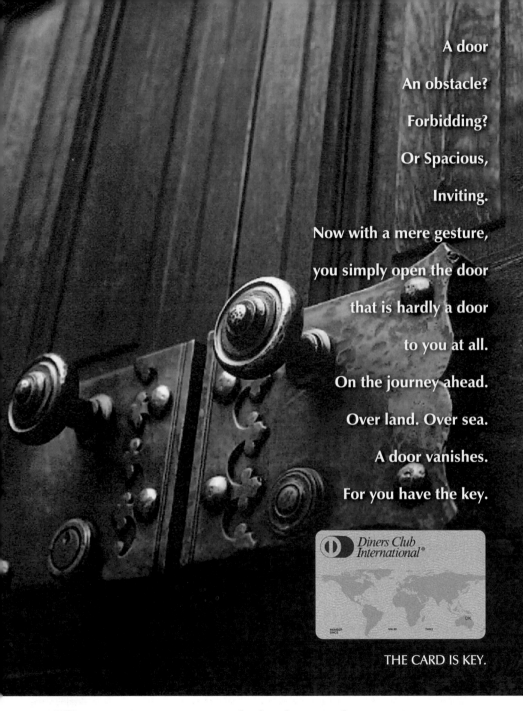

A door

An obstacle?

Forbidding?

Or Spacious,

Inviting.

Now with a mere gesture,

you simply open the door

that is hardly a door

to you at all.

On the journey ahead.

Over land. Over sea.

A door vanishes.

For you have the key.

THE CARD IS KEY.

Diners Club
International

Global Card Service L.L.C

P.O. Box 2666, Postal Code 112, Ruwi, Sultanate of Oman
Tel: 771 2591 / 771 2495 / 771 3020, Fax: 771 2058
E-mail: dcoman@omantel.net.om, Website: www.dinerscluboman.com

Exchange Centres	
Abu Mehad	24 566 123
Gulf Overseas	24 834 182
Hamdan	23 296 903
Laxmidas Tharia Ved	24 712 562
Modern Exchange Co LLC	24 832 133

Credit Cards

Larger shops, hotels and restaurants in Muscat and Salalah accept major credit cards (American Express, Diners Club, MasterCard and Visa) and they will often have the card logos displayed at the entrance. However, if you are travelling in the interior, or are shopping at souks and smaller shops, often cash is the only form of payment accepted.

Tipping

An increasing number of hotels and restaurants automatically include a service charge of at least 5% (check the bottom of your bill!), although it is unlikely to end up with your waiter. Tipping is optional although a few hundred baisas are greatly appreciated, particularly in smaller restaurants.

Media & Communications

Newspapers/Magazines

Newspapers and magazines are available from bookshops, supermarkets, petrol stations, grocery shops and hotel shops.

The Oman Daily Observer, the *Times of Oman* and the *Oman Tribune* (200 baisas each) are the three daily English newspapers. *The Week* is a free tabloid published every Wednesday. The Arabic language newspapers are *Al Watan*, *Al Shabiba* and *Oman*.

Foreign newspapers, mainly American, Asian, British, French and German, are available in hotel bookshops and supermarkets, although they are usually a lot more expensive than they are back home and a few days out of date. Hobby magazines, such as computing, photography, sports and women's magazines are also available, but are very expensive (expect to find blacked out portions, or sometimes even whole pages missing if they contain images considered offensive to Islam). The Press Act allows the government to censor publications for political and cultural reasons.

Further Reading

There is a wide selection of books and magazines on Oman, ranging from coffee table books to specialist/hobby books and travel books. One useful publication is the monthly *Oman Today*, a mini guidebook costing RO 1. It features a variety of articles on what's happening around town, interesting places to visit and things to try.

History buffs will appreciate *Arabian Sands* by the great explorer Wilfred Thesiger, a pictorial account of his crossing of the Empty Quarter with Bedouins in the early 60s. For adventurous souls, the following are indispensable *Off-Road in Oman*, *A Field Guide to the Geology of Oman*, *Wadis of Oman*, *Bluewater Fishing in Oman*, *Caves of Oman*, and *Snorkelling and Diving in Oman*.

> **Why Pay Full Price?**
> *Bargaining is a traditional part of doing trade in Oman and it is still widely used today, especially in the souks. You can sometimes end up paying half of the original asking price. A discount of 10% is usual, even in appliance stores, but not in supermarkets or department stores. It can also be a fun way to do business; vendors will square up to 'do battle', courteously offering their customers some kahwa, and in return customers should bargain hard!*

Post & Courier Services

Other options → Postal Services [p.78]

The government operated General Post Office (GPO) is the sole provider of postal services in Oman, although there are other courier companies operating both locally and internationally. The GPO is reasonably efficient and, in addition, there is an express mail service called EMS. Omani stamps (six new issues annually) are very colourful and make good souvenirs.

As a guide, postcards cost 50 baisas within the Sultanate and to other GCC countries, 100 baisas to other Arab countries and 150 baisas to everywhere else. Letters cost from 50 baisas internally (15g maximum) and from 250 baisas internationally (10g maximum). Airmail letters take ten to 14 days to reach USA, Europe or Australia, and half the time using EMS.

Opening times vary, but most branches are open 07:30 - 14:00 from Saturday to Wednesday. They close at 11:00 on Thursdays and are not open on Fridays. Post offices at the Al Harthy Complex (Al Qurm) and As Seeb are open longer hours.

There is no home address postal service. Incoming mail is delivered to post office boxes at a central location, from where you can collect it.

Courier Companies	
DHL	24 563 599
Federal Express	24 833 311
TNT	24 489 170
UPS	24 700 165

Radio

Oman has a number of commercial radio stations, broadcasting mostly in Arabic. The government-owned English language radio station (90.4 FM in Muscat and Salalah) plays a mixture of news, talk shows, classical music and modern music. The station operates daily from 06:00 to midnight and the schedule is printed in the local newspapers. News headlines, weather forecasts and a list of pharmacies on duty are read frequently. The BBC World Service broadcasts on 15575 Hz. If you want to hear Arabic music, tune in to 89.0 FM and 107.7 FM.

Television/Satellite TV

Other options → Satellite TV & Radio [p.78]
Television [p.78]

There is only one local television channel, Oman TV (Channel 6 in Muscat and Channel 10 in Salalah). The shows on this channel are mainly Arabic, although you'll get the occasional film or series in English. The daily English news broadcast is at 20:30, and news in Arabic is shown at 11:00, 15:00 and 18:00. It also broadcasts by satellite throughout the world. Go to www.oman-tv.gov.om for the schedule of English programmes on Oman TV.

There is a wider choice of programmes offered by satellite TV, ranging from international entertainment and films to sport, cartoons and current events. Most leading hotels have satellite television for guests, and it is usually quite straightforward for a resident to have installed (see [p.78]).

Telephones

Other options → Telephone [p.75]

All communication is provided by the government-owned Oman Telecommunications Company (Omantel), except for mobile telephony which has two providers – Oman Mobile and Nawras Telecom. Mobile phones, or the numbers, are often referred to as 'GSM', although only true GSM connections can make and receive international calls.

National call charges are based on the area to which the calls are made. International direct dialling is possible to over 170 countries and surprisingly enough the charges are often reduced rather than increased. Rates are published in the telephone directory and the Omantel website (www.omantel.net.om).

New Telephone Number Formats

All phone numbers will become eight digit numbers. The emergency number will remain as 999.

At time of going to press, the number changeover was nearing an end, with most areas having been successfully changed. If you dial an old Oman number, a voice recording will give you the new number. Check the Omantel website for new number formats (www.omantel.net.om)

To prepare for future privatisation of the communications sector, the Telecommunications Regulatory Authority decided to convert all numbers in Oman to eight digits, following a phased schedule by region. Most areas have already been successfully changed. The changeover dates and the new numbers are published in the daily newspapers and on the Omantel website. If you dial an invalid number a voice recording will give you the new number. Otherwise, dial 198 for directory assistance. And keep checking the Omantel website for updates on the changeover.

Public pay phones accept phone cards or coins. Cards are available in values of RO 2 and RO 5 from petrol stations, supermarkets and some smaller shops. Pagers are a cheap alternative to mobile phones and are mainly used in business.

Area Codes & Useful Numbers	
Oman Country Code (landlines & mobiles)	00968
Directory Enquiries – National	198
Directory Enquires – International	143
International Operator	195
Fault Reports	192
Billing Information	24 632 124
GSM Helpdesk	196
Speaking Clock	140
Electricity	154
Water Emergency	153
To call an Oman number from overseas, dial ++ 968 xx xxx xxx	

Simple, Effective, Appealing – three qualities essential to great design.

The **Explorer Designlab** team approaches every project with this in mind, creating perfect solutions to everyday design problems while challenging trends and exploring the boundaries of creative design.

Design is central to your company's image, and has a direct effect on how you are perceived by your customers. Contact us to learn how you can benefit from our services.

CORPORATE IDENTITY • BROCHURES & REPORTS • PACKAGING • ADVERTISING • PRINT • WEB

PO Box 34275 Dubai, UAE
Phone (+971 4) 335 3520 **Fax** (+971 4) 335 3529
Email Info@Explorer-Publishing.com

www.Explorer-Publishing.com

Internet

Other options → Internet Cafés [p.260]

Internet use is still in its infancy in Oman, with about 5% of the population subscribing to it. Omantel is the sole provider of internet services and all sites are accessed through its proxy server. Some sites, particularly those considered incompatible with Islamic values, are blocked to maintain the country's moral and cultural values. You can surf the internet without being a fixed subscriber using the 'Log n Surf' system. All you need is a computer with a modem and a regular phone line. Only a few areas of Muscat are currently wired for high speed broadband connections so the transmission rate varies considerably. Your email address will be an eight character user name, along with the omantel suffix (username@omantel.net.om). See the New Residents section [p.77] for how to get connected. Internet cafés in Muscat provide easy and cheap access, but there are no wi-fi hotspots.

Websites

There are a number of websites about Oman, some more relevant and interesting than others. New sites are cropping up all the time. The table on [p.41] lists those that we have found to be the most useful – if you come across any helpful sites that are not listed here, please let us know and we'll include them in the next edition.

Annual Events

Oman Annual Events

Throughout the year Oman hosts a number of annual events, some of which have been running for years. The events described below are the most popular and regular fixtures on Oman's social calendar; most of them, except for the Khareef Festival in Salalah, are held in and around Muscat and the Batinah coast.

Bullfighting

In the true sense of the word, two gargantuan Brahmin bulls butt heads and lock blunt horns sumo-style until one of them stumbles, flees or is knocked out of the arena. Human handlers restrain over-aggressive bulls rather than incite them. The bulls are bred for fighting and winners can fetch up to RO 2,500. Matches start at around 16:00 during the winter months in Barka and As Seeb. Admission is free.

Camel Racing

Time spent watching this traditional sport is an extraordinary experience. Races are spread over several days, with different sprints organised daily for different age groups of camels. The camels are bred and trained for racing; those with Omani bloodlines are the most coveted. Winners can fetch up to RO 250,000. Camel races are held at tracks in As Seeb, Salalah, the Interior and Batinah regions during public holidays and National Day celebrations. Admission is free.

> **Dynamic Dubai**
>
> *Dubai has its fair share of annual events too - if you fancy a road trip don't leave home without your trusty copy of the Dubai Explorer. It's the ultimate pleasure and leisure companion to this vibrant and cosmopolitan city, and it's packed with pointers to help you make the most of your trip.*

Eid Al Adha

Meaning 'Feast of the Sacrifice', this four day holiday marks the end of the annual pilgrimage to Mecca. The ritual involves the slaughtering of many animals and giving of alms and food to the poor. The holiday is celebrated 70 days after Eid Al Fitr.

Eid Al Fitr

This Islamic holiday lasts three days and celebrates the 'Feast of the Breaking of the Fast'. It is held at the end of Ramadan. Check the newspapers, radio and television for exact dates as it depends upon an official sighting of the moon.

Exhibitions

With the increasing importance of MICE (Meetings, Incentives, Conferences, Exhibitions) tourism to Oman, the government-owned Oman International Exhibition Centre has seen a full calendar lately. It is located a stone's throw from the As Seeb International Airport and is adjacent to the Golden Tulip Seeb Airport Hotel. See [p.43] for a monthly listing of exhibitions.

Websites

Business/Industry

www.businessdirectoryoman.com	Business Directory for Oman
www.cbo-oman.org	Central Bank of Oman
www.chamberoman.com	Oman Chamber of Commerce and Industry
www.gcc-sg.org	what the GCC is all about
www.kom.com.om	Knowledge Oasis Muscat – Oman's IT park
www.mctmnet.gov.om	Muscat Municipality
www.mocioman.gov.om	Ministry of Commerce and Industry
www.moneoman.gov.om	Ministry of National Economy
www.mrmewr.gov.om/environmental.htm	Ministry of Regional Municipalities & Environment & Water Resources
www.muscatmall.com	Online shopping
www.omanet.om	Ministry of Information
www.omantourism.gov.om	Ministry of Tourism
www.oeronline.com	Oman Economic Review
www.oite.com	Oman International Trade Exhibitions Center
www.omantel.net.om	Internet and telephone services provider; search for mobile and fixed phone numbers
www.omantel-yellowpages.com	Online Yellow Pages
www.tenderboard.gov.om	Tender Board

Embassies

www.oman.org/gov90.htm	Websites of embassies in Oman
www.embassyworld.com	Phone numbers of Omani embassies abroad and foreign missions in Oman

Hotels/Sports

www.motorsport.com	Motor sport rallies in the Middle East

Hotel details listed in General Information [p.25], and sporting organisations in Activities

Oman Information

www.apexstuff.com/common/omanessentials.asp	Oman Today – The essential leisure guide
www.arab.net	News of the Arab world
www.beautifuloman.com	With hotel coupons to download!
www.destinationoman.com	All about Oman and getting here
www.geocities.com/Baja/Dunes/5260/index.htm	Travelling in Oman - in French, English, German - with photos
www.khareefsal.om	About Dhofar and the 2001 Khareef Festival
www.nizwa.net	Environment and culture, plus many links to Oman websites
www.oman.org	Oman Studies Centre - links to many websites
www.omanglobe.com	News about the Middle East
www.omannews.com	Oman News Agency; daily updates
www.omanobserver.com	Daily newspaper
www.oman-radio.gov.om	Oman radio broadcasts schedule
www.oman-tv.gov.om	Oman TV programmes schedule
www.outpostexpat.nl	Outpost Expatriate Network, for expats living or relocating abroad
www.rop.gov.om	Royal Oman Police – visa information and viewing traffic fines
www.soukofoman.com	On-line shopping for traditional clothes and art
www.timesofoman.com	Daily newspaper
www.clinics-oman.com/clinics.htm	Private Clinics, Dentists, Private & Government Hospitals, Opticians and Pharmacies

General Info

Annual Events

General Info

Annual Events

Al Fahal Island Swim

Petroleum Development Oman has been hosting this challenging, yet fun, competition every May since 1989. Brave competitors get up at 06:00 to swim four kilometres from Al Fahal Island to the Ras Al Hamra Recreation Centre beach. Anyone can participate; swimmers just need to fill in the entry form, pay the fee of RO 5 and organise boat support.

Horse Racing and Show Jumping

Oman is famous for its pure-bred Arabian horses, which originate from Zad-ar-Raakib, the stallion given by the Prophet Solomon to the Azd tribe. The Oman Equestrian Federation (24 490 424) organises the Annual Royal Meeting, national show jumping competitions every winter, and the Royal Equestrian Show every five years, at the Enam Equestrian Grounds in As Seeb.

Islamic New Year's Day

This day marks the start of the Islamic Hijri calendar, which is based on the lunar calendar.

Khareef Festival

This festival is held in Salalah each year, from late June to September, to celebrate the monsoon season. There are music and dance performances from different regions of Oman, the exhibition and sale of Omani handicrafts, and sports events. It is a chance to witness rare performances such as the Zanooj dance, which involves a cast of thousands.

Lailat Al Mi'raj (Ascension of the Prophet)

This day celebrates the Prophet's ascension into heaven. In 2005 it is expected to be on 1st September.

Muscat Festival

This 22 day event is designed to showcase Oman's vibrant history and culture, in order to boost tourism. It is organised by Muscat Municipality in January and February. Traditional dances, camel races, concerts, sporting and educational events, and various activities for adults and children are held in different venues throughout Muscat. Some hotels and commercial centres offer discounts.

Musical Events

Fete de la Musique, a traditional French festival of music organised by the French Embassy, is held every year on June 21. The Ras Al Hamra Music Ensemble, composed of PDO employees and their families, hosts five concerts a year – two ensemble concerts (one in a wadi!), one piano evening, and two children's concerts. Contact Pat Wind (Chairperson), on 24 678 522, or RAHRC (PDO) office (24 677 321) for timings. Admission is free.

National Day

Oman's National Day is on 18 November, as is his Majesty's Birthday. Therefore celebrations continue on 19th November. There are parades, fireworks, camel races and bullfights throughout the country. Many Omanis return to their home villages to celebrate, so the roads may be busier than usual.

Renaissance Day

Held on 23 July, this day commemorates the accession of His Majesty Sultan Qaboos to the throne.

ROSO Concert Series

Although Oman has no tradition of classical music, the Sultan's passion for it led to the creation of the Royal Oman Symphony Orchestra in 1985. It is composed entirely of young Omanis trained locally by foreign experts. A lively series of public concerts is held in the winter season, usually at the Oman Auditorium of the Al Bustan Palace Hotel. Enquire at the hotel for the concert schedule.

Wahiba Challenge

Usually held in October, this motor sports event involves crossing the Wahiba Sands from east to west in a 4 WD. The organiser, PDORC Land Rover Adventure Club, emphasises that it is not a race, but rather a test of skill and endurance – you will have to cross about 31 dune ridges in 60 km! More information is available on www.omanlandrover.com.

Muscat Festival

Main Annual Events – 2005

January

01	New Year's Day (fixed)
02	Royal Oman Symphony Orchestra
13	Flat Horse Races (Bahla)
16	Port & Maritime begins
21	Eid Al Adha (moon)
21	Muscat Festival begins
24	Royal Oman Symphony Orchestra
25	Eid Fair begins
27	Flat Horse Races (Sinaw)
27	Football Tournament (As Seeb Beach Park) begins
30	Bowling Tournament begins

February

02	Royal Oman Symphony Orchestra
02	Eid Fair ends
03-11	Hockey Tournament (As Seeb Beach Park)
06	Bowling Tournament ends
08-10	Oman Travel Market
08-12	GCC Men's Beach Volleyball Championship
10	Islamic New Year's Day (moon)
10	Cycling Championship
10	Flat Horse Races (Al Khaboura)
11	Terry Fox Run
11	RAH Music Ensemble 'Music in the Wadi'
16-26	22nd Al Khartoum International Exhibition
18	Muscat Festival ends
18	Football Tournament (As Seeb Beach Park) ends
19	Port & Maritime ends
23	Muscat Int'l Book Fair begins

March

03	Flat Horse Races (Jaalan-Sur)
04	Muscat Int'l Book Fair ends
11	Flat Horse Races (Bidiye, near Sinaw)
13-17	Indian Trade Fair
14	RAH Music Ensemble Evening
16-18	Oman International Rally 2005 (FIA MidEast)
22-26	Wedding 2005 Exhibition
31	Flat Horse Races (Ibra)
31	Ideal Home Exhibition begins

April

08	Ideal Home Exhibition ends
12-14	Ghedex/Trainex/Jobex 2005
13	RAH Music Ensemble Concert

21	Prophet Mohamed's (PBUH) Birthday (moon)
25-29	Comex 2005

May

06-14	Furniture Exhibition
09	RAH Music Ensemble Piano Evening
09	Syrian Trade Fair begins
22-30	Arabian Catering Show
tbc	Al Fahal Island Swim

June

03	RAH Music Ensemble Concert for Children
17	Syrian Trade Fair ends
21	Fete de la Musique
27	Pakistan Solo 2005 Exhibition Begins

July

03	Pakistan Solo 2005 Exhibition ends
15	Khareef Festival begins
23	Renaissance Day

August

31	Khareef Festival ends

September

01	Ascension of the Prophet (moon)
13-16	Motor Show
22-30	Autumn Trade Fair

October

04	Ramadan begins
19-23	Lifestyle Exhibition
tbc	Wahiba Challenge

November

03	Eid Al Fitr (moon) Ramadan ends
4-12	Eid Festival
18	National Day
18	Birthday of HM Sultan Qaboos
21-28	Oman Desert Express

December

05-7	GCC Water & Power Exhibition
11-17	Woman Exhibition
23-31	International Beauty Exhibition
31	Bank Holiday

tbc – to be confirmed   For more information on these events, see [p.40].

Denotes public holidays

We make good health happen!

We have always strived to bring good health to homes with our products,
our services and our expertise. In your well being lies our success.
It's a commitment we've maintained all these years and what we'll pursue till the end.

Muscat Pharmacy & Stores, we bring good health to you!!!

• Pharmaceuticals • Medical & Hospital Equipment & Furniture • Laboratory Equipment • Glassware & Furniture
• Veterinary Medicine & Instruments • Medical & Surgical Goods & Hospital Disposables • Perfumes
• Cosmetics & Toiletries • Baby Foods & Baby Care Items • Consumer Products • Watches
• Fashion Jewellery & Gift Articles

24 Hours Service Branches:

• Ruwi Main: 24702542/ 24794186 • Al Sarooj: 24695536 • Al Khuwair: 24485740/ 24487980
• Al Ghubra North: 24497264 • Al Mawelah: 24537080 • Sohar: 26840211/ 26842703 • Al Hail: 24535977
• Hamriya: 24833323 • Salalah: 23291635

Muscat Pharmacy & Stores LLC

An ISO 9001:2000 Company

We bring good health to you!

P.O. Box 438, Postal Code 113, Muscat, Sultanate of Oman.
Tel.: (+968) 24814501 Fax: (+968) 24815202

New
Residents

New Residents

Highlights...

Housing   p.60

Moving house can be a major headache, especially in a foreign country, but fear not – our comprehensive housing section will guide you through all those accommodation conundrums. In addition to advice on rental procedures and avoiding property pitfalls, there's an overview of all the main residential districts and a Setting Up Home section to help you settle in without too many headaches.

Get Support   p.84

Relocating to a new country, particularly one where the cultural differences to your home country are significant, can lead to feelings of isolation, stress and depression. Don't go it alone – there are medical professionals and support groups that can help you through the tough times. Or you can find a group or network to help you make new friends.

New Residents

Table of Contents

Overview

Oman offers the best of many worlds and has become a popular destination in the Middle East. It is relaxed and friendly, modern and full of character, and is developing all the time, but not too fast. Omanis are wonderfully warm and charming and will make you feel very welcome. In comparison with neighbouring Dubai, Oman is still relatively conservative, so be aware of local customs and expectations of behaviour – especially in the way you dress and behave in public. Things may move a little more slowly than you are used to, but if you can respect the Omani way of life and reciprocate their courtesy your patience will be rewarded. Just keep a sense of humour and an *insh'allah* (God willing) attitude, and you'll be fine.

Seasoned expats say that life in Oman has a distinctive quality. The expat community is small and tightly knit so you get to know people very quickly and you can't go anywhere without bumping into someone you know (or several people you know, several times a day!). That can be comforting or frustrating, depending on your point of view. It's a cosmopolitan place so you'll have opportunities to make friends from all countries, all backgrounds and all walks of life. The pace of living and the outdoor lifestyle particularly suits families with young children, giving Oman society a more settled quality. People tend to stay longer, often requesting extended contracts. However, there isn't a great deal on offer for young adults and those with older children sometimes decide to move on after many happy years.

Oman's continual development means that things change regularly, sometimes quickly and without warning, so the following information is intended only as a guide to what you will have to do to become a car owning, house renting, fully connected resident of Oman. Always check procedures and details beforehand; your sponsor/employer will be able to help.

This chapter gives information essential for new arrivals, with the aim of reducing the difficulties of relocation and helping you to make a smooth transition into the new area. The main focus is on Muscat and the surrounding areas as more than half of the country's economic activity is concentrated in Muscat, the industrial centre of Rusayl next to it and the surrounding Batinah region. All the major companies, ministries, foreign embassies, training institutes and the university are located in this area. Oman is a big country with eight administrative regions, each with several wilayats (towns), and 45% of expatriates live in Muscat while the remainder are spread throughout Oman.

In The Beginning...

...there was a sponsor. To become a resident in Oman you need someone to legally vouch for you. This is usually your employer, who becomes your legal sponsor. Once you have residency you can then sponsor your spouse, parents or children, as long as you meet the specific requirements to do so.

The first step to acquiring residency is to enter the country on a valid entry visa (see Documents [p.48]).

If you are entering Oman because you have a job, your employer in Oman will usually provide your visa. If you do not already have a job secured, you may obtain a visit visa to enter the country for a short time (see Visas – Entering Oman [p.18]). If you live in Oman and wish to apply for a visa for a family member or friend, you can do so at the immigration department at Seeb Airport or you can leave it up to them to get a visa on arrival (if they hold passports that allow them to do this) – either way, it will cost RO 6.

The original entry visa documentation must be presented to Immigration officials on arrival at the airport, and your passport will be duly stamped.

Once you have entered the country on a work visa, you can apply for residency. This should be done within 60 days of entering Oman or a fine will be incurred. You also require a labour card. Your employer will usually process all required documentation for you, and sometimes for your family as well.

Residence visas are valid for three years and can be renewed (although this does not apply to elderly parents or maids – see Residence Visa [p.48] and Domestic Help [p.72]). Labour cards and health cards are valid for one year. As long as you are a qualified professional with a university degree or have an established employment history, you'll face few difficulties in obtaining the necessary paperwork to become a resident.

Useful Advice

When applying for a residence or work visa, resident card, driving licence or any type of permit, you will always need a bundle of Essential Documents (see below). You'll also have to complete countless application forms, which usually have to be typed in Arabic. Although this will probably be organised by your sponsor, most government offices and hospitals have small cabins where typists offer translation services in English and Arabic for between 300 baisas and RO 1. Most also offer photocopying services and some of the larger ones can take instant passport photos.

Essential Documents

To save repetition in the following section, Explorer has devised a list of Essential Documents. These are standard documents that you will always need to produce for administrative procedures. Additional documents will be referred to in the appropriate paragraph.

- Original passport (for inspection only)
- Photocopy of the personal details and visa pages in your passport
- Passport size photographs
- Copy of labour card (if you are working)
- Copy of sponsorship certificate for non-working residents

You will need countless passport photographs over the next few months, so save time and get about 30 taken at once. There are plenty of small photo shops around; ask for the negative so you can get reprints quickly and cheaply. Photo booths are commonly found in shopping centres but unfortunately not where you need them quickly, such as vehicle licensing offices.

Usually two passport photocopies and two photographs will be required each time you apply for anything. For other documents you may also have to supply the original (for inspection) with the photocopy.

Documents

Entry Visa

Other options → Visas [p.18]

It's always smart to keep the happenings of the city in consideration when planning your journey. Whether you are on holiday or moving to live, plan your arrival to fall between October and March if you can. Oman is extremely hot and humid in the summer and apart from a mad dash from your air-conditioned house to your air-conditioned car to

the air-conditioned shops, you won't want to spend much time outdoors.

If you are in Oman on a visit visa and want to work you must first find an employer (who will be your sponsor), then transfer to an employment visa in order to apply for your residence visa and labour/resident card. This is done through the immigration department and, again, your sponsor will make the arrangements. Although visas can be exchanged at the immigration office, you can also do a 'visa run' – leave the country for a few days and re-enter on a new visa. The usual destination of choice is Dubai so it's a good excuse for a shopping trip and a bit of exciting nightlife.

The Oman government has recently begun to promote tourism more actively and has revamped the visa system, making it easier for tourists and short-term visitors. Refer to the new visa classifications in the General Information section [p.18].

Health Card

Although most expats have private medical insurance provided by the company they work for, public hospitals and health centres are still an option for any resident of Oman.

To get free medical care, apply for a 'health card' at your nearest health centre. On your first visit to the Ministry of Health centre nearest to where you live, or hospital in case of emergency, take along your labour/resident card, passport and passport photograph. People who haven't received a labour card can also use the facilities by providing proof of their employment in Oman.

For a full list of government health centres and hospitals to find one nearby, check the Ministry of Health website at the following address: www.moh.gov.om/ mohhospital.php

Residence Visa

Other options → Visas [p.18]

Before getting a visa you must get a no objection certificate (NOC). This is an official document stating that neither your Omani sponsor nor the government has any objection to your entering the country (see below).

There are two types of residence visas – one for employment (when you are sponsored by your employer) and one for residence only (when you are sponsored by a family member). Normally, you or your employer will apply for a residence visa at the

Omani embassy in your country of origin, before you leave for Oman. Your sponsor should organise everything related to your visa, including payment. On arrival your company's PRO or your sponsor will take you to the Royal Oman Police (ROP) station on Death Valley Road to be fingerprinted. Those working must have labour clearance and an employment residence visa; spouses and family members are each issued with a 'joining family' residence visa. It is illegal to work on a joining family residence visa, even part time. If you wish to work you must get an employment visa. If you are working for the same sponsor as your spouse, exchanging the visa is usually a simple process. If you obtain a job elsewhere you must transfer sponsorship to your new employer and go through the whole process from the beginning. Your new sponsor will do what's necessary.

It is advisable, if possible, to try to avoid doing this (or anything which requires the involvement of government departments) during Ramadan, when everything tends to slow down until after Eid, by which time there will be a huge backlog! The ROP is located near Muscat Private School on Madinat As Sultan Qaboos Street (Death Valley Road), and the phone number is 24 600 099.

All expats seeking employment or applying for residency in Oman must have a health certificate from their home country, stating that they are free from illness and not carrying any communicable diseases.

Sponsorship by Employer

Your employer should handle all the paperwork, and will usually have a staff member (who is thoroughly familiar with the procedure) dedicated to this task alone. After your residency is approved they should then apply directly for your labour card (see below). You will need to supply the essential documents and your education certificates. You must have your certificates attested by a solicitor or notary public in your home country and then by your foreign office to verify the solicitor as bona fide. The Oman embassy in your country of residence must also sign the documents. While this sounds like a runaround, it is much easier if you get this done before you arrive in Oman.

Family Sponsorship

Once you are sponsored by your employer you can arrange sponsorship for your family members. Many employers will help you with this task. If yours doesn't, the process can be lengthy and

tedious. There are two family sponsorship options available – a Family Joining Visa or a Family Residence Visa.

A Family Joining Visa is for your spouse and children only. The Family Residence Visa is for relatives that do not fall into the Family Joining Visa category, such as siblings or elderly parents. Brothers and sisters of the resident must be younger than 18 years and a document must be provided stating that there is no other family income outside Oman. People on family sponsorship may not work in Oman, paid or unpaid. Once a visa has been granted, the holder has up to six months from the date of issue to enter Oman. The visa is valid for two years from the date of entry. This visa is renewable and allows multiple entries.

No Objection Certificate (NOC)

Once the NOC has been issued, a number will be sent by telex or fax to the airline from the Omani Immigration Department, authorising them to board you on the flight to Muscat. If the airline does not have this authorisation, you will not be allowed to board the plane. On arrival at the airport in Muscat you must go to the NOC counter where you will receive a small piece of paper, which you take to passport control and exchange for your visa.

Oman national flag

The NOC can only be collected from Seeb International Airport. Most hotels can arrange an NOC in about a week. You just need to make a reservation and send a copy of your passport, a list of the countries you have visited in the past year and, in some cases, passport photos. The hotel will usually charge a small fee for the service and ask for your commitment to stay with them for a minimum of three nights. Some people, for example journalists or Palestinians, find it more difficult to get an NOC; women travelling on their own usually find it easy.

Labour Card

The labour card, issued by the Labour Department, is a legal document certifying the employment status of an individual. To work in Oman you have to hold a valid labour card, which should be renewed annually. You can only apply for your labour card once you have residency. If your employer is arranging your residency, your labour card should be processed directly after your residency has been approved. If you are on family residency and decide to work, your employer (not your visa sponsor) will need to apply for your labour card. Your sponsor should supply an NOC. Women on their husband's or father's sponsorship are not allowed to work unless they have a labour card (also known as a work permit). The labour card is very important; if an officer asks you to produce your card, and you are unable to do so, you can be heavily fined.

From 2005, the Government intends to start issuing resident cards to all citizens. This card replaces the labour card, which will be phased out. Using biometric recognition, the resident card is multi-functional and features the holder's personal details, driving licence, emergency medical data and electronic validation at immigration checkpoints. It will also serve as an electronic cash card for transactions at government organisations and some business institutions. Cards are issued by the Directorate General of Civil Status. You will need a completed application form, passport, medical certificate, labour clearance from the Ministry of Manpower (private sector workers) and two photographs. Non-working residents (family members) need a completed application form, passport, birth certificate, medical certificate and two photographs. Further information can be requested from the Directorate General of Civil Status, located off the Seeb Airport Roundabout.

Free Zones

Free zones have not developed in Oman in the same way they have in other Gulf states, but Muscat has one small development called Knowledge Oasis Muscat. The first stage of this venture is situated in Rusayl, north-west of Muscat near the Sultan Qaboos University, and is now fully occupied by a collection of Omani, regional and multinational companies. There are plans to build another phase.

Companies can set up in Knowledge Oasis with 100% foreign ownership and receive other benefits including no personal or company taxes, exemption from import duties and competitively priced, high standards of infrastructure.

Certificates & Licences

Driving Licence

Other options → Transportation [p.88]

Though Oman is one of the more tranquil Middle Eastern countries, the driving is still fast and furious and accident statistics are alarming. In response, the Government has initiated a road safety campaign and is active on the Arab Countries' Council for Road Safety. Crashed vehicles are on display outside Death Valley Road police station in Al Qurm, where they serve as a grisly warning to passing motorists (although it could be argued that rubbernecking at the more dramatic examples constitutes a hazard in itself), and weekly accident statistics are published in the press. Many of the larger business organisations conduct road safety workshops. Muscat is essentially a driver's city – there is very little provision for pedestrians and driving on the highway can be nerve wracking, particularly at peak times. However, many pedestrians still risk dashing from one side of the highway to the other through the speeding traffic, rather than walk to one of the pedestrian crossings built in an effort to prevent such suicidal behaviour.

Automatic Licence Transfer

The following driving licences are transferable in Oman without taking a driving test: All Gulf Cooperation Countries (GCC), Australia, Belgium, Brunei (Sultanate of), Canada, Denmark, Finland, France, Germany, Ireland, Italy, Japan (after translation), Jordan, Lebanon, Luxembourg, Monaco, Morocco, the Netherlands, New Zealand, Norway, Spain, Sweden, Tunisia, Turkey, United States of America, United Kingdom

To apply for a driving licence you must be a resident over 18 years of age. Visitors may drive a hired or borrowed car on a valid international or home country licence (see Vehicle Leasing [p.88]). Residents from many countries, including the UK and US, may simply exchange their national licence for an Omani one as long as they've had that licence for at least one year. The transfer is done at the traffic police headquarters on Death Valley Road, and costs RO 20. You will need to have an eye test done before you can transfer your licence. Your company's PRO should take you to the police station (located near Muscat Private School) and help you through the process of licence exchange or test booking. Driving licences are valid for ten years but can be renewed. Roads are policed rigorously by the Royal Oman Police. Drinking and driving is illegal, and if you are caught you will be in quite deep trouble and may face hefty fines and probably even jail time. If you have an accident and you've been drinking, your insurance will be invalidated. Remember, it's zero tolerance – even one drink puts you way over the limit. You are not allowed to use your mobile phone while driving unless you are connected to a hands-free device. If you are caught talking on your handset, you face a fine of up to RO 70. Always carry your driving licence when driving; you may be fined if you fail to produce it at a spot check. If you have any queries on driving licence transfers or traffic regulations, you can contact the ROP Directorate of Traffic on 24 600 099.

Driving Licence Documents

- Licence Exchange form with signature and stamp of sponsor
- An NOC from your sponsor/company (in Arabic)
- Two photographs
- Passport and resident permit copy
- Original driving licence along with a photocopy (and translation, if requested by the Traffic Police)
- Blood Group Certificate

Additional requirements for Female Applicants:

- NOC letter addressed to the Director of Licensing brought in person by the guardian or substitute
- If married, marriage certificate or birth certificate of a child
- If unemployed, a copy of husband's labour card and a letter from his sponsor/company

Driving Test

Those not on the automatic licence transfer list, or who haven't driven in their country of origin, will need to take a driving test. The first step is to obtain a learning permit – start by picking up an application form from the traffic police. To do this you'll need to take the 'Essential Documents' (see [p.48]) and RO 5. You will be given an eye test at the traffic police. Your next step is to find a reputable driving school.

No Omani Licence?
The traffic Law permits expatriates on a visit visa to drive rental cars for 3 months. Expats on employment visas should have Omani driving licences.

There are only a few, recently opened, driving schools in Oman that advertise in the local paper. Most instructors work individually and you find them by word of mouth. Many driving instructors operate out of Death Valley Road police HQ, although some will come to your house. They drive white cars, easily recognisable by the red diagonal stripes. You can usually pick up a recommendation by word of mouth or through your company. There are female driving instructors for women although no female test inspectors.

When your instructor feels you are ready to take the test you will have to sit a three part driving test, comprising a reversing test, a road test and a highway code test. The first involves reversing between oil drums placed in two parallel rows barely wider than your car; you have to get it right first time and you can't take the road or theoretical tests until you've passed this test (known, with fear and loathing, as 'the barrels'). Once you've passed all three tests you have to apply for your licence through the authorised driving school. The police are known to be strict in issuing new licences and this process can take several months. You'll need perseverance!

Driving Schools	
Al Firsan United Enterprises	24 565 776
Morning Star	99 441 688

Liquor Licence

Other options → Alcohol [p.152]

Attitudes to drinking are quite relaxed in Oman, as long as it is done in an appropriate place – being drunk in public or behaving badly while under the influence of alcohol are dealt with severely. Do not take this lightly; rowdy, drunken behaviour can even result in you being deported. There are no

New Residents
Certificates & Licences

pubs as such, but you can drink in hotel bars, licensed restaurants and private clubs, and at the many social events that are generously sponsored by the major alcohol retailers. Recently, some hotel bars' opening hours have been extended to 03:00, brightening up the social life considerably. To buy alcohol to drink at home you must have a liquor licence. Only non-Muslim residents with a labour card are permitted to apply. For married couples, the wife can only be included on the permit if her husband works in the Interior. Licences cannot be used outside the city in which they are issued.

The licence entitles you to spend up to a specified amount each month. This is usually not more than 10% of your salary, although if your job entails corporate entertaining you can apply for a larger allowance. The licence is valid for two years. You can't 'bank' your allowance – if you don't spend the full allowance in a particular month, you lose it. This explains the frantic 'stocking-up' queues in the shops on the last day of each month, especially before Ramadan and Eid, when all bars and retail outlets are closed and restaurants do not serve alcohol.

New liquor permits and renewals are available from the Liquor Licensing Office (located at the ROP Station at the end of Ruwi Street). You will need an NOC in Arabic and English, a copy of your passport and labour or resident card, a copy of your employment contract, a copy of your labour card statistical form (issued by the Directorate of Labour Affairs), two passport photographs and 3% of your monthly salary. For renewals, you will also need your previous permit and a copy of the previous permit's front page.

It is illegal to carry alcohol around in your car so you must go straight home from the shop. Drunk driving is illegal and rigorously policed; if you are caught you are likely to be imprisoned immediately for at least 24 hours and if you have an accident and have been drinking your insurance will be invalid.

The Liquor Licensing Office is open from 07:30 to 12:30 (Saturday to Thursday), and the phone number is 24 704 666.

Birth Certificate & Registration

The birth of an expat child should be registered within two weeks of the date of delivery. If you don't have the correct documentation you may face difficulties when you next try to leave Oman. You'll get an official birth certificate from the hospital where your child was born (it costs RO 6), and you then need to have this certificate stamped at the

Ministry of Foreign Affairs Attestation Office (Consular section – 24 699 500) in Al Qurm. Then you need to go to your embassy, where your baby will be issued with a passport, before applying for your baby's residence visa through the usual channels. If you are British you can register your child's birth with the British Consulate – this is not compulsory but it means your child will have a British birth certificate and will be registered at the General Registry Office in the UK. Before the birth, it is worth checking the regulations of your country of origin for citizens born overseas (see [p.22] for a list of embassies and consulates in Oman).

To register your child with the Omani authorities, you will need a completed application form, birth notification from the Ministry of Health (birth certificate), resident cards or passports of both parents and the parents' marriage certificate. Legal responsibility for registering the child's birth rests with the father, although in his absence it may also be done, in the order of their listing, by any adult relative present at the birth, any adult residing with the mother, the doctor or any midwife who attended the event.

Explore the world outside

Marriage Certificate & Registration

While the singles' scene in Oman may not set your heart on fire, you just never know when you'll turn a corner and meet the love of your life. Most couples prefer to return to their countries of origin to get married, but if you are planning to marry in Oman you have a number of options (see below). All marriages should be registered, within 30 days, at the Department of Notary Public in Al Khuwayr. To do this you'll need a completed application form, marriage notification from the Ministry of Justice, or a marriage certificate authenticated by the Omani Diplomatic Mission in the country where the marriage took place (if it took place abroad). If one of the newly-weds is Omani you'll also need his/her resident card or passport and ID card, as well as an approval letter from the Ministry of Interior. The marriage can be registered by the husband or the wife, or by their fathers. While the Department of Notary Public in Al Khuwayr is part of the Ministry of Justice, it is separately located in Dohat Al Adab Street, one street down from the Radisson SAS Hotel. The phone number is 24 485 795, but not many speak English here, so unless you have an Arabic speaking friend a visit may be more effective than a phone call. The opening hours are 07:30 to 14:30.

Muslims

Two Muslims wishing to marry should apply at the marriage section of the Sharia Court in Al Wutayyah. You will need two witnesses, both Muslims. The woman does not need the permission of her father or brother to marry, unlike in other parts of Arabia. Passports and passport photocopies are required and you may marry immediately. The Sharia Court is located just off the Al Wutayyah Roundabout, next to the ROP football stadium.

Civil Weddings

Couples wanting a non-religious ceremony should contact their local embassy or consulate as they may have regulations and referrals to arrange for a local civil marriage, which can then be registered at their embassy.

Christians

There are Catholic and Protestant churches in Muscat (Ghala and Ruwi) and Protestant churches in Salalah and Sohar. Protestants should contact the Pastor at the office in Ruwi for an appointment (24 799 475/24 702 372). Both partners should be resident in Oman and must provide proof of their marital status, this can take the form of a letter from their sponsor or embassy. Partners from different countries must provide evidence from their respective embassies that they are free to marry. Widowed or divorced people must produce appropriate original documents indicating they are free to marry. Four witnesses, two from the bride's side and two from the groom's, must attend the

wedding ceremony. Copies of the passport information page and visa of each partner must be provided. The church requires at least one month's notice to perform the ceremony and pre-marital counselling is recommended. The marriage certificate must be attested by both the Ministry of Foreign Affairs (Consular section) Attestation Office and by the couple's respective embassies. There is no fee for the ceremony but a donation is welcomed. To marry in the Salalah or Sohar Protestant churches, contact the pastors (23 235 677 in Salalah or 26 840 606 in Sohar).

Catholics should contact the priest at the Catholic Church of Saints Peter & Paul in Ruwi (24 701 893) or at Holy Spirit Catholic Church in Ghala (24 590 373). The couple is expected to take instruction before the wedding ceremony takes place. You will need your original baptism certificates and a no objection certificate from your priest stating that you have not previously been married in a church. A declaration of your intent to marry is posted on the public noticeboard of the church for a period, after which, if there are no objections, the priest will fix a date for the ceremony. The parish priest will advise you of his fee accordingly.

Hindus

Hindus can be married through the Shiva Temple (24 737 311), the Darsayt Temple (24 798 548) and the Indian Embassy (24 814 274). Contact the Indian Embassy for further details.

Divorce

All divorces occurring in the Sultanate need to be reported within 30 days from the date of the event. You will need a completed application form, divorce notification from the Ministry of Justice or divorce certificate authenticated by the Omani Diplomatic mission in the country where the divorce took place. If one of the married couple is an Omani citizen, their resident card or passport and their ID card should be produced, along with an approval letter from the Ministry of Interior. Divorces are finalised at the Department of Notary Public (24 485 795). See Marriage Certificates & Registration (above) for location details.

Death Certificate & Registration

In the unhappy event of the death of a friend or relative, the Royal Oman Police (ROP) must be informed immediately. The ROP will make a report and you must also inform the deceased's sponsor, who is responsible for registering the death with the authorities; this must be done within two weeks. To register the death, the sponsor should produce a completed application form (which you get from the ROP), a notification from the Ministry of Health, the ID of the deceased, the resident card or passport, and a letter from an official authority notifying that the burial has been carried out or that the body has been sent out of the country. Remember that in Muslim societies, bodies must be buried by sunset on the day of death, so things can happen very fast. If there are any suspicious circumstances, the ROP will take photographs of the body. Post mortems, which are carried out at the ROP hospital in Al Wutayyah, are only performed in the event of a suspicious or accidental death.

In the case of an accident, Accident and Emergency (A&E) doctors will release the death certificate unless there is a post mortem pending, in which case the ROP will do so. The certificate is usually released to the sponsor. There is no charge for the death certificate, although it will not be released until all hospital bills are settled. Ensure that the cause of death is stated on the death certificate. From A&E, the deceased is taken to the mortuary. In order to release the body, you or your sponsor must obtain a letter from the relevant embassy authorising the removal of the deceased from the hospital. This letter should be taken to the ROP who will issue a letter for the hospital. You or your sponsor must arrange transport for the body, so you will need to buy a coffin and hire an ambulance. If you can't afford an ambulance, the deceased can be transported in your car.

Resting in peace

Should you wish to fly the deceased home to your home country, you must talk to the relevant airline and get a release letter from your embassy. The ROP hospital will embalm bodies for RO 120 and Khoula hospital charges RO 100.

If you wish to perform a burial in Oman, you should obtain a letter to that effect from your embassy. Give this to the ROP who will supply you with a letter for the hospital to release the body. Contact the church of your choice to perform the funeral service. Your embassy will contact the municipality. For non-Muslims, there is a cemetery at PDO.

On a precautionary note, if you intend to stay in Oman for some time you should seriously consider making a will under Sharia law, particularly if you are married. If one partner dies, it is so much easier for the remaining partner to sort out legalities quickly. Otherwise, it can take a long time to resolve questions of inheritance – such as how do deal with the car, the boat, and the bank account, which are in your partner's name – and you can't leave the country until it's done.

Work

Working in Oman

Expat workers share a common mission – to seek a better quality of life. They come from various countries and lifestyles, and many are skilled, educated and have a lot to contribute. There are those who have been seconded by companies based in their home country, and those who have come to Oman in search of the expat lifestyle. However, don't be fooled – it's not all coffee and sunshine. Setting up life here and establishing a network is still hard work. Additionally, you only have developing labour laws to protect you.

There are two major factors that make finding work in Oman more complicated than in other places – the Omanisation programme and the foreign capital investment law.

The Omanisation programme has been in place since 1988 and works toward replacing expatriates with trained Omani Personnel. There is a reward system in place for companies that meet the Omanisation targets.

The Foreign Business and Investment Law of 1974, which restricts the amount of capital a foreigner can invest in any given business, affects some sectors more than others. The general rule is that 51% of any business has to be owned by an Omani national. This law is being revised, giving more allowances to foreign investment. In general terms the more cash you are willing to invest the bigger portion of the company you can own.

Your skills and degree of specialisation will dictate how easy it is to find a job in Oman. Expats are always needed in the oil industry, the medical sector (doctors, nurses, physiotherapists, dieticians, pharmacists, etc) and in education (school teachers, language teachers and translators).

Ramadan, all Muslims and the public sector work a six hour day, as stipulated by Article 69 of the Omani labour law. Some companies reduce their working hours for all staff, including expats.

Clocktower Roundabout

Working Hours

Working hours vary largely depending on the company you work for. Employees work either a straight shift or split shifts. The split shift allows for an afternoon sleep (or a quick shopping trip!) and timings are usually 08:00 – 13:00 and 16:00 – 19:00. Shopping centres open 09:00 – 13:00 and 16:30 – 21:30, most supermarkets stay open all day from 8.00 till 21.00 and more and more shops in big shopping malls do the same. Both private and public sector organisations work straight shifts. Government organisations work 07:00 – 14:30 and private companies 07:00 – 16:00 with an hour lunch break, although there are variations. The weekend is Thursday and Friday, but most people also work on Thursdays till 13:00.

Public holidays are declared by the Government. Most public holidays are religious holidays and thus dependent on the Hijri Calendar (and the moon) – the holiday cannot be declared until the new moon has been seen by the moon-sighting committee. Consequently, it's difficult to plan and book holidays because, despite intense speculation, it is impossible to know the exact day or duration of the holiday until the moon is sighted the night before. Many people just book and go anyway. The beginning of Ramadan is also declared by the Government and is not announced until the moon sighting committee agrees. During

Finding Work

You may find it particularly hard to get work while on a visit visa in Oman –thanks to the slow pace of life. While the free paper The Week, The Observer, and the Times of Oman all have classified sections, most adverts are for Omani nationals or labourers. You can get related digital publications on www.apexstuff.com. The best way of finding work here is through contacts, the internet or just sending out your CV. Alternatively you can contact companies and ministries directly, but word of mouth seems to be a more efficient strategy. A good source of information for job searching is the Apex Business Directory of Oman where you can find information, addresses and telephone numbers of most of the companies and businesses in Oman. You can pick up a copy at the Apex office (24 799 388) in Ruwi, Muscat. If everything else fails try the noticeboards outside the shops.

If you have come to Oman with your spouse who is working and you wish to find a job for yourself, the options are very limited unless you are in the teaching or medical professions. To find a job in these sectors, it's best to ask directly at schools, hospitals and clinics. The rigorous Omanisation programme does not permit an expat to hold a job that an Omani is qualified to do, which cuts out most administrative jobs and many others. Well-qualified

New Residents

Work

teachers of English as a second language are sought after. There are several institutes offering English courses to non-native speakers, so call to see if there are vacancies. These include the Polyglot Institute (24 831 261), Hawthorn College, Khimji Training Institute (24 783 997); the Centre for British Teachers – CFBT (24 485 290) and the British Council (24 600 548). The latter two also offer CELTA courses if you wish to train. For other languages you can try the Centre Franco-Omanais (24 697 579) and German Language Courses (24 832 164).

Omantel

Recruitment Agencies

Virtually non-existent, recruitment agencies generally cater for manual labourers from Asian countries. The only agencies that might offer more interesting expat jobs are listed in the table.

Get Hunting!

Useful contacts:
Omani Centre for Investment Promotion and Export Development (OCIPED): Tel 24 812 344/24 817 600, Fax 24 810 890
Ministry of Commerce and Industry: Tel 24 810 209, Fax 24 817 238
Ministry of Social Affairs & Labour and Vocational Training: Tel 24 602 444, Fax 24 699 357
Chamber of Commerce: Tel 24 707 674, www.omanchamber.org

Useful websites:
www.smartgroups.com/groups/oman-skillpool
www.careermideast.com/
www.ociped.com/index.asp
www.expatnetwork.co.uk/index.asp

To register, check with the agency to find out if they take walk-ins. Most accept CVs via fax or email these days and will then contact you for an interview. The agency takes its fee from the registered company once the position has been filled. It is illegal for a recruitment company to levy fees on candidates for this service.

Recruitment Agencies	
CFBT Education Services & Partners LLC	24 481 938
Ideas Management Consultants	24 791 876
Modern Centre for Business Services	24 482 283
Renaissance Services SAOG	24 796 636
National Training Institute	24 605 273
Oman Resources Development	24 693 502

Business Groups & Contacts

For in-depth information about business in Oman refer to your local business group (see the table) or the commercial attaché at your embassy or consulate. Also worth contacting are the Chamber of Commerce (24 707 684) or the Omani Centre for Investment Promotion and Export Development (OCIPED – 24 812 344). Alternatively, the Oman Economic Review (www.oeronline.com) is a monthly business publication that makes for very interesting reading.

Business Groups & Contacts	
American Business Council of Oman	24 797 623
British Council	24 681 000
Oman Chamber of Commerce & Industry	24 707 674

Employment Contracts

Once you have accepted a job offer you will be asked to sign an English and Arabic copy of your contract. While it is rare for there to be any discrepancies between the two contracts, it is the Arabic one that will hold up in a court of law. If you have any doubts about the integrity of your employer you should get a lawyer or Arabic-speaking friend to read through it. You should also check a copy of the Omani labour law – if your contract reads differently from the labour law and you have signed it, then it is the contract that is binding, not the law. The labour law is your friend and benefits you more than your employer. You should receive a copy from your employer but, if not, you can get a copy from the Ministry of Manpower.

If you are sponsored by your spouse and wish to work, you will need to obtain an NOC (see [p.49]) from his employer before signing a contract with your new employer. Your employer will then apply for your labour card, see [p.50]

Labour Law

The current version of the Oman labour law was promulgated in 2003. The law outlines everything from employee entitlements (end of service gratuity, workers' compensation, holidays, etc) to employment contracts and disciplinary rules. The labour law is considered fair and clearly outlines the rights of both employees and employers. Labour unions and strikes are illegal, but adherence to the law is rigorously policed and disputes are adjudicated by the Labour Board. Copies of the labour law can be obtained from the Ministry of Manpower (24 816 591).

'Banning'

While it is natural to seek out better work opportunities, job hopping in Oman isn't that easy. Many expats have to accept that they face an employment ban if they change employer – the important lesson here is that if you do find a job in Oman, make sure it's the one you want because after you've signed the contract you may find it difficult to switch jobs. If you come to Oman with your company, or to take up a new post, you would normally stay in that job until you leave the country. If you want to change jobs while in Oman, for any reason, you must obtain a release letter from your employer (in English and Arabic) verifying that you have met all your obligations to him and that he permits you to work elsewhere. A release letter isn't guaranteed by any means and whether you get one will depend on your relationship with your employer/sponsor and the reason for leaving your job. Without this letter you are obliged to leave the country as soon as you leave your job and you may not return, even as a visitor, for between six months and two years.

People resigning from jobs fall into two categories; those who resign to return to their own country and those who resign to work for a different Omani company. If you are returning to your own country, your residence visa will be cancelled on departure at the airport. If you wish to return to Oman in the future you'll need to find a new sponsor and apply for residency again from the beginning. If you want to change jobs and work for a different company, you need to obtain a release letter in order to transfer.

You are generally not permitted to live in Oman if you are not employed, because you must have sponsorship, and that sponsorship normally ends when your employment does. In rare cases, your sponsor may be generous enough to continue sponsorship until you find another job.

Successful Socialising

- *Circle of Friends – Try to be open minded and make an effort to get to know people from all cultures and backgrounds – it's such a good opportunity. There are numerous clubs and groups that you can join.*

- *Networking – networking is an invaluable way of keeping your finger on the pulse and keeping track of what's hot and happening.*

- *The Rumour Mill – Oman has a good grapevine and people's reputations often go before them! However, it's best to make your own judgements, and remember that walls have ears...*

- *Life's a Catwalk – Being stared at (both men and women) is just commonplace here – it's not a threat, but can be irritating. You can't do anything to stop it, so just learn to ignore it.*

- *Chat line – Local calls are cheap, so you can chat for a few hours before the guilt sets in. Mobile and public phones are charged at the same local rate too.*

- *Top Tap Tips – In the summer, your cold water will run hot, so turn off your heater and your hot tap will run cold.*

- *Dodgy Driving – Oman boasts the best driving in the Arabian Peninsula, but it can still be scary. There are some very fast cars around so practise defensive driving and keep your eyes peeled for the boy racers, the impatient businessmen and the just plain insane. Lunatic overtaking is the greatest hazard.*

- *Social Life – Muscat has a good social life, from afternoon tea at the Bustan palace to quiz night at Al Ghazal. You can do more for less in Oman, so there are no excuses to stay home.*

- *Friends – You'll find everyone friendly and there are plenty activities to join in with; soon you'll be part of the worldwide expat community with invitations to holiday in many countries. Open your mind – leave your prejudices at home. Oman has a multi-national, cosmopolitan population and kindness comes from all quarters. Keep this in mind and you'll make friends easily.*

New Residents

Work

Financial & Legal Affairs

Bank Accounts

Oman has plenty of international banks offering standard facilities such as current, deposit and savings accounts, as well as ATM facilities, chequebooks, credit cards and loans. You'll find ATMs all over Muscat, mostly around the shopping areas, though increasingly in residential areas too — location details can be obtained from the banks. Most Muscat-based banks are linked so that you can use other banks' ATMs, and some offer global access links. Some banks set a minimum balance limit and you must keep this amount in your account or you will be charged.

To open a bank account in Oman you need to have a residence visa, or to have your application underway. You will need a copy of your passport, showing your personal information page and visa page, and your original passport.

Opening Hours: timings of the banks vary, but are generally 08:00 – 12:30 from Saturday to Wednesday, and 08:00 – 11.30 on Thursday. No banks are open in the evenings. Money exchanges are open from 16:00 – 19:00.

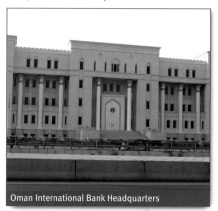

Oman International Bank Headquarters

Financial Planning

Planning for the financial future (unless you take the head in the sand approach) is an important aspect of modern day life and especially necessary for expats. Before you do anything you should contact the tax authorities in your home country to ensure that you are complying with the financial

Cost of Living

Drinks	
Beer	RO 2
Fresh Fruit Cocktail	RO 2
House Wine (glass)	RO 2 – 2 5
House Wine (bottle)	RO 9 – 12
Milk (1 litre)	500 bs
Water	
1.5 litres (supermarket)	100 bs
Water 1.5 litres (hotel)	RO 1 – 1 5

Food	
Big Mac	900 bs
Bread (large)	350 – 850 bs
Cappuccino	RO 1.1 – 1 3
Chocolate bar	150 – 200 bs
Eggs (dozen)	600 bs
Fresh Fruit	100 bs – RO 3/kg
Fresh meat	RO 1-7.5/kg
Sugar	150 bs – RO 2/kg
Shawarma	200 bs
Tin of Tuna	300 – 600 bs

Miscellaneous	
Cigarettes (per packet)	600 bs
Film (often free with processing)	RO 1
Film processing (colour, 36 exposure)	RO 3.5
Hair Cut (female)	RO 13
Hair Cut (male)	RO 1.500 – 5
Postcard	200 bs

Getting Around	
Car Rental (compact)	RO 12/day
Taxi (airport to Muscat)	RO 7
Taxi (metered)	1km/250 bs
Taxi (without meter)	negotiable
Bus from airport to Muscat	200 bs
Wadi trip (half day)	RO 65 per car

Entrance Fees	
Beach Club	RO 6
Cinema	RO 2-2 5
Museum	300 – 500 bs
Nightclub	Men – RO 2-5
Nightclub	Women free
Park	300 – 500 bs

Sports	
Go Karting (15 min)	RO 4
Golf (18 holes)	RO 5
Jet ski hire (30 mins)	RO 10
1 Dives – full equipment	RO 12-19
1 Dives – tank and weigh	RO 9-10
Night Dive	RO 3-10
Snorkelling 1/2 day	RO 10-20
Dolphin watching	RO 12-15

Big business

Housing | New Residents

laws there. Many countries will exempt you from paying income tax once you prove your Oman residence or your non-residence in your home country (a contract of employment is normally a good starting point for proving non-residence). As a non-resident, however, you may still have to fulfil certain criteria (such as only visiting your home country for a limited number of days each year). Generally, the main reason for accepting an expat posting is to improve your financial situation. It is recommended not to undertake any non-cash investments until you know your monthly savings capacity, even though this may take up to six months to ascertain. In fact, one of the first steps you should take with your new earnings is to begin paying back as much debt as possible (starting with your credit card/s!).

If you have a short-term contract, avoid long term investment contracts. Once you've decided expat life is for you and you are ready to plan for the future, you might want to establish an emergency cash buffer (three to six months' salary), a retirement home, retirement income, and adequate insurance (life, household and medical).

If you wish to seek the advice of a professional financial planner, try any of the major international firms, or make a few enquiries through word of mouth.

Cash round the clock

Taxation

Oman levies no personal taxes and withholds no income tax. The only taxes you are obliged to pay as an expatriate are as follows: an obligatory 8% service tax in hotel food and beverage outlets, a 4% tourism tax, a 5% municipality tax, and a 3% municipality tax on rental accommodation. There is also a tax on alcohol bought at retail shops, and on pork (6 slices of bacon costs RO 5, the equivalent of filling your car up with petrol!).

Legal Issues

For most people, any brush with the law can be a worrying experience, but in an unknown country with a foreign language this can be particularly unnerving. If you do find yourself on the wrong side of the law you should contact your embassy or consulate as soon as possible and follow their advice. You should also get yourself a lawyer.

Oman is governed by international civil law, with the exception of religious affairs (including marriages, divorces and child custody cases) which are governed by Sharia law – Islamic canonical law based on the teachings of the Prophet Mohammed (PBUH) and the teachings of the Quran. To practice law in Oman a lawyer must have an internationally recognised legal qualification and be registered with the Ministry of Justice. All court proceedings are conducted in Arabic and you may be unaware of what is being said regarding your case, so it is important to hire legal representation that you trust.

Warning: Do not fall for any fantasies of opiate nights in the Middle East – drug use is highly illegal here and even your embassy won't be able to get you out of trouble with the local authorities if you break this law.

Law Firms	
Al Alawi Mansoor Jamal & Co	24 814 466
Denton Wilde Sapte	24 573 000
Said Al Shahry Law Office	24 603 123
Trowers & Hamlins	24 682 900

Housing

Rented accommodation is currently the only option for anybody who is not a citizen of Oman or the GCC, although future development projects may allow expats to purchase property (see Purchasing a

Bringing you the best in banking

At BankMuscat, our customers are our driving force. Through the years, our focus has remained unchanged: meeting - and exceeding - our customers' needs. As the nation's premier bank, we are committed to bringing the best in banking services to Oman and to our growing operations across the region. Thinking ahead for our customers helps us stay ahead!

- *Over 90 branches across Oman* • *Largest ATM network* • *Call Centre* • *Internet Banking*
- *Mobile Banking* • *Kiosk Banking* • *eTrade* • *A growing international presence*

بنك مسقط
BankMuscat

www.bankmuscat.com

Home [p.69]). Oman has no central listing of available properties for rent. In the main cities you'll find numerous boards with houses for rent but to get the home you want and the right terms a reliable estate agent can save you a lot of grief. The capital, Muscat, is spread out into distinct residential areas mostly divided by mountains, valleys or highways. The main areas are Muscat, Mutrah, Ruwi, Watya, Al Qurm, Shati Al Qurm, Madinat As Sultan Qaboos, Al Khuwayr, Ghubbrah, Al Azaiba and Seeb.

New residents arriving in Oman on a full expat package may have accommodation included in their employment contract. If you are not so lucky, don't be dazzled by the charm of the expat lifestyle – living in Oman is expensive and you should make sure the package you negotiate is sufficient to cover all your costs.

Renting in Oman

Despite Omanisation, expat numbers are stable and perhaps even increasing so there remains a steady demand in the rental market, especially for the better quality properties, and rent levels are maintained. Whether this will be affected if expats are eventually allowed to buy Omani property (as has been proposed) remains to be seen.

Rent Disputes

Should the need arise, the Ministry of Justice (24 697 699) will assist both tenants and landlords in rent disputes.

Search Tips

Location, location, location
Check proximity of potential homes to mosques, rubbish bins, schools, and the airport flight path.

New Buildings
Look out for buildings under construction – it's often a good way to find a place you like and be one of the first on the waiting list. The guys on site should be able to give you the name of the real estate agent or landlord.

Noise Control
In the less built up areas, beware that the area around your new home could be ripe for development – few people really appreciate a noisy building site just a few metres from their bedroom window! Construction work starts at about 06:00 and finishes by 22:00 or 23:00, with the occasional 01:00 concrete pour, six days a week. You may even find the odd builder working on Fridays but if you find this interferes with your weekend lie-in you can request them to stop.

Real Estate Agents

The entire leasing process in Muscat is governed by well-drafted legislation and the lease is prepared on a standard Municipality form. The standard lease, which can have minor changes made to it, is normally for one year (which is automatically renewable unless three months notice is given before expiry by either the landlord or the tenant). Annual rent for villas is often requested in advance in one cheque, although it is sometimes possible to agree with the landlord that six-month's rent is paid upon signing of the lease and the remainder of the amount by post dated cheque. Rent for apartments is usually payable quarterly, or in some cases monthly. In most cases, no security deposit is payable by tenants.

If you decide to let an agent help you find your new home, you can choose from somebody local or from an internationally recognised agency. The more reputable agencies (see table below) will arrange all the paperwork for your tenancy agreement and ensure that the required Municipality procedures are followed. It is worth trying to negotiate over the rent, especially if the market is slow or if you offer to pay in one cheque (rather than three). Many people can organise an estate agent through their company PRO but it is always wise to check that the recommended agent is a registered real estate broker, authorised to conduct leasing in Muscat.

You may find that some agents don't have access to a car and you will have to pick them up to go to viewings. Landlords pay the agent's commission so you should pay nothing to the agent. The other option is to drive around the area you would like to live in looking for 'To Let' signs, which may be agency or private landlord.

Real Estate Agents	
Al Alawi Real Estate	24 700 983
Al Habib & Co LLC	24 702 666
Al Khalili & Al Bahar Real Estate Co LLC	24 509 000
Al Qandeel Real Estate	24 696 519
Cluttons	24 564 250
Eamaar Real Estate	24 699 733
Gulf Real Estate	24 814 371
Hamptons International P.63	24 563 557
Hay Al Rahbah	24 693 877
Hilal Properties P.65	24 600 688
Oman Homes	24 488 087

Price is temporary.

Integrity is permanent.

Take the stress out of buying and renting property. Talk to the people in Oman
who believe that a traditional personal touch is still required
in today's fast moving real estate market.

It's not that we don't make effective use of technology- far from it.
We just ensure that our clients are treated as people, not job numbers.

**For all your property and relocation needs in the Sultanate of Oman,
please call 00968- 24563557
or visit www.hamptons-int.com**

When you have decided on a property the landlord should registers the lease with Muscat Municipality (at his/her own expense). Tenants should be aware that the registering of a lease is compulsory in Oman. Failure to register the lease or registering it at a rental cost that is in fact less than the amount being paid by the tenant is against the law. All reputable agents undertake this process automatically but some unregistered brokers and landlords try to avoid it when dealing direct with a tenant. Without a registered lease, the tenant has no protection and can be ordered to leave the property at any time without legal recourse. Also, you should only make payment to the landlord upon signing a formal letter of intent preceding the lease.

Tenants obligations extend to paying for all utilities and for basic maintenance of the property. Landlords are responsible for the upkeep of the property structure and any major maintenance works and the lease agreement usually specifies that at the time of taking possession, the landlord will ensure that the villa/apartment is in good condition.

The Lease

To take out a personal lease – that is, not through your company – you must be a resident. The real estate agent will need a copy of your passport and visa, a no objection letter (NOC) from your company, a copy of your salary certificate, a signed rent cheque and up to three post-dated cheques covering the remainder of the year's rent. You will be required to sign a lease for one year and, unlike elsewhere in the world, you must pay the whole year's rent up front. Because of this, it's extremely important to choose carefully when deciding on accommodation, as you are tied in for a year, unless you are lucky enough to have a benevolent landlord who lets you break your lease. If you do develop a good relationship with your landlord you can sometimes negotiate three or six-month leases after the first year is up. In most cases no security deposit is required. If, like many people, you don't have a year's rent just conveniently sitting in your account, your bank will be quick to offer you a loan, as long as your salary is paid directly into an account held at that bank. To rent through your employer, the agent or landlord will require a copy of the company's trade licence, a passport copy of the person signing the rent cheque and, of course, the rent cheque itself. The landlord will register the lease with the relevant municipality. The registering of

leases showing rental at less than the real amount is against the law and this is a big risk for tenants who effectively have no protection in the event of dispute. In most cases tenants pay for all utilities (gas, water, electricity) and the general maintenance of the property. The landlord must ensure the house is in good condition when new tenants move in, and he is generally responsible for any structural work and major maintenance.

Renters' Nightmare

Most leases in Oman are fixed for one year and unless you find a really nice landlord who lets you break your lease or sub-let, you are locked in for the remainder of the year. The penalty? You might lose your deposit, and you certainly won't get the remainder of your rent back! So be careful when you sign your lease, as you have to pay your entire year's rent up front (in one to three cheques) and make sure the apartment or villa you've just found is really the one you'd like to call home for the next year!

Main Accommodation Options

There are various types of housing available in Muscat for the new resident, such as serviced apartments, standard apartments, garden courts or villas. There is also the option of apartment or villa sharing. Some of those arriving to work in Oman will have employment packages that include company accommodation and, in some cases, may not move to their own choice of property within the first two years. However, most employees are now given a rental allowance and permitted to choose their own house. Rents range from RO 300 to RO 2,500 per month for villas, and RO 150 to RO 650 per month for apartments. Most villas and apartments available for rent are unfurnished, so you have to provide all furniture, air conditioners, kitchen and laundry appliances. You can buy everything you need in Muscat, although you may have less choice than you would back home. Most apartments, and nearly all villas, have bedroom and bathroom facilities for housemaids.

Serviced Apartments

Serviced apartments are fairly expensive and therefore more suited for shorter stays. Some people live in serviced apartments for a month or two until they find the house they want, or while they await the arrival of their family members. Apartments can be rented on a daily, weekly, monthly or yearly basis and are fully furnished right

Housing **New Residents**

H I L A L
PROPERTIES

-  Sales
- Leasing
- Property Management
- Relocation Services

down to the last detail, with a cleaning and laundry service included. The main contacts for serviced apartments are ASAS Residence (24 57 1509), Al Noorah Gardens (24 697 203), and Safeer Hotel Suites (24 691 200).

Apartment/Villa Sharing

Sharing an apartment or villa with colleagues or friends is a great way to cut accommodation costs. It can also be a welcome loneliness antidote if you're ever feeling homesick. Many villas have a majlis area as well as a lounge, so even if you're sharing with numerous other people you should be able to find a peaceful corner of the house. To search for housemates, check the noticeboards outside supermarkets – especially the Sultan Centre and branches of Al Fair – for people advertising shared accommodation.

Standard Apartment

Apartments are found all over the Muscat area and vary from tiny with a communal bathroom, to vast penthouses. Muscat's hilly terrain means that people living on the top floors usually have a great view. Rents are usually between RO 150 and RO 600 per month.

Apartment building

Garden Court

Garden courts consist of a few small semidetached villas built around a communal garden. There is often a swimming pool. There are quite a few in the Madinat As Sultan Qaboos area.

Villas

Villas range in price from RO 300 to RO 2,500 per month. You can sometimes find older villas (in reasonable condition) in good areas for upwards of RO 300. In some areas, RO 500 will get you a six bedroom mansion with a view, but you might not have any garden or outside space. Some villas cost as much as RO 2,500, and these are equipped with central air conditioning, carports, electric security gates, swimming pool and more.

Residential Areas

Other options → Exploring [p.97]

All towns have their more desirable areas, and Muscat's are Shati Al Qurm, Al Qurm and Qurm Heights. These areas feature huge marble villas with beautiful exteriors and luxurious interiors, and more bathrooms than you can shake a stick at. They are high quality, elegant homes situated in leafy, tranquil streets, usually with high gates and shaded parking. Though some have pools, sometimes the garden space is limited. You'll also find upmarket complexes with shared pools and fitness facilities. These locations are also popular because they are near the main shopping malls and services. Rents are usually between RO 700 and RO 2500 per month. Shati Al Qurm is beautifully landscaped and runs along the beach – many of the villas have sea views and beach. Al Qurm and Qurm Heights are two of the older developed residential areas. Villas there can be up to 30 years old and while they may be less luxuriously finished, they often have more character.

You will find similar large villas in Al Khuwayr, Al Azaiba and Ghubbrah for much lower prices. These districts are less picturesque and they lack some of the amenities, but they are still popular with expats looking for big houses and small rents. While it may be tempting to rent the largest place you can afford, remember you'll need lots of furniture, curtains and rugs to make your 'palace' feel like home – of course, the larger the house, the larger your electricity and water bills will be.

Madinat As Sultan Qaboos (known as MQ or MSQ) is an old residential area that is currently undergoing a revamp. It continues to be popular with expats because the houses are a manageable size and the area has a slightly European feel. Centred around a small shopping complex, it has a village atmosphere and many amenities. Many of the houses are 20 to 30 years old and some of the interiors have seen

Housing options in Muscat

better days. Housing options vary and include villas, garden courts and apartments, ranging in price from RO 300 – RO 600 per month. MQ has lots of garden courts and you either love 'em or hate 'em – a dozen, two or three bedroom, terraced houses built in a square around a shared garden with pool. If you're used to a compact house you may feel more comfortable in one of these — they have low ceilings, small kitchens and are usually carpeted, unlike the larger villas with their expanses of marble floor. The central court is enclosed and thus suitable for children (as long as they can swim) who will often have a ready-made gang of friends. Garden courts are great if you're the sociable type, but if you prefer your own space you might find garden court life pretty claustrophobic.

The grander MQ villas are lived in mainly by locals, and the smaller three or four bedroom ones are rented by expats. Built when land was not at a premium in the central area, these villas often have spacious, mature gardens, although there is an increasing trend to demolish single villas and build several new houses on the same plot. There are also a number of brand new apartment blocks and housing developments, some commissioned by PDO (Petroleum Development Oman, the national oil and gas company and a large employer) for their employees.

MQ is close to the British School-Muscat, the American-British Academy (both multi-cultural) and the French school. There are also several nursery schools in the area, so it is often first choice for families with young children.

Cheaper housing is found in Ruwi, Al Wutayyah, and Mumtaz; or further out of town in Al Hail or Seeb to the west, or Qantab to the east. These areas are fine for those who work close by but are a 30 – 40 minute drive from the commercial areas. Al Hail, Seeb and parts of Al Azaiba are on the flight path and many flights come in at night so if you're a light sleeper this could be a problem!

You may also want to consider whether there is a tarred road to your house and what kind of water supply and A/C it has. Newer properties usually have split A/C, while older ones have wall A/Cs (known as wallbangers). Some houses have central A/C. Central and split A/C is always more expensive. Not all areas of Muscat are connected to the main water supply; if yours is not you will have to order a tanker (blue truck) of water every few days. Many houses seem to have plumbing problems and whether you get them sorted out will depend on how reliable your landlord is.

Al Ghubbrah, Bawshar   Map Ref → 6-E3

Home to a mixed community, Ghubbrah is on the right of the highway going from town to Seeb, and Bawshar (South Ghubbrah) is on the left, nearest to town. North Ghubbrah has some impressive beachfront villas. You'll find a fair share of marble palaces here, but they are much cheaper than in Shati and Al Qurm. The Muscat Private Hospital, the Chedi Hotel and the American International School of Muscat are nearby. On the downside, some areas are still not connected to the main water supply, some of the roads are not tarred, and the traffic during rush hour can be frustrating (although new road building programmes have eased the congestion a little).

Al Hail/Seeb   Map Ref → 1-B1

These areas used to be considered 'out of town', but with the opening of City Centre and Markaz Al Bahja on the doorstep, they are now conveniently located for some of the best shopping in town. Rents are reasonable and properties here tend to be popular with those who work up the coast, at SQU or on the Rustaq loop. The main kind of accommodation is rural-type villas with larger gardens, and some compounds.

Al Khuwayr   Map Ref → 7-B3

Al Khuwayr has a variety of large villas and apartments, at reasonable rents. It is a commercial district and therefore is less picturesque than the traditional residential areas; it is home to a large mixed community. It is close to the Holiday Inn and Radisson SAS, and features some good quality, new villas. However, only some areas are connected to the main water supply.

Al Khuwayr

New Residents

Housing

Al Azaiba   Map Ref → 6-A2

Al Azaiba is a spacious new residential area between Ghubbrah and As Seeb. Villas here are new, large and of high quality. The gardens are larger than elsewhere and the streets wider, but the area is perhaps not as pretty as Shati or Al Qurm. The area has recently been connected to the main water supply. It is only ten minutes from City Centre and Markaz Al Bahja, but while this means convenient shopping, it also means heavier traffic.

Madinat As Sultan Qaboos   Map Ref → 7-E2

This is a sought after residential area with a variety of housing and rents. It has large villas, small villas, old and new apartments, garden courts, and mature, spacious gardens. Some of the older villas can be a little bit run down. The area is undergoing a regeneration programme with new residential buildings and a shopping complex planned. The local services are good and there are schools and nurseries nearby. The area has a friendly, village feel and is popular with both expats and nationals.

Al Qurm   Map Ref → 8-D3

This area is also much sought after by nationals and expats. These localities on built on hilly land, so many properties have good views over the city and the sea. Although in general the properties are older than the ones in Shati, there is lots of new building going on and the area features a mix of independent villas with good sized gardens, and new compounds. The area has nearby shopping centres, and is close to the Crowne Plaza Hotel.

Ruwi   Map Ref → 12-D2

This low rent area features mainly apartments, and is home to a mostly Asian community. It is near the CBD, so the traffic can get pretty frantic.

Shati Al Qurm   Map Ref → 7-D1

This is the ultimate address in town, and popular with nationals and expats. It is the embassy district, and is very upmarket and exclusive. Palatial villas line wide, leafy streets. The area stretches along the beach, so most of the properties have fabulous views. Houses here are not permitted to exceed two storeys, so gardens tend to be small as landlords increase the size of ground plans. The Grand Hyatt and InterContinental Hotels are nearby, and so is the Al Shatti Private Hospital. There is also a shopping centre with Starbucks and Costa Coffee.

Other Rental Costs

Additional costs to be considered are a 3% municipality tax and sometimes a deposit (although this is fully refundable when you vacate the premises). If you are renting a villa with a garden, your water costs will be higher – the grass and plants will need watering every single day in Oman's hot climate. If you are not happy doing the gardening yourself, you can pay someone to do it for you.

Purchasing a Home

Real estate purchase is restricted to Omani/GCC nationals. However, proposed legislation (scheduled for 2005) will allow expats to buy property in Oman for the first time. The government is observing the booming property market in Dubai, where foreigners have recently been given permission to purchase property in designated areas. Details of expat property ownership in Oman have not been finalised – restrictions and conditions may be applied and there is uncertainty about how the law will be linked to residence visas. Traditionally, Omanis have bought a plot of land, employed a builder, and built a house on an independent and individual basis. The population boom in the 70s and 80s has resulted in a growing class of young Omani professionals looking for property and, in anticipation of the new law, developer-built schemes of villas and apartments are proposed, aimed at both locals and expats.

Moving Tips

- Book moving dates well in advance
- Don't forget insurance and purchase additional insurance for irreplaceable items
- Make an inventory of the items you want moved (keep your own copy!)
- Ensure everything is packed extremely well and in a way that can be checked by customs and repacked with the least possible damage; check and sign the packing list
- Keep a camera and film handy to take pictures at each stage of the move (valuable in case of a dispute)
- Do not pack restricted goods of any kind
- If moving to Oman, ensure videos, DVDs and books are not offensive to Muslim sensibilities

New Residents

Housing

Setting up Home

Moving Services

When moving your furniture to or from Oman, you can choose to ship it either by air or by sea. Airfreight is quick (usually just a few days) and is good for small consignments and the essential stuff you can't live without. To move a houseful of furniture though you need to send a container by sea, which will take several weeks. You can get either a 20 or 40 foot container, depending on how much you need to move. If you're really lucky you could share container space with somebody moving to the same place. Either way, ensure you employ a reputable professional moving company to pack your goods and make the arrangements. If you are moving to Oman in the summer, your belongings will travel at sustained high temperatures in the container ship, so expect some of your plastic items to warp and some of your china might have little surface cracks as a result of the heat. A company with a wide international network is usually the best and safest option but, more importantly, you must trust the people you are dealing with. Relocating can be very unsettling, especially if it's your first move (it definitely gets easier). Ensure the company is competent in the country of origin and has reliable and knowledgeable agents in the country of relocation. Most removal companies offer free consultations, give advice and demonstrate packing materials. Some will supply an information pack and video. Often your employer will have an arrangement with one or more removal companies.

When your shipment arrives in Muscat you may be called to Customs to be present when your crates are opened, to make sure nothing illegal or inappropriate is brought into the country. If you are lucky, someone from your company may stand in for you and you may only have to go if something is found which customs officers object to. This process can be exhausting; the search may take place outdoors, over the space of a few hours and it can be frustrating to watch your carefully packed boxes being unceremoniously rummaged through. The customs officers may retain certain items, such as CDs, DVDs, videos, books and even photo albums, for further investigation. Once items are checked you will get them back, though it may take several weeks, and anything which contravenes the law or is considered culturally offensive will be confiscated. It is wise to have copies made of home videos and leave them at home.

Renting the Smart Way (Help for Renters)

Like anywhere else in the world, Oman has its fair share of cons. To avoid falling into a landlord trap, it is advisable that both parties produce a written agreement. This contract reduces the risk of either party falling out on the rental terms discussed. Remember to ask for a copy of the estate agent's identification card and make sure you save copies of all receipts, contracts and other documents. Make sure that any maintenance work that needs to be done in your new house is finished before you move in. Once you accept the keys and move in there is no guarantee that any pending jobs will be finished.

Relocation Experts

Relocation experts offer a range of services to help you settle into your new life in Oman as quickly as possible. Practical help ranges from finding accommodation or schools for your children to connecting a telephone or information on medical care. In addition, they will often offer advice on the way of life in the city, putting people in touch with the social networks to help them get established in their new lives.

Removal/Relocation Companies

Eagle Global Logistics LLC	24 495 417
Gulf Agency Co (Oman) LLC P.71	24 479 155
Inchcape Shipping Services	24 701 291
Inchcape Shipping Services (Salalah)	23 219 033
Khimji Ramdas (Project & Logistic Group)	24 786 123
Middle East Shipping & Transport Co LLC	24 790 024
Yusuf Bin Ahmed Kanoo & Co	24 712 252

Furnishing Accommodation

Other options → Home Furnishings
& Accessories [p.164]
Second-Hand Items [p.170]

For good quality furniture at reasonable prices the most popular outlets are Home Centre (City Plaza), Alasfoor Furnishing, Fahmy Furnishing (in Al Khuwayr) and ID Design (Markaz Al Bahja). Another option is to take a trip to Abu Dhabi or Dubai and shop at one of the furniture superstores located there, such as IKEA, Home Centre or Marina Gulf Trading. There are transport companies who will bring items down from Dubai for between RO 10 and RO 30, if the store doesn't deliver. For second-hand furniture, look on the noticeboards outside branches of Al Fair, or just keep your ears open for friends leaving Oman, and make them an offer!

Garage Sales

When you know you're leaving and have sorted all the stuff you want to take with you from the stuff your friends have had their eye on, and the stuff you can donate to schools and good causes, haul the rest into your carport and hold a garage sale. Ask your friends if they want to contribute unwanted items or join forces with other departing families for a mega bazaar. Advertise on supermarket noticeboards, at work, in schools and in the local free paper, The Week. Tie balloons outside your gate for easy identification. Price up your goods, arm yourself with lots of change, plastic carrier bags and newspaper, and be prepared to stand up to hordes of people determined to buy your possessions for 100 baisas. Don't think about what you paid for it and you'll be fine – concentrate on the benefits of not having to lug it home with you and the bit of extra income to boot.

Household Appliances

Carrefour, Sultan Centre, Salman Stores, Lulu Centre, Panasonic and Philips outlets and many little shops in Ruwi Suq Street all have good selections of household appliances and general domestic goods. Make sure your purchases come with a warranty. Sockets correspond to the British three-pin plug but most appliances come with a two-pin fitting so you'll have to change the plug or use adaptors. Note that the two-pin plug with external metal earthing strip must be plugged into the appropriate adaptor (not so easy to find but the Sultan Centre has them) – don't use a standard two-pin adaptor because your appliance will not be earthed, it's dangerous and some appliances short out and break down. New appliances are reasonably priced but there are also plenty of second-hand ones available on the noticeboards and at garage sales, often in good condition. You won't get a guarantee though and you should test the appliance before you buy.

Household Insurance

As you probably won't own your house in Oman, it's easy to take a more relaxed attitude towards household insurance. The Sultanate is very safe and the crime rate extremely low but burglaries do occur and predominantly expat residential areas can be targets. Many national and international insurance companies have offices in Muscat, offering all the standard services – check the Yellow Pages for details. To take out a policy you will need confirmation of your address, your passport, a list of household contents and valuation, and invoices for any items over RO 250.

Household Insurance	
ALICO AIG	24 561 209
Arabia Insurance Co LTD	24 793 299
Norwich Union Insurance	24 694 040
Oman National Insurance Co SAOC	24 795 020
Royal & Sun Alliance Insurance PLC	24 478 318

Laundry Services

There are no self-service launderettes in Oman but plenty of outlets where you can drop off your laundry for washing, ironing or dry cleaning. You can have clothes ironed for only 100 – 150 baisas a piece — a bargain, and useful for bachelors who don't have a housemaid.

Domestic Help

Though the idea of having domestic help may be strange to you at first, it's amazing how quickly you get used to it! It's probably one of the hardest aspects of expat life to give up when you move on. Having someone to help gives you more time to spend with your family and takes the hard work out of entertaining. For an affordable sum you can have your home always spotlessly clean and, given the grand scale of most houses, that's no small consideration. Domestic helpers (both male and female) come mainly from India, Sri Lanka, Bangladesh and the Philippines, and many gardeners are from Pakistan. You are not permitted to employ someone related to you or of the same nationality as you. As the employer, you must sponsor your helper and (in most cases) provide accommodation – most villas have a servant's quarters. You have a duty of care to your domestic helper and are responsible for organising and paying for his or her residence visa, medical test, labour/resident card, medical bills and a return flight home every two years. The visa will cost you RO 20 and the labour/resident card, RO 70. A domestic helper will normally do general cleaning, washing, ironing and babysitting. Many will also be able to cook and can produce a range of European, Arab and Indian food. Rates vary but, generally speaking, you will pay RO 70 – 100 per month for part time (two to four hours a day, five days a week), RO 100 – 120 per month for full time (eight hours a day, six days a week) and RO 1 per hour for anything extra (part-time helpers usually negotiate babysitting separately, for example). The best way to find someone is by word of mouth but there are plenty of ads on the noticeboards and in the local press. There are also several reliable agencies. Good domestic helpers rapidly gain a reputation and if you find one he or she can become an indispensable part of the family you may find your friends queuing up to take him or her on when you leave. Standards of spoken and written English vary enormously and you may want to take this into account. If you choose someone from an advert rather than recommendation, ask for two references, and check them.

Domestic Services

Unless specifically stated otherwise in your lease, any plumbing or electrical work needed in your house is the responsibility of the landlord. Not only should he arrange for such services, he should foot the bill as well. Many landlords use a specific maintenance company to look after their properties, and even if you know that another company could do the job better and faster, he is paying, so he gets to choose!

In most cases you'll find your accommodation through an estate agent or your company and they should provide you with information on these services. As a general rule, be cautious of using services from the yellow pages or adverts without a recommendation.

Pets

Bringing Your Pet to Oman

Many people have brought their pets to Oman but it does involve paperwork and time. However, it's worth the effort if your good times are even better with your furry friend by your side. The following steps need to be taken to import pets into Oman.

- Have your pet vaccinated and its booklet updated (in English) by your vet in your home country (the rabies vaccination must be up to date and clearly shown in the booklet). Ask your vet which vaccinations are required. You'll need two health certificates – one should be dated no more than six months before your departure and the second should be obtained ten days prior to the date of travel.

- With the help of your sponsor, get an import certificate (RO 5) from the Ministry of Agriculture and Fisheries Animal Health Department (24 696 300). This, along with a copy of the vaccination records and health certificates, must accompany your pet on arrival into Oman. Certificates must be produced at the airport, on arrival of the animal, to the Quarantine office. If for any reason the authorities are not satisfied with your certificates, they can quarantine your pet for six months (for this reason, it's essential that you check with your local vet and/or the Oman embassy in your home country about the exact requirements).

- Book a space for your pet with your airline (after checking which airlines allow pets).

Clearing the animal at Seeb International Airport will take two to three hours. Although there are no special facilities for animals, they are placed in a special ventilated area where they won't suffer from the high temperatures. If you are visiting a neighbouring country and want to take your pet with you check with the relevant ministry authorities within that country.

Taking Your Pet Home

When it's time for you and your pet to move on from Oman, you will need to start the procedure a few weeks before departure. Check with your airline about their policy on pets – some may allow you to take your pet (if it's small enough, of course) as carry on luggage, rather than as cargo. The regulations for 'exporting' your pet depend on the country to which you are moving, but the basic requirements are:

- A valid vaccination card (which should have been issued not more than one year and not less than 30 days ago)

- A health certificate issued by the Municipality or the Ministry of Agriculture and Fisheries, normally issued one week before departure

- A travel box that meets airline regulations (normally made of wood or fibreglass)

Your local vet, kennels, or the airline that you are using can inform you of the specific regulations, such as quarantine rules, pertaining to your destination.

Vets

While there is not an abundance of vets practising in Muscat, you will still be able to find good quality healthcare for your pet. Austrian Vets 4 U offer a good level of care with highly qualified vets trusted by many pet owners. In addition to veterinary services, Dr. Khaled can arrange the paperwork and procedures involved in bring your pet into Oman, having it registered, or taking it out of the country. He also offers boarding kennels for cats and dogs, which is very useful if you go away in the summer.

Veterinary Clinics	
Dr Khaled	24 562 263
Austrian Vets 4 U	24 566 311

Cats & Dogs

In the Middle East, animals are treated with much less sympathy than you may be used to. Although Islam forbids the maltreatment of animals, dogs are not highly regarded and are certainly not seen as fluffy, loveable members of the family. That said, there are many dog owners in Oman. All dogs must be registered with the Municipality and inoculations must be kept up to date. Puppies must be vaccinated at six weeks old and then annually. It is recommended that cats and dogs are sterilised to stop them roaming, but this is not compulsory. Some people adopt stray dogs, or the local 'string' cats (so called because they are as thin as pieces of knotted string – until you start feeding them, of course). There are stray cats everywhere – occasionally the Municipality has a crackdown, rounding up and shooting strays (make sure your own pet is safe inside when this happens). If you do adopt a local animal be sure to have it vaccinated, dewormed and sprayed for fleas. Oman is not a rabies-free country, so be very careful. If you are bitten by a stray animal (cats can carry rabies as well as dogs), go to Accident & Emergency at Khoula Hospital in Al Wutayyah for an anti-rabies shot (only government hospitals have stocks of the vaccine).

Pet Shops

There is only one pet shop in Muscat, located downstairs in Sabco Centre. They have fish, birds, mice, hamsters, rabbits, dogs, cats and even a snake or two. Conditions in which the animals are kept leave something to be desired and they are not cheap. You can pay RO 200 – 400 for a dog and RO 150 – 200 for a 'pedigree' cat (sort of Persian or Siamese), but you won't get papers. These cats are locally bred – genuine pedigree animals, with papers, come from Eastern Europe and will cost you twice as much. You can have your cat or dog vaccinated at the pet shop and the first set of jabs is free but they don't give all the vaccinations your pet will need. It's better to pay a visit to Dr. Khaled who can provide the essential rabies vaccination and give your new pet a checkup.

Pet Services	
Creatures Trading	24 563 721

Utilities & Services

Electricity & Water

Electricity and water services are supplied by the Government and are generally efficient and reliable. There is no mains gas service but bottled gas (LPG) is available for cooking. Power cuts – lasting from a few minutes to several hours – occur every now and then but rarely pose a major inconvenience. It helps to have a stock of candles and torches handy, just in case. Utility bills are paid at Oman Investment & Finance Company (OIFC) or through your bank or an ATM. To use the ATM service you have to register your details by phone (the bank will have the number). Once you are registered, you can pay your bills outside banking hours (and without standing in queues). The bank transfer system is slower than paying directly to OIFC so allow a few extra days to avoid being disconnected. Wherever you pay, make sure your bill is stamped and that you keep it for reference – you may need it for proof of payment at a later date.

Electricity

The electricity supply in Oman is 220/240 volts and 50 cycles. Sockets correspond to the British three-pin plug but many appliances are sold with two-pin plugs so you will need lots of adaptors (available in any supermarket or corner shop) – better still, change all the plugs.

Water

Though some water comes from natural wells there is not enough to service the country's needs so most of the supply is from the sea, processed at the desalination plant at Al Ghubbrah. The main supply of water is very reliable but not all of Muscat's residential areas are connected to it. If your house is not you will have to rely on a water bowser to fill up your tank every two or three days. Water trucks for domestic use are blue (the green ones carry non-potable water, for municipal garden watering and industrial use) and they are everywhere – just flag one down or ask your neighbours which 'water-man' they use. You will often see several trucks filling up at one of the water wells dotted around the city. Expect to pay around RO 25 a month for truck water. Global Water Services will deliver 24 hours (24 487 575).

If you are connected to the main supply, keep an eye on your bills and water meter; if you have an underground leak within your property boundary you could be held responsible for a hefty bill, even if you weren't aware of the leak.

In the heat of summer it's unlikely you'll have the chance to take a refreshing cold shower. Water tanks are usually located on the roof where they are heated to near boiling point by the sun, and you can't even stand under the shower it's so hot. Between April and October, the only way to get a cool shower is to turn off your water heater, and use the hot tap.

Oman's water is safe to drink as it is purified eight times. However, it is heavily chlorinated (which affects the taste) so most people prefer to drink one of the many local bottled mineral waters. Apart from the coffee shops, all restaurants will supply bottled water. If in doubt, ask for a sealed bottle to be brought to your table. You can get 20-litre bottles of purified water for use at home, either with a hand pump or a water cooler. These are available from shops and supermarkets, you pay a RO 6 deposit per bottle and refills cost RO 1. Alternatively, get a company to deliver the water to your house.

Water Suppliers	
Al Afia Water	25 544 555
Al Bayan	24 594 634
National Mineral Water Company	24 590 095
Oasis Water Company LLC	24 446 392

Sewerage

All properties in Oman have septic tanks, which must be emptied regularly by one of the yellow sewage trucks. The cost for having a septic tank emptied is between RO 10 and RO 14 a time, you'll probably have to get it done about once a year (you'll know when it's time from the smell!). If you need to order a sewage truck the easiest way is to call the number on the back of one of the yellow tankers, or ask your neighbour. Alternatively call Oman Wastewater Services Company (24 693 412). The Oman Wastewater Services Company is about to embark on a RO 350 million sewage recycling project.

Gas

Oman doesn't have mains gas but there are many suppliers of bottled gas. Gas canisters are available in various sizes, you pay RO 15 – 20 as a deposit, and RO 3 per refill. Gas is delivered to houses by orange trucks – they drive around residential areas and you just need to flag them down. Popular times for the gas run are late morning, early evening and on Fridays. Once you've found a supplier, get his mobile number and you'll be able to call him whenever you need more gas. Most will deliver any time up to 21:00.

Gas Suppliers	
Bidarco	24 811 689
Mohsin Haider Darwish LLC	24 703 411
Noor Al Ghroob Trading	24 812 224
Oman Industrial Gas CO	24 813 012

Telephone

Omantel (the Oman Telecommunications Company) used to be the sole provider of landline, mobile and internet services, but at time of going to print, a new GSM service provider – Nawras – had just started operations in the Oman mobile phone market. For more information on Nawras, which is operated by QTel, visit www.qtel.com.qa.

Recently privatised, Omantel has invested in the latest technology and offers an efficient service. At peak times you may experience connection problems with your mobile phone, and the internet service also hangs occasionally. On the plus side, the Omani Government's 'access for all' policy keeps charges low and rates usually decrease rather than increase. You need to be resident to get a landline but you can buy a Hayyak 'pay-as-you-go' SIM card without residency. The Omantel Yellow Pages can be accessed online at www.omantel-yellowpages.com.

Landline Phones

It is unlikely that your accommodation will have an active phone line when you move in. To apply for a landline connection you should submit the following documents to Omantel: a completed application form (in English), your passport (and a copy), your visa, and a copy of your tenancy agreement. Once you have submitted your application it will be one to two weeks before you are connected. If you need additional phone sockets, be sure to ask at the time of application. You pay a deposit of RO 200 and RO 10 per line installation. Quarterly rental is RO 3 and calls are charged according to distance and time, ranging from 0.003 to 0.075 baisas per minute (emergency calls are free). Off-peak rates apply on long distance calls all day Friday and on national holidays. Omantel offers many additional services such as call waiting, call forwarding and conference calling. You can also use the Jibreen service – a prepaid phone card that can be used to make local or international calls from any landline or payphone. The card is available in denominations of RO 1.5, RO 3 and RO 5, is valid for 90 days from first call and is charged at the payphone tariff. For more information and details visit the Omantel website (www.omantel.net.om), which lists services and charges.

Mobile Phones

Mobile phones, commonly referred to as GSMs, are an integral part of Oman life. Everybody has at least one, and they're probably used more than landlines. You can use your own handset or buy one in Oman – handsets are always sold independently of contracts and there's a wide range of brands available at reasonable prices. You'll usually find a good deal on a handset in Carrefour or the smaller mobile phone shops in shopping malls. For help with your GSM, voicemail, SMS or other mobile services, call 196 (toll free).

Non-Resident

The GSM section of Omantel is called Oman Mobile. If you're just visiting Oman, or still waiting for your residency to come through, you can use the Hayyak pay-as-you-go system. There are no contracts or monthly bills it is a popular option among residents too, both local and expat. You can use any GSM handset – just buy a Hayyak kit from Oman Mobile (RO 30), which includes a SIM card and a RO 5 top-up card. Top-up cards (RO 3, RO 5 and RO 10, valid for one, two and three months respectively) are available from supermarkets and smaller shops displaying the Hayyak sign. Calls are more expensive than with a contract, at 70 baisas for the first minute and 35 baisas for each 35 seconds thereafter but charges are irrespective of distance. There is no roaming facility with Hayyak. Oman Mobile has recently introduced Hayyak Plus and Hayyak Al Zayer. Hayyak Plus makes your GSM number valid for one year, with a 60 day grace period. The extension card costs RO 10 and your call credit can be topped up using standard Hayyak

cards. The Hayyak Al Zayer kit is aimed at tourists or business visitors – it costs only RO 10 and offers full airtime for 30 days. It is not rechargeable, nor does it support SMS (text messaging). National calls are charged at 0.075 baisas per minute and international calls at 0.425 baisas per minute. Hayyak kits are available from the Omantel office in Al Khuwayr (behind the ice rink).

Resident

Once you are a resident you can apply for a GSM contract; you'll need an application form and a copy of your passport, visa and labour/resident card. You pay RO 100 deposit (RO 200 for international access and RO 300 and a sponsor's letter for roaming) in addition to the RO 10 connection fee and the RO 4 monthly charge. A SIM card is RO 7. Calls within a 20 km radius cost 25 baisas per minute peak time (06.00 – 20.00) and 12.5 baisas per minute off-peak. This rises through a scale to 150 baisas and 75 baisas per minute respectively for calls over 200 km. Roaming is charged at 15% on top of the relevant standard tariff. Oman Mobile supports most familiar GSM features including local and international SMS text messaging, caller ID and call waiting, and has roaming agreements with 33 countries.

Thuraya

Oman Mobile also supports the Thuraya system – a satellite-based GSM service which, though comparatively expensive (just less than international call rates) and thus not a viable option for daily use, is valuable for emergency communication when travelling outside standard GSM range. Although Oman's populated areas have GSM network coverage there are still empty spaces with no reception. If you're a regular camper and wadi basher, you may consider it worth buying a Thuraya phone – especially if you travel with small children or need to be accessible at all times for some reason. Thuraya currently

Missing Mobile

Lost your mobile? Call 196 to temporarily or permanently disconnect your number. You will have to provide the number of the document that you presented when you applied for your SIM card (probably your passport or labour card). To replace the SIM, you'll need to go to a branch of Omantel with your essential documents in hand and a fee of RO 7. As soon as you have the new SIM card, your old one will be permanently disconnected. You can keep the same telephone number.

provides access to 99 countries in Europe, the Middle East, Africa and Asia. The handset costs around RO 300 and doubles as a GPS receiver.

Bill Payment

Bills are sent monthly and include rental charges and call costs. Only international calls are itemised on the bill, although the number of local and mobile calls and text messages is listed. You can pay your bill at the Omantel office in Al Khuwayr (behind Al Zawawi mosque, next to the ice rink) which is easy and efficient, and the best way to ensure continuity of service. You can also pay through some banks (such as Bank Muscat or HSBC) or through the ATM, but these services have a processing time of up to ten days. If you do not pay when you receive your bill Omantel will helpfully send an email reminder. If you ignore that, they will cut you off without further warning. Landlines continue to receive calls for several days but outgoing calls will be barred. If you do get cut off, take your bill to the Al Khuwayr office, pay all outstanding debts and a reconnection fee of RO 1, and your service will be

> ### No mobile when mobile
>
> *It is against the law to use a mobile phone handset while you are driving, if you like to talk behind the wheel you should use a hands-free kit. Failure to do so can result in you being pulled over and given a spot fine of RO 70.*

Post box

reconnected immediately. Always keep your bills and receipts for proof of payment.

Bill Enquiry Service

You can check your GSM and internet bills on Omantel's website. Apply online for a PIN and just log in to find out how much you owe.

Internet

Other options → Internet Cafés [p.260]
Websites [p.40]

You can access the internet from any Omantel landline using a computer and a 56 Kbps modem. To get connected using your own landline (or one in your company's name), you need to apply at Omantel. There are several Omantel Customer Service Outlets in Muscat – check the website for details of the one closest to you. You'll need to hand over a completed application form, copies of your passport, visa and labour/resident card (plus the originals, just in case!), and a letter from your sponsor. There is also a registration fee of RO 10. The monthly charge for internet connection is RO 2, and each hour's surfing is charged at 0.180 baisas. You can have one email address – you@omantel.net.om. If you need extra email space it costs 0.200 baisas per megabyte. If you register for a PIN on the Omantel website, you can also access your Omantel email account from any computer anywhere in the world.

If you need assistance with the internet, you can call 1313 toll free. Broadband (ADSL) is available in many areas of Muscat, with plans for expansion ongoing.

Log 'n' Surf

This facility allows you to surf the internet without a contract or subscription to Omantel. All you need is a computer with a modem, and a phone line. The charge will be billed to the line you are connecting from. To connect from a PC just double click on 'My Computer', then on 'Dial-up Networking' and then on 'Make a New Connection'. Type in 'omantel' for both your username and password, dial 1312 and click connect. Charges are a little higher – 25 baisas per minute from a landline and 50 baisas per minute from a mobile (to access the internet using your mobile you need to subscribe to the data service for an extra RO 3 per month).

New Residents

Utilities & Services

Postal Services

Other options → Post & Courier Services [p.36]

The postal system is reliable and efficient but there is no house address mail delivery in Oman; all mail is routed through the Central Post Office then distributed to post office boxes. While most people use their company address, it is possible to get an individual PO box number – just apply through your local post office. There is a regular airmail service and an express mail service. Most of the leading international courier services have branches in Oman. Post office opening times vary.

Post Offices	
Al Hamriya	24 789 311
Al Harthy Complex	24 563 534
Jawharat A'Shati Complex	24 692 181
Madinat As Sultan Qaboos	24 697 083
Mina Al Fahal	24 565 465
Muscat	24 738 547
Ruwi	24 701 651
Seeb	24 519 922
SQU campus	24 413 333

Television

There is only one local channel – Oman TV – and although it shows the odd English programme, broadcasts are mainly in Arabic. Programme details are published in the local press. All broadcast material must comply with Oman's moral code, so certain films and programmes may be censored. TVs are in PAL format (UK standard), so certain videos will not work unless you have multi-system equipment. However, almost any TV, VCR or DVD player you buy in Oman is multi-system and will work anywhere in the world.

Satellite TV & Radio

In contrast, satellite TV offers a huge choice of channels. Every house seems to have at least one satellite dish attached. Pay TV channels require you to pay for equipment (dish, decoder), installation and subscription (monthly, quarterly or annually) for the channels you want to watch. Free-to-air channels require only the equipment installation, there is no subscription fee. There is a greater variety of English language programmes on the pay channels rather than on the free-to-air channels, which are mostly in Hindi or Arabic. Most satellite providers offer bundled packages of channels.

Equipment

Equipment can be bought from main dealers or any of the small electrical shops. Second hand dishes and decoders are often advertised on supermarket noticeboards and in the classified ads. The majority of dealers will offer installation. Many apartment blocks have satellite channels already fitted. If not, ask your landlord about a cost share system.

Satellite/Cable Providers	
Al As'hab Trading Co LLC	24 837 477
Al Hamli Telecommunication	24 830 550
Mohd & Partners Electronic Store LLC	24 832 725
Orbit Direct	24 489 499
Salim Al Humaidi Trading	24 836 708
Shanfari & Partners	23 290 139
Showtime P.vii	971 4 367 7160

Health

General Medical Care

Medical care in Oman is excellent. There are many private specialist clinics, private and government hospitals, all staffed by qualified professionals. Most people who receive medical treatment in Oman can say their experience was a positive one. However, private medical care is costly and visitors and non-residents are strongly advised to take out medical insurance. Although there are no specific health risks facing visitors it's a good idea to keep your tetanus and hepatitis protection up to date.

The most common health threats are heat and dehydration. Summers in Oman are hot and humid and, unless you've lived in this part of the world before, you'll probably underestimate just how hot it can get. Wear a strong sunblock all year round, especially on your face and neck, and drink plenty of water (a minimum of two litres a day). Take special precautions to protect children from the heat and make sure they wear UV protected sunsuits and plenty of sunscreen on the beach. Whenever you can, stay out of the sun – park in the shade where possible and wear a hat.

Hotels, restaurants and shopping malls often have arctic air conditioning to combat the heat outside, and the constant temperature changes can leave you prone to colds for the first few months.

Omani nationals and resident expats receive healthcare for a nominal cost at government

hospitals, although expats must have a referral from a health centre to receive treatment. Although costly, the walk-in convenience of private medical care is handy. Waiting times are longer at government hospitals, which are very busy. You'll have to wait to get an appointment and then wait again when you arrive for your appointment; whereas at Muscat Private Hospital and Al Shatti Hospital you can usually get an appointment almost immediately.

Hospitals

Government Hospitals	
Al Nahda Hospital	24 837 800
Ibn Sina Hospital	24 875 363
Khoula Hospital	24 563 625

Private Hospitals	
Al Shatti Hospital	24 604 263
Muscat Private Hospital P.79	24 592 600
Royal Armed Forces Hospital	24 331 997
Sultan Qaboos University Hospital	24 413 355

Health Centres

Government Health Centres	
Al Wutayyah Hospital	24 571 744
Azaiba Hospital	24 497 233
Bawshar Hospital	24 593 311
Ghubbrah Hospital	24 497 226
Muscat Hospital	24 737 696
Mutrah Hospital	24 711 296
Royal Hospital	24 599 000
Ruwi Hospital	24 786 088
Wadi Kabir Hospital	24 812 944

Private Health Centres	
Lama Polyclinic	24 707 566
Qurm Medical Centre	24 692 898

Diagnostics

Al Afaq Medical Diagnostic & Imaging Centre LLC	24 501 162
Al Amal Medical & Health Care Center	24 485 052
Al Hassan Medical Center	24 481 135
Al Hayat Polyclinic LLC	24 565 941
Ibn Sina Hospital	24 875 363

Dermatologists

Abu Musafir Skin Clinic	24 706 453
Al Amal Medical & Health Care Center	24 485 052
Al Shatti Hospital	24 604 263
Bio Carre	24 707 444
Hatat Polyclinic LLC	24 563 641

Muscat Pharmacy branches at Al Khuwayr Commercial Centre, Al Sarooj and Muscat Private Hospital, and the Scientific Pharmacy in Al Qurm, are open 24 hours. Locations and numbers of duty pharmacies are listed in the daily press.

Maternity

There are three hospitals in Muscat where you can have your baby: Muscat Private Hospital, Al Shatti Hospital and Sultan Qaboos University Hospital. Expatriate children can no longer be delivered in government hospitals. These three hospitals will provide ante and postnatal care packages, as will many private clinics. If your child is not an Omani citizen you'll get an official birth certificate at the hospital where delivery took place (at a cost of RO 6). Take this certificate to the Ministry of Foreign Affairs (Consular section) Attestation Office to be stamped (this will cost another RO 6) and then to your country's Embassy, where your baby will be issued with a passport. You can then apply for a visa for your baby through the usual channels. To register your child with the Omani authorities you will need a completed application form, the birth notification from the Ministry of Health, labour/resident cards or passports of both parents, and the parents' marriage certificate. Legal responsibility for registering the child's birth rests with the father, although in the absence of the father it may be done by the mother, any adult relative present at the birth or any adult staying with the mother.

Muscat Private Hospital

Ante & Post Natal Care	
Al Shatti Hospital	24 604 263
Hatat Polyclinic LLC	24 563 641
Medident Centre	24 600 668
Muscat Private Hospital P.79	24 592 600

Gynaecology & Obstetrics	
Al Massaraat Medical Centre	24 566 435
Al Shatti Hospital	24 604 263
Hatat Polyclinic LLC	24 563 641

Paediatrics

Muscat Private Hospital has an excellent paediatrics department run by two paediatricians on back-to-back shifts, providing 24-hour cover and a walk-in clinic. They also operate a free 24-hour GSM hotline, open to parents and young people up to 18, offering invaluable medical advice and counselling. The principle behind this, on the basis that prevention is better than cure, is to give parents immediate reassurance and advice and to provide confidential support to teenagers who need a sympathetic and objective ear. The number for the hotline is 99 474 989 or 99 474 992.

Dentists/Orthodontists

In the many dental clinics in Muscat there are practitioners and specialists of all nationalities. As usual, word of mouth is the best way to find the one who suits you.

Private Dentists/Orthodontists	
Al Amal Medical & Health Care Center	24 485 052
Al Massaraat Clinic	24 566 435
Emirates Medical Centre P.83	24 604 540
Harub Dental Clinic	24 563 814
Hatat Polyclinic LLC	24 563 641
Medident Centre	24 600 668
Precision Dental Clinic	24 696 247
Qurm Medical & Dental Centre	24 692 898

Opticians

There are plenty of opticians in Oman, with most outlets selling a range of sunglasses and prescription lenses. For more information, see Eyewear [p.161].

Opticians	
Al Ghazal Opticians	24 563 546
Grand Opticals	24 558 890
Oman Opticals	24 562 981
Yateem Opticians	24 563 716

Hairdressers

There's no shortage of salons where you can get your hair cut although prices range from the reasonable to the ridiculous. Many of the more popular salons are located within hotels or shopping malls.

Hairdressers	
Al Hana Saloon	24 561 668
Beauty Centre Al Harthy Complex	24 566 188
Beauty Centre Al Wadi Centre	24 563 321
Beauty Centre Jawharat A'Shati Complex	24 602 074

Alternative Therapies

Muscat is a cultural crossroads and many of its residents come from countries where traditional therapies are practised. Consequently, there is a good balance of holistic treatments and orthodox Western medicine available. Natural medicine can be very effective and, because the treatments are aimed at balancing the whole person, your therapist will need to know a lot about you. Be prepared to spend up to two hours on the first consultation so that your therapist can build up a picture of your background and medical history. Alternative treatments can cost as much as Western medicine. While they rarely offer the quick fix that one expects from orthodox practice, they work slowly and gently with the body's natural processes, so be prepared to stick with it to get a result. As always, word of mouth is the best way to find the most appropriate treatment. Some of the more common disciplines are listed below, but for general advice on a range of alternative medical treatments, contact the Al Kawakek Complex Ayurvedic Clinic, Al Qurm (24 564 101 or 99 340 138), or the All Seasons Ayurvedic Clinic, Madinat As Sultan Qaboos (24 604 178).

Acupressure/Acupuncture

One of the oldest healing methods in the world, acupressure involves the systematic placement of pressure with fingertips on established meridian points on the body. This therapy can be used to relieve pain, soothe the nerves and stimulate the body, as determined necessary by the therapist. Acupuncture is an ancient Chinese technique that uses needles to access the body's meridian points. The technique is surprisingly painless and is quickly becoming an alternative or complement to Western medicine as it aids ailments such as asthma, rheumatism, and even more serious diseases. It has also been known to work wonders on animals!

Acupressure/Acupuncture

Acu-Magnetic Treatment Clinic	24 487 828
Al Maaqooq Clinic	24 491 988

Homeopathy

Homeopathy, which has been practised in Europe for centuries, is a safe and effective treatment for jump starting the body's formidable self-healing powers. Working at both the physical and emotional levels it treats the whole person rather than the symptoms and uses remedies derived from a variety of natural sources. Practitioners undergo rigorous training and many are also qualified Western medical doctors. Homeopathic remedies are not available over the counter in Oman as they are in many countries, but there are several practising homeopaths and clinics.

Homeopathy

Bait Al Dawa Homeopathic Clinic	24 489 031
Hatat Polyclinic LLC	24 563 641

Reflexology & Massage Therapy

Reflexology is another scientifically detailed method of bringing the body and mind back into balance. Based on the premise that reflex points on the feet and hands correspond to the organs and body systems, and that massaging these points improves and maintains health, reflexology works by stimulating the body's natural self-healing process. While many spas and salons offer massage and reflexology, there are those which offer a more focused therapeutic approach to the holistic healing qualities of reflexology and massage.

Reflexology/Massage

Acu-Magnetic Treatment Clinic	24 487 828
Noor Al Madeena Ayurvedic Clinic	24 797 273
Oman Ayurvedic Health Resort LLC	24 692 262

Aromatherapy

Chedi Muscat, The	24 498 035

Back Treatment

Back problems can seriously affect your quality of life. Chiropractic and osteopathy treatments focus on manipulating the skeleton in a non-intrusive manner to improve the functioning of the nervous system or blood supply to the body. Chiropractic is based on the manipulative treatment of misalignments in the joints, especially those of the spinal column, while osteopathy involves manipulation and massage of the skeleton and musculature. Building core muscle strength is an excellent way to support a fragile back. There is no osteopathy clinic at present. Physiotherapists work out of Muscat Private Hospital and Al Shatti Hospital.

Pilates is said to be the safest form of neuromuscular reconditioning and back strengthening available. Les Mills' Body Training System classes are also extremely effective, particularly BodyPump, BodyBalance and RPM. The Palm Beach Club at the InterContinental Hotel (24 600 500) has five Body Training System licences. A number of clinics offer therapeutic massage for back pain, and word of mouth is a good way to get a recommendation.

Back Treatment

1st Chiropractic Clinic, The	24 698 847
Palm Beach Club	24 600 500

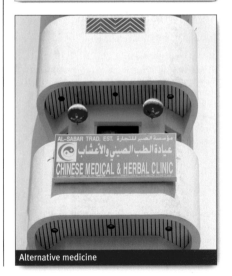
Alternative medicine

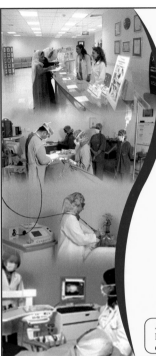
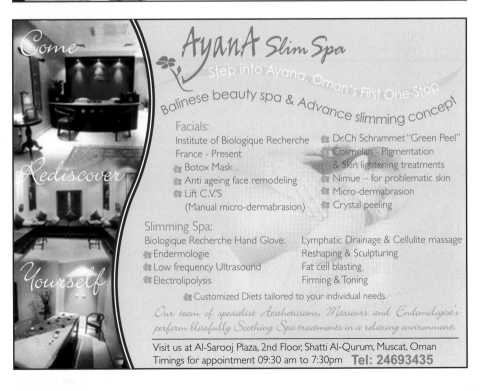

Mental Health

In addition to the normal pressures of modern living, expat life can have its particular challenges. Moving to a different culture, leaving friends and family behind, changing jobs or just dealing with the heat in Oman can be stressful, even for the most resilient personalities. If you have moved to Oman with your spouse and can't find a job, time can hang heavy on your hands. Although people are generally friendly here, they have their own busy lives. It can be lonely until you settle in. If you need someone to talk to there are places you can go for support. Al Shatti Hospital, Muscat Private Hospital (MPH), University Hospital and Hatat Polyclinic can put you in touch with counsellors, psychologists and psychiatrists. There are a wider range of services on offer in Dubai.

Counselling/Psychology

Al Shatti Hospital	24 604 263
University Hospital	24 413 355

Psychiatry

Al Shatti Hospital	24 604 263
Hatat Polyclinic LLC	24 563 641
MPH	24 592 600

Support Groups

One of the toughest parts of expat life is the loss of your immediate support network back home (friends and family). In 1992, Unicef, together with the Ministry of Health, set up CSG (Community Support Groups). With the help of the Omani Women's Association, CSG holds workshops and training to implement support networks throughout the region.

- Muscat Mums is a friendly support group for mums to be and mums with children under the age of ten. They organise various activities and coffee mornings throughout the year. Check out their website http://muscatmums.tripod.com

- Alcoholics Anonymous (AA): The Oasis Group meets Saturday, Monday and Wednesday from 19:30 to 20:30 at the Medident Medical Centre (Madinat As Sultan Qaboos, behind Pizza Hut). The Candlelit Group meets Sunday and Tuesday at the Top Care Medical Centre in Al Azaiba. You can call the 24-hour hotline on 99 447 109, email serenity@aa-oman.org

- Narcotics Anonymous meets at Hatat Polyclinic in Al Azaiba on Monday at 19:30 and Thursday at 19:00. There is a further NA meeting at the Medident Clinic on Friday at 19:00. For more information call 99 264 347.

Support Groups

Alcoholics Anonymous	99 447 109
Muscat Mums	99 509 449
Narcotics Anonymous	99 264 347
Omani Women's Association	24 602 800
UNICEF	24 602 624

Education

There are international schools catering for all major cultural or population groups in Oman. Most of the schools are fee paying. Ask around about schools and visit all those you are interested in – try to go during a school day and ask to see a class in progress. If you can, talk to pupils, staff and other parents. There are often waiting lists for the most popular nursery groups and schools so, if possible, it is best to register early.

To enrol your child at a school you'll need to submit the following:

- School application form
- Passport size photographs
- Copies of student's birth certificate
- Current immunisation records
- Reports from previous schools, if any

The school will inform you if there are any other documents they require in order to process the application.

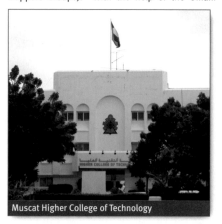

Muscat Higher College of Technology

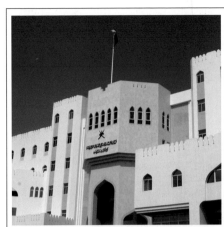

Government Ministry buildings

Nurseries & Pre-Schools

(Age: 2 – 4½ years)

Children are generally interviewed before being accepted for nurseries. English is often the chosen teaching language and fees vary tremendously.

Hours: Usually four to five hours in the morning.

Fees: Ranges from RO 650 to RO 1,300 per annum.

Nurseries & Pre-Schools	
Abu Adnan	24 605 704
Al Shamoos	24 561 871
Bright Beginnings	24 699 387
Middle East Nursery	24 787 127
Indian Nursery	24 479 662
Little Flower Nurseries	24 478 512
National Nursery Montessori	24 478 512
Tenderbuds	24 691 055

Primary & Secondary Schools

(Age: 4½ – 11 years) (Age: 11 – 18 years)

Most schools will require proof of your child's previous school academic records, although some may also require children to take a grade level entrance exam and appear for an interview.

Depending on your nationality and educational requirements, most national curriculum syllabuses can be found in Oman's schools, including GCSEs, A-levels, International Baccalaureate and American high school diploma, as well as all the Asian equivalents.

The standard of education is high and most schools have excellent facilities and offer plenty of extra curricular activities. All schools must be approved by the Ministry of Education and are subject to regular inspections to ensure rules and regulations are being upheld. Many schools also offer nursery education.

Primary & Secondary Schools	
Azzan Bin Qais Private School	24 503 081
Bangladesh School	24 497 127
British School-Muscat, The P.87	24 600 842
Ecole Francaise	24 601 007
Indian School	24 707 567
	24 811 521
Muscat Private School	24 565 550
Pakistan School	24 702 489
Sri Lankan School	24 811 005
Sultan School	24 536 777

Fees range from RO 200 to RO 3,800 per year.

Hours: most schools run from 07:30 – 13:30, although times vary, particularly between kindergarten, primary and secondary.

University & Higher Education

Most expat teenagers return to their home country by university age, or earlier, or go abroad for further education. Choices in Oman are limited. For its own nationals the Sultanate is expanding its system of further education and training, although Sultan Qaboos University is still the main centre.

Universities	
Caledonian College of Engineering	24 535 522
Modern College of Business & Science	24 482 802
Muscat College of Management Science and Technology	24 594 783
Sultan Qaboos University	24 413 333

Special Needs Education

There are no dedicated schools in Oman for expatriate children with special needs. Schools with learning support departments may be able to accommodate children with basic learning difficulties. The American International School of Muscat (TAISM) has a support unit of professionals including a special education teacher. You can contact them on 24 595 180 for more information.

Learning Arabic

Other options → Language Schools [p.222]

Living in a foreign country can be a great opportunity to learn the language and expand your horizons. Any attempt to communicate with local people in their own language always goes down well. It also helps you understand the culture better. As English is the second official language of Oman, however, almost everyone speaks it (except for the people you really need to communicate with – policemen and taxi drivers) and it's easy to get by without knowing a word of Arabic. If you want to progress beyond *a salam'aleikum* there are a number of private institutions that offer Arabic language courses (try the Polyglot Institute Oman, 24 835 777). If you want just a few words to help you get by, have a look at the Basic Arabic table [p.14].

The British School - Muscat

Tel.: 24600842, Fax: 24601062, E-mail: admin@britishschool.edu.om
www.britishschool.edu.om

• Registrations open from September onwards.
Contact our Registrar, Mrs. Deirdre Selway for further details on 24600842

Give your child the best you can.

You have the choice to give your child the best education possible. At The British School - Muscat, we give children an opportunity to take a chance on a road that leads to creativity, within the boundaries of a sound education system.

Transportation

Other options → Car [p.28]
Getting Around [p.28]

Cars are the most popular form of transport in Oman and the cost of purchase, maintenance, insurance and fuel are up to 50% less than in many parts of the world. New residents will delight in the chance of owning a five litre fuel injected American sports car or a top of the range 4 WD and still have enough money left over for fuel! In fact petrol is cheaper than bacon.

It is illegal to drive a dirty car; if you do so you risk being stopped by the police and told to wash your car, or even fined. So after a weekend of off road adventuring you'll have to roll up your sleeves up or make a trip to the carwash – the Rainbow Carwash at Al Sarooj is excellent and you can have a coffee while you wait.

The following section covers leasing, buying and renting cars, registration and insurance for buyers, and fines and accident procedure for buyers, renters and leasers.

Vehicle Leasing

Leasing a vehicle has many advantages over buying. Not only is it a good option for shorter or uncertain periods, but the leasing company will deal with breakdowns, accidents, insurance and re-registration for you and will offer 24-hour assistance. Cars can be leased on a weekly, monthly or annual basis. You can choose from a range of models from saloon cars to four-wheel drives. Prices vary according to the model and the length of lease, but a one-year lease on a basic saloon car will cost about RO 200 per month. For short-term rental, many of the local and international companies offer daily rates. Check the newspapers or the Oman Business Directory for the most competitive. To hire any vehicle you will need to provide a passport copy and driving licence.

Hi There Neighbour!

Did you know that the glitzy, glamorous city of Dubai is just a short drive from Muscat? And did you know that Dubai is packed with hundreds of star-rated restaurants, luxurious hotels, buzzing nightspots and glorious beaches? And did you know that the Dubai Explorer is the ultimate guidebook to this amazing, progressive city? Well now you know!

Buying a Vehicle

To own a car in Oman you must have a labour/resident card. If you decide to buy a car you'll find that it is considerably cheaper to buy, maintain and run a car in Oman compared with most other countries. Every expat resident is allowed to own up to three vehicles. Whether you are buying a brand new car or a second-hand one, when it's time to close the deal you'll need to present certain documents. You'll need your Essential Documents [p.48], a vehicle purchase form (available from the police station or the showroom), plus your valid driving licence and a copy. The vehicle purchase form should be signed by your sponsor or company and then taken to your insurance provider. In the case of a private sale, the seller should be with you as the car must be insured in your name before the registration can be finalised. Once the car is registered you will get a vehicle registration card (a 'mulkia'). You should always have the mulkia with you in the car, although many people keep a copy in the car and leave the original mulkia at home.

Vehicle Leasing Agents

Al Maha Rent A Car	24 603 376
Anwar Al Shaikh Trdg Est	23 298 085
Avis Rent a Car Salalah	23 202 581
Avis Rent a Car Muscat	24 607 235
Global Car Rental	24 697 140
Mark Car Rental & Tours	24 562 444
Sixt Rent A Car	24 489 082
Thrifty Car Rental	24 489 248
Unic Rent-A-Car	24 691 108
United Finance Co SAOG	24 565 151
Value Plus Rent A Car	24 597 264

New Vehicles

Most new car models are available through the main dealers. Many car dealerships have showrooms between the Al Wutayyah and Wadi Adai roundabouts, although there are others located all along the highway (Porsche, Land Rover, GMC and Mitsubishi are all situated between the Bawshar and Al Azaiba Roundabouts). Some dealers sell several makes of car – Zubair sells Chrysler, Yamaha and Mitsubishi.

Don't forget to haggle – most dealers will offer a discount on the advertised price of a new car. The best time of year to get a good deal is during Ramadan, when all the dealers have promotions. Some dealers even offer a 'buy one, win one' raffle

Make way
for the Legends

The all-new 2005 Toyota 4WDs. The ultimate in power. The utmost in performance. And the highest in status. Totally unchallenged for over five decades. Visit the nearest Toyota Showroom and meet these legends, now.

LAND CRUISER
THE ALL TERRAIN CONQUEROR

- Choice of 4.5 L EFi, 4.7 L V8 & 4.2 L Diesel Engines
- Blue Tooth Telephone Kit
- Active Traction Control (ATC)
- Wood Paneling & Wood Combination Steering Wheel

PRADO
POWER PACKED. FEATURE PACKED.

- Choice of All New 2.7 L, VVTi & 4.0 L, V6 and 3.0L Diesel Engines
- All New 6-speed Manual and 5-speed Automatic Transmission
- Electronically Modulated Air Suspension
- Active Height Control (AHC)

RAV4
THE 4WD FOR SERIOUS FUN

- 2.0 L EFi VVTi Engine
- Full-time 4WD
- CD Player with 6 CD Changer
- Multiple Rear Seat Adjustment

ticket that gives you the chance to win a second car! You might save money if a new batch of cars arrives, as last year's models immediately drop in price.

The dealer will take care of all the paperwork involved in the car purchase on your behalf, including registration and arranging finance. They will also usually offer good warranties and free servicing for the first few years. Unless you are paying cash for the car you will need to get a bank loan or leave a post-dated cheque for every month of the finance period (typically 12, 24 or 36 months). When you collect your car you will drive with green licence plates until the vehicle registration is complete.

Fill 'er up

New Car Dealers

Al Hashar & Co	24 596 434
Al Rumaila Motors LLC	24 490 627
Auto Plus (International Commercial House LLC)	24 478 080
BMW – Al Jenaibi International Automobiles LLC	24 560 889
Lexus – Bahwan Automotive Centre	24 561 377
Mitsubishi – Zubair Automotive	24 591 772
Oman Gulf Enterprises	24 793 072
Oman Marketing & Services Co (OMASCO)	24 561780
Oman Trading Establishment LLC	24 793 072
Sata LLC	24 492 544
Saud Bahwan Group (Toyota) P.89	24 578 000
Suzuki – Moosa Abdul Rahman Co	24 571 110
Towell Auto Centre LLC P.138	24 564 048
Wattayah Motors LLC	24 562 729
Zawawi Trading Company LLC	24 713 311

Used Vehicles

With cars being relatively cheap, and expats coming and going all the time, the second-hand car market is thriving. The main areas for used car dealers are Al Wutayyah, Al Khuwayr and Wadi Kabir, although you'll find dealers in other locations too. The advantage of buying through a dealer is that they'll arrange the registration and insurance for you. In general, dealers do not offer warranties unless you are buying a car that is still protected under its manufacturer's warranty. Newspaper classifieds offer little in terms of second-hand vehicles for sale, except for Sunday's *Times of Oman* supplement and the classified section of *The Week*. Supermarket noticeboards are a good source of cars for sale, and there is the car souk at the Friday Market. If you do buy a second-hand car privately it's a good idea to have it checked for major faults before you buy. Reputable car dealers will perform a thorough check-up of a vehicle for about RO 15.

Used Car Dealers

Al Fajer Cars	24 491 112
Al Hamriya Car Marketing (Used Cars)	24 830 551
Al Hasin Trading	24 453 731
Al Itihad Cars Showroom	24 542 990
Al Jazeera Motors	24 600 127
Al Majaini	24 831 133
Al Sharouq Rent A Car	24 832 833
Al Siyabi Used Cars	24 698 195
Al Wathbah Trading	24 421 828
General Automotive Co LLC	24 492 143
Johrat Al Hail Trading	24 831 931
Khamis Bin Saud Bin Ali Al Amari	24 421 610
Modern Cars Exhibition	24 786 011
New Zahra Trading	24 833 953
OK Used Cars	24 691 218
Real Value Autos	24 560 508

Ownership Transfer

To transfer a private vehicle into your name you need to fill in a form which details the buyer's personal information and bears the signatures of both buyer and seller. The seller must appear in person before the Directorate of Licensing at the Traffic Police department. If the seller still has a loan outstanding on the vehicle the bank must give its approval, and if the loan has been paid the bank will issue a letter of discharge. All transactions related to buying or selling second-hand vehicles should go through the Royal Oman Police.

Perfectly covered

Motor Insurance

Get better protection and exclusive advantages

- Discounts for careful drivers
- Breakdown service with full cover
- Emergency medical expense cover
- Replacement car during accident repair
- No depreciation on spare parts
- Home and Travel insurance available

Together we're stronger

NORWICH UNION

Vehicle Import

If you are importing a vehicle you will need to go with your shipping agent to the port to get the import papers from the Port Authorities (if you're lucky your shipping agent will do this without you). They'll give you a form with some details of the car on it, such as engine number, chassis number, date of production, etc. Depending on the age of the vehicle, and the mood of the person helping you, you might have to pay tax.

The next thing you need is insurance. Even though the car is not registered you can insure using the engine number or chassis number to identify the car. The insurance company will give you a form, all in Arabic, which you'll need for the registration. They will fill in the form for you. You'll also need a letter from your sponsor to say they approve of you importing the vehicle. The next step is to go to the Ministry of Commerce in Ruwi, behind Lulu shopping centre. Take the vehicle export papers from the country of origin, the import papers from the shipping agent, the registration form in Arabic from the insurance company, the insurance papers, the sponsor's letter, passport copies, your Oman driving licence, a copy of your labour card, and the original ownership papers. To be on the safe side, just take any document remotely connected with the vehicle, plus a few spare copies! After paying a fee of RO 1 you'll be given an approval form. Armed with all your papers, your next stop should be the police station on Death Valley Road to have your car checked at the Annual Inspections section. Once your vehicle has been inspected, collect the inspector's report (from the small office in the inspection area) and proceed to the main office of the police station. Here you'll have to present your documents before being directed to the customs counter (in the same room). After customs, you'll be sent back to the inspector's office and this is when you'll have to pay a fee of RO 20 – remember to keep the receipt! You will then get your licence plates which you'll take home to affix to your car. The following day you should go back (to the same counter) and hand over the receipt (take all the other papers too, just in case). They will give you the final registration card, it is the same size as a credit card. Finally, go back to the insurance company and give them the registration number and show them the card.

Vehicle Insurance

You must have adequate insurance before you can register a car in your name. The minimum requirement is third party insurance, but fully comprehensive insurance is advisable. Many insurance companies, both local and international, are listed in the Yellow Pages. To insure your car you'll need copies of your driving licence, your labour/residence card, and the mulkia for your car. In some cases the insurance company will want to inspect the car first.

It is simple and inexpensive to insure your car for the UAE, should you wish to drive across the border. Remember, your insurance will not be valid if your licence is not valid, or if you have an accident while under the influence of alcohol.

Registering a Vehicle

All cars must be registered annually with the police; the registration document is called the 'mulkia'. Along with your Essential Documents [p.48] the following documents are also required:

- New registration form filled in by the applicant or their representative and stamped by the sponsor
- Insurance certificate
- Proof of Purchase certificate
- Copy of a valid driving licence

There is a detailed list on the ROP website (www.rop.gov.om) of all documents required when registering your vehicle. Additional documents are required if you have imported your vehicle or purchased it at an auction. It's advisable to check the website before heading out to register the vehicle.

The Process

If you are buying your car from a dealer they will usually do this for you. If you have bought a vehicle privately you can do it yourself or pay an Omani to do it for you – many advertise their services on supermarket noticeboards (they'll probably charge around RO 10 to RO 15 – well worth it!).

If you decide to do it yourself, collect the necessary documents (and some spare copies, just in case), and head down to the police headquarters on Death Valley Road. Across the road from the station you'll see a group of Omanis fitting registration plates — approach one and wait your turn (it's usually less busy in the afternoon).

It is at re-registration that you find out if you've picked up any traffic fines, so take extra money with you in case you have to pay your fines (you can find out if you've been caught on the ROP website – www.rop.gov.om — before you go).

If your car is ten years or older it will need to pass a roadworthiness test. This involves an inspection to check that the chassis and engine numbers match those on the mulkia; that the lights and brakes work; that the level of smoke emission is acceptable; and that the paintwork is not damaged or fading. Once the car has passed the test you can proceed with registration. If your car fails the test you must first sort out the problem(s) and then start the process again.

There is also a traffic police branch at Seeb, which is open 24 hours a day.

Traffic Fines & Offences

If you are caught driving or parking illegally, you will be fined (unless the offence is more serious, in which case you may have to appear in court). Around Muscat are a number of police-controlled speed traps, fixed cameras and mobile speed traps which are activated by cars exceeding the speed limit by nine km/hr. Fines start at RO 10 and go up in increments of RO 5. All traffic fines should be paid at the Traffic Fines Section of the Death Valley Road police station. Your fines are 'banked' and you only have to pay them once a year when you re-register your car and you can check whether you've received any fines online at www.rop.gov.om/trafficfine.

Breakdowns

If your car breaks down the chances are good that someone will stop and help you – everyone knows the dangers of being stuck in the heat. If a police car or breakdown truck doesn't pass by, a kind motorist will usually stop to offer assistance, particularly if you have a flat tyre. You can call the Arabian Automobile Association (AAA), which is a 24-hour breakdown service (similar to the AA in the UK). Their number is 24 605 555.

Traffic Accidents

Other options → Car [p.29]

If you have an accident don't move your car until the police arrive, even if you are causing a major road blockage. They will usually arrive pretty quickly. In case of an accident call 24 560 099 (don't call 999, it is reserved for the Fire Department and emergency cases only). Expect a crowd of rubberneckers to gather around the accident – at least you'll have someone there who can translate from Arabic to English when the police arrive. The police will decide (on the spot) which party is responsible for the accident, and then all involved parties should go to the nearest police station. If your car can't be driven the police will arrange for it to be towed away. When you get to the police station you might have to wait around for quite some time, so be patient. You'll need to present your driving licence and mulkia (registration card). If any of your documents are invalid you will immediately be blamed for the accident. If your company has a PRO it's a good idea to get him to come down to the station to help you translate and fill in the many forms. If there is a fine to be paid, the police will hold your licence until you've paid it.

The police will fill in an accident report and you will be given a reference number. The car must be sent to a garage that is approved by your insurance company. The garage is not allowed to carry out repairs to any vehicle without the police report.

If you are involved in an accident where someone is hurt or killed, and the case goes to court, you will not be allowed to leave the country until the case is settled.

Repairs (Vehicle)

By law, no vehicle can be accepted for repair without an accident report from the Traffic Police. Usually your insurance company will have an agreement with a particular garage to which they will refer you. The garage will carry out the repair work and the insurance company will settle the claim. Generally there is RO 100 deductible for all claims but confirm the details of your policy with your insurance company.

Drive safely

Exploring

EXPLORER

Exploring

Highlights...

Forts

p.122

You'd be hard pushed to travel too far in Oman without spotting the familiar turret of one of the country's ubiquitous forts. A telling reminder of the country's history of conflict and defence, these buildings today act as fascinating reminders of a turbulent past. You could find yourself bewildered by the sheer number out there, so read this section first to get the lowdown on our favourite forts!

Get Out of Town!

A high percentage of Oman's population lives in the region of Muscat, and it's true that the city has the highest concentration of entertainment and leisure facilities. However, there's so much more for you to see and do than just explore the capital city, and a trip out of town will really open your eyes to the staggering sights and breathtaking beauty of this charming country.

Exploring

Oman, the fabled land of Sindbad the Sailor, has been a place of great attraction to explorers for centuries. During his expedition, Marco Polo visited the region of Dhofar in the late 13th century, and then sailed up to the coast of Qalhat, once a city of high prosperity. Fifty years later he was followed by the Moroccan explorer Ibn Battuta, who had begun his pilgrimage to Mecca in 1325. Twenty nine years later Battuta had seen the whole of Arabia, referring to Oman as 'the coast of the fish eaters' (not surprising as he arrived in Oman by sea at Sur). The more recent desert explorations of Britain's Wilfred Thesiger are most fondly remembered in Oman and the UAE today. Thesiger crossed the Rub Al Khali (Empty Quarter) twice between 1946 and 1948, both times disguised as a Syrian Bedouin.

There are still countless reasons to visit Oman. The Gulf of Oman's rich sea life, the variety of unspoilt landscapes, the vast deserts, the rugged mountains, the numerous forts, the wildlife and, last but not least, the friendly Omani people, are all things that you will remember fondly. The Omanis treasure their past and therefore abundant remains of ancient cities and local heritage can be admired. Adventure seekers can enjoy activities such as desert driving, wadi bashing, diving and trekking. Other local attractions include shopping in the souks or a visit to the camel races, both of which provide perfect opportunities to mingle with the locals and get a taste of everyday life in Oman.

Also known as the Pearl of Arabia, Muscat still lies embedded in a traditional culture. With all its greenery, beaches, museums, the famous Mutrah Souk and other commercial centres, visitors should take at least a few days to discover this friendly city, and become adjusted to the pace and way of life in Oman. The modern city of Muscat has grown and developed and there are now many separate areas making up the whole, which is usually referred to as the Greater Muscat area. Hence, there is no one place which you can visit to get a 'feel' of Muscat — the areas are divided by low craggy hills and each part has its own distinctive character.

After exploring Muscat you can move on to other, more rugged regions of the country. Travelling north will bring you to the cities of Barka, Nakhal

and Sohar. If time allows, the Mussandam peninsular to the north-west is highly recommended, with its main cities of Khasab and Bukha, and with scenery totally different from the rest of Oman. It features beautiful fjords and lagoons and is becoming an increasingly popular tourist destination. Travelling inland leads you to Rusayl, Rustaq, Nizwa, Bahla, Jabrin and also to the tranquil mountains of Jebel Al Akhdar, an experience not to be missed. Going south via the interior route, you will pass the cities of Rusayl, Fanja, Sumail, Ibra, Al Mudayr, Al Mintrib, Sur and Ras Al Hadd. On the coastal route Tiwi Village is worth a stop, as is the ancient city of Qalhat, if only for the fact that this historical city, now in ruins, was of such particular interest to Marco Polo and Ibn Battuta.

The southern province of Dhofar, and its capital Salalah, provides a welcome change in climate in the hot summer months. While the rest of Oman is paralysed by heat, the monsoon (khareef) blowing in off the Indian Ocean ensures a high percentage of rainfall in this area, resulting in cool weather and beautiful greenery. Salalah attracts international as well as local visitors for its peace and tranquility.

Apart from the major regions to visit in Oman, this section also includes its largest island, Masirah, which is off the south-east coast.

Wherever you go, don't forget to take along the best guide available – the pull-out map from the back of this book.

So old, but so beautiful

Oman Visitor Checklist

The checklist below features the must-see, must-do activities while you are visiting this beautiful country.

From beaches and parks to desert and mountains, there is plenty of exploring to be done. Muscat is an atmospheric city and features numerous restaurants serving food from every corner of the world. Of course you should take the opportunity to sample traditional Omani food, which is widely available.

Omani Food [p.16]

Enjoy the taste of Omani food, as well as the traditional customs involved in eating. The menu varies from spicy to mild, and has delicious fish, meat and vegetarian options. Dishes are usually served with rice, and the lunchtime meal is often the main meal of the day.

Museums in Muscat [p.125]

The Natural History Museum in Muscat is fascinating, featuring an informative tour of Oman's wildlife. For an insight into the traditions and lifestyles of the Omanis, a trip to the Bait Al Zubair Museum offers a glimpse into the past.

Camel Riding & Racing [p.129]

This is a chance for you to ride on the back of the 'ship of the desert'. The experience of riding a camel is one you won't forget in a hurry! If you prefer your camels at a distance, get involved in the competitive camaraderie as a spectator at a camel race.

Sultan Qaboos Mosque [p.129]

The notable Sultan Qaboos Mosque along the main Sultan Qaboos Road is one of the largest in the region, and also one of the highest, with one of its minarets reaching almost 100m. It is open to visitors from Saturday to Wednesday (08:00 – 11:00).

Wadi Driving [p.212]

Oman's wadis are often filled with running water, and offer spectacular driving opportunities for off-road enthusiasts. Navigating along the narrow rocky tracks can be tough, but if you need to take a break you can swim in one of the freshwater pools.

Nizwa [p.114]

Once the capital of Oman and the centre for trade between the coastal and the interior regions, Nizwa is still one the largest towns in the interior. Embedded in a beautiful palm oasis, with its large fort and various souks, visiting Nizwa is an absolute must.

Desert Safari

Experience the adventure of dune driving, ride a camel, watch the beautiful desert sunset, dance along with belly dancers, sleep under the stars and wake up with the sunrise in total tranquility. Refer to tour operators for more information [p.141].

Sindbad the Sailor (Sohar) [p.112]

Don't miss out on a trip to Sohar, the birthplace of the legendary Sindbad the Sailor. The Sohar Fort Museum, located in the fort, is the ideal place to learn all about Sohar's history. The museum covers subjects from geology to anthropology to historic trading.

Beaches [p.132]

Oman has many beautiful beaches, most of which are public. The Al Bustan Palace Hotel in Muscat has a private beach – If you want to experience this luxury version, it costs RO 15, which includes lunch and one drink.

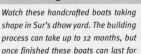

Dhow Building

Watch these handcrafted boats taking shape in Sur's dhow yard. The building process can take up to 12 months, but once finished these boats can last for over a century. To arrange a trip on a dhow, check with various tour operators about arranging a cruise [p.141].

Exploring

Oman Visitor Checklist

Dolphin & Whale Watching [p.144]

While sailing the open waters of the Gulf of Oman, it is not unusual to come across a school of playful dolphins. While the chances of seeing a whale are not as favourable, keep your eyes peeled and your patience might be rewarded.

Bird Watching [p.128]

Oman has a wide variety of birds, thanks to its landscape which varies from lush green slopes, open sea and beaches, to tidal mudflats, coastal lagoons and arid desert plains. Keen birdwatchers will have plenty to see and may even spot a lifer or two.

Water Delights

The beautiful Gulf of Oman has some amazing diving and snorkelling spots. Many hotels and major tour operators (see [p.141]) run various activities such as surfing, sailing and fishing. For more information on tour operators, see Activities [p.141].

Souks [p.182]

Experience the sounds, smells, sights and tastes of Oman at the local markets. It's a unique chance to mingle with locals, practice bargaining and sample Omani cuisine. Even if you're just browsing, it's a great way to experience some local flavour.

Horse Riding [p.206]

Explore the mountains or desert landscapes on horseback for a unique and unforgettable experience. Your steed is trained to cope with rugged ground, so put your trust in your horse's sure-footedness and relax.

Glitter and Gold

Muscat's architecture is inspired by gold and you'll see several buildings with that golden glow. Look out especially for the headquarters of Oman International Bank in Al Khuwayr, with its ten-metre high, gold-plated doors.

Mountain Biking [p.208]

Avid mountain bikers will love the challenging tracks that wind their way through Oman's rocky mountains, the wadis and along the coastline. Even the most hardcore bikers will find routes that test their skills. There are also some easier tracks for beginners.

Frankincense [p.170]

In ancient times frankincense was more valuable than gold, because of its rich aroma and scarcity. Oman was a major frankincense producer, and you can follow the history of this industry in the Dhofar region, or sample the product itself in one of the souks.

Hiking [p.205]

Oman's spectacular mountain scenery and roughly worn paths make it ideal for those who want to explore the country by foot. The climate in higher areas is usually cooler, which can be a relief after the heat of the plains and coastal areas.

Camping [p.194]

Nature lovers and happy campers will love Oman, where you can pitch your tent just about anywhere for a night out in the rough. Choose from the white beaches, the rocky mountains or the desert dunes, set up camp, and then just relax and enjoy your surroundings.

Caving [p.196]

Oman's caves are a mystical world of glittering stalagmites and stalactites, white gypsum crystal and underground lakes. These natural treasures are there for you to explore, but remember to respect and preserve them, since they are part of Oman's natural heritage.

Turtles [p.131]

A trip to see the nesting turtles is essential. Watching these huge creatures lumber up the beach to lay their eggs, then making their way back into the sea is to see nature at its most miraculous. You are virtually guaranteed a sighting in Ras Al Jinz.

Muscat (Old Town)

The old town of Muscat is situated on the coast at the eastern end of the Greater Muscat Area between Mutrah and Sidab. It is a quiet, atmospheric area and like Mutrah it is based around a sheltered port, which was historically important for trade.

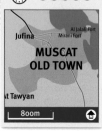

The striking Alam Palace, home of Sultan Qaboos, was built on the waterfront in the 1970s and dominates the town. It is flanked by two Portuguese forts, Jalali Fort and Mirani Fort, both of which overlook the harbour (see Forts [p.122]).

Since the forts around the palace are used by Omani authorities, they are rarely open to visitors, although you are allowed to take photographs from the outside. The city wall of Muscat connects to mountain hills behind the old town along the

Area Highlights

Alam Palace
Experience the fairy tale image of the Sultan's palace, which is easily accessible from the road. You can walk right up to the gates, have a peek into the gardens, and have your photo taken in front of this wonderful example of Arabian architecture.

Bait Al Zubair
This museum is home to a fascinating collection of ancient artefacts and modern displays that provide an insight into how life was for Omanis a long time ago. One of the displays is a realistic recreation of an Omani mountain village.

Omani French Museum
This museum celebrates the French-Omani relationship over the past few centuries. It showcases various materials of historical importance, some dating right back to the 1700s.

natural bay. You can walk from the bay to the front side of the palace by passing the beautiful Al-Zawawi Mosque, then turn left into Qasr Al-Alam Street. You can take photos at the palace entrance without being asked any questions.

Evidence of the city walls that used to completely surround the old town can still be seen, as well as the three gates which were closed to protect the city from intruders. At one of these town gates is the

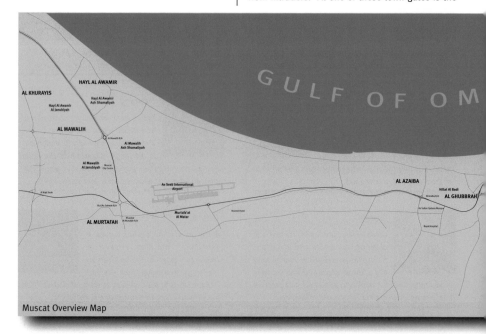

Muscat Overview Map

Muscat Gate House Museum, which opened in 2001 and offers, among other attractions, a great view over the town from its roof. Within the old city walls you'll find the Omani French Museum (Bait Fransa). Also the Bait Al Zubair museum is located just outside the walls on Al-Saidiya Street.

Sights of Muscat

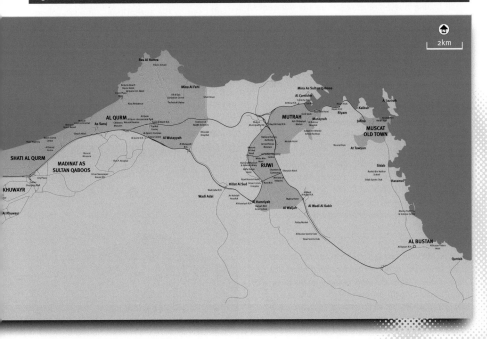

Mutrah

Nestled between the sea and a protective circle of hills, and neighboured by Al Qurm, Ruwi and the old town, is Mutrah. The town grew around its port, which today is far more vibrant than the port of Muscat's old town.

Area Overview

Epitomising Oman's efforts at beautification, Mutrah Corniche shows how far Oman has come since the early 1970s. The Corniche runs for about three kilometres along the Mutrah harbour, and is lined with pristine gardens, parks, waterfalls and statues. At the northern end, the old traders' houses and the Lawati Mosque showcase traditional architecture, with windtowers designed to capture the slightest cooling breeze.

Also at the northern end, on the edge of the Dhow harbour, is the fish market where you can witness the hustle and bustle of the fishing trade. The earlier you get there the better – from 06:30 the small fishing boats are dragged up the adjacent beach to unload catches ranging from sardines to

Area Highlights

Mutrah Souk

Whether you're in the market for a specific purchase or just want to wander around and soak up the atmosphere this is the souk to head for. Bargaining is all part of the experience and spices, incense and jewellery, along with a few hidden gems make this traditional Arabian at is very best.

Mutrah Fish Market

Once you get used to the smell of fish, you can browse the stalls looking for a fresh catch. After you've haggled with the fisherman for the best price, walk round to the back of the market where, for a few baisas, you can get someone to clean and gut the fish for you.

Mutrah Fort

This picturesque fort is 400 years old and is situated on a small outcrop of rock overlooking the corniche and harbour. When the Omanis captured the fort in 1654 it was a significant point in their fight to oust the Portuguese. It was restored in 1980 using traditional materials.

Catch of the day

sharks. Right next to the fish market is an excellent fruit and vegetable market with a colourful array of exotic produce. Both markets generally offer cheaper produce than the supermarkets. Slightly further down is the entrance to Mutrah Souk, one of the best souks in the region, which is always buzzing with activity. For more information refer to [p.184] in the Shopping section.

During the cooler months it is a pleasant walk from the souk area along the seafront to Mutrah Fort. Notable are the Portuguese towers and the Omani walls in between. Unfortunately, the picturesque fort is rarely open to visitors since it is still used by the authorities, although you are permitted to take photographs from outside.

Further east, you will find the Al Inshirah restaurant and Al-Riyam Park where a huge incense burner sits high on a rocky outcrop. Behind Al Inshirah is an ancient watchtower overlooking Mutrah. The view at the top is lovely and well worth the steep, 100-step climb.

There are parking meters in certain areas along the corniche, so have some loose change ready.

Giant incense burner in Al-Riyam Park

20 ADVENTUROUS ROUTES

Oman

Off-Road

EXPLORER

What are you doing this weekend?

Detailed maps and step-by-step instructions will lead you and your 4 WD over stunning mountains, through lush green wadis, and across dramatic sand dunes. Don't get behind the wheel without it!

Al Qurm

The area known as Al Qurm (meaning 'mangrove' in English) lies in the centre of the greater Muscat area, stretching along the coast north of Madinat As Sultan Qaboos and Ruwi, and is divided into two districts – Al Qurm and Shati Al Qurm, each with quite different characteristics.

Al Qurm

Al Qurm is a mixture of residential and commercial buildings and is home to one of the main shopping areas of Muscat. It is also notable for having the largest park in Muscat, the Qurm National Park & Nature Reserve.

The park incorporates a large boating lake, a fountain, 'Waterfall Hill', Sultan Qaboos' Rose Garden and many meandering pathways. In 1999 the Ministry of Regional Municipalities and Environment (MRME) established a mangrove nursery in this park, which has since provided thousands of mangrove seedlings every year for transplantation in other parts of the country. The aim is to stimulate the growth of mangrove trees – mangrove rich areas are productive for fish breeding and nursery. A pleasant side effect of this conservation effort is that mangrove areas offer beautiful spots for recreational activities such as canoeing.

Shopping in Al Qurm is centred in the area around Al Qurm Roundabout where a number of Muscat's major malls are located, including Al-Araimi Complex, Sabco Commercial Centre, and Capital Commercial Centre. They are all well-established, pleasant places to shop, with a wide range of goods and services and plenty of free parking.

Further north is the main residential area built on a small peninsula with excellent views along the coastline, especially to the west. The west side of this

Permits

Oman is home to many historical forts and in this section you'll find a rundown on some of the well known ones. To get access to certain forts around the country you will require a permit – these are available free of charge from the Ministry of Culture and National Heritage in Muscat (24 602 555). The Ministry is located next to the Natural History Museum. Occasionally the fort watchman will be quite relaxed if you happen to turn up without the correct paperwork, but there is a chance you will be turned away. Most hotels provide booklets with more detail on various forts, or you can see the book Forts of Oman.

area, known locally as Qurm Heights, consists of medium to high-end accommodation, while the eastern side is housing exclusively for PDO (Petroleum Development Oman) staff with private leisure facilities.

Area Highlights

Qurm National Park & Nature Reserve
Muscat's main park featuring large lawns, a boating lake, water fountains and shady pergolas. It is the home of HM Sultan Qaboos' famous Rose Garden, a tranquil, fragrant area that is full of rose varieties from all over the world. Mondays are for families only.

Majan Beach
This small and quiet beach, which is not far away and easily accessible, is ideal for snorkellers as it has superb coral reefs. On good days you can see parrot fish, rays and turtles. The beach is equipped with manmade sunshades and barbecue pits.

Beach Promenade
In the hour or two before sunset the beach and shoreline stretching from the Hyatt Regency Muscat to the InterContinental Hotel becomes a lively promenade. People come here to walk, jog, jet ski, play football and barbecue, and it is a pleasant spot to relax and watch the world go by as the sun goes down.

As well as the small green Qurm Heights Park, a popular spot with Al Qurm residents, Majan Beach, close to Ras Al Hamra Recreation Club, is a great place for a barbecue or some snorkelling with a surprising variety of fish and a coral reef within a short distance of the beach.

Also in Qurm Heights, from its cliff top location the Crowne Plaza Hotel offers a good range of leisure facilities as well as a number of dining choices with seating on the terrace, all offering commanding views over the hotel's gardens down to the beach.

From Qurm Heights, the road snakes down the hill to the sea front, where a new road has been built linking up the previously unconnected areas of Al Qurm and Shati Al Qurm along the coast. This road has opened up access to this area which includes a long stretch of beach, two inlets which wind inland through mangroves, and an attractive beach park with palm trees, sunshades and seats close to Qurum Beach Hotel. The Marina Café sits right on the corniche road and is a great place to take in the views from its first floor terrace.

Shati Al Qurm

Shati Al Qurm stretches along the coast from Al Qurm to Al Ghubbrah, just north of the main Muscat–Seeb highway. This upmarket residential area is home to many of Muscat's foreign embassies and some top hotels, but it also has a great stretch of public beach and a small, friendly shopping centre.

Area Overview

In the mornings, evenings and at weekends, the strip between the Hyatt Regency and the InterContinental comes alive with people walking, playing sports and generally enjoying the beach. The Hyatt Regency Muscat aims to impress, with its breathtaking lobby with sparkling gold leaf and crystal trimmings. The beautiful décor continues outside with palm trees, traditional Arabic tents, and torches illuminating the gardens all the way down to the beach. The Muscat InterContinental is an older hotel, but with a relaxing friendly atmosphere and a range of restaurants and bars that still rivals any hotel in Muscat. The leisure facilities, pools and beach are popular with guests and Muscat residents.

The Jawharat A'Shati Complex right beside the sea near the InterContinental has a small community feel and is the heart of café culture in Muscat. Big brand coffee shops sit alongside independent outlets where you can order hot coffees and delicious food throughout the day. This is a great spot to relax and take in the sea views.

There is also the Children's Museum where kids of all ages can enjoy interactive displays. Entrance is free but the museum gets quite crowded on Thursdays.

See also: *Children's Museum; Oil & Gas Exhibition Centre – Museums & Heritage [p.126]; Parks [p.133]; Shopping Malls (Shopping) [p.173].*

The comings and goings in Shati Al Qurm

Exploring

Muscat – Main Areas

Ruwi

Less than 30 years ago, the valley (Wadi Kabir) in which Ruwi lies was completely undeveloped. Today it is the bustling commercial district of Muscat, commonly referred to as the central business district (CBD). Before 1970 the area consisted only of Bait Al Falaj, the aeroplane runway and the Al Hamriyah village. Now it is notable for fine modern architecture, particularly along Bank Street, which is home to the Central Bank of Oman and Bank Muscat headquarters. Wadi Kabir is like the main artery of Ruwi, since all main buildings are found along its side. While there are modern buildings in the area, regulations are restrictive and discourage the construction of any excessively high skyscrapers. Although it may not be a hotspot for tourists to stay in, it is worth having a wander round if not just for the plentiful local restaurants selling excellent Arabic and Indian cuisine at reasonable prices.

A good point to begin your exploration of Ruwi is the Omantel Tower next to the main post office,

Area Overview

🚗	⬤⬤⬤⬤◯
📷	⬤⬤◯◯◯
🕐	⬤⬤◯◯◯

RUWI
1.6km

which you will find near the centre of the CBD. On Al Jaame Street, on the south side, you'll find the Sultan Qaboos Mosque, the central bus and taxi stations and the clock tower.

On the north side of the Omantel Tower, the Bait Al Falaj (in the army base) houses the Sultan's Armed Forces Museum. You'll find the National Museum in Al Noor Street (in the north-west part of Ruwi). It is located close to the intersection with Al Burj Street.

The Ruwi Souk, also known as Ruwi High Street, is the place to go for anything from souvenirs to diamond rings.

Area Highlights

Sultan's Armed Forces Museum
Located in the Bait Al-Falaj fort, the museum provides a fascinating insight into the military history of Oman, as well as illuminating day-to-day traditions and activities from the past.

Ruwi Souk
Apart from being able to get your everyday household goods here at bargain prices, you'll also find an abundance of Omani souvenirs to take home for your friends and family.

Sheraton Oman Hotel
One of the first and still the tallest building in Muscat, it dominates the Ruwi skyline and is perfect for the business traveller or serious shopper. The culinary theme nights, particularly Seafood Night on Wednesdays, make it an enduring favourite among both expats and locals.

Ruwi

Exploring

Muscat – Main Areas

Al Bustan & Sidab

The villages of Al Bustan and Sidab provide an interesting diversion from the main Muscat areas. Heading south along Al Bustan Street out of Ruwi, the spectacular mountain road takes you over the rise from Wadi Al Kabir, where you can see the village of Al Bustan nestled in the bottom of the hills with the sea in the background.

On Al Bustan Roundabout at the foot of the hills is the Sohar dhow. In 1980, it set sail on an eight-month journey from Sur to Canton, captained by Tim Severin. This journey was made to commemorate a voyage made by an adventurous trader, Abu Ubaida bin Abdullah bin Al Quassim, in the eighth century. It was constructed at the Sur dhow yard and is made in the traditional manner, entirely from local materials and with no nails, and sits at 24m in length.

Just past this landmark is the Al Bustan Palace InterContinental Hotel, one of the most famous hotels in the Gulf. It is an international award winner and ranked among the top five hotels in the world. You can spend a leisurely day drifting around the hotel and grounds, having a cocktail on the beach or afternoon tea in the atrium. The surroundings are beautiful and the service is first class. The Seblat Al Bustan restaurant offers a traditional Omani experience – traditional Arabic tents are set up in the hotel gardens every Wednesday night during the cooler months.

Area Highlights

Al Bustan Palace InterContinental Hotel
Even if your budget doesn't stretch to a night's stay in this luxury hotel, you should still experience the royal treatment with the legendary 'afternoon tea' in the Atrium Tea Lounge. If it's activity you're looking for, the Al Bustan Palace also has some amazing sports, leisure and recreation facilities.

From the Al Bustan Roundabout you can head up the coast towards Muscat's old town, where along the way you will find the scenic harbour area of Sidab. Fishing is the lifeblood of this area and traditions have been passed down through the generations. The Marine Science & Fisheries Centre is an academic institution that undertakes studies of different fish stocks, but it also has a very interesting public aquarium and library (for

more information, refer to museums on [p.126]. On your way to Sidab you will pass Marina Bander Al-Rowdha and the Capital Area Yacht Club, both offering the chance to get closer to the ocean with various marine activities for members and guests.

Al Bustan Roundabout and the Sohar Dhow

Al Khuwayr

Heading towards central Muscat from Seeb, Al Khuwayr (also known as Al Khuwair) is on the south side of As Sultan Qaboos Street. Right opposite the main ministries district of Shati Al Qurm, Al Khuwayr also has a few ministry buildings as well as banks and embassies, some housed in impressive buildings.

The head office of the Oman International Bank is located here and is interesting from an architectural point of view. The interior of the building is as beautiful as the exterior, which has imposing front doors that are ten metres high and 24-carat gold plated! You'll see them being polished on a daily basis if you walk past early enough. This area is also home to the impressive Zawawi Mosque, just off the motorway.

Area Highlights

Natural History Museum
This museum is a fascinating and informative collection of exhibits relating to Oman's wildlife. You can see stuffed animals in their different natural habitats, many of which are unique to Oman and the Gulf region. The Whale Hall should not be missed – it is dominated by the suspended skeleton of a 25 year old sperm whale. Entrance is free.

Also worthy of a visit is the Oman Natural History Museum located within the Ministry of Heritage and Culture (24 641 300). It contains some very interesting displays on Oman's wildlife and natural heritage. Al Khuwayr has a souk (also known as the Al Khuwayr Commercial Centre), found in the middle of Al Khuwayr, although it is more of a shopping centre than a traditional souk.

Bandar Al Jissah & Qantab

Further down the coast from Al Bustan, the mountains increase in height and the landscape gets more rugged. However, this undulating rocky coastline hides a number of beautiful secluded coves. These bays, mostly reachable by road winding over the mountain, are home to the beaches of Qantab and Jissah, the Oman Dive Centre and the new Barr Al Jissah Resort.

Many of the bays in this area have stretches of sandy beach sheltered by rocky cliffs and with crystal clear waters that are perfect for snorkelling, diving and fishing. At Qantab Beach friendly local fisherman occasionally offer to take you fishing.

The beach of Bandar Al Jissah can be very busy on Fridays, but its attraction is twofold – firstly it is accessible by car, and secondly it is the best place to catch a sea taxi. Sea taxis are the small fishing boats you see loaded up with fresh fish during the week, and on weekends they try to catch much bigger fish – tourists! For a very small fee they will transport you and all your gear to one of the secluded beaches further down the coast, such as Al Khayran, and leave you there until a specified

Area Highlights

Oman Dive Centre

Live out your 'stranded on a desert island' fantasies by spending the night in a barasti bungalow on the beach – the Oman Dive Centre has various accommodation options as well as a restaurant and dive shop. For more information, visit their website (www.diveoman.com).

Barr Al Jissah Resort

The Barr Al Jissah development, situated in its own bay, is set to become one of the most exciting resorts in the Gulf region. With three luxury hotels, a full range of leisure facilities (including private beaches, pools, a planned 19 restaurants, cafés and bars), a heritage centre and an Omani souk, this resort will certainly become one of Muscat's 'must-do' destinations. Even the construction process for this resort has been attracting a lot of interest. Barr Al Jissah is scheduled to open by the end of 2005.

time when they will come and pick you up. Don't worry about being stranded – it is accepted that you don't pay the fee until after your return journey. Snorkelling gear is recommended as the marine life in the area is stunning.

A little further south is the Oman Dive Centre (www.diveoman.com.om), reputedly one of the top dive centres in the world. It offers dive training, trips and accommodation in rooms or barasti huts on the beach (whether you are diving or not).

To get there, follow the road from Ruwi and Wadi Al Kabir to Al Bustan – you will see the village of Qantab signposted to the right just past the top of the hill. Take this right turn and follow the road until the new roundabout where you can turn left for Oman Dive Centre or go straight for the Barr Al Jissah Resort at the end of the road.

Beach traffic

Madinat As Sultan Qaboos

Moving further east, the next area is Madinat As Sultan Qaboos (MQ or MSQ), also on the south side of As Sultan Qaboos Street, running between to Al Khuwayr and Al Qurm. Primarily a residential area, and home to some foreign embassies, this is one of the most popular addresses for expats in Muscat. It has a small but friendly shopping centre with a useful range of shops, cafés and restaurants. One of the main landmarks in this area is The Omani Museum. Try and fit in a visit to Kargeen Caffé, where excellent food and drink can be enjoyed in one of the most surprising and pleasant venues in the city.

The Omani Museum

The Omani Museum, perched atop Information Hill, offers spectacular views from the outside. Inside it houses some fascinating exhibits showcasing Oman's rich history and cultural heritage. For more information, see the entry under Museums – Muscat [p.127].

Kargeen Caffé

Rusayl

Located to the south-west of Seeb, there are not many visitor attractions in Rusayl. However, a visit to the Amouage perfume factory is worthwhile, especially considering Oman's proud history as the source of the best incense in the world.

Abu Dhabi Explorer

Muscat – tick.
Dubai – tick.
Make Abu Dhabi next on your list of GCC cities to explore. As the capital city of the UAE, it's full of culture and tradition. It's also absolutely packed with shops, restaurants, and plenty of fun lovin' expats. So go forth; and let the Abu Dhabi & Al Ain Explorer be your guide...

The Amouage factory (24 540 757) produces 'the most valuable perfume in the world'. A tour around the factory illustrates the production process and allows visitors to sample various fragrances before splashing out on a bottle or two! Tours of the factory are available for individuals or groups (maximum of 30 people). There are two guides and the tour, which is free of charge, can be taken in either English or Arabic.

The factory is open from Saturday to Wednesday (08:00 - 13:00 & 14:30 - 17:00) and on Thursday mornings (08:00 - 13:00).

See also: Flora & Fauna [p.11]; Ubar – City Tours Other (Exploring)

Seeb

Although it is a fair drive from the centre of Muscat, Seeb is home to some good shopping centres and other attractions. Located on the outskirts of the city, on the main road to the UAE, Seeb is about 35 km from the main commercial area of Muscat. As it is the location of Oman's only international airport, this is the first area many travellers see.

The two big shopping malls in Seeb are Muscat City Centre and Markaz Al Bahja – both of which are located to the right of the main highway. Shoppers flock to these centres for major retailers like Carrefour, Next, Monsoon and Mothercare. The Oman International Exhibition Centre also attracts plenty of business travellers to Seeb.

On the right hand side of the Seeb – Muscat road is the Sultan Qaboos Grand Mosque. Apart from admiring the impressive Arabian architecture and opulent trimmings, it is a rare opportunity for non-Muslims to see the inside of a mosque. It is one of the largest mosques in the Arab world, with the point of its highest minaret reaching almost 100m. This landmark mosque, which can hold up to 20,000 worshippers, is open to non-Muslims in the morning (08:00 – 11:00) from Saturday to Wednesday. Visitors should wear appropriate clothing – long trousers for men and loose, modest clothing for women.

Area Highlights

Sultan Qaboos Grand Mosque
This beautiful example of Islamic architecture provides a wonderful insight into the cultural heritage of Oman. hours for the tour are strictly between 08:00 and 11:00 from Saturday to Wednesday.

Muscat City Centre
This is currently the busiest, biggest and most modern mall in Oman. Not even its location past Seeb Airport deters people who come from far and wide to shop here. The mall is open from 10:00 (except for Carrefour, which opens an hour earlier) to 22:00. None of the shops close for lunch.

Markaz Al Bahja
This enormous new shopping mall is still quite quiet, probably because of its out-of-town location towards Seeb. But it is well worth a shopping trip – the mall is spacious and relaxing and there is plenty of free underground parking.

The main attractions are Marks and Spencer and Toys R Us, both of which are on the top floor.

Exploring

Muscat – Other Areas

Muscat City Centre

Al Dhahirah Region

With a name meaning 'the back', the Al Dhahirah region is in Oman's interior, to the west of the magnificent Hajar mountains and bordering the UAE and Saudi Arabia. It contains the towns of Ibri and Buraimi, and the ancient tombs at the prehistoric site of Bat are featured on Unesco's list of World Heritage Sites.

Buraimi

Buraimi is the Omani half of the main town in the Buraimi Oasis; the UAE half of the town is called Al Ain. While effectively spanning an international border, there are no checkpoints within the town itself and the Oman/UAE border is located about 50km east of Buraimi. Non GCC residents travelling from Oman will require a road permit. Buraimi can trace its history back to its strategic position at the intersection of various caravan routes to and from Oman. There is an extensive falaj system, which keeps the region fertile. Being an oasis town, Buraimi is pleasantly green and full of date palm plantations. The area has a cooler and less humid climate than the coastal regions, making it a popular destination during the summer months.

On the Al Ain side of Buraimi is the main fort, Hisn Al Khandaq, which has been extensively restored recently and is open to visitors.

There is also the camel souk, where merchants are more than happy to show you around and will even make a serious attempt to sell you a camel. Watching the camels being loaded into pick-up trucks is a show you won't want to miss! For further information on Al Ain refer to the *Abu Dhabi Explorer.*

Ibri

Ibri lies 300 km to the west of Muscat, between the foothills of the Hajar Mountains and the vast Rub Al Khali desert (the 'Empty Quarter'). With its central location it was historically an important stopover for merchants travelling between the different regions of the Arabian Peninsular, and trading remains active in the area today. The bustling souk sells a variety of merchandise including locally produced woven palm goods. The daily auctions (which take place in the mornings) are fascinating – you'll be able to watch local residents, farmers and traders haggling over dates, vegetables, honey and livestock. The souk is situated near Ibri's impressive fort, which is notable for the large mosque set within its walls.

Batinah Region

With a coastline stretching north-west from Muscat to the UAE border, Batinah has many charming coastal towns and villages including Barka and Sohar. Inland towards the western Hajars there are dramatic peaks and wadis, and numerous areas of historical interest, such as Rustaq with its large fort.

Barka

Barka is a small coastal town, approximately 75 km west of Muscat. It makes an interesting day trip from Muscat or a breakpoint on a drive to Sohar, which is further along the coast. It is famous for its fortnightly bullfights and large central fort, located only a few hundred metres from the coast. Barka is still home to craftsmen who practise traditional trades such as weaving. The historical Bait Naa'man [p.126] and the Ostrich Farm (see below) are attractions worth exploring whilst in Barka.

Bullfighting

Unlike Spanish bullfighting, the Oman version is bloodless and the animals suffer little or no injury. It is not a gory sport, but rather a contest of strength between two powerful animals. The Brahmin bulls used in fighting are often pampered family pets. At the beginning of a fight, two bulls of similar size are led into the centre of the ring to lock horns for battle. The fight is over when the weaker of the two is forced to its knees or out of the ring, or when one of the bulls simply gives up and runs away. Each fight lasts just a few minutes, and usually the worst injury suffered is a bruised ego for both the losing bull and its owner!

This historical form of entertainment is loved and treasured by Omanis, and you'll find that half the fun is watching them cheer on their favourite bull, and trying to recapture it at the end of the fight. The best bulls can change hands for substantial amounts of money.

Bullfights are held in several places along the Batinah coastline; usually on Friday afternoons at around 16:30. Barka and Seeb are the two main bullfighting sites, and a smaller ring is located in Al Sawadi. Entrance is free, and visitors are welcome. Fights are not held during the hottest summer months and Ramadan.

Ostrich Farm

The Ostrich Breeding Farm in Barka is surprisingly interesting. Visitors can see the 100 adult birds or the eggs being incubated and also chicks between February to June. The farm started in 1993 when the eggs were imported from South Africa, and it is also home to about 30 crocodiles.

Ostriches are farmed for various purposes and the aim of the farm is to sustain a 300-bird breeding group to meet the ever-increasing demands for healthy meat, fine leather and exquisite feathers. Ostrich meat is considered an excellent alternative to beef, since has a very similar consistency and texture but is very low in cholesterol.

Entry fee is 500 baisas per adult and 200 baisas per child. You can visit the farm any time except for during lunch (12:00 – 14:00), but phone first to let them know you are coming (26 885 535).

Location: From the Barka Roundabout, turn onto Nakhal Road. After four kilometres you'll see the Majan Water Factory on the right. Turn right into the private road just before the factory, and the ostrich farm is the first farm on your left.

Nakhal

Nakhal is 30 km inland from Barka and about 100 km from Muscat. The town has an imposing, restored fort set on a hill, and if you stand at the top of the watchtowers, you'll have magnificent views of the surrounding countryside and town. Inside the fort kitchen and living quarters of the Wali (leader), the men's and women's majlis, and the prison. The area is also well known for the Al Thowarah hot springs which can be found a short distance beyond the fort. The natural spring water is channelled into the falaj system to irrigate the surrounding date plantations, and it's possible to paddle in the run-off water. There's a car park and picnic facilities, making it a popular destination for locals and tourists.

Rustaq

In the Middle Ages, Rustaq (or Rostaq) was the capital of Oman. However, today it is best known for its large and dramatic fort, which has been extended over the years. Rustaq is located in the western Hajar Mountains about 170 km south-west of Muscat. The fort has been restored and the large main watchtower is believed to be of Sassanid origin. It was well equipped to withstand long sieges, since it has its own water supply. Legend has it that a tunnel once connected the Rustaq Fort to the nearby fort at Al Hazm.

Nearby attractions include a souk selling various items, and the renowned hot springs (that also flow at Nakhal). The hot springs in Rustaq have been enclosed into bathhouses for men and women.

About 20 km from Rustaq, travelling north back to the coast, is the village of Al Hazm, which is home to an interesting fort. It was built around 1700 AD and has a falaj system that is still working today. There is also an excellent view of the surrounding countryside from the top of the watchtower.

Snake Gorge (Wadi Bimah)

Snake Gorge, in the mountains west of Rustaq, is part of Wadi Bani Awf and a popular destination for adventurous hikers. The route involves some spectacular scenery, and those intending to carry out the walk should be warned that it does involve some daring jumps into rock pools and a fair bit of swimming through ravines. It is vital that you keep

Exploring

Batinah Region

a very close eye on the weather, as any rain in the mountains higher up (and many miles away) can cause the wadis and ravines to become raging torrents in just a few minutes.

Sohar

Sohar lies about halfway between Muscat and Dubai, 200 km north-west of the capital. Situated on the Batinah Coast, it was once the maritime capital of Oman and an important distribution centre for locally produced copper. Sohar is renowned for its fort (with in-house museum), the lively fish souk (just off the corniche), and for being the birthplace of legendary Sindbad the sailor. As in the rest of Oman, the people here are friendly, although in Sohar they may be less used to visitors and cameras. However, as the country opens up to tourists, residents are becoming more familiar with foreigners.

See Also: *Sohar Fort in Exploring [p.125].*

Dakhiliya Region

Despite being isolated from the sea, Dhakhiliya was historically important as many trade routes between the coast and the interior passed through the region. The Sumail Gap is a valley that divides the eastern and western Hajars. Also in this region is the ancient town of Nizwa, which was once Oman's capital.

Bahla

The ancient walled city of Bahla is only two hours drive from Muscat, and just 40 km from Nizwa. It has a small population of around 60,000, and contains 46 separate villages. While it is not yet on the mainstream tourist map (although efforts are being made to attract more tourists to the area), archaeology buffs and history enthusiasts will find that it is well worth a visit. It is believed to be one of the oldest inhabited regions in Oman, and archaeologists have found artefacts here dating back to the third century BC. It was historically a strategic stopover on the old trading route from Muscat to other parts of the Arabian Peninsula. Apart from the historical buildings and the traditional way of life, Bahla also has a rich and diverse ecology – a balanced mixture of fertile land, mountains, wadis and desert. The productive soil, fed by an continuous

supply of water from Jebel Akhdar, has in the past yielded crops of wheat, barley, cotton and sugar cane, and today it is still home to many viable date plantations.

The town is characterised by its many winding roads, some so narrow that you have to pull over to let an oncoming car pass. Whether you explore the town of Bahla on foot or by car, you will find an eclectic balance between the new, functioning town, the ancient, fascinating ruins, and the many date plantations that make perfect picnic spots.

Bahla is enclosed by a protective, fortified wall that stretches for 12 km around the town. Although large sections of the wall are still standing, parts of it are in ruins and earmarked for eventual reconstruction.

Forts and Ruins

The Bahla Fort, situated on Balhool Mountain, is one of the main attractions in Bahla. It is included on Unesco's list of world heritage sites, and is currently undergoing careful and extensive renovation under Unesco's sponsorship and supervision. The ruins of the fort tower 50m above the village, and although its famous windtowers have been almost totally destroyed by time, they were once thought to be the tallest structures in Oman.

In the area around the fort you can wander through deserted mud-brick villages, the largest of which is Al Aqar. You can explore the ancient houses at your leisure, and in some houses you can even go up to higher storeys and look through the old window frames for a unique perspective. It is a fascinating glimpse into the past, showing you what life was like in Oman's olden times. The ruins of the mosque are particularly interesting.

The Jabrin Fort, which is a very short drive from Bahla, has been extensively restored and redecorated. The Imam Bilarab originally built it in the 1600s as a grand country residence. His tomb is still located within the fort, to the left of the main entrance. It is believed that Jabrin Fort was home to one of the first schools in Oman, way back in the 17th century.

The Souk

There is no better place to rub shoulders with the friendly people of Bahla than at the traditional market or 'souk'. Locals gather here to trade in livestock and socialise under the shade of a huge central tree. Goats are tethered to this tree before being bought or sold. In the alleyways leading away

Beautiful Bahla

from this central livestock trading area, you'll find many small shops that sell traditional crafts, Omani antiques (a particularly good spot to hunt for a genuine antique khanjar), rugs, spices and nuts. You can watch the local silversmith at work, repairing khanjars and jewellery in the same way it has been done for generations. The souk also has sections for fruit and vegetables, all of which are locally produced, and the locally grown dates are delicious.

You can't visit the area without buying some distinctive Bahla pottery to take home with you. Bahla is a good source of high quality clay, and there are many skilled potters in the area (all male – it is only in the southern regions of Oman that you'll find female potters). You can see them working at the traditional pottery site, which is just past the souk. There is also a pottery factory, built by the government in the late 1980s, and the Alladawi clay pots workshop that boasts four industrial kilns, each able to produce around a hundred pots each month. While you will probably buy a piece of pottery for ornamental purposes (plant pots, vases, incense burners or candle holders), clay pots are still used for practical purposes in Bahla, such as carrying and cooling water, and storing food and dates.

Fanja

The picturesque village of Fanja is situated next to an extensive palm grove that runs alongside Wadi Fanja. Seventy kilometres from Muscat, the approach to Fanja is one of the most scenic routes Oman has to offer. The village has a dramatic tower, perched on top of a hill, offering spectacular views of the surrounding scenery and the wadi below. Fanja is renowned for its pottery and visitors can wander round the market bargaining for locally produced pots, plus local fruit, vegetables, honey and woven goods made from palm leaves.

Nizwa

About 140 km from Muscat, Nizwa is a popular destination for tourists and residents of Oman alike. In the sixth and seventh centuries, Nizwa was the capital of Oman and the centre for trade between the coastal and the interior regions. It is still the largest and most important town in this area of the interior. Historically the town enjoyed a reputation as a haven for poets, writers, intellectuals, and religious leaders, and for centuries it was considered the cultural and political capital of the country.

Positioned alongside two wadis, Nizwa is a fertile sea of green with an oasis of date plantations stretching eight kilometres from the city. Its two notable attractions include Nizwa's 17th century fort and the magnificent Jabrin Fort, noted for its wall and ceiling decorations and its secret passageways and staircases. Many ancient ruins such as Bahla Fort and mud brick villages can be seen among the date palm plantations and the wadis.

The Nizwa Souk is an interesting and atmospheric place where visitors will find many examples of the local silversmiths' art, especially ornately engraved khanjars.

Sumail

The town of Sumail (or Samail) sits in the Sumail Gap, a natural valley that divides the Hajar Mountain chain into the eastern and western Hajars. As the most direct path between the coastal regions and the interior of the country, this route has always been an important artery. Irrigated by countless wadis and man-made falaj systems, the area is green and fertile, and the dates produced here are highly rated.

Mazin bin Ghaduba

Mazin bin Ghaduba was the first Omani to embrace Islam. He travelled to Medina to meet the prophet Mohammed (PBUH) and upon his return built the country's first mosque, the Masjid Mazin bin Ghaduba. Bin Ghaduba's grave can still be visited in Sumail, located beside a falaj system across the road from the fort. The mosque is also still standing (after numerous renovations) and can be found in the old town beyond the souk.

Dhofar Region

Dhofar is the southernmost region of Oman, bordering Saudi Arabia and the Republic of Yemen. The frankincense produced here is regarded as the finest in the world, and once made the area immensely wealthy and important. Visitors still flock to the coast to enjoy the lush greenery and cool weather.

Salalah

Salalah is the capital of Dhofar, and is over a thousand kilometres from Muscat. It is possible to get there by road, but the drive is long and boring,

Salalah – it's a different world

with little of interest to see or do along the way. You may prefer to fly there instead, and Oman Air operates two flights a day from Muscat. Salalah has a museum, and the souks are worthy of a visit; especially the Al Husn Souk (next to the palace) where you'll find silverware, frankincense and locally made perfume. There are also a number of beautiful beaches to be found along the coast.

Plenty of trees beautify the landscape, mainly at the border of the desert near the lower reaches of the jebels. You will also find an impressive grouping of trees in Wadi Qahshan, which runs through the mountainous backdrop of the Mughsayl – Sarfait road that links Salalah with the Yemen border. Here frankincense trees grow and are farmed by local villagers – they cut into the trunks and allow the sap to harden into lumps that are then scraped off and traded in bulk.

The Khareef

The coastal region is subject to weather conditions quite different from the rest of the country, and as such the scenery in the south forms a stark contrast to that in areas further north. From June to September the monsoon rains (or khareef) active in the Indian Ocean clip southern Dhofar and the countryside becomes an area of lush greenery, with vast swathes of pasture, rivers and waterfalls. The foothills of the mountains a few kilometres inland are often covered with a thick blanket of fog during this time. The rain and fog cause a significant drop in temperature, making Salalah a popular destination for residents of other Gulf countries trying to escape the summer heat.

Frankincense

The Dhofar region was historically the centre of the frankincense trade, with local trees producing what was (and still is) considered the best frankincense in the world. As a result, the area became prosperous as this precious commodity was exported by sea to India and by land throughout Arabia and as far as Europe. Locally produced frankincense is still widely available in souks throughout Oman. The Frankincense Souk is packed with merchants selling incense, perfumes and traditional artefacts.

Ubar

The legendary lost city of Ubar (referred to as Iram in the Holy Quran) is said to have been a wealthy trading post at the junction of numerous caravan routes, where merchants would come from afar to buy much sought after incense. Traders in Ubar would sell pottery, spices and fabric from India and China in return for the unique silver frankincense of Oman. The trade made Ubar a city of unrivalled wealth and splendour and when Marco Polo visited, he called it 'paradise'. According to the Quran the wickedness of the inhabitants led Allah to destroy the city and all roads leading to it, causing it to sink into the sand. For a thousand years the city's location remained unknown, until in the 1990s British explorer Sir Ranulph Fiennes, in a 20-year search using modern satellite technology, discovered the city of Ubar beneath the shifting sands of Omani desert near Shisr, north of Salalah. Excavations have revealed the thick outer walls of a vast octagonal fortress with eight towers or pillars at its corners, and numerous pots and artefacts dating back thousands of years. Debate rages as to whether this is indeed Ubar, but the site is fascinating nonetheless for being the location of what was surely an important desert settlement many years ago. Tour companies offer full day tours to Ubar through the Qara Mountains and stunning landscape.

Mussandam Region

Other options → Weekend Breaks [p.146]

The Mussandam Peninsula is the Omani enclave to the north, which is divided from the rest of Oman by the United Arab Emirates. It has only recently been opened to tourists and is a beautiful, largely unspoilt area. The capital is Khasab, a quaint fishing port largely unchanged by the modern world. The area is of great strategic importance since to the north lies the Strait of Hormuz, with Iran across the water, while the Arabian Gulf is to the west and the Gulf of Oman to the east.

The Mussandam region is dominated by the Hajar Mountains, which also run through the UAE and into the main part of Oman. It is sometimes called the 'Norway of the Middle East' since the jagged mountain cliffs plunge directly into the sea and the coastline is littered with inlets and fjords. The views along the coast roads are stunning. Inland, the scenery is equally breathtaking although to explore properly a 4 WD and a good head for heights are indispensable! Just metres off the shore are beautiful coral beds, with an amazing variety of sea life including tropical fish, turtles, dolphins and occasionally, sharks.

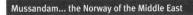

Mussandam... the Norway of the Middle East

To reach Mussandam from Muscat, the journey can be made by either plane or car. The flight takes about 1½ hours using Oman Air (24 707 222), the only airline offering internal flights in Oman. The cost is RO.40 return and flights are daily from Saturday to Wednesday. Visitors do not need any additional visa to fly to Mussandam. However, the downside of flying is that to explore the region properly a car is needed and car rental in Khasab is quite expensive.

To drive to Mussandam from Oman you need to travel through the UAE. GCC nationals and Omanis are free to come and go as they please. However, non-GCC expats resident in Oman will need to apply for a road permit to be able to leave Oman by car and will be turned back at the border if they do not have the necessary paperwork. There is no UAE customs or border post, but there is an Oman border control. Visitors to the Sultanate on a single entry visa will not be allowed back into the country once they have been stamped out. Entry for expats into Mussandam can only be made at the Ras Al Khaimah border post, not at Dibba.

Bukha

Bukha is located on the western side of the Mussandam peninsular, with a coastline on the Arabian Gulf. The area borders the UAE emirate of Ras Al Khaimah and is 27 km north of Khasab. This small town is overlooked by the ruins of an old fort, but there is little to see other than the remains of one watchtower. The Bukha fort however, beside the main road and just metres from the sea, is more impressive. Built in the 17th century it was restored in 1990 and is certainly the town's biggest landmark. The area's traditional occupations are fishing and boat building, and Bukha has a small harbour. There is also a pleasant strip of sandy beach with a number of shelters. The village of Al Jadi, about three kilometres north of Bukha, is picturesque and has a couple of fortifications, amongst which are two restored watchtowers.

Khasab

Khasab, the capital of the Mussandam area, is surrounded by imposing and dramatic mountains which dominate the entire region, with some peaks above 2,000m. The town of Khasab is relatively spread out and has numerous date plantations. There is a small souk and a beach, but the port is the main area of interest. The town subsists on fishing, trade (mostly with ports in Iran) and agriculture – producing a range of fruit and vegetables. In fact khasab means 'fertile' in Arabic.

At one end of the bay is the restored Khasab Fort which is open to the public. There's not that much to see inside, but its setting against the mountainous background is spectacular. Kumzan Fort is just outside Khasab. It was built around 1600 AD by the Imam (ruler) but little is left of it today, apart from the two watchtowers. About 10 km west of Khasab is the village of Tawi, where there are prehistoric rock carvings of warriors, boats and animals.

One of Khasab's biggest draws is the diving. These waters are not recommended for beginners, but experienced divers can enjoy spectacular underwater cliffs and an abundance of marine life at sites just a short boat ride away.

Sharqiya Region

Sharqiya is a region of contrasts. The coastline extending south and east from Muscat features numerous fishing villages and ports. The area's beaches are home to some of the most important turtle breeding grounds in the world, and breathtaking wadis and dramatic expanses of sand dunes can be found just a few kilometres inland.

Masirah Island

Masirah Island lies 20 km off the south-east coast of Oman and is the Sultanate's largest island. It is about 80 km long by 18 km wide with hills in the centre and a circumference of picturesque isolated beaches. The island is off the coast of the Barr Al Hikman area, and can be accessed via ferry from Shana'a – but only during high tide. The crossing takes around 90 minutes. There is a military base on the island, and the main town of Hilf, which has 8,000 residents. Hilf has a hotel, some shops, and a couple of restaurants, but otherwise the island is relatively undeveloped.

The highest point of the island is Jebel Hamra at 275m and graded roads run through the middle as well as around the island.

Turtles

Masirah's beaches are internationally recognised for their importance as turtle breeding grounds. Four species of turtle come ashore to lay their eggs here – Green Turtles, Hawksbill, Olive Ridley and Loggerheads. Masirah is thought to be home to the world's largest nesting population of Loggerhead turtles, estimated at 30,000 females.

Beaches

The beaches off Masirah Island's east coast offer some of the best surfing in the region, with waves of seven or eight feet on a good day. The summer months are also a good time for windsurfing, but the strong winds that lash the island during this time can be unpleasant and make camping on the beach quite uncomfortable. The beaches are also a great location for camping – the donkeys, camels, goats and gazelles who roam the island make excellent companions.

Shell collectors will be in their element here as the beaches are home to a vast range of shells, some of which are quite rare.

If camping is not for you, the other option is to stay at Masirah Hotel in Hilf (25 504 401) – their capacity is only six rooms, so book early!

See also: Masirah Island Watersports Club – Masirah Island (Sporting Activities) [p.118]; Camping (Exploring Muscat) [p.99]; Environmental (Pleasure & Leisure) [p.220]

Sur

Sur is an old fishing and trading port 300 km south-east of Muscat. For centuries the town was famed for its boat building and became quite prosperous as a result. Its fortunes did decline somewhat with the advent of more modern vessels and construction techniques, but Sur is enjoying something of a revival, and with its pretty corniche, forts and interesting Marine Museum the town is definitely worth a visit, as is the Sunaysilah Fort which overlooks the town, offering breathtaking views of the area and coast. For more information on both of these refer to Museums, Heritage & Culture [p.120]. The Arabic word Sur means a walled fortified area and there is evidence of the ancient defences throughout the town. Sur was the first port of call in Arabia for traders from the Far East and Africa, and it is believed that trading with the African coast dates back to as early as the sixth century AD.

From Muscat there are two roads to get to Sur. If you are more into a smoother ride, the Sur highway (route 23) is the best option. The 300 km single tarmac road, leading through the mountains and crossing some wadis, takes about three and a half hours from Muscat (direction Nizwa – Sur).

Alternatively if you have a 4 WD and don't mind a rocky ride you can take the coastal road (direction Quriyat – Sur). In terms of distance this route is much shorter (only 150 km) but it takes at least four hours. In Quriyat turn right to Sur at the roundabout, then follow the asphalt road and keep following the Sur signposts (not Tiwi). From there the tarmac soon changes into gravel. A few highlights along the way are the Bimmah Sinkhole, located six kilometres after Dibab village, just 500m off the road on your right. Tiwi Beach (also known as White Sand Beach) makes a good stop for some relaxing and snorkelling (although it is very crowded on public holidays). Just past Tiwi Village you'll find the signpost for Wadi Shab, one of the most picturesque wadis in Oman. The end of the coastal road is marked by an oasis and the ancient city of Qalhat, famous for its dry stone walls, the remains of ancient water cisterns and the scattered headstones of a cemetery. From here you progress into the mountains, with some steep slopes and descents.

Coming from the coastal road, the first thing that will appear in front of you is the enormous LNG plant (Liquefied Natural Gas). If you drive about 15 km south you will head into Sur – coming from the highway you will first pass Sur Bilad, a suburb of Sur, with its impressive Bilad Fort [p.123].

Dhow Building Yard

While Sur no longer produces vessels in the quantities or sizes that it once did, boat building is still an important industry in the town. A visit to the boatyards is a fascinating chance to watch workmen crafting wooden boats without technical drawings or modern tools, using skills that have been passed down from one generation to the next. The yard is open from Saturday to Thursday and is run by Mr. Juma Hasoon and his son. When they are there they can guide you around, but they only speak a few words of English. Alternatively you can just wander around by yourself.

Tiwi

Tiwi is a small fishing settlement about 30 km up the coast from Sur, situated in a little cove between two of the most beautiful and picturesque wadis in the area – Wadi Tiwi and Wadi Shab. These green oases are a must-see for their crystal clear pools and lush vegetation, including date palm and banana plantations. The residents of Tiwi are spread across nine small villages and there are endless opportunities for walking and exploring.

Exploring

Sharqiya Region

In Wadi Shab you can start your walk with a trip across the water courtesy of a small boat operated by locals. Further along the wadi you can swim through pools and access a cave with a waterfall inside. Tiwi Beach, located on the way to Fins and also known as the White Beach, offers a tranquil spot for passers by.

Al Wusta Region

In contrast to Oman's other regions, Al Wusta has few sites of historical interest and is often only seen from a car window as people make the long drive between Muscat and Salalah. However, the region does boast many areas of natural beauty and an abundance of wildlife. The Jiddat Al-Harasis Arabian Oryx Sanctuary [p.130] has successfully reintroduced the species to the wild after it was hunted to extinction, and the coastal mangroves are home to a number of rare and endangered bird species.

Museums, Heritage & Culture

Archaeological Sites

Archaeological excavations in south-eastern Arabia only started in the 1950s. It was then that Danish archaeologists found evidence of settlements and temples of the city-state of Dilmun, dating back over 4,000 years, in the grave mounds of Bahrain. Some time later, these archaeologists were surprised by an unexpected discovery on the island of Umm an Nar, off Abu Dhabi (UAE), of another previously unknown culture contemporary with Dilmun.

Encouraged by the discoveries at Dilmun and Umm an Nar, Danish archaeologists excavated 200 single-chambered burial cairns in 1961 near Jebel Hafit in Al Ain, just on the Oman-UAE border, showing a culture even older than those found at Dilmun and Umm an Nar. In literature, sites are often referred to as either the Umm an Nar or Hafit Periods.

Umm an Nar is well known for its large, circular tombs – these were used by families for collective burials over several generations. In some cases, archaeologists have found the remains of more than a hundred people buried in one tomb. The Hafit period is characterised by smaller cairns, originally with a beehive-like appearance, designed for one or two burials.

It is only recently that these Omani tombs have been 'discovered' by the outside world, although of course local people have always known their whereabouts and had their own stories about their origin.

Bat & Al Ayn Tombs	
Location ➜ See below	na
Web/email ➜ na	Map Ref ➜ 1-B2

There are two exits, signposted to Amlah and Al Ayn, in between Bahla and Ibri (Route 21). In the distance, Jebel Misht acts as a dramatic backdrop with its lopsided, triangular peak. Near the village of Al Ayn (on the left-hand side of the wadi) you'll find the best examples of beehive tombs, standing in a row of about 20 on the crest of a small hill. A few kilometres before Al Ayn is a turnoff to the left, signposted 'Bat'. There is a burial site located 1.5 km north of Bat, consisting of 100 tombs, which was found in 1976 by Danish archaeologists.

The tombs in this area date back to the third millennium BC. They are circular in shape, are constructed from blocks of local stone, and incorporate two walled enclosures – showing parallels with the Umm an Nar period. It was the second Omani site listed by Unesco as a world heritage site.

Eastern Hajars – Shir Tower Tombs	
Location ➜ See below	na
Web/email ➜ na	Map Ref ➜ 1-B1

Some of the tower tombs in Shir, discovered in the 1990s, are still in pristine condition even though they are around 4,500 years old. Unfortunately, the site is only accessible to truly experienced 4 WD drivers with a GPS system. Follow Route 23 to Ibra, and after Ibra turn left to Wadi Naam. Turn right into the wadi after 16 km, just before the An Niba palm plantation. After about 32 km, two tracks merge and lead directly to the eastern Hajars. Follow this track for about 22 km to a junction turning to the east

Oops!

Oman - it's a big country, and whilst we endeavoured to explore every nook and cranny you may feel there's a particular place worthy of a mention that we overlooked. Well don't keep it to yourself! Email Info@Explorer-Publishing.com and give us the details. We'll send our resident researchers to check it out and you'll read all about it in the next edition.

The fascinating sights of Tiwi

Exploring

Museums, Heritage & Culture

(right). Here you start climbing to an altitude of 1,700 m over about 22 km, with some very steep gradients. Descending the mountains on the eastern side, as you drive towards Fins on the coast, guarantees some spectacular scenery with the Gulf of Oman as backdrop.

Halban Tombs

| Location ➜ See below | na |
| Web/email ➜ na | Map Ref ➜ 1-B2 |

The large, beehive-shaped tombs in Halban are believed to date from the Umm an Narr period. They are situated on an elevated coastal terrace at the edge of the Batinah coastal plain and the ophiolite hills, just at the back of the small Halban Oasis (an easy drive of about 80 km from Muscat). To get there, take the highway to Sohar and about seven kilometres before Barka, at the 'Hut' Roundabout, make a left turn. Then turn immediately right, and after about one kilometre turn left towards Halban.

Lost City of Ubar

| Location ➜ See below | na |
| Web/email ➜ na | Map Ref ➜ 1-E3 |

The discovery of the 'Lost City of Ubar' in the 1990s was worldwide news. Ubar is said to have existed from 2800 BC to around 300 AD, as a remote desert outpost where caravans assembled to transport shipments of valuable frankincense across the desert. The legend of Ubar says that God punished the people of 'Ad for their wealthy, sinful lifestyle, and for neglecting his warnings, by sinking them in the sand (a story not unlike that of Sodom and Gomorrah in the Bible). It appears that Ubar was built on a limestone cavern that collapsed, causing the city to actually sink in to the sand. It was rediscovered with the help of remote satellite sensing. Ubar is in the Shisr area, which is about 85 km north-east from Thumrayt in southern Oman, north-west of Salalah. You may need a 4 WD, since most of the roads are graded.

Art Galleries

Other options ➜ Art [p.155]
Art Supplies [p.155]

Art is valued highly in the Arab world, so art galleries in the region tend to stock high quality works in various styles. Although Oman has no art museums, its galleries do offer peaceful surroundings where you can browse or buy. Most of the galleries also offer a framing service.

The Omani Society for Fine Arts (24 694 969 or www.omanartsociety.net) encompasses all mediums, such as painting, photography, sculpture and more. They can also provide details of any upcoming exhibitions or art-related events.

For a complete listing of art galleries, see [p.122] in the Shopping section.

Art Galleries	
Al-Araimi Complex	24 566 180
Al Madina Art Gallery	24 691 380
Bait Muzna Gallery	24 739 204
Gallery, The	92 154 827
Lamsat	24 698 338
Murtada A.K Trading	24 711 632
Yiti Art Gallery	24 796 073

Forts

The mud brick and stone architecture of Oman's many forts provide a constant reminder of the country's past. Whether you travel the interior, the coast or the mountains, you are sure to happen across the remains of a fort, each with its own story to tell of Oman's defensive history. The Omani government takes great care of these national treasures, and many of the forts are either heavily restored or in the process of restoration, sometimes against the wishes of archaeologists who would rather see the forts in their original states.

While forts were built primarily as structures of military defence, they also served as points of convergence for political, social and community activity. Therefore, some forts have palatial, luxurious interiors hidden behind their stark exteriors.

Despite there being official opening times, it is not uncommon to arrive at a fort and find it is closed off for restoration. To avoid disappointment, you can check with the Ministry of National Heritage and Culture (www.mnhc.gov.om) in Al Khuwayr beforehand.

Oman is renowned for its forts and there are literally hundreds around the country. The list below as a brief selection of some of the best forts around Oman but for more information on other forts most hotels have leaflets and booklets from the Oman Tourist Board or you can check out the book, Forts of Oman, available in bookstores.

Barka Castle

Location → Barka	na
Web/email → na	Map Ref → 1-B2

This vast and rambling fort is 800 years old and was originally built for Imam Ahmed bin Said. In 1984 it was fully restored. As you approach the fort you will see what is left of the walls of a much larger compound, the corners of which are marked by semi-ruined round towers. The small door in the huge carved gates leads into a cool dark stairwell. At the top of the stairs the fort opens out and you can then get an idea of the size of this building. Although there are no furnishings, other than cannons and cannonballs, and no guide available, you can spend a fascinating few hours wandering around the fort's towers, prisons and prayer rooms. The towers offer an excellent view of the surrounding area and out to sea. Entrance to the fort is free.

Bilad Sur Castle

Location → See below	na
Web/email → na	Map Ref → 1-B1

Just inland from Sur, on the road to Muscat, is Bilad Fort. Open daily, this is probably the most impressive of the town's forts. It was built in around 1800 AD to defend Sur from attacks from tribes in the interior, and is based around a courtyard with watchtowers at each corner. Interestingly, the two main towers have small extensions, enabling the defenders to get a higher vantage point from where to spot the enemy. It is situated in an attractive setting, surrounded by palm trees, and makes for a very pleasant outing. To get there from Muscat, get on the highway to Sur and turn right at the Clocktower Roundabout (also identifiable by the Shell petrol station). Turn left after exactly one kilometre, just before a large brownish/pinkish building. A permit to visit can be obtained from the Ministry of Culture & National Heritage in Muscat (www.mnhc.gov.om).

Off-Road Pioneers

Once you've conquered the rugged trails and hilly terrain that Oman has to offer, continue your quest for off-road domination of the region by heading for the natural delights of the UAE. With maps and suggested routes, off-roading tips and safety recommendations, the UAE Off-Road Explorer is the essential accessory for modern-day adventurers.

Jabrin Castle

Location → See below	na
Web/email → www.omantourism.gov.om	Map Ref → 1-B2

Jabrin is about 220 km south-west of Muscat, near Bahla and Nizwa. The large and imposing Jabrin Fort dominates the surrounding plain. It was built in the 1700s as a palace and later converted to a fort. Inside, visitors can see the living quarters of the Imam, his family and their servants, including the dining room, kitchen, prison, school and majlis (the traditional meeting room). There are various household items and military equipment on display among the maze of passageways and staircases. The fort has been restored and now has many wall and ceiling decorations.

To get to the fort from Nizwa, follow the Ibri road for about 45 km and turn right at the signpost for Jabrin. After about four kilometres, turn right at the small roundabout. The fort is open daily and admission is free. Although you actually need permission from Muscat to enter the fort, this is not usually enforced. For more info, contact the Ministry of National Heritage and Culture (www.mnhc.gov.om).

Jalali Fort & Mirani Fort

Location → Muscat Bay · Muscat	na
Web/email → na	Map Ref → 10-D4

These two forts flank the Sultan's palace on the waterfront, overlooking Muscat Bay. Built on the site of earlier Omani fortifications, both forts were extensively renovated in the late 1500s by the Portuguese when they controlled Muscat.

It is difficult to enter these forts due to their proximity to Alam Palace, although special permits can be obtained to visit Jalali Fort. Contact the Ministry of National Heritage and Culture for more information (www.mnhc.gov.om).

Khasab Castle

Location → Khasab	na
Web/email → www.omantourism.gov.om	Map Ref → 1-A2

Khasab Castle was built in the 1600s by Portuguese invaders as a stronghold in Khasab Bay. Within its low walls is a large central watchtower, which is thought to have existed even before the Portuguese built the castle itself. At the entrance you'll see three small cannons facing the sea – these were still in use as recently as the

Exploring

Museums, Heritage & Culture

Exploring

Museums, Heritage & Culture

1990s, not for defence purposes but rather to announce the sighting of the moon and the beginning of Eid celebrations.

Inside the castle is a small gift shop where you can buy some interesting Omani crafts and souvenirs. Entrance to the castle is free, and you don't need a permit from the Ministry to enter. The castle is open from Saturday to Wednesday from 07:30 to 14:30.

Bahla Fort

Kumzan Fort

Location → Khasab | na
Web/email → na   Map Ref → 1-A2

The Kumzan Fort is just outside of Khasab. It was built around 1600 AD by the Iman, and today there is very little left of the fort apart from two watchtowers. You could combine a visit to this fort with a trip to the nearby village of Tawi, where there are prehistoric rock carvings of warriors, boats and animals.

Mutrah Fort

Location → Above corniche · Mutrah | na
Web/email → na   Map Ref → 10-A3

Mutrah Fort is one of the few Portuguese forts left in the country. It was built in about 1600 AD on a small outcrop of rock overlooking the corniche and harbour, a position from which the harbour trade could be neatly controlled. In 1654 it was captured by the Omanis and this was a significant turning

point in their fight to oust the Portuguese. There have been many additions to this fort over the years, and it was fully restored in 1980 using traditional materials. As it is still used by the authorities it is rarely open to visitors. However, you are allowed to take pictures of this picturesque building from the outside.

Mutrah Fort

Nizwa Fort

Location → Town Centre · Nizwa | na
Web/email → www.omantourism.gov.om   Map Ref → 1-B2

The Nizwa Fort is the oldest in Oman. Although the building, as it stands, dates back to the mid 1600s, it has been built on a far earlier structure dating from the 1100s. It is surprisingly large and although it is not as visually impressive as others, it is one of the most interesting forts to visit. You can wander through the maze of passageways and rooms that were specially designed to confuse attackers – a glance at the map by the main entrance is useful to orientate yourself. The fort was the home of the Imam (the effective ruler of the interior) for about 300 years.

The views from the upper levels show the sheer size of the oasis, with palm trees extending as far as the eye can see in several directions. It is also a good vantage point for viewing the town's distinctive blue-domed mosque up close, as well as the surrounding Hajar Mountains.

The fort is open from Saturday to Thursday (09:00 – 16:00) and on Fridays (08:00 – 11:00). Admission costs 500 baisas.

Sohar Fort

Location ➜ Nr the coast · Sohar	26 844 758
Web/email ➜ na	Map Ref ➜ 1-B2

This big square fort is one of the largest in Oman, and since it was whitewashed it has become a dazzling landmark in central Sohar. The main fort is fairly plain, with open spaces and small gun towers, but the most interesting part of your visit will be when you enter the keep, which houses the Sohar Fort Museum. Spread over three floors, this museum details the archaeological, geological and anthropological history of Sohar. It also touches on parts of greater Arabian history that have influenced the development of the town, such as the silk route and copper mining. Each exhibit is clearly explained and well illustrated.

From the top floor of the museum there are steps to the tower's roof where you'll have incredible panoramic views over plantations, across the mosque to the mountains or out to sea.

An English-speaking guide is usually available in both the fort and the museum. The fort is open from 08:00 – 14:00 and 16:00 – 18:00 (Saturday to Wednesday), and from 08:00 – 12:00 and 16:00 – 18:00 on Thursday and Friday. Admission is 500 baisas. To get there, take the City Centre exit off the Muscat-Dubai highway, and after about two kilometres turn right at the second roundabout.

Sunaysilah Fort

Location ➜ Sur	na
Web/email ➜ na	Map Ref ➜ 1-B1

The main fort in Sur overlooks the town and offers commanding views of the area and the coastline. It is built on a relatively simple square design, with a tower at each corner, and is probably about 300 years old. It was restored in 1989 and is open daily to visitors. However, to enter you need a permit from the Ministry of Culture & National Heritage in Muscat (www.mcnh.gov.om). The fort is open from Sunday to Thursday between 08:30 and 14:30; admission is 500 baisas.

Museums – Muscat

Other options ➜ Art [p.155]
Mosque Tours [p.129]

The Omani government plays an active role in preserving Oman's past, and museums are an important way of preserving the country's prestigious heritage and history. You can spend hours learning about the achievements of Oman's ancestors, gaining valuable insight into the history of life in each specific area.

You'll find a limited number of museums outside Muscat, but the few that do exist are interesting excursions for history buffs.

Entrance to museums costs very little, and information on exhibits is given in both English and Arabic. Opening times often change during summer, Ramadan, Eid and on public holidays, so check before you go to avoid a wasted journey.

Bait Al Zubair

Location ➜ Al Saidiyah Street · Muscat	24 736 688
Web/email ➜ bazubair@omantel.net.om	Map Ref ➜ 10-D4

A collection, rather than a museum, the Bait Al Zubair offers a fascinating insight into the Omani lifestyle and traditions, mixing ancient and modern. It is located in a beautiful restored house in Muscat, and each display is accompanied by excellent explanations and descriptions. There are also knowledgeable and helpful staff on hand, making this a highly recommended stop for all visitors.

The four major displays cover men's jewellery, khanjars and attire; women's jewellery and attire; household items including kitchenware, incense burners and rosewater sprinklers; and swords and firearms. There is a central photo gallery with fascinating pictures from the 1920s up until the present day.

Outside you'll find full size recreations of stone-built Omani homes, a small souk, fishing boats and a flowing falaj. There is also a gift shop selling a variety of Omani items and paintings, custom-made miniatures of the pieces on display, and other museum souvenirs. The museum is open from 09:30 – 13:00 and 16:00 – 19:00, Saturday to Thursday. Admission costs RO 1 for adults, and 250 baisas for children under 15. Educational groups may enter for free.

Bait Naa'man

Location ➜ Barka (see below) | na
Web/email ➜ na | Map Ref ➜ 1-B2

Although it looks like a small fort from the outside, this is more of a fortified palace with all the comforts of home. It was built 360 years ago for Imam Saif bin Sultan as a resting place on journeys from Muscat to Rustaq. In 1992 the palace was restored, and stocked with antique Omani household items. A wander through the rooms, prisons, secret meeting places and cannon towers will uncover some interesting details about the lives of the inhabitants and their unique methods of defence, such as how they poured hot date honey onto unwelcome guests.

To get there from the main road, go past the Barka Roundabout and after four kilometres turn right at the sign for Naa'man. Follow the road until the fort appears on the left. To get there from Barka, go past the new bullring and take the next road on the left (200m before the roundabout).

Bait Al Zubair

Children's Museum

Location ➜ Nr Qurm Nature Reserve · Al Qurm | 24 605 368
Web/email ➜ na | Map Ref ➜ 8-C4

Kids of all ages will enjoy this interactive science museum. Solidly built displays clearly explain holography, lasers, the human body, energy, faxes, computers and many other fascinations of daily life. Plenty of button-pressing, handle-turning, pedalling, balancing, jumping and running

space for kids to exhaust themselves before lunch. This museum is popular and can get crowded on Thursdays. Entrance is free.

Marine Science & Fisheries Centre

Location ➜ Marina Bander Al-Rowdha · Sidab | 24 740 061
Web/email ➜ www.marinaoman.com | Map Ref ➜ 13-E4

The Marine Science & Fisheries Centre was set up in 1986, near Sidab on the coast near Muscat, with the support of Unesco. In cooperation with the Sultan Qaboos University, the Centre is intended to develop sea-based aquaculture on a large scale. It has a public aquarium that displays local aquatic flora and fauna, and a modern library, both of which are interesting for visitors. You can view Loggerhead, Hawksbill and Green Turtles up close in the turtle pool.

The Centre shares an entrance road with Marina Bander Al-Rowdha, near the Al Bustan Palace InterContinental Hotel. Entrance is free.

Muscat Gate Museum

Location ➜ Al Bahri Rd · Muscat | na
Web/email ➜ na | Map Ref ➜ 10-D4

Located in one of the fortified gates of the old city walls, the Muscat Gate House is the newest museum to open its doors to visitors. It illustrates the history of Muscat and Oman from ancient times right up to the present day with a special display on the city's springs, wells, underground

Muscat Gate Museum

Exploring

Museums, Heritage & Culture

waterways, souks, mosques, harbours and forts. The awe-inspiring view from the roof over the old town of Muscat is almost worth the visit alone.

National Museum

| Location ➜ Nr Al Falaj Hotel Muscat · Ruwi | 24 701 289 |
| Web/email ➜ na | Map Ref ➜ 12-C1 |

A small but fairly comprehensive museum showcasing silver jewellery, ladies' costumes from around Oman, pottery, a selection of scale-model dhows, crockery, coffee pots, and guns. Additionally, there is a selection of unique items of furniture from the old palace in Muscat, clothes, pictures and medals from the Zanzibar rulers; as well as correspondence and pictures of the last five sultans of the Al Said Dynasty. Your English-speaking guide will probably offer you the chance to sample the legendary Omani hospitality, by inviting you to have some traditional kahwa (coffee), halwa and dates afterwards. Entrance costs 500 baisas, and the museum is open from 09:00 – 13:00 and 16:00 – 18:00 from October to March, and from 09:00 – 13:00 and 17:00 – 19:00 from April to September.

Natural History Museum

| Location ➜ Al-Wazarat St · Al Khuwayr | 24 641 374 |
| Web/email ➜ na | Map Ref ➜ 7-B2 |

This museum, housed within the Ministry of National Heritage and Culture, is a fascinating and informative collection of exhibits relating to Oman's wildlife. You can see stuffed animals, many of which are unique to Oman and the Gulf region (such as the oryx and the Arabian leopard), in replicas of their natural habitats. The 'Oman Through Time' exhibition (sponsored by PDO) follows the history of Oman through fossils, and includes the development of oil and gas reserves.

The Whale Hall should not be missed – it is dominated by the suspended skeleton of a 25 year old sperm whale. The quiet blue hall is filled with the sounds of whale and dolphin calls, and offers a wide range of information about the unique selection of whale species found off the Omani coast. The dolphin and whale skeletons that are displayed in the Whale Hall have all been recovered from Oman's beaches.

If you visit during the winter months, you can tour the botanical gardens adjacent to the museum building. These carefully tended gardens feature Omani trees, shrubs and flora, including frankincense, desert rose, henna and aloe.

Children will love this visitor attraction. Entrance is free.

Oil & Gas Exhibition Centre

| Location ➜ Mina Al Fahal (PDO) | 24 677 834 |
| Web/email ➜ na | Map Ref ➜ 8-E3 |

The Exhibition Centre was given to the Omani people as a gift from Petroleum Development Oman (PDO), the largest oil and gas production company in the country. It provides a well-designed, interactive journey through the development, discovery, extraction and use of fossil fuels in Oman. Kids will love the interesting displays that include seismic computer games, nodding donkeys, and gigantic rotating drill bits. There is a café serving light meals and refreshments, as well as a computer playground featuring familiar computer games.

Omani French Museum

| Location ➜ As Saidiyah Street · Muscat | 24 736 613 |
| Web/email ➜ na | Map Ref ➜ 10-D4 |

This museum is on the site of the first French Embassy, and is a carefully preserved example of 19th century Omani architecture. It celebrates the close ties between France and Oman over the past few centuries. Although the museum exhibits have French captions, there are usually brief English translations. The ground floor of the museum features exhibitions on early French contacts, the history of Omani-Franco trade and on HM Sultan Qaboos' visit to France. Upstairs you'll find records, furniture, clothes and photographs that belonged to early French diplomats. One room holds not just regional Omani women's clothing, but also some antique French costumes. Entrance is free.

Omani Museum

| Location ➜ Nr Ministry of Information · MSQ | 24 600 946 |
| Web/email ➜ na | Map Ref ➜ 11-A1 |

The Omani Museum sits on top of Information Hill and is almost worth visiting for the view alone. It is run by the Ministry of Information, and although it is fairly small, it is very informative. It is the only museum in Muscat that offers detailed

Museums, Heritage & Culture

archaeological information and artefacts. It also has displays on agriculture, minerals, trade routes, architecture, dhows, arts and crafts, jewellery and weaponry. Entrance is free.

Sultan's Armed Forces Museum, The

Location ➜ Bait Al-Falaj Fort · Ruwi | 24 312 654
Web/email ➜ na | Map Ref ➜ 12-D1

This showcase of Oman's military history is set in the main building and grounds of the beautiful Bait Al Falaj Fort. The fort was built to be the Garrison Headquarters for the Sultan Said bin Sultan's Armed Forces in 1845. It features descriptions of the origins of Islam in Oman, tribal disputes and the many invasions of the coast by foreign powers. While these exhibits are a little on the dry side, the more recent military history is lavishly represented with uniforms, antique cannons, early machine guns, weapons confiscated from the rebels in Dhofar, models of military vehicles and planes, instruments, medals and even an ejector seat and parachute.

Outside you'll find the exhibits of military hardware such as planes, helicopters, boats, rough terrain vehicles and the first car owned by HM Sultan Qaboos when he became Sultan — a Cadillac with inches-thick bulletproof glass. You can also have a wander around wartime field headquarters and a military hospital. A representative of the army, navy or airforce will guide you around the museum, which is a definite must-do for military enthusiasts. Entrance is 500 baisas.

Museums – Out of Muscat

Other options ➜ Tours & Sightseeing [p.134]

Salalah Museum

Location ➜ An Nahdah St · Salalah | 23 294 549
Web/email ➜ na | Map Ref ➜ 1-E3

The museum is the cultural centre of Salalah and offers visitors an extended display of traditional literary works, ancient scriptures and coins dating back to the 11th century, pottery dating back to the middle ages and traditional irrigation tools and manuscripts. In the lobby there is an exhibition of Wilfred Thesiger's photographs of Salalah and other parts of Arabia taken in the 1940s and 1950s. Entrance is free.

Sohar Fort Museum

Location ➜ Sohar Fort · Sohar | 26 844 758
Web/email ➜ na | Map Ref ➜ 1-B2

This small museum, situated in one of the towers of the Sohar Fort, provides an interesting insight into Oman's geology, geography and ancient history. It includes an extended display on the copper trade, which was once very important for Oman. You can also see the tomb of Sayyid Thuwani bin Said bin Sultan Al-Busaid, the ruler of Oman from 1856 to 1866. On the first floor, the history of Oman's notable forts is illustrated. A walk up to the roof of the fort gives you beautiful panoramic views of Sohar and the sea. To get there, take the 'City Centre' exit off the Muscat-Dubai road, and after two kilometres turn right at the second roundabout. Entrance is free.

Sur Maritime Museum

Location ➜ Al-Orouba Sports Club, opp Sunaysilah Fort · Sur | na
Web/email ➜ na | Map Ref ➜ 1-B1

The local youth sports club in Sur runs this small marine museum. It gives an idea of what life is like at sea and the importance of fishing and trade to the area. Highlights include old photographs, wooden models and maritime artefacts, as well as examples of local weaving and fabrics embroidered with silver. The museum is located on the premises of the Al-Orouba Youth Sports Club, near the main entrance of Sunaysilah Fort. The small white building that houses the museum is identified by a ship's wheel on the wall. If you are planning to visit the museum, it is advised to call Mr. Abdullah M. Al-Araimi (25 541 466/99 387 155). He is the secretary of the sports club, and he will gladly open the museum for you if it is closed, and give you the grand tour. Entrance is free.

Other Attractions

Birdwatching

Other options ➜ Birdwatching Groups [p.218]

Birdwatchers can take advantage of Oman's fortunate location in the path of thousands of exotic birds migrating between Asia and Africa. The beaches and lagoons along the coastline are good places to spot a rich variety of marine birdlife, from storks and herons to flamingos and ducks.

For a detailed introduction to the colourful birdlife in Oman, the *Birdwatching Guide to Oman* (Hanne & Jens Eriksen and Panadda & Dave E. Sargeant) is invaluable. You can also refer to the website www.birdsoman.com.

Muscat Diving and Adventure Centre	
Location → Nr Radisson Hotel · Al Khuwayr	24 485 663
Web/email → www.holiday-in-oman.com	Map Ref → 7-B3

Birdwatching tours through this company are usually on Thursday mornings, although full day tours are also available upon request. You will be accompanied by an experienced birder who can help you identify your sightings and provide further information on the birdlife of Oman. Muscat Diving and Adventure Centre require 24 hours notice to organise a birdwatching tour, and there should be a minimum of four people. A half day tour costs RO 15 (RO 10 for children) and a full day tour costs RO 30.

Bullfighting

If you think bullfighting is a cruel and bloody sport, you'll be pleasantly surprised by Oman's bullfighting tradition. It is a clash of wills between two pampered (and valuable) Brahmin bulls, who lock horns until one either gives up or is forced out of the ring. No blood, no guts, no gore! Bullfights are held along the Batinah coastline, usually on Friday afternoons. For more information, see p.111.

Camel Racing

Other options → **Camel Rides [p.192]**

Camel racing is a popular traditional sport and you shouldn't miss the chance to see it up close. The camels are bred especially for the track, and it is still Bedouin families that raise and train them. The racing season runs from August to April, and races are held mainly on Fridays and public holidays during the winter months. Races start at around 06:00 and continue until 09:00, so you may have to forsake your lie-in! Announcements for camel races appear mostly in the Arabic newspapers, but if you are keen to go you can find out details from one of the tour operators. Race tracks can be found all around the country, including Seeb (the main location) in the north and Salalah in the south. In the interior you'll find

many other racing tracks, sometimes clearly signposted, along the main roads. A visit to any of these might give you the opportunity to see the camels being trained, although usually only before 08:00.

Mosque Tours

Other options → **Museums – City [p.125]**

Sultan Qaboos Grand Mosque	
Location → As Sultan Qaboos St · Al Khuwayr	na
Web/email → na	Map Ref → 6-C4

This beautiful example of Islamic architecture provides a wonderful insight into the cultural heritage of Oman. It is also one of the few mosques that allow entry for non-Muslims. Apart from being a place of worship, this huge mosque is a centre for scholars and houses an Islamic reference library containing over 20,000 sources of information on Islamic sciences and culture. The mosque is lavishly decorated, and features a 263m prayer carpet, 35 crystal chandeliers (the central one is 14 metres high and eight metres wide), and a floor entirely paved with marble. The tour takes you into the men's and women's prayer halls, where you are even allowed to take pictures. There are strict rules governing entry of non-Muslims into the mosque – you have to take your shoes off before entering, and both men and women should wear conservative clothing (women should be covered up, including their hair), and children under ten years are not permitted. The hours for the tour are strictly between 08:00 and 11:00 from Saturday to Wednesday.

Sultan Qaboos Grand Mosque

Nature Reserves

There is significant emphasis on the care and protection of the Omani environment, such as conserving biodiversity and promoting eco-tourism. Nature reserves have been established to prevent damage to the natural habitat of many different species, including leopards, oryx and various birds and fish.

Arabian Oryx Sanctuary

Location → Jiddat Al Harasis (see below) | na
Web/email → na   Map Ref → 1-D2

This reserve is located in the isolated area of Jiddat Al Harasis, the home of Arabia's last true nomads. The environmental resources in this area (flat plains, sand dunes, high hills and rocky slopes) support a unique desert ecosystem that benefits diverse species of flora and fauna. The Arabian Oryx is a medium-sized antelope that is well adapted to its desert existence, particularly because it has the capacity to conserve water. Unfortunately, wild Oryx died out in 1972, but thanks to the efforts of HM Sultan Qaboos, the first Oryx from a captive herd was successfully released into the wild.

An entry permit for the sanctuary is available from the Office of the Adviser for Conservation of the Environment, Diwan of Royal Court (24 693 536). For more information, see www.oryxoman.com.

To get there from Muscat, follow the main Salalah highway about 500 km to Hayma, and then follow the Duqm graded road to the Habab Junction. Head north on a secondary graded road for a further 23 km, and then head due east following a desert track for another 23 km. It is recommended that you travel in a convoy with at least two 4 WD vehicles.

As Saleel Natural Park

Location → See below | na
Web/email → na   Map Ref → 1-C1

The As Saleel Natural Park in Al Kamil w'al Wafi, approximately 55 km south-west of Sur, is divided in three vegetation areas; alluvial plain covered with acacia woodland, wadis in the higher mountains, and sparsely vegetated hills and rocky outcrops forming the northern boundaries. These zones provide good habitat for some of the medium-sized wildlife species in Oman, such as gazelles, wild cats, wolves and foxes. The park has been designated for the future development of wildlife education and tourism, protecting the wildlife in its own habitat. Unfortunately unrestricted access in the past has made the animals quite shy, so a visit to this park comes with no guarantee of a sighting.

Daymaniyat Islands Nature Reserve

Location → Btn As Seeb & Barka | na
Web/email → na   Map Ref → 1-B2

The Daymaniyat Islands are a cluster of nine islands along the coast of Seeb and Barka. The islands are surrounded by rocks and shallow seas, and they can only be reached by boat. They are of great environmental significance, as they are home to some endangered species and the nesting sites for several species of migratory birds. The islands themselves are off limits to visitors. You can anchor

Rugged Good Book

Many of Oman's most beautiful spots can only be reached in a 4 WD. So load up your vehicle with tents and supplies and head off into the rocky mountains, desolate dunes and winding wadis. Oh, and don't forget to take the Oman Off-Road Explorer – it's the essential guide to roughing it like a pro! Available late 2005.

just off the islands and dive or snorkel in the surrounding waters, although you need to get permission to do this. The waters feature an abundance of marine life and the greatest diversity of corals in the region. Each year, 250 – 300 Hawksbill turtles nest on the islands – this species is the most endangered of all marine turtles, and they usually nest in small numbers over a large geographical area. Therefore, this congregation of such a large group on such a small cluster of islands is of global importance.

Jebel Samhan Nature Reserve

Location → See below | na
Web/email → na   Map Ref → 1-E3

The immense Jebel Samhan Nature Reserve is located close to Salalah in the south of Oman, and stretches from Marbat in the south to Shuwimiya in the north-east. The limestone highlands, scalloped mountain peaks, wadis and canyons and the 1,500m high escarpment overlooking foothills and the coastal plain between Marbat and Sadh provide ideal habitat for the last-known wild population of Arabian leopard. Other wildlife present in the area includes Nubian ibex, Arabian gazelle, striped hyenas, caracal, wild cats, foxes and wolves. Whales can sometimes be seen along the coast between Hadbin and Shuwaymiya. Green and Loggerhead turtles also nest on the sandy beaches, and the adjacent cliffs provide a resting place for migrating birds.

To get there, turn left at the signpost marked Tawi Atayr (32 km before you reach Taqah). In Tawi Atayr, turn left following the signpost for Khis Adeen. Turn right after one kilometre, and then drive along the graded road for about 66 km, at which point you will reach the plateau on top of the Jebel Samhan.

Khors of the Dhofar Coast

Location → See below	na
Web/email → na	Map Ref → 1-E4

The Dhofar coast Khors are valuable resources with an abundance of wildlife. One of the most important reasons for protecting the Khors is their use by large numbers of migratory birds for food and rest during their annual migration – over 200 species of birds have been recorded in these Khors. The Khors were traditionally used by the local people to water and graze their livestock, while the marine life provided rich fishing territory. With the increase in population and the expansion of the Salalah area, some of the Khors' resources became threatened by over-utilisation. The Oman Government has therefore decided to proclaim these valuable resources as protected areas. To witness some of the Khors' beauty go to Khor Rouri Beach, a few kilometres east of Taqah Village (east of Salalah).

Ras Al Jinz Turtle Reserve

Location → Ras Al Hadd · Sur	na
Web/email → na	Map Ref → 1-C1

Turtle nesting sites on the coast of Oman have been recorded on over 275 beaches along the coast, from the Mussandam in the north to near the border with Yemen in the south. Five out of the seven recognised species of marine turtle are found in Oman's waters, while the Green turtle, the Loggerhead, Hawksbill and Olive Ridley are

known to come ashore and nest. The giant Leatherback turtle, which can weigh up to a ton, feeds in the waters off Oman's coast, but does not regularly nest here. Turtles face many threats to their survival, not least being caught in fishing nets and having their nesting sites destroyed by man. Green turtles are estimated to lay up to 60,000 egg clutches each year in Oman; the effort of about 20,000 female turtles. While they nest all along the coast, the majority of nest sites are along a 50 km stretch of coastline around Ras Al Hadd (the most eastern point of the Arabian Peninsula). Here, the government has set up a reserve to allow the public to view the amazing spectacle of nesting females and newborn hatchlings. The area has been limited to the beaches at Ras Al Jinz, with access to the other beaches being prohibited. To visit the turtle reserve at Ras Al Jinz you must apply for a permit to the Directorate General of Nature Protectorates by phone (24 692 574/24 692 550) or fax (24 602 283). Places are limited to about 60 people and it is advisable to book well in advance if you can. A fee of RO 1 is charged, per person, for those aged ten and above. You will need to supply names and nationalities of all visitors, plus a contact phone number, visit date and your car registration number. The permit allows you to stay on the government campsite at Ras Al Jinz and to have access to the beach. When you receive the permit you will also get an information pack on using the campsite and watching the turtles.

Nesting instinct

Tawi Atayr & Wadi Darbat

Location → East of Salalah (see below) | na
Web/email → na | Map Ref → 1-E3

The Wadi Darbat Natural Park in the Dhofar region provides stunning views of waterfalls, lakes, mountains, and lush vegetation. There are also caves to explore (rich in stalactites and stalagmites) and a wide range of wildlife. During the khareef season (in summer), there is a monsoon waterfall that is a hundred metres high.

To get there from Taqah, drive towards Marbat and after 32 km you'll find the turn-off for Tawi Atayr (famous for its 'Well of Birds' – a natural sinkhole that is over 100m wide and 211m deep – which homes many species of birds, particularly during the khareef). From the Tawi Atayr turn-off, turn left after a few hundred metres to get onto the track that will lead you down into Wadi Darbat.

Showjumping

Oman Equestrian and Camel Federation

Location → Various locations | 24 490 424
Web/email → na | Map Ref → na

This federation organises a variety of equestrian events and camel races. At least one showjumping competition takes place each week, normally on a Sunday or a Tuesday. The Enam ground is the main showjumping arena in Oman, and it hosts several national and international events. Showjumping is only held during the cooler winter months. Events are published in the newspapers, or you can contact the federation to get a current schedule.

Beaches & Parks

Beaches

Other options → **Beach Clubs [p.216]**
Parks [p.133]
Swimming [p.211]

With over 1,700 km of coastline it is hardly surprising that Oman offers some wonderful stretches of sandy beach. Many of them are unspoilt areas where you will find seclusion and isolation. The following are some of the main beaches that are popular with visitors and residents alike.

Azaiba Beach

Location → See below | na
Web/email → na | Map Ref → na

Also known as Aviation, Strabag or Shell beach (or as Seeb beach further up the coast), this long stretch of beach is backed by dense bushes that act as a good windbreak. Access is mainly by 4 WD, although if you don't mind a short walk you can get there in a normal car. It is not the best beach for snorkelling as there is no coral, but it is a good windsurfing site. Because it is a quiet beach, it is suitable for taking your dogs for a run – just make sure you don't disturb the fishermen, as this is still a working beach and they can get a bit grumpy if you get in their way. But on the other hand they are usually more than happy to sell you some fish, show you how their nets work and teach you how to cast sardine nets.

To get to this beach, turn right off the main highway at the signpost for the Aviation Club (about a kilometre past the Zubair complex/Shell station in Al Azaiba). When you reach the Aviation Club, follow the track to your left if you are in a 4 WD, or leave your car here and walk the rest of the way.

Bandar Al Jissah

Location → See below | na
Web/email → na | Map Ref → 15-C2

While this beautiful (although quite short) stretch of beach can be very busy on Fridays, its attraction is twofold – firstly it is accessibly by

Bandar Al Jissah

saloon car, and secondly it is the best place to catch a sea taxi. Sea taxis are the small fishing boats you see loaded up with fresh fish during the week, and on weekends they go for much bigger fish – tourists! For a very small fee they will transport you and all your gear to one of the secluded beaches such as Khayran, leave you there until a specified time and then will come and pick you up. It is widely understood that you need not pay the fee until you have been picked up. Snorkelling gear is recommended as the marine life here is stunning.

To get there, head towards the Al Bustan InterContinental Palace Hotel from Wadi Al Kabir – you will see the village of Qantab signposted to the right as you reach the top of the hill. Take this right turn and follow the road until you see a signpost for Oman Dive Centre – Bandar Al Jissah is at the end of this road.

Beach Promenade

Location → Nr Hyatt Regency & InterCon Htl · Shati Al Qurm	na
Web/email → na	Map Ref → 8-A4

In the hour or two before sunset the beach and shoreline stretching from the Hyatt Regency Muscat to the InterContinental Hotel becomes a lively promenade. People come here to walk, jog, jet ski, play football and barbecue, and it is a pleasant spot to relax and watch the world go by as the sun goes down. Don't be confused by the concrete wall that you'll see about half way down – while this appears to be the end of the beach it is possible to walk out onto a concrete ledge and continue along until the end of the beach.

Dibab – Tiwi Coast

Location → Btn Dibab & Tiwi · Nr Sur	na
Web/email → na	Map Ref → 1-B1

The south-east coastal road from Muscat to Quriyat takes you to the most beautiful white sandy beaches between Dibab and Tiwi Village. It makes for a great day trip if you want to escape the city and don't mind driving for about two and a half hours. A 4 WD is recommended as the road consists mostly of gravel. Snorkelling can be magnificent here, especially along the rocks. It is also an ideal spot for a picnic or early evening barbecue. With its picturesque and restful setting between the mountains and the coast, it is also an excellent camping spot.

Majan Beach

Location → Nr Ras Al Hamra Club · Qurm Heights	na
Web/email → na	Map Ref → 8-D1

This small and quiet beach, which is not far away and easily accessible, is ideal for snorkellers as it has superb coral reefs. On good days you can see parrot fish, rays and turtles. The beach is equipped with manmade sunshades and barbecue pits.

To get there, go past the Ras Al Hamra Recreation Club, keeping it on your right, and continue over the slight rise for another 150 metres. Parking for the beach is on the opposite side of the road.

Ras Al Hadd Beach

Location → Nr Sur (see below)	na
Web/email → na	Map Ref → 1-B1

The beaches around Ras Al Hadd are famous for nesting turtles. They are also popular with visitors who like the relaxing atmosphere and tropical surroundings. The Turtle Beach Resort (99 007 709/25 543 400), located on the end of a beautiful turquoise bay, is a good choice for those who like to combine simplicity with a little bit of luxury. The resort has an outdoor, dhow-shaped restaurant where you can have a drink overlooking the bay. Lunch and dinner are also served. You don't need to pack your tent, as the resort offers 25 cottages, each one supplied with two beds and a ventilator.

You should definitely take your snorkelling or diving gear; this is a prime spot to see turtles, rays, Murray eels and a range of colourful fish. The resort has a small motor boat and on request they will take you out to see the turtles in the summer season (this will cost you around RO 15, excluding drinks).

The drive from Muscat will take you between four and five hours, so many people make a weekend trip out of it. To get there from Sur, follow the sign to Ras Al Hadd. After about 60 km you'll reach a T-junction, where you should turn left. Turn left again after about three kilometres, following the sign for Turtle Beach Resort.

Parks

Other options → Beaches [p.132]

In 'desert' countries such as Oman, the lack of lush greenery is something that you might miss from back home. Fortunately, Oman has a good selection of parks and gardens that are welcome patches of green. Parks are well looked after by the municipality and usually include lawns, sandy play areas and playground equipment for children, and maybe a water feature or two. Before you load your bicycle, rollerblades or dogs into the car, check the park's policy on these – some might allow certain activities, while others don't. Entry to many of the parks is free.

Kalbooh Park

Location → Kalbooh · Mutrah | na
Web/email → na | Map Ref → 10-C3

Situated along the coast by the village of Kalbooh, this small park is a picturesque spot for an evening stroll. It features paved walkways and a grassed amphitheatre. A selection of kiosks and a small Pizza Hut sell snacks and drinks. The views are amazing, with the sea to one side and sheer, rocky hills to the other. In the daytime there is a beautiful view along the coast of Mutrah.

Naseem Park

Location → Past Seeb Airport · As Seeb | na
Web/email → na | Map Ref → na

This large park, opened in 1985, is located on the highway leading to the Batinah, area about 30 km from Seeb International Airport. There is a train ride that goes round the park, a mini falaj system, and jasmine maze and a well-tended Oriental Garden, built to commemorate the strong ties between China and Oman. A cafeteria selling drinks, icecreams and snacks is situated in the centre of the park.

Qurm Heights Park

Location → Nr Crowne Plaza Hotel · Qurm Heights | na
Web/email → na | Map Ref → 8-C2

This small park is perched high on the cliffs in Al Qurm, next to the Gulf Forum Hotel. Its grassy lawn is surrounded by shady trees and plenty of plants and shrubs. At one end of the park is a collection of stone benches on a small paved area complete with Roman-style pillars – the perfect spot for a few minutes of contemplation at the end of the day. This tranquil park is very popular in the evenings with people living in the area.

Qurm Park & Nature Reserve

Location → Al Qurm St · Al Qurm | na
Web/email → na | Map Ref → 8-C4

This sprawling park and nature reserve runs from the side of the main coastal road right down to the public beach. It is Muscat's main park, and features large lawns, a boating lake, fountains and shady pergolas. It is the home of HM Sultan Qaboos' famous Rose Garden, a tranquil, fragrant area that is full of rose varieties from all over the world. The large fountain shoots water as high as 30 metres into the air, and is lit up at night. For 500 baisas you can ride one of the park's horses around a short loop in the park – RO 3 gets you a ride around the whole garden and for RO 10 you can ride down to the beach on horseback, for about an hour. The horses are there every day from 16:00 to 23:00 (in the winter only).

The park incorporates a nature reserve, which is made up of tidal wetlands and mangroves – good for spotting migratory birds. You can expect to see Sooty Gulls, White-cheeked Terns, Crested Terns and, at low tide, various herons and waders. The reserve also runs a mangrove nursery, providing thousands of mangrove tree seedlings every year. The park is home to the City Amphitheatre, which seats up to 4,500 people. This is a popular venue for events. Mondays are for families only.

Riyam Park

Location → Above corniche · Mutrah | na
Web/email → na | Map Ref → 10-B3

Riyam park is located on Mutrah Corniche and offers pretty views of the harbour. It is home to a huge model of an incense burner, which is visible from the road. You can climb up the incense burner to get even better views of the harbour, sea and cliffs. It is a particularly child-friendly park, featuring a playground and a small funfair, shady gardens and a pond.

Tours & Sightseeing

Other options → **Activity Tours [p.142]**
Out of Muscat [p.136]
Weekend Breaks [p.146]

Oman is a wonderful place to explore, with its varied landscape and abundant coastline. Good weather and interesting scenery make it ideal for

outdoor activities. There are many companies that specialise in helping visitors make the most of their time in Oman. They are run by experienced people with good local knowledge who can take you off the beaten track to explore Oman's most fascinating sights.

Various tours and safaris are available, from city tours to desert safaris, and from excursions into the wilderness of the interior to trips to villages in the northern parts of the Sultanate. Tours can be half day, full day or even overnight, camping in the desert or mountains.

The following descriptions will give you an idea of what is commonly offered on various tours. On full day, evening or overnight tours your meals will usually be provided, and on half day city tours you will usually return in time for lunch. Check what is included in your tour package – sometimes you may have to pay for your own meal at a designated rest point (usually a hotel). Most tours include soft drinks and water.

The Tour Operator table lists a selection of tour companies operating locally. Some of these companies will be more flexible than others in terms of customising a tour specifically for your group. For something a little more adventurous, refer to Activity Tours [p.142].

City Tours – Muscat

Muscat City Tour

This half-day tour shows a selection of Muscat's sights and attractions, and includes visits to Oman Museum, the Natural History Museum, Al Alam Palace, Jalali Fort, Mirani Fort, Mutrah Souk, the corniche, the fish market and Muscat Old Town area.

Muscat Cultural Tour

Concentrating more on the history and heritage of Muscat and Oman, this tour visits Oman Museum, the Natural History Museum, the Oil & Gas Exhibition Centre, the Children's Museum, the French-Omani Museum, the Marine Aquarium and the Marine Science and Fisheries Centre. The exact itinerary and museums visited can vary with different tour operators.

City Tours – Out of Muscat

Nizwa

Nizwa is the largest city in Oman's interior, and this full-day tour explores the fascinating sights and heritage of this historically significant place. After driving deep into the Hajar mountains, you arrive at the oasis city of Nizwa, which is home to the Nizwa Fort (which dates back to the 17th century) and the magnificent Jabrin Fort, notable for its wall and ceiling decorations and secret passageways. Many ancient ruins, such as Bahla Fort and various mud-brick villages, can be seen among the date palm plantations and wadis.

Rustaq / Batinah

Batinah, the north-west region of Oman, has always been an important area for its abundant agriculture and strategic position as the trading centre between the mountains and the coast. It is home to many forts including the oldest and largest in the country, Al Kersa Fort. En route you will also visit the ancient souks, hot springs and sandy beaches, all amid spectacular mountain scenery.

Ubar

The discovery of the 'Lost City of Ubar' in the early 1990s caused great excitement in the archaeological world. This full-day tour takes you through some stunning scenery as you drive through the Qara Mountains to the site of Ubar. This ancient city was at the crossroads of significant trade routes, making it a place of unrivalled wealth and splendour – when Marco Polo visited Ubar, he called it 'paradise'. However, at the height of its glory it sank into the desert sands, leaving no trace of its existence. Legend had it that to punish the residents of Ubar for their greed and lavish lifestyle, God caused the sand to swallow the city. When the lost city was uncovered, less than 20 years ago, it was discovered that a huge limestone cavern underneath Ubar had collapsed, causing the city to sink into the sand.

After leaving Ubar you'll continue off-road as the tour ventures into the famous sands of Rub Al Khali (the Empty Quarter), for some dune driving.

Exploring

Tours & Sightseeing

One of Oman's greatest attractions... its people

Safari Tours

Dune Dinner

After being collected in the mid-afternoon, you will be driven inland towards the Hajar mountains and then off-road through the lush green scenery and freshwater pools of Wadi Abyad. You'll then head for the undulating dunes of the nearby Abyad desert for some exciting dune driving before stopping to watch the sun set over the sands. After a sumptuous barbecue, you'll head back to Muscat.

Full-Day Safari

This trip combines a visit to one of Oman's most spectacular wadis, Wadi Bani Khalid, with the breathtaking expanse of the Wahiba Desert. Different tour operators have different itineraries, but on the way from Muscat you will visit places such as the ruined fort of Mudairib, Shab Village and the town of Sur. Some of the unforgettable sights you may see on the way are traditional mud-brick homes clinging to steep valley walls, clear streams carrying fresh water into deep pools, and manmade irrigation systems ('falaj'). As you leave the mountains you'll head for the Wahiba desert for an exhilarating ride over the dunes, some of which are 200 metres high.

Mountain Safari

The height and extent of Oman's mountain ranges surprise many visitors. This trip heads into the highest range, Jebel Akhdar, and up to Jebel Shams, which is Oman's highest peak at over 3,000m. On the way, you'll pass through towns (such as Nizwa) and remote villages set on terraces cut into the mountains. Ancient irrigation channels bring water to the villages to feed the crops. The top of Jebel Shams feels like the top of the world, with the entire mountain range and the awe-inspiring 'Grand Canyon' of Oman (a rocky canyon dropping thousands of metres from the plateau), way below.

Overnight Turtle Watching

All tour operators offer trips to the famous Ras Al Jinz Turtle Sanctuary, where you can watch the rare sight of turtles coming onto the beach to lay their eggs. On your way to Ras Al Jinz you'll pass Quriyat, Wadi Shab and Wadi Tabi, and the town of Sur, home to the most skilled dhow builders in Oman. After arriving at the Turtle Sanctuary, you'll be served a beach barbecue before night falls and the turtles come lumbering onto the beach to lay their eggs and bury them in the sand. After a few hours sleep, you'll return to the beach and watch the mass of tiny hatchlings struggle out of their eggs and make their journey into the sea. On your return journey to Muscat you will get to see more of the countryside and historical settlements.

Wadi Drive

An off-road tour through the wadis can either be half-day, full-day or overnight, camping in the peaceful surroundings of the rocky wilderness. You'll get to see falaj irrigation channels, in place for centuries, bringing water from underground springs to irrigate palm plantations and vegetable terraces. Natural streams run all year round in several wadis, transforming the dry, rocky landscape into fertile areas of lush greenery and clear rock pools that are often home to fish, frogs and other wildlife. Hidden villages in the mountains, seemingly trapped in time, illustrate how people used to subsist in times gone by.

Somewhere over the rainbow...

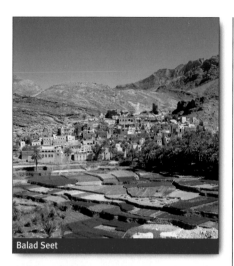

Balad Seet

Wahiba Desert

The Wahiba Desert stretches all the way from the coast to the mountains. This tour travels into the middle of seemingly endless dunes of red and white sand. Dune driving is a must do; a ride up and down the steep slopes, courtesy of a very skilled driver, is like a natural rollercoaster. A visit to a traditional Bedouin homestead for Arabic coffee and dates follows, as well as the chance to try camel riding, the oldest form of desert transport.

Overnight Desert Safari

Leave the noise of the city behind you and experience the peace of the desert for a night. After an exhilarating drive through the dunes you will set up camp in a remote area of Wahiba, where Bedouin tribes have lived traditionally for thousands of years. At sunset, enjoy a camel ride while a barbecue is prepared and then relax in comfortable surroundings under the starlit sky. In the morning, after a leisurely start, visit the flowing wadis to see the greenery and rugged mountain landscape, which form a complete contrast to the desert sights of the previous day.

East Salalah Tour

Leaving from Salalah and travelling east, this tour visits many historical sites and places of interest along the picturesque coast, including the fishing village of Taqa with its watchtowers and castle. Further on is Khor Rouri, a fresh water creek now separated from the sea. It is the site of the ancient city of Samharam, known for its frankincense and for being the former capital of

the Dhofar region. Also on the tour is Mohammed Bin Ali's Tomb, the Ayn Razat ornamental gardens, the Hamran Water Springs and the historical trading centre of Mirbat.

West Salalah Tour

Venture inland from Salalah to the northern part of the Qara Mountains, where the road winds up hairpin bends and eventually leads to the border with Yemen. The tour goes to the Tomb of the Prophet Job, a place visited by many Islamic pilgrims, and the wadis and green pastures where they grow the finest frankincense in the world. Returning from the mountains, you will head to the spectacular Mughsail Beach where, at high tide, seawater gushes through natural blowholes in the limestone, reaching dizzying heights. On the way back to Salalah, visits will be made to the bird sanctuary and Mina Raysut.

Tour Operators

The following guidelines are just to give you an outline of how tour operators do business. Each operator may offer something different, and tour itineraries, timings and prices will vary from one operator to the next. Most companies have head offices in Muscat, although they all offer tours both in and out of the capital.

When booking a tour it is normal practice to do so three or four days in advance. In some cases bookings can be made at shorter notice. You usually pay a 50% deposit when you make the booking, with the remainder payable when you are picked up at the start of the tour. Cancellation policies differ from company to company; although cancelling your tour without an appropriate notice period may result in the loss of your deposit.

Tours are often priced per vehicle rather than per person, although some tours offer fixed individual rates and do not stipulate minimum numbers.

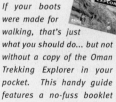

Proud to be a Trekkie

If your boots were made for walking, that's just what you should do... but not without a copy of the Oman Trekking Explorer in your pocket. This handy guide features a no-fuss booklet and a series of detailed route cards (with easy to follow maps and tips for each route) that will really take you places! Lara Croft or Indiana Jones outfits are optional...

Exploring

Tours & Sightseeing

On the day of your tour you will be picked up either from your hotel, residence or an agreed meeting point. Tours usually leave on time, and no-shows do not get a refund. At most times of year it is advisable to wear cool, comfortable clothing such as shorts and T-shirts. Hats and sunglasses are also recommended. If you are going on a desert or mountain tour, you should wear strong, flat-soled shoes as there is usually some walking involved. Other items you will probably want to take include sun protection, a camera and money (in case there is an opportunity to buy souvenirs or postcards).

Off-road driving is exhilarating but extreme, and people who suffer from motion sickness may not enjoy the experience very much. You can rest assured that your driver is a skilled professional and knows exactly what he is doing. However, remember that you are the client and you have the right to request him to slow down or tackle less challenging routes, if you feel the ride is too bumpy for your group. Most drivers will take an easier route if you are with young children, elderly people or people with special circumstances (note: it may not be safe for pregnant women to go on an off-road tour).

Activity Tours

Other options → Tours & Sightseeing [p.134]

In addition to city and safari tours, several companies offer more adventurous or specialist activities. Check out the individual companies below to find out what each offers. A basic level of fitness may be required for some of the tours. As well as safari tours, there are several camping resorts across Oman with fixed tents and/or barasti huts. They offer

a good basic facilities and a wide range of activities including dune buggies, star gazing, experiencing real Omani food and entertainment and getting to see Oman's wildlife including dolphins, turtles and birds. See Camping [p.194].

I'm the tallest of all the camels

Al Ghadeer Tours

| Location → Marbellah · Bawshar | 24 425 557 |
| Web/email → abulait@omantel.net.om | Map Ref → na |

Al Ghadeer specialises in trips into the Wahiba Sands, complete with camel trekking and meeting traditional Bedouin communities. However, they also offer tours such as historical and cultural tours, 4 WD safaris, camping trips, hiking and dhow cruises.

They can also take care of airport pickups, internal flights and car rental.

Tour Operators

Adventure Tours	24 786 916	touroman@shanfari.com	na
Al Ghadeer Tours	24 425 557	abulait@omantel.net.om	na
Bahwan Travel	24 704 455	topclass@omantel.net.om	na
Desert Discovery	24 593 232	tours@omantel.net.om	www.desert-discovery.com
Global Tours	24 695 959	globtour@omantel.net.om	www.globaltoursoman.com
Khasab Travel & Tours	26 730 464	khastour@omantel.net.om	www.khasabtours.com
Mark Tours	24 562 444	marktour@omantel.net.om	www.marktoursoman.com
Mezoon Travel	24 796 680	mzt@omzest.com	www.mezoontravel.hypermark.net
National Travel & Tourism	24 566 046	nttoman@omantel.net.om	www.nttoman.com
Nomadic Adventures & Tours	99 336 273	nomadiccamp@gmx.net	www.nomadicdesertcamp.com
Oman Discovery	24 706 424	omandisc@omantel.net.om	na
Oman United Agencies	24 700 326	na	na
Oman Orient Tours	24 485 066	otmct@omantel.net.om	www.orienttours.ae
Premier Tours	24 700 272	premier@omantel.net.om	na
United Tours	24 787 448	utours@omantel.net.om	www.unitedoman.com
Zubair Travel & Tourism	24 695 678	zubairtr@omantel.net.om	na

Bahwan Travel Agencies

Location → Gen Business Distr · Ruwi   **24 704 455**
Web/email → www.bahwantravels.com   Map Ref → na

Apart from the usual city tours (half and full day), dhow cruises, 4 WD safaris, camping trips, camel trekking and scuba diving tours offered by most tour operators, Bahwan can also offer assistance with cruise ship shore excursions, multi-destination holidays (UAE, Iran, Jordan, Bahrain, Qatar & Yemen), self-drive holidays and dive packages. Their guides are either Omani, German or Dutch, and languages spoken include English, French, German, Arabic, Dutch and Spanish.

Desert Discovery Tours

Location → Way 4852 · Al Azaiba   **24 493 232**
Web/email → www.desert-discovery.com   Map Ref → na

Desert Discovery offers a range of activity and sightseeing tours under the guidance of officially appointed Omani guides. Whether you want to camp overnight in luxury tents in the Wahiba Sands, try sand skiing or dune driving in the desert, ride a camel or watch turtles nesting on the beach in Ras Al Jinz, this tour operator can organise an itinerary for you. For a unique chance to explore Oman off the beaten track, you can book a tour in one of Desert Discovery's mobile camping units. Each unit consists of a large entertainment tent (including groundsheet, table and chairs), plus smaller tents, equipped with camp beds and sleeping bags, for sleeping. For more information, call the above number or visit their website.

Empty Quarter Tours

Location → Madinat As Sultan Qaboos   **99 387 654**
Web/email → www.emptyquartertours.com   Map Ref → na

Experienced Omani guides (who speak both English and Arabic) will lead you in the tour of your choice, be it crossing the Rub Al Khali (Empty Quarter), watching nesting turtles lay their eggs on the beach, spending the night in a traditional Bedouin campsite or camel trekking over the Wahiba Sands. Empty Quarter Tours can organise customised tours for special occasions such as weddings, birthdays or Christmas parties, and educational trips for schools. If you are arriving in Oman by air, they can arrange an airport meet and greet service, and they offer accommodation at their Nahar Tourism Oasis (near Ibra), which has its own restaurant and pool.

Muscat Diving and Adventure Centre

Location → Nr Radisson Hotel · Al Khuwayr   **24 485 663**
Web/email → www.holiday-in-oman.com   Map Ref → 7-B3

The Muscat Diving and Adventure Centre specialises in diving tours and adventure activities for the energetic tourist. They offer a comprehensive and personal service during your stay in Oman, including airport pickups, transport from your hotel to the centre, car rental and customised tours.

They organise various land and water activities, such as kayaking, game fishing, dolphin watching, archery, climbing, trekking, caving and bird watching. In addition, they also offer desert safaris, wadi tours, 4 WD self-drive holidays and sunset cruises. The centre specialises in diving, and can arrange diving tours according to your requirements. There is a shop onsite, selling diving and climbing equipment.

Coastal Cruises

The following companies run excellent coastal cruises in a variety of packages. Sidab Sea Tours also run Coastal trips, see review under Fishing, [p.203] for company details.

Marina Bander Al-Rowdha

Location → Marina Bander Al-Rowdha · Sidab **24 737 288**
Web/email → www.marinaoman.com   Map Ref → 13-E4

Marina Bander Al-Rowdha is located on the western coast of Oman, and is one of the best launch spots for fishing, diving and sailing. It has 140 wet berths and 90 dry berths, and is fully equipped for launch, recovery, service and marine control. The Marina can organise tours for whale and dolphin watching, watersports, diving and fishing. For a more relaxing excursion, take a cruise on a traditional dhow or be transported to a secluded beach for an afternoon's sunbathing. The Marina has its own restaurant, the Blue Marlin, as well as the welcoming Lighthouse Bar.

Moonlight Dive Centre

Location → Nr Grand Hyatt Muscat · Shati Al Qurm **99 317 700**
Web/email → na   Map Ref → 7-D1

The Moonlight Dive Centre can deliver a customised cruise package to meet your requirements. They offer trips for groups (from four to 25 people) in one of their two boats, which are based on the beach in Shati Al Qurm next to the Hyatt Regency Muscat. A typical cruise heads south along Muscat's spectacular coast, visiting rocky islands, secluded beaches or even marina cafés for breakfast or refreshments. But time can be allocated for other activities as per your requirements, such as fishing, snorkelling, sunbathing or watersports. For a three-hour trip, expect to pay around RO 25 per person.

Dolphin & Whale Watching

There are more than 20 species of whales and dolphins either living in or passing through the seas off the coast of Oman. Although no tour operator can guarantee a sighting of these beautiful sea creatures, the odds are definitely high that you will get to see a school of dolphins swimming alongside your boat, playing in its wake.

Whales are not so frequently seen – these gentle giants travel in smaller groups and stay under the surface for a lot longer, so you have to be a little bit more patient. Early mornings and evenings, when the seas are at their calmest, are the best times for whale sightings. It is possible to see them from the shore (usually in cliff areas, such as Mussandam) but it is better to be out at sea in a boat, where the experience is closer and infinitely more exciting.

Sidab Sea Tours also run Dolphin trips, see review under Fishing, [p.203] for company details.

Arabian Sea Safaris

Location → Htl InterContinental · Shati Al Qurm | 24 693 223
Web/email → www.arabianseasafaris.com | Map Ref → 8-A4

Every Arabian Sea Safaris tour has a dolphin and whale specialist onboard who talks about the behaviour, ecology and lifestyle of these magnificent animals. So although sighting is not guaranteed, you will still increase your knowledge and understanding of Oman's marine life and environment. If you do spot dolphins (and the chances are very high that you will), underwater microphones give you the unique opportunity to listen to the communication between them. If you are very lucky you might even come across one of the many species of whales that can be found just a few kilometres off Muscat's coast.

Special onboard activities for children are designed to increase their understanding. The

cost per person is RO 25, which includes breakfast and soft drinks. It is possible to kayak with the dolphins, but this will cost extra.

Marina Bander Al-Rowdha

Location → Marina Bander Al-Rowdha · Sidab | 24 737 288
Web/email → www.marinaoman.com | Map Ref → 13-E4

Marina Bander Al-Rowdha offers dolphin sightseeing excursions a little way off the coast of Muscat. For more information, see Activity Tours [p.142].

Muscat Diving and Adventure Centre

Location → Nr Radisson Hotel · Al Khuwayr | 24 485 663
Web/email → www.holiday-in-oman.com | Map Ref → 7-B3

This upbeat tour operator can take you out to sea to spot dolphins, and estimate the chances of a sighting at around 90%. The most common species seen are Common, Spinner and Bottlenose. The boat seats up to ten people, and departs daily at 07:00, 11:00 and 15:00. Cruises last for three to four hours, and the cost per person is RO 20 (which includes soft drinks).

Oman Dive Centre

Location → Bandar Al Jissah · Al Bustan | 99 340 096
Web/email → www.diveoman.com.om | Map Ref → 15-E3

Every morning, the Oman Dive Centre organises a boat trip to go and spot dolphins off the coast of Muscat. Your chances of seeing Dolphins (usually Common, Spinner, Bottlenose or Indo-Pacific species) are high at any time of year. Your chances of seeing whales are not as high, although they have been spotted from time to time (usually from December to February). The boat trip includes breakfast served onboard.

Oman Whale & Dolphin Research Group

Location → Various locations | 24 696 912
Web/email → www.whalecoastoman.com | Map Ref → na

This group of volunteers is involved in the conservation of whales and dolphins. They undertake scientific research and collect information about the marine life of Oman. They also give up their spare time to work with tour companies (such as Arabian Sea Safaris and Z Tours), giving talks to tour groups or helping to maximise the chances of a sighting. They keep records of all sightings and strandings, and if any dolphins or whales wash up on the beaches, they will investigate to ascertain the cause of death. If you find a beached whale or dolphin, contact either Robert Baldwin of the Oman Natural History Museum (24 604 500) or Mohammed Al Barwani (24 566 664).

Out of Oman

UAE Overview

The United Arab Emirates borders the Sultanate of Oman to the north-west. It is a small country covering an area of 83,600 km², with a population of 4,041,000 at the end of 2003 (UAE Ministry of Planning). Made up of seven emirates, with the Abu Dhabi emirate as the capital, the others are Ajman, Dubai, Ras Al Khaimah, Sharjah, Umm Al Quwain and Fujairah, the only emirate entirely on the east coast of the peninsula. The Emirates were once independent states but came together in 1972 on the withdrawal of the British from the region to create the Federation. Each emirate has a certain degree of autonomy and rules and regulations may differ slightly between them.

The UAE has a reputation as being the most relaxed and westernised country in the Gulf. Dubai, in particular, is a shopper's paradise and is well set up to cater for a large tourist industry with plenty of hotels, shopping centres, sports activities, etc., as well as an amazing array of restaurants, bars and nightclubs.

Abu Dhabi is about five hours by car from Muscat, while Dubai is about four hours. There are two crossing points by road into the Emirates which are open to expatriates – one at Hatta and one at Buraimi/Al Ain. Dubai, Abu Dhabi and Al Ain have excellent airports and flights from Muscat are frequent.

The exchange rate at the time of publication was RO 1 to Dhs.10. Visitors to the UAE will find the Dubai Explorer and the Abu Dhabi Explorer useful guides to the region.

Visas

Visa requirements for entering the UAE vary greatly between different nationalities, and regulations should always be checked before travelling, since details can change with little or no warning.

All visitors, except Arab Gulf Co-operation Council nationals (Bahrain, Kuwait, Qatar, Oman and Saudi Arabia), require a visa. However, citizens of the countries listed below automatically get a visit visa stamp in their passport upon arrival. In most cases this will be valid for 60 days. If you plan to extend your stay you will either need to renew this visit visa, or get a new one by leaving and re-entering the country.

> **Visa on Arrival**
>
> *Citizens of Andorra, Australia, Austria, Belgium, Brunei, Canada, Cyprus, Denmark, Finland, France, Germany, Greece, Hong Kong, Iceland, Ireland, Italy, Japan, Liechtenstein, Luxembourg, Malaysia, Malta, Monaco, The Netherlands, New Zealand, Norway, Portugal, San Marino, Singapore, Spain, Sweden, Switzerland, United Kingdom, United States of America and Vatican City now receive an automatic, visit visa on arrival in Dubai.*

Expat residents of other nationalities who meet certain criteria may obtain a non-renewable 30-day visa on arrival. Residents of Oman, of certain nationalities, may enter the UAE on a free of charge entry permit.

Tourist nationalities (such as Eastern European, Chinese, South African and members of the former Soviet Union) may obtain a 30 day, non-renewable tourist visa sponsored by a local entity, such as a hotel or tour operator, before entry into the UAE. The fee is Dhs.100 for the visa and an additional Dhs.20 for delivery. The visa must be applied for before the visitor enters the country.

Other visitors may apply for an entry service permit (for 14 days exclusive of arrival/departure days), valid for use within 14 days of the date of issue and non-renewable. Once this visa expires the visitor must remain out of the country for 30 days before re-entering on a new visit visa. The application fee for this visa is Dhs.120, plus an additional Dhs.20 delivery charge.

For those travelling onwards to a destination other than that of original departure, a special transit visa (up to 96 hours) may be obtained free of charge through any airline operating in the UAE.

Costs: Companies may levy a maximum of Dhs.50 extra in processing charges for arranging visas. The DNATA (Dubai National Airline Travel Agency) visa delivery service costs an extra Dhs.20.

Visit visas are valid for 30 or 60 days, not one or two calendar months, and as the arrival and departure dates are counted in this number it is safer to consider the length as 28 or 58 days. If you overstay,

Exploring

Weekend Breaks

there is a Dhs.100 fine for each day plus a Dhs.100 fee. If you overstay a significantly long time, the matter may go to court where a judge will decide the penalty. Also, Israeli nationals or travellers whose passports bear Israeli stamps will be denied a visa.

Abu Dhabi Emirate

Since the discovery of oil in 1958 Abu Dhabi, the capital emirate of the UAE, has become a modern infrastructure – visitors will find a city of skyrise buildings, a large port, corniche and hotels, hospitals and all the latest facilities. Al Ain is the second most important town in the Emirate, while the Liwa oasis to the south is made up of a number of small villages over a large area. It lies on the border with Oman and shares the Buraimi Oasis with the Sultanate.

Dubai

Dubai has a reputation in the Middle East for being a liberal and 'happening' place and it certainly has its far share of cosmopolitan restaurants, bars and nightclubs. It is also often described as the 'shopping capital of the Middle East' and is sure to satisfy even the most devoted shoppers.

Two areas of interest outside the main city are Hatta and the Hatta pools, which are nestled in the Hajar Mountains very near the border with Oman. Jebel Ali is south of the city on the road to Abu Dhabi and is famous for its large port and industrial complex.

Ras Al Khaimah

This is the most northerly emirate, sharing a border with Mussandam. Like all the coastal cities it relied on a seafaring existence and served as an important port for pearling, trading and fishing. It is one of the more fertile and green areas of the UAE and, although a quiet town, is a good starting point for exploring the surrounding countryside and the Hajar Mountains. It is also the start and finish point for a spectacular trip through the mountains via Wadi Bih to Dibba on the east coast.

Fujairah

This is the only emirate located entirely on the east coast and is a beautiful relaxing spot, with golden beaches and bordered by the Hajar Mountains. It is often known as the youngest of the Emirates since it was a part of Sharjah until 1952. It is popular with residents from the west coast of the Emirates, as well as Omanis.

Local attractions include the old fort, which is about 300 years old, Fujairah Museum, Fujairah Heritage Village, Kalba Lagoon and the oldest mosque in the UAE.

Khorfakkan

Another popular destination for a quick break, Khorfakkan is a charming town, set in a bay and flanked by two headlands – hence its alternative name – 'the Creek of the Two Jaws'. It is part of the Emirate of Sharjah and has an important modern port. Ships discharging their cargo here can save a further 48-hour journey through the Strait of Hormuz to the west coast.

Weekend Breaks

Hotels [p.24]
Out of Muscat [p.136]
Tours & Sightseeing [p.134]

Taking a break from routine, even just for a couple of days, can help tide you over until your next long holiday. There are many beautiful locations in and around Oman that you can get to in a few hours (or less) for a relaxing weekend break.

Below is a list of hotels in Oman that are suitable for short trips. If you want to go further afield, you can hop over the border for a weekend of glitz, glamour and shopping in Dubai or Abu Dhabi, where there's no shortage of luxury hotels, white sandy beaches, excellent restaurants and enormous shopping malls. For more information on planning your weekend break in the UAE refer to the table of hotels below, and get hold of a copy of the *Dubai Explorer* or the *Abu Dhabi Explorer.*

Hotels in this region almost always give discounts on the published or 'rack' rate. And during the summer months there are often promotions and price cuts. When making a hotel reservation, check whether the rate includes breakfast or whether it is for the room only. Also, check whether the various

Crossing the Border

As lovely as Oman is, a weekend break to Dubai will satisfy all your 'bright lights, big city' longings. And when you do cross the border, make sure you take a copy of the Dubai Explorer – it's so full of useful info that it's a more important travel document than your passport!

taxes and service charges are included – these can add a whopping 20% to your bill otherwise.

Weekend Break Summary

Sultanate of Oman (+968)

Emirates	Hotel	Phone	Email	Rate (RO)
Al Buraimi	Al Buraimi Hotel	25 652 010	alburaimihotel@yahoo.com	21.5 (+17%)
Barka 250km	Al Sawadi Resort	26 795 545	sales@alsawadibeach.com	50 (+17%) (B)
Muscat	Al Bustan Palace	24 799 666	albustan@interconti.com	129 (+17%)
450km	Chedi Muscat, The	24 505 035	chedimuscat@ghmhotels.com	85 (+17%) (B)
	Crowne Plaza	24 560 100	cpmct@omantel.net.om	41 (+17%)
	Grand Hyatt Muscat	24 602 888	hyattmct@omantel.net.om	98 (+17.4%)
	Holiday Inn Muscat	25 587 123	mcthinn@omantel.net.om	34 (+17%)
	InterContinental	24 600 500	muscat@interconti.com	56 (+17%)
	Mercure Al Falaj	24 702 311	accorsales@omanhotels.com	25 (+17%)
	Radisson SAS	25 505381	sales@mcdzh.rdsas.com	37 (+17%)
	Sheraton Oman	24 799 899	sheraton@omantel.net.om	52 (+17.4%)

Mussandam

Khasab 150km	Golden Tulip Khasab	26 730 777	info@goldentulipkhasab.com	35 (B)
Nizwa 350km	Falaj Daris	25 410 500	fdhnizwa@omantel.net.om	29.5
Salalah	Holiday Inn Salalah	23 235 333	hinnsll@omantel.netcom	40 (+17%)
1,450km	Salalah Hilton Resort	23 211 234	sllbc@omantel.net.om	40 (+17%)
Sohar 250km	Sohar Beach Hotel	26 841 111	soharhtl@omantel.net.om	35 (+17%)
Sur 650km	Sur Mercure	25 543 777	reservationssur@omanhotels.com	28 (B)

United Arab Emirates (+971)

				(Dhs)
Abu Dhabi	Abu Dhabi Hilton	02 681 1900	auhhitw@emirates.net.ae	900 (+16%)
180km	Beach Rotana	02 644 3000	beach.hotel@rotana.com	1,050 (+16%)
	InterContinental	02 666 6888	auhha-reservation@interconti.com	950 (16%)
	Le Meridien	02 644 6666	meridien@emirates.net.ae	1,300 (+16%)
	Mafraq Hotel	02 582 2666	mafraq@emirates.net.ae	550 (+16%)
	Millennium	02 626 2700	sales.abudhabi@mill-cop.com	550 (+16%)
	Sheraton Abu Dhabi	02 677 3333	sheraton@emirates.net.ae	720 (+16%)
Al Ain	Al Ain Rotana	03 754 5111	alain.hotel@rotana.com	700 (+16%)
130km	Al Ain Hilton	03 768 6666	alhilton@emirates.net.ae	350 (+16%)
	InterContinental	03 768 6686	aanha@icalain.ae	696 (+16%)
	Mercure Grand	03 783 8888	resa@mercure-alain.ae	520 inc
Jazira 60km	Al Diar Jazira Beach	02 562 9100	reservations@jaziraresort.net	750 (+16%)
Dubai	Al Maha Desert Resort	04 832 9900	almaha@emirates.net.ae	5,880 inc
	Al Qasr Hotel	04 366 8888	reservations@madinatjumeirah.com	2,500 (+20%)
	Bab Al Shams	04 832 6699	info@babalshams.com	2,040 inc
	Jumeirah Beach Hotel	04 348 0000	reservations@thejumeirahbeachhotel.com	1,850 (+20%)
	Mina A' Salam	04 366 8888	reservations@madinatjumeirah.com	1,850 (+20%)
	One&Only Royal Mirage	04 399 9999	reservations@one&onlyroyalmirage.ae	1,560 (+20%)
	Ritz-Carlton Dubai, The	04 399 4000	rcdubai@emirates.net.ae	2,150 inc
Hatta 110km	Hatta Fort	04 852 3211	hfh@jaihotels.com	780 inc

Note   Rate = Price of one double room; +xx% = plus tax; B = Inclusive of breakfast.
The above prices are peak season rack rates. However, many hotels will offer a discount off the rack rate if asked.

Exploring

Weekend Breaks

YOU CLICK
PHOTOCENTRE
You needn't go anywhere else
OTHER SERVICES
Developing & Printing
Digital Printing
Custom Enlargements
Image Archiving
Framing
Lamination
Mounting
Canvas
Slide Processing
GSM Phone Prints
Retouching
WE PRINT
Whether you click with cameras or mobile phones. Digital or on film. Great pictures deserve to be preserved forever. And no one does that better than PHOTOCENTRE. No one. You get high quality prints at a low price and on-time delivery, every time.
Muscat, Sultanate of Oman
Ruwi (+968 24 831 162)
CCC (+968 24 561 015)
Zakher Shopping Mall (+968 24 479 296)
Zeenah

Shopping

EXPLORER

Highlights...

Mutrah Souk [p.184]

Considered by many to be the best souk in the Gulf, Mutrah Souk is a haven for bargain hunters, explorers and history lovers alike. You can lose yourself (quite literally) amongst the winding alleyways of shops and stalls where little has changed for hundreds of years. Almost anything can be found here, from ornate silver khanjars, frankincense and spices, to cheap plastic toys and mosque alarm clocks. The experience is not to be missed, and offers you a perfect opportunity to brush up on your haggling skills.

Clothing Sizes

Women's Clothing

Aust/NZ	8	10	12	14	16	18
Europe	36	38	40	42	44	46
Japan	5	7	9	11	13	15
UK	8	10	12	14	16	18
USA	6	8	10	12	14	16

Women's Shoes

Aust/NZ	5	6	7	8	9	10
Europe	35	36	37	38	39	40
France only	35	36	38	39	40	42
Japan	22	23	24	25	26	27
UK	3.5	4.5	5.5	6.5	7.5	8.5
USA	5	6	7	8	9	10

Men's Clothing

Aust/NZ	92	96	100	104	108	112
Europe	46	48	50	52	54	56
Japan	S	-	M	M	-	L
UK	35	36	37	38	39	40
USA	35	36	37	38	39	40

Men's Shoes

Aust/NZ	7	8	9	10	11	12
Europe	41	42	43	44.5	46	47
Japan	26	27	27.5	28	29	30
UK	7	8	9	10	11	12
USA	7.5	8.5	9.5	10.5	11.5	12.5

Measurements are approximate only; try before you buy

Shopping

Table of Contents

Shopping

Muscat is the shopping capital of Oman and offers a cosmopolitan range of shops and goods. From expensive boutiques to handicraft stalls and everything in between, shoppers are never far away from finding what they want. The tax-free status means that some items, like carpets, textiles and gold, are much cheaper than elsewhere. Many imported goods are comparably priced to other places in the world. The key to shopping like a pro in Muscat is to bargain where possible or wait for sales when discounts can be as high as 70% off the normal retail price.

Oman has some of the liveliest, most authentic and colourful traditional markets ('souks') in the region. Distinguished old men in their 'dishdashas' sit behind the counters in small shops, while bejewelled women in their 'abayas' haggle with authority. Modern shopping centres, replete with world-renowned brands and ample parking, are pivotal social settings for many residents and visitors. They provide air-conditioned entertainment for a mix of nationalities that are there to see and be seen, or just pass the time.

The busiest shopping times are Wednesday, Thursday and Friday nights when it can get a little too crowded, even for the serious shopper. Many shops have sales during the annual Muscat Festival in January and in the months covering the two Eid holidays. During Ramadan, some shops are open until midnight, supermarkets are packed to the brim with unbelievable amounts of food, and the queues are long, especially in the evenings. There are usually numerous promotions and raffles offered by shopping malls and even restaurants during these periods.

The following section covers the various shopping areas around Muscat and Salalah, and some towns in the interior noted for their traditional markets. It also provides relevant information for all shoppers – from what to buy to where to buy it, plus a few tips on how to stretch your rial.

Refunds and Exchanges

In general, there is no problem exchanging goods that are faulty or that you have changed your mind about as long as they are unworn, unused, preferably in their original packing, and you have the receipt. However, most retailers will only either exchange or give store credit, very few will give a full cash refund.

Some of the larger shops clearly display their refund policies (for example, underwear is non-returnable) and only allow exchanges for a limited period (usually seven days from date of purchase). Many international department stores are more proactive in their customer service policies, so for products that are more expensive, it may be best to stick with the big name shops.

Shop assistants are always willing to help and, in general, exchanging goods or getting store credit is an easy task. Unfortunately this is not usually the case when asking for a refund. If you insist on a refund, ask to see the manager or leave your number and ask the assistant to call you when they have spoken to their supervisor. You might have to do some chasing up but with a bit of persistence you can sometimes get your money back. Getting angry rarely works; it is better to be unfailingly polite at all times. If you really feel you've had a bad experience, see the following section on consumer rights.

Consumer Rights

Taking a retailer to court in Oman would be a very lengthy and costly procedure and could cause you a lot more stress than the original problem. First try to resolve the dispute with compromise, by negotiating for an exchange of goods or upgrade of services. You will probably have more success if you remain calm. If you do have a major problem that can't be sorted out by persistence or the inclusion of an Omani friend in the proceedings, try the Oman Association for Consumer Protection – they have offices at the Al Harthy Complex in Al Qurm. There is also a helpline for consumer complaints (24 817 013). You might struggle to get through, but they may be able to help you with your issue.

Shipping

Sending purchases abroad can be a tedious business but there are many shipping and cargo agencies that make it much easier. Items can be sent by sea freight (the least expensive option), air freight or courier. It is best to contact the agency directly as rates vary considerably – for contact details look in the Omantel Telephone Directory under 'Courier Services', 'Cargo Services' or 'Shipping Companies', or in the classified ads of local newspapers. Most airlines also have a cargo service division, but do not necessarily fly to the destination you want.

If you buy carpets or furniture, some shops may arrange shipping for you but always ask first – that antique wooden chest may not seem like such a bargain after adding in the shipping costs. Shops will sometimes issue a certificate stating that the item is worth less than it is to save you money on import duty. This is highly illegal, of course, but they seem to have no qualms about doing it. Ironically, it is easier to arrange for a whole houseful to be shipped than for a couple of boxes – what a great excuse to buy more!

How to Pay

You will have no problems paying for your shopping in Oman. International credit cards like Visa, MasterCard, Diner's Club and American Express are widely accepted by established retailers in Muscat and Salalah. Small traders in the souks and local convenience stores only take cash, though some jewellery shops in the Mutrah Souk will accept credit cards. You might be able to pay with postdated local cheques when purchasing expensive items like cars – but this all depends on your credentials and the reputation of the vendor.

Retailers will not look kindly on visitors who try to use their own currency; even dirhams from the UAE are usually refused. There are exchange houses in Al Qurm, Ruwi, Mutrah, City Centre in Muscat, and in Salalah. Money can be changed in hotels but the rate is usually less favourable than in exchange centres or banks.

For the best bargains, always keep some Omani rials with you – bigger discounts are given to those who pay cash.

Bargaining

Other options → Souks [p.182]

For many visitors, bargaining can be an alien and uncomfortable way of doing business but it is a time-honoured tradition in this part of the world. In the souk, you are expected to haggle and vendors will often drop the price substantially for a cash sale. In contrast to other countries, where you may be badgered into buying something after accepting a glass of mint tea, bargaining in Oman is less stressful and it can be great fun if you just relax and take your time. Sellers remain polite and normally do not push desperately for a sale.

The key to bargaining is to decide on how much you want to pay for the item (get an idea of the value by scouting other shops) and be prepared to walk away if you don't get it for that. Start with a customary greeting and ask the shop assistant how much it costs. In return, drop the price by about half and start the negotiations from there. At all times, remain polite and never use aggression as a bargaining tool.

Once you have agreed on a mutually beneficial price, you must buy the item as you have made a verbal contract. If you don't get the price you want, walking away will sometimes do the trick – it is not uncommon for a shop assistant to chase after you while reducing the price at every step.

Away from the souks or stores in Ruwi, bargaining is not common practice although many shops will give a set discount, saying that the price shown is 'before discount'. In some instances, even if you don't ask for a discount, the assistant will pass it on to you anyway – this can be a welcome surprise when it is time to pay.

What & Where to Buy

You can get most things you need in Muscat although the areas are a bit scattered across the city and you'll need a car or taxi to move from one to another. The following section covers the main categories of items to be found in Oman, from beer to biscuits, clothes to cars, and where you can find them.

Alcohol

Other options → Drinks [p.229]
Liquor Licence [p.51]
On the Town [p.261]

Anyone aged over 21 years can buy alcohol at licensed bars, restaurants and some clubs for consumption on the premises. However to buy alcohol for home consumption you need to have a liquor licence, which looks like a mini passport and has to be requested by your employer. Not all companies will assist their employees with this – it depends what kind of business it is and their attitude towards alcohol. Muslims are not allowed to apply for a liquor licence. For more information on how to get your licence, see [p.50] in the New Residents section.

Alcohol is not sold in supermarkets, but is available in the many specialist stores around Muscat. These are usually hidden away and there is no indication from the outside that these shops sell alcohol. Look for names like African and Eastern LLC, Gulf

AMOUAGE

The most valuable perfume in the world

To discover the grandeur of ultra-luxury Amouage, please visit our Perfumery between Saturday and Wednesday.

Experience the handcrafted ultra luxury of Amouage at our boutiques at Sabco Centre and Muscat City Centre.

www.amouage.com
Tel: 24540757, 24540161

Supply Services, Oman United Agencies (OUA) and Onas. Ask around because everyone knows where they are. You can buy alcohol on the black market, but this is a bit of a dodgy practice and can't be recommended. And remember, the cheaper the tipple, the worse the hangover!

It is illegal to transport alcohol unless you are taking it from the shop or the airport duty free to your house (even then you should make sure you have a receipt in case you are stopped by the police). Drinking alcohol in public places is not allowed and there are stiff penalties for drinking and driving. If you do decide to take a few drinks with you on your next wadi trip be discreet about it and stay well away from any villages.

Pick up supplies at the bottle shop!

Alcohol

African & Eastern LLC	Al Khuwayr	24 486 513
	Ruwi	24 799 045
	MSQ	24 602 121
	Salalah	23 467 817
Gulf Supply Services	Al Khuwayr	24 483 122
	MSQ	24 696 869
	Ruwi	24 810 709
Oman United Agencies	Ghala	24 504 109
P.ix	MSQ	24 603 892
	Ruwi	24 704 031
Onas	Al Qurm	24 565 467
	Ruwi	24 817 669

Arabian Souvenirs

Other options → Carpets [p.158]

Shopping for presents in Oman is really tough because you always want to buy one for yourself as well. And why shouldn't you? The only thing you have to fear is exceeding your baggage allowance.

Traditional Arabic items make good gifts and ornaments for the home. Popular local gift items include the traditional coffee pot and small decorated cups used for drinking 'kahwa' (Arabic coffee), incense burners, wedding chests and traditional Omani khanjars (daggers). Khanjars are almost always sold encased in an elaborately wrought sheath, and are arguably the most recognisable symbol of Oman – if you do buy one though, make sure you pack it in your suitcase rather than your hand luggage.

Incense Burners

Incense burners are usually small clay pots in which various items are burned to give off a distinctive smell. Different regions of Oman have their own unique incense burners. For example, the burners found in Dhofar are painted in very bright colours. When teamed with a packet of frankincense or 'oudh', these burners make excellent gifts.

Other souvenirs that should evoke memories of your time in Arabia are miniature dhows crafted from wood or silver, Quran holders, pottery camels, the traditional hat worn by Omani men (a 'kumah'), natural or glazed clay pots and jars from Bahla, woven milking baskets with leather bases, and ancient rifles. The authenticity and quality of these items is usually directly proportionate to the price.

Omani wedding jewellery, crafted in heavy silver, makes a good souvenir and occasionally you'll find a rare piece or collector's item.

Many of the items are made in India but sold as the real thing – some are easy to spot as fakes, others less so. Although the souks generally offer the best buys, it may be difficult to tell how genuine and old a particular article is unless you are an expert in Omani crafts.

The Omani National Heritage Gallery, near the InterContinental Hotel in Shati Al Qurm, is a government run shop that sells genuine Omani craft items. It was set up to keep traditional skills such as pottery and weaving alive in the face of modern development.

The shop staff can tell you all about the stock and give you a full insight into where a particular piece originated and how long it took to create. The goods are more expensive than in other places but they are genuine. Plus you can be sure you are helping to keep these traditions alive by providing income for the people who practise them.

If you want a comprehensive reminder of Omani crafts, you can pick up the hefty, highly informative and beautifully illustrated *The Craft Heritage of Oman*, a two-volume coffee table book that covers everything on the subject.

Oman Heritage Gallery

For tourists who love humorous 'kitsch', there are loads of bargains. In the souks you'll find singing camels (singing either the Macarena, or 'Habibi' for a more authentic feel), T-shirts (featuring the adventures of Tintin and Snowy in Oman), the famous mosque alarm clock, a brightly coloured plastic mosque that wakes you up with the call to prayer. Don't leave Oman without one!

Arabian Souvenirs

Oman Heritage Gallery	Jawharat A'Shati Complex	24 696 974
Sabco Souk	Sabco Commercial Centre	24 566 701

Art

Other options → Art Classes [p.218]
Art Galleries [p.122]
Art Supplies [p.155]

Muscat has a reasonable selection of galleries selling mainly paintings and a few selected pieces of sculpture, jewellery and pottery. These are often produced by local or expatriate artists in a variety of styles. Foreign artists and photographers with an interest in Omani culture and landscapes often hold exhibitions in museums and galleries; check the local papers or The Week for details of upcoming events. Mutrah Souk, Capital Commercial Centre (CCC) and Al Harthy Complex (both in Al Qurm), the Omani Fine Arts Society, and the Bait Muzna Gallery are treasure troves of local and Arabian art. For more information, see Art Galleries on [p.122].

Art

Al Jawahiz Trading Co	Al Harthy Complex	24 562 269
Bait Muzna Gallery	Nr Bait Zubair Museum	24 739 204
Oman Society for Fine Arts	Nr Ramada Hotel	24 694 969
Yiti Art Gallery	Capital Commercial Centre	24 564 297

Art Supplies

Other options → Art [p.155]
Art Classes [p.218]
Art Galleries [p.122]

Shah Nagardas Manji stores, in Al Qurm, Madinat As Sultan Qaboos and Ruwi, carry basic art supplies like oil paints, acrylics, pastels, brushes and drawing paper but you may not always find what you want. Serious artists are better off bringing their materials from home or ordering over the internet. When you're ready to display your work, the many framing shops in Ruwi High Street provide quick, professional and inexpensive service.

Art Supplies

Office Supplies Co. LLC	Al Qurm	24 563 033
Oman Society for Fine Arts	Nr Ramada Hotel	24 694 969
Shah Nagardas Manji	Al Qurm	24 562 656
	Madinat As Sultan Qaboos	24 600 532
	Ruwi	24 703 803

Beach Wear

Beach wear sold in Muscat generally veers towards the no-nonsense, one-piece styles for competitive swimmers rather than teeny-weeny bikinis for lounging around the pool. BHS, Woolworths, Marks & Spencer and Monsoon have good ranges, but if you want something unique it is better to buy abroad or order online. Sports shops carry a

Shopping

Art • Beach Wear

limited selection of beach wear for children. You can get beautiful but inexpensive sarongs (made in Thailand) and fashionable imitation label swimming shorts for men in Mutrah Souk and on Ruwi High Street.

Beach Wear		
BHS	Beh Sabco Centre	24 562 456
Marks & Spencer	Markaz Al Bahja	24 536 035
Monsoon	Muscat City Centre	24 558 902
SLT Beach Shop	Al Khuwayr	24 489 303
Woolworths	Muscat City Centre	24 558 131

Books

Other options → Libraries [p.223]
Second-hand Items [p.170]

The range of imported books and magazines available in Muscat is relatively limited due to the laws of supply and demand. To bring a title into the country, it must first be checked for its content, so often the latest releases are out of date before they make it to the shelves. The situation seems to have improved recently, so either the authorities are getting more relaxed in applying censorship rules, or more efficient! Prices for paperbacks are almost the same as in other countries.

Latest releases aside, there are some beautiful coffee table books full of inspired photographs of Oman and its people – these are really good for taking home to show people that you don't live in a country filled with nothing but sand.

Foreign newspapers and magazines are flown in regularly but are expensive. Magazines that contain illicit material are censored with the aid of a black marker pen, as opposed to being banned completely. Subscription magazines may take longer to reach you, because some poor soul has to go through the racy pictures of scantily clad women and dress them up with ink!

The Family Bookshop (with branches in Al Qurm and in Madinat As Sultan Qaboos) and Turtle's (Lulu Hypermarket and Seeb Airport Departure Lounge) cater primarily for English speakers, but also stock Arabic titles. They have good selections of children's books. Al Batra Bookshop (Al Wadi Commercial Centre and Sabco) stocks mostly reference books, hobby books, some children's books and older fiction titles. Most of the larger hotels have small bookshops that stock a limited choice of fiction, travel books and books on Oman. Supermarkets like Carrefour, Al Fair and The Sultan Centre also

carry a reasonable selection of books and magazines. If you can't find what you're looking for, you can order books online although the cost of postage may double the price.

A little out of the ordinary is House of Prose in the Al Wadi Commercial Centre, Al Qurm. This is a second-hand bookshop stocking mainly fiction, travel and biography titles. A buy-back policy offers half price on any of their books returned in good condition (remember to keep your receipt), and a 'look out list' is useful if you have a request for a particular title. They stock about 20,000 books in Muscat and another 20,000 at their shop in Dubai and books can be sold back to either store. Alternatively, the American Women's Group holds periodic second-hand book sales and exchanges.

Bikini Babes!

Wearing bikinis on the public beaches may offend local sensibilities, so wear them only in private beach clubs or in hotels. One-piece swimsuits are a safer option but even then always carry a long shirt with you for a quick cover up, unless you don't mind being stared at by the locals.

Books		
Al Batra Bookshop	Al Wadi Commercial Centre	24 563 662
	Sabco Commercial Centre	24 568 460
Al Fair	Shati Al Qurm	24 561 905
Al Marifa Bookshop	Nr Naseem Hotel	24 713 607
Al Mutanabbi Bookshop	Al Wadi Commercial Centre	24 563 662
Carrefour	Muscat City Centre	24 558 140
Family Bookshop	MSQ	24 786 461
	Nr Sabco Centre	24 564 391
House of Prose	Al Wadi Commercial Centre	24 564 356
New Academic Bookshop	Ruwi	24 830 006
Sultan Centre	Al Qurm	24 567 666
Turtle's	Seeb Airport	24 510 478
	Lulu Hypermarket	24 584 353

Camera Equipment

Other options → Electronics & Home Appliances [p.161]

Those who enjoy photography will find that Oman has a reasonable selection of cameras and accessories (mainly in Muscat) both for the professional and the amateur, although not all the models of a particular brand may be available. Prices are comparable to those in duty free shops.

Shopping

Books • Camera Equipment

Abstracts of Oman

Department stores usually have a small photography section with cameras from Nikon, Canon, Pentax, Olympus and Samsung. Professional photographers or serious hobbyists should check out Salam Stores in Al Qurm. They carry medium format cameras (Bronica and Signa), lenses and camera accessories like tripods from Manfrotto. They will also help to install your dark room, provide a Durst enlarger and train you in its use.

For the average holiday snapper there are plenty of choices. Most electronics shops sell a variety of film and digital point-and-shoot cameras. You should be able to find the brand and price of camera to suit your needs. Sales staff are helpful and patient even with technophobes! If you find a camera you want to buy, try haggling over the price a little – it might just work.

Foto Magic is a reliable outlet for buying and developing films, and downloading images from digital cameras, they can even print out pictures on greeting cards, T-shirts or mugs. They have a branch in most shopping areas.

Camera Equipment

BOSCH	Nr Sabco Centre	24 566 557
Capital Store LLC	Ruwi	24 561 888
Foto Magic	Ruwi	24 796 256
OHI Electronics	Al-Araimi Complex	24 561 459
Photocentre P.148	Ruwi	24 814 752
Salam Studio & Stores LLC	Nr Al Qurm R/A	24 564 071

Cards & Stationery

Other options → Art Supplies [p.155]
Books [p.156]

Larger supermarkets like Carrefour, Sultan Centre and Al Fair carry a good supply of English greetings cards, wrapping paper and stationery. Specialist card shops such as Carlton Cards can be found in Sabco and Muscat City Centre. Birthdays and most holidays (Christmas, Easter, Mother's Day) are catered for and you can surprise your friends back home with special cards for Eid! You may find that cards here are a bit on the slushy or sentimental side, but if you prefer sending jokey cards you'll probably find a wider range in Carlton Cards or the Sultan Centre.

While postcards can cost as little as 100 baisas, greeting cards and wrapping paper are more expensive. Cards with Omani themes, which are produced by local artists, can be found in museum gift shops and at Murtada AK Trading in Mutrah

souk. Aside from costing less, they are good quality and make original alternatives to standard greetings cards.

Pick up a postcard

Cards & Stationery

Al Fair	Shati Al Qurm	24 561 905
Al Fikri Centre	Al Khuwayr	24 478 870
Carlton Cards	Muscat City Centre	24 558 887
	Sabco Commercial Centre	24 562 799
Carrefour	Muscat City Centre	24 558 140
Murtada AK Trading	Mutrah Souk	24 711 632
Sultan Centre	Al Qurm	24 567 666

Carpets

Other options → Arabian Souvenirs [p.154]
Bargaining [p.152]

Weaving is one of Oman's major handicrafts and skills have been passed down through the generations. Camel hair, goat hair, sheep wool and cotton are used in weaving, either in their natural state or dyed with plant dyes or murex shells. Designs are usually simple stripes and occasionally geometric figures. You can find local carpets in the Omani National Heritage Gallery in Shati Al Qurm, or buy them directly from the weavers on the long, winding road to Jebel Shams (a 1.5m x 2.5m rug of sheep wool will cost around RO 30). To learn more about this handicraft, get a copy of the book *Traditional Spinning and Weaving in the Sultanate of Oman*.

Imported carpets, mainly from countries such as Turkey, Iran, Pakistan, Central Asia and China, are easy to find in Muscat. Apart from carpets in a variety of designs and colours, you can also buy camel bags and cushion covers (either stuffed or unstuffed).

All of the shopping centres have at least one carpet shop – good news for those people who like to shop in an air-conditioned environment. It is not that easy to find good carpets in other regions, although Salalah and Nizwa may have a few.

Carpet shopping can be a minefield for those who know little about the product, so it is a good idea to read up about it first and visit a number of shops to get an overview of designs and price ranges. The quality of the carpet is reflected in the price, with silk being more expensive than wool and cotton. There is also a significant difference between hand-made and machine-made carpets – hand-made carpets are more uneven in design and weaving, and are usually more expensive. You will also pay more for carpets with more knots per square inch than those with less.

Magic carpets

Carpets

Gulf Shells Trading	Al-Araimi Complex	24 571 630
Oman Heritage Gallery	Shati Al Qurm	24 696 974
Oriental Carpets & Handicrafts	Al Wadi Commercial Centre	24 564 786
Persian Carpets LLC	Al Wadi Commercial Centre	24 562 139

Many shops sell authentic antique carpets from Iran or Afghanistan, and will provide you with a certificate stating the age and value. You'll also find a good choice of Turkish kilims.

Bargaining is an expected stage in the buying process, you'll disappoint the seller if you don't even try (see a guide to bargaining on [p.152]). The seller will elaborately roll out countless carpets for you to view, but don't let this make you feel that you are obliged to buy one.

Some carpet shops will let their regular customers take a carpet home for a few days, to 'try it out' with your furniture.

Cars

Other options → Buying a Vehicle [p.88]

New arrivals in Oman are pleasantly surprised to find that cars are much cheaper here than in their own countries due to very low import duties. All the major car manufacturers have their own enormous showrooms displaying the latest and most expensive models. It is not uncommon for representatives from car dealers to pay you a visit at your new company, shortly after you arrive in Oman, to try to persuade you to buy a car from them. They can take care of all car buying headaches, such as financing and registration, and can have you on the road before the ink on your signature is dry. Good discounts are given towards the end of the year (when next year's model is due in the showroom) and during Ramadan. Japanese brands are popular and have an excellent resale value.

Most of the big garages have a second-hand car section. When buying a used car, make sure you see the car's service history and check that there have been no major accidents. You can pay an independent garage RO 10 to check the car for you for any mechanical faults.

Buying a car on Oman is easy and straightforward, and the most stressful part is probably the bargaining. Prices are never final so be firm if you are determined to close the sale. Remember, the dealer has paid the original owner a lot less than the price he is now asking you to pay.

If you decide to avoid the dealership route, keep an eye on supermarket notice boards or in the newspapers for used cars. Go with an Arabic-speaking friend to the car market in Wadi Kabir on Fridays and you may be lucky enough to find a used Porsche or 4 WD at a bargain price. Strangely, people occasionally stop each other at

Shopping

Cars

traffic lights or garages to ask if they want to sell their car – you could try this if you see something you really want.

Clothes

Other options → Beach Wear [p.155]
Kids' Items [p.166]
Lingerie [p.167]
Shoes [p.172]
Sporting Goods [p.172]
Tailoring [p.173]

Over the last few years the choice of clothes in Muscat has expanded dramatically. This is largely thanks to the opening of City Centre, which is quite far out of town past the Seeb Airport but well worth a trip. It has a number of international brand shops that you may recognise from home, including Mango, Monsoon, Promod, Splash, Woolworths and Next. These shops get new stock in every four to six months. There is also an inexpensive clothing section in Carrefour where serious bargain hunters have been known to find Gap sweatshirts for RO 3.

Oops

If you're a fashionista that puts Carrie Bradshaw to shame and we've missed any of your favourite frock shops then please let us know. Whether it's vintage chic or rocker retro from backstreet boutiques we'd love to know about your fashion faux pas! Maybe you even have a shop of your own?!

Markaz Al Bahja, past City Centre, has a Marks & Spencer and a few smaller shops where you can pick up some good bargains. Some of the places will even alter garments for you if necessary. Lulu Hypermarket and Safeer Hypermarket have an extensive clothes section and The Sultan Centre has limited range of sportswear.

The Al Qurm shopping area contains five shopping centres and numerous shops within walking distance of each other. City Plaza, just off the Al Khuwayr Roundabout, has Western-style clothes for all ages and sizes, as well as an accessories department that stocks earrings and necklaces, shoes and handbags at reasonable prices. Just make sure you look out for their frequent sales.

Signature designer stores for women have yet to make their debut in Muscat, although brand names can be found in some stores and surprisingly there are a number of shops in Al Qurm and City Centre that carry designer suits, jackets, shirts and casuals for men (try Tahani, Cerruti, Jazz and Moustach in Sabco). Capital Store carries suits by Loewe while Salam Stores is where you'll find Hugo Boss.

Shopping spree in the sale

Sana Stores and Ruwi High Street are good places to pick up ready-made outfits (especially Indian-style outfits such as saris or salwar kameez), textiles and cheap clothes for men, women and children.

If you want an alternative to buying off the peg, you could enlist the services of a tailor. Workmanship can vary but generally the quality is very high for the amount you pay. Once you've bought your choice of fabric, you can get an item copied from a photo, drawing or sample garment. Shop around, as some tailors charge RO 20 to copy a dress while others charge as little at RO 6, particularly in Ruwi. Word of mouth is usually the best way to find a tailor.

There are often good sales on during Ramadan and the Eid holidays, as well as in January and September/October when shops are clearing old stock to bring in the new. Discounts of 70% are not uncommon, although go prepared to sort through a rack of odd sizes and last season's styles.

Clothes		
Carrefour	Muscat City Centre	24 558 140
City Plaza	Madinat As Sultan Qaboos	24 698 988
Giordano	Muscat City Centre	24 558 139
Hang Ten	Muscat City Centre	24 558 870
Mango	Muscat City Centre	24 558 244
Marks & Spencer	Markaz Al Bahja	24 536 035
Monsoon	Muscat City Centre	24 558 902
Next	Muscat City Centre	24 558 801
Promod	Muscat City Centre	24 558 240
Woolworths	Muscat City Centre	24 558 131

Computers

Other options → Electronics &
Home Appliances [p.161]

There are many computer shops throughout Muscat
that are stocked up to the ceilings and staffed by
knowledgeable people. The best places to go are Al
Wadi Centre (Al Qurm), Computer Street in Ruwi and
Carrefour in City Centre. There are authorised
dealers for Apple (in Al Harthy Complex) and Dell
Computers (Al Khuwayr slip road). Prices are better
than in a lot of places but as usual, you must bargain
before you close the deal. Carrefour frequently has
good deals on laptops. You can also get offers in
shops where you tell the vendors what you want and
they'll set you up with PC, printer, scanner, desk and
chair, bring it all round and install it for you. Getting
computers fixed is easy and usually cheap, but you
may get frustrated that the deadline you are given is
not met. Outside Muscat you won't find much in
terms of technology and may have to wait a long
time for anything you order to come.

The Omani government has been clamping down on
the sale of pirated software since it became a
member of the World Trade Organization. But copies
of PC and PlayStation games are still sold in small
shops in Ruwi and Al Qurm for as little as RO 1.

Computers		
Al Morsad Trading Est.	Al-Araimi Complex	24 562 118
Carrefour	Muscat City Centre	24 558 140
Computer Point	Sabco Commercial Centre	24 565 848
Computer Xpress	Ruwi	24 835 631
Faisal Al Alawi Trading	Ruwi	24 702 812

Electronics & Home Appliances

Other options → Camera Equipment [p.156]
Computers [p.161]

Muscat's shops stock a reasonable selection of
electronics and home appliances, from well-known
brands to knock-offs. Prices are competitive and can
be brought down even further by bargaining. Wide
screen televisions and home theatre systems are
cheap compared to back home, although it is smart
to shop around comparing prices and brands,
whatever you want to buy. Warranties, after-sales
service, delivery and installation should all be
discussed before making any purchase. If you want
to take anything overseas with you, check on the
compatibility for your system or power supply.

Carrefour in City Centre has a wide range of
inexpensive items that are good for people
furnishing a house without an allowance from their
company, but prices are fixed. Larger appliances
such as washing machines and fridges are delivered
and installed free of charge. They also stock smaller
items such as stereos and kitchen appliances.
Twelve-month warranties are given on most items.

Ruwi High Street is a good place to go browsing and
compare prices since all the major showrooms are
here. If you don't see what you're looking for, ask,
as it may be hidden in the back room. Department
stores like Salman and Salam have home appliance
sections and frequent sales. People living in Salalah
can usually find good deals on appliances in town,
so there is no need to go all the way to Muscat.

For second-hand items, check supermarket
noticeboards or newspaper classifieds. Expats
who are leaving will often sell things at reasonable
prices in order to get rid of them quickly. This is
especially good if you're looking for large
appliances or air conditioners.

Electronics & Home Appliances		
Carrefour	Muscat City Centre	24 558 140
Salam Studio & Stores LLC	Nr Al Qurm R/A	24 564 071
Salman Stores	CCC	24 560 135
	Ruwi (1)	24 707 620
	Ruwi (2)	24 795 881
	Al-Araimi	24 566 286
	Seeb	24 422 213
	Salalah	23 293 146
Sony	Al-Araimi Complex	24 564 485

Eyewear

Other options → Opticians [p.81]
Sporting Goods [p.172]

The strength of the sun in Oman means that
sunglasses are a must. With long drives up and
down the motorway and days at the beach the sun
is often in your eyes. All kinds of sunglasses are
available in the malls, in Ruwi and in the souk,
from designer eyewear to rip-offs and everything in
between. Prices range from a few rials to many
hundreds and shops often have to cut prices to
compete so you might get a good bargain on
designer shades. Make sure you buy sunglasses
with 100% UVA and UVB protection. They must be
large and dark enough to protect the eyes from the
sun's glare.

Shopping

Computers · Eyewear

Shopping

Flowers · Food

Most shopping centres have opticians that will make prescription eyeglasses, prescription sunglasses and contact lenses (hard, soft, gas permeable and thoric). They usually offer free eye tests if you order from them. Disposable contact lenses and coloured contact lenses are also available. Opticians and pharmacies carry lens-cleaning solutions.

Eyewear

Al Ghazal Opticians	Sabco Commercial	
	Centre	24 563 546
Grand Opticals	Muscat City Centre	24 558 890
Oman Opticals	Al Khamis Plaza	24 562 981
Yateem Opticians	Al Khamis Plaza	24 563 716

Flowers

Other options → Gardens [p.163]

Given Oman's desert climate, flowers are a total luxury. There is a reasonable selection of florists in Al Qurm selling both fresh and dried flowers. Caravan in the Al Harthy Complex and The Flower Shop in Sabco have good selections. Bella La Rose in Capital Commercial Centre specialises in (you guessed it!) roses – a stunning arrangement of ten roses sprinkled with gold dust is reasonably priced at around RO 8. Simple bouquets can also be bought in The Sultan Centre, Al Fair and Carrefour, and cost between RO 2 and RO 7, depending on the number and kind of exotic flowers included.

To send flowers internationally it is much cheaper and faster to order online rather than through a local shop – very useful when you forget your mum's birthday!

Flowers

Al Fair	Shati Al Qurm	24 561 905
Bella La Rose	Capital Commercial Centre	24 566 766
Caravan	Al Harthy Complex	24 566 795
Carrefour	Muscat City Centre	24 558 140
La Bonita	Markaz Al Bahja	24 535 197
Sultan Centre	Al Qurm	24 567 666
The Flower Shop	Sabco Centre	24 560 043

Food

Other options → Health Food [p.164]

Oman has a good range of supermarkets and grocery stores that cater to the culinary needs of its multinational population. Although there are some speciality items that you won't find, most things are available somewhere if you look hard enough or ask around. Prices vary considerably, even among supermarkets. Items imported from Europe are sometimes double what they would cost in their country of origin and locally made counterparts (like dairy products) are much cheaper and just as good.

There are plenty of local convenience stores in residential areas, some of which even have a small produce section with onions, garlic, ginger, bananas and a limited range of vegetables. Carrefour, the Sultan Centre, Lulu Hypermarket, Al Fair and Safeer Hypermarket are the biggest and most popular supermarkets. There are smaller ones (Al Jadeed, Pic n Save and Family Shopping Centre) that are not as upmarket or modern, but that still carry a wide range of goods, sometimes even cheaper than in the hypermarkets. During Ramadan mountains of food, both fresh and tinned, are on sale – this is a good time to stock up on non-perishable food items. Even on non-festival days, offers seem to cater towards feeding large families – products are bundled up with sticky tape and sell for RO 1.

Carrefour, the well-known French hypermarket, sells everything from laptops and French cheeses to shoes and stationery, as well as an excellent selection of fresh produce – fruits, vegetables, meats and seafood. It has a good bakery where croissants, baguettes, European style breads, cakes, and Arabic and Indian sweets are made on the premises. It also has a separate small section for Filipino and Indian food. Al Fair supermarket, with branches in Qurm, Madinat As Sultan Qaboos, Jawharat A'Shati, Al Sarooj and Zakher Mall, is favoured by expats for British, European and Asian food. It is the only supermarket that sells frozen pork and other pork products like paté, proscuitto, salami and ham. Al Fair also has a 'Monday Market' when special items are on sale. The recently opened Lulu Hypermarket in Al

Time for the weekly shop

Ghubbrah has a good fresh produce section and sells fresh Thai herbs and grated coconut.

Petrol stations have also entered the food market with their own forecourt shops – these little shops sell necessities from quick, hot snacks to washing powder, and some are open 24 hours a day. Look out for Select shops at Shell stations, and Souk shops at Al Maha.

Food		
Al Fair	Shati Al Qurm	24 561 905
Al Jadeeda Supermarket	Al Khuwayr	24 601 010
Carrefour	Muscat City Centre	24 558 140
Family Shopping Centre	Ruwi	24 799 635
Lulu Hypermarket	Ruwi	24 811 449
Pic n Save	Al Khuwayr	24 479 211
Sultan Centre	Al Qurm	24 567 666

Fruit & Vegetables

Middle Eastern cuisine uses a lot of fresh fruits, vegetables and herbs, and produce coming from this region can be amazingly cheap. A carton of Jordanian oranges, for example, costs only one rial – a bonus for people who love freshly squeezed orange juice. Excluding imported fresh produce, fruits and vegetables are, in general, very affordable, especially if bought from places like the fruit and vegetable markets in Wadi Al Kabir (Ruwi), Mutrah and Al Mawaleh (on the road to Nizwa).

Fish

Go to the Mutrah fish souk early in the morning for the freshest catch off the boats. A browse among the stalls reveals an amazing variety of fish and seafood, some still squirming or struggling to get out of the baskets. If you're in the Al Azaiba beach area, the fishermen may sell their daily catch. The larger supermarkets also carry fresh seafood and fish (whole, fillet or steaks) in sterile surroundings.

Vegetarians

Vegetarians should not have too much difficulty finding suitable food products in Oman. The proliferation of Asian expatriates means there are some excellent vegetarian restaurants in town. Fresh and imported fruits and vegetables are widely available and cheap, especially in open-air markets. Spices and nuts imported from all over the world are sold by the scoop in large supermarkets. Al Fair also carries some soya based products, but the choice is limited.

Gardens

Other options → Flowers [p.162]
Hardware & DIY [p.163]

Gardening in the heat requires passion and dedication, if you have these then you can find everything you need. Most of the good garden centres are roadside open-air areas on the road towards Seeb Town. They open in the morning until about 13:00 and again from 16:00 to 21:00. The staff can offer good advice, and plants are not expensive. There are also some nurseries in Muscat that sell indoor plants, bougainvilleas, border plants and brightly coloured seasonal plants. The Sultan Centre and Al Fair also stock some pot plants.

You can buy glazed and unglazed clay pots from Bahla, some of which seem too decorative to merely put plants in. Garden furniture is available in many styles upstairs at City Plaza, and inexpensive plastic garden furniture can be bought in The Sultan Centre, Carrefour and on Ruwi High Street. Again, look on the supermarket notice boards because expats going back to cooler climates are unlikely to take their outdoor furniture with them.

Gardens		
Alaas Services & Trdg	Majan House	24 482 070
Al Fair	Shati Al Qurm	24 561 905
Bahjat Ghala Trading	Ghala	24 502 988
Carrefour	Muscat City Centre	24 558 140
City Plaza	Nr Al Khuwayr R/A	24 698 988
Fahmy Furniture	Al Khuwayr	24 489 812
Palms Garden Centre	Nr Fort R/A	24 546 349
Sultan Centre	Al Qurm	24 567 666
Truckoman	Al Wutayyah	24 565 248
Wadi Adai Garden Centre	Nr Hatat House R/A	na

Hardware & DIY

Other options → Outdoor Goods [p.169]

DIY enthusiasts can have fun browsing Honda Street in Ruwi, a long street of nothing but hardware, tools, paints and construction materials. Parking can be a problem, particularly on Thursdays. Carrefour, Sultan Centre, Safeer and Lulu Hypermarket also have some DIY equipment, but the smaller shops are sometimes better because you can negotiate the price. The shops have counters directly inside the door, so you have to ask for what you want rather than browse around looking for it.

Shopping

Gardens • Hardware & DIY

If you are not inclined to put up your own shelves, ask in the shops and someone can come round and do it for a couple of rials. DIY furniture bought in City Plaza is assembled in your home free of charge.

Hardware & DIY		
Carrefour	Muscat City Centre	24 558 140
Durrat Al Sahil Est.	Nr Al Ghubbrah R/A	24 592 232
Lulu Hypermarket	Ruwi	24 811 449
Safeer Hypermarket	Al Azaiba	24 496 019
Sultan Centre	Nr Al Harthy Complex	24 567 666

Health Food

Other options → Food [p.162]
Health Clubs [p.217]

Organic food is almost impossible to find and specialist shops are yet to arrive in Oman. Al Fair has some non-dairy, low fat, low calorie products but these are usually mixed in with the regular items. The Sultan Centre also has a very limited range in its dietetic section.

Health addicts might find it hard to get all the supplements and vitamins they need but Muscat Pharmacy, in Al Sarooj, is probably the best bet. The supermarkets have a limited selection of multivitamins for kids and adults, but check the sell by dates. Sports enthusiasts who swear by protein and food supplements should check out Sport One in CCC.

Health Food		
Al Fair	Shati Al Qurm	24 561 905
Muscat Pharmacy & Stores LLC	Ruwi	24 814 501
Sport One	Capital Commercial Centre	24 563 230
Sultan Centre	Al Qurm	24 567 666

Home Furnishings & Accessories

Other options → Furnishing Accommodation [p.70]
Hardware & DIY [p.163]

It is possible to furnish a house quite cheaply in Oman although you may have trouble finding what you want if your tastes are on the simple or modern sides. On the Al Khuwair service road, parallel to Sultan Qaboos Street, are huge shops selling what Europeans call 'Arabic Style' furniture, but confusingly Arabs call it 'European Style" (think plastic horses, mirrors looming over you on your headboard and bright sofas with silver carved lion's feet legs). You can dilute the gaudiness of these pieces by ordering them in different colours or sizes to the display models. These shops also stock curtains and orthopaedic mattresses. City Plaza, just around the corner, sells wooden and leather furniture imported from Malaysia and India, and houses a branch of Home Centre. The Danish shop ID Design, in Markaz Al Bahja, sells Scandinavian furniture. Watch out for the sales during Ramadan and around September.

There are some excellent shops selling wooden furniture, sometimes rather dubiously called antique shops. Most items are mass-produced in India and artificially aged. There are a few furniture shops in Al Qurm, around Al-Araimi and Sabco. Marina (in Al-Araimi) and Bombay (in Markaz Al Bahja) have lovely Anglo-Indian colonial and prices are fixed so you don't have to worry about haggling. Some people make special trips to IKEA in Dubai and have the furniture delivered. Alternatively, the many woodworking and metalworking shops in Wadi Al Kabir in Ruwi will custom make any piece of furniture for a reasonable price. Ruwi is also a good place to find readymade furniture and home furnishing shops - try Al Baladiyah Street and Souk Ruwi Street up to the Al Hamriyah Roundabout.

You can reduce prices of furniture quite a lot by bargaining. Things are not always in stock and can disappear so if you see something you really love, buy it right away.

Every area has shops that can make curtains and blinds. You'll probably have to wade through books and books of fabric samples before you find what you want, but the end result (custom-made curtains that fit your windows perfectly) will be worth it.

Home Furnishings & Accessories		
Bombay	Markaz Al Bahja	24 545 658
City Plaza	Off the Al Khuwayr R/A	24 698 988
Fahmy Furniture	Al Khuwayr	24 489 812
Home Centre	City Plaza	24 698 988
ID Design	Markaz Al Bahja	24 545 658
Marina Gulf Trdg	Al-Araimi Complex	24 562 221
P.iv	Shati Al Qurm	24 698 884
United Furniture	MSQ	24 603 416

Jewellery & Watches

Other options → Souks [p.182]

Jewellery

A big advantage of living in this region is the wide range and excellent prices of watches and jewellery (particularly gold). Apart from the obvious 'bling' factor, quality watches and jewellery pieces are good

Shopping

Health Food · Jewellery & Watches

Muscat's many doors

forms of investment. Gold is sold by weight and priced according to the international daily gold rate published on the internet or the local papers. 22 or 24 carat gold is popular here, as opposed to Europe where 18 carat gold is more common. In addition to being priced by weight, there is also a price for workmanship – this varies according to the intricacy of the design. As the international gold price is fixed, it is this workmanship fee that you can negotiate on.

Jewellery comes in many forms, from traditional Omani silver to cultured pearls from Japan and ethnic creations from India. More modern designs can be found in exclusive jewellery shops. If you are a serious gold shopper, check out the Mutrah Souk and Ruwi High Street where you can find various designs at various prices for various tastes. Have a good shop around until you find something you love – if you buy something you are not sure about you might regret it when you turn the corner and see your dream piece on display in the next shop! You can also design your own jewellery, or get a copy of a photograph made up.

Silver

Throughout its history, Omani silverwork has been held in high regard in Gulf countries, and some silver is sold as 'Omani' to increase its value. Silver was used not only to make various forms of jewellery, but also to decorate weapons and create everyday objects such as coffee pots, pipes and ear-cleaners. Each region in Oman has its distinctive designs. The books *Silver, the Traditional Art of Oman* and *The Craft Heritage of Oman* are indispensable guides to this important craft.

Silver Currency

Maria Theresa (1717-1780) was a Hapsburg by birth and the wife and Empress of the Holy Roman Emperor Francis I. The Maria Theresa thaler made its debut in 1751 at a time when Omani traders were desperately in need of an internationally acceptable and reliable currency. They liked the touch and texture of the coin, and the consistent silver content. Craftsmen used the thalers to develop and intricate pieces of silver jewellery. Oman's own currency was introduced in 1970, so the need for the thalers died out.

Take a short walk around any of the main souks in Muscat or the interior and you'll find a variety of dusty, tarnished silver that can be polished back to shiny brilliance. There are small boxes used to hold kohl and huge earrings which are hooked over the top of the ears rather than through pierced ears. A lot of it is wedding jewellery and although it looks ancient, it is unlikely to be very old. Traditionally, a woman's wedding jewellery was

melted down and sold or refashioned on her death, but inherited pieces are not uncommon. Bedouin women may also sell their silver jewellery, as Eid approaches, in order to have some cash for celebrations; the souk in Sinaw is a good source. You may also see Maria Theresa dollars (or thalers) which were the legal currency in Oman until 1968. Spend time, browse and you can dig up some real treasures.

Jewels of Oman

Watches

As with jewellery, watches are cheaper here than in Europe. Supermarkets stock cheap to medium-priced watches, while dedicated watch showrooms stock pieces priced from average to outlandish!

Jewellers		
Al Felaiij Jewellers	Muscat City Centre	24 558 518
Al Qurum Jewellers	Sabco Commercial Centre	24 562 558
Khimji's Watches	Ruwi 🅿	24 703 142
Ruwi Jewellers	Al Khamis Plaza	24 565 977
Watch House	Muscat City Centre	24 558 838

Kids' Items

Other options → Clothes [p.160]

Children's clothes, shoes and toys to suit all tastes and budgets can be found practically anywhere, from shopping centres to souks. While the variety of clothes for girls is fantastic, from frilly and lacy frocks to MTV hipsters, it is a bit more challenging finding fashionable clothing for teenage boys. The Baby Shop, Mothercare and Adams have a good selection of reasonably priced clothes for infants to barely-teens, toys and baby equipment. Sana Store, in Ruwi, has racks and racks of inexpensive children's clothes. Also check out the kids' sections in department stores (like Woolworths) and supermarkets, especially Carrefour, Lulu and Safeer.

Toys R Us, in Markaz Al Bahja, City Plaza, and the toy shop in Muscat City Centre carry everything from dolls to computer games and are great for one-stop shopping. Supermarkets also carry a good selection of toys. Supermarket noticeboards are great for finding second hand equipment like buggies, cots and larger toys and don't forget Ruwi High Street for lower priced items. Some churches and societies will lend out baby equipment to families in need.

Kid's Items		
Adams	Muscat City Centre	24 558 914
Baby Shop	City Plaza	24 698 988
Carrefour	Muscat City Centre	24 558 140
Early Learning Centre	Muscat City Centre	24 558 866
Lulu Hypermarket	Ruwi	24 811 449
Mothercare	Beh Sabco Centre	24 562 456
Safeer Hypermkt	Al Azaiba	24 496 019
Sana Fashions	Wadi Al Kabir	24 810 289
Smart Kid's Toys	Al-Araimi Complex	24 564 898
Toys 'R' Us	Markaz Al Bahja	24 540 360
Woolworths	Muscat City Centre	24 558 131

Lingerie

Other options → Clothes [p.160]

Lingerie is big business in the Middle East and you might be surprised by what is lurking under someone's conservative clothes. A browse in a specialist lingerie shop, like Women's Secret, Inner Lines (both in City Centre) and High Lady (Al Wadi Centre), can be an eye opening experience.

If you're looking for something a bit more conservative and functional, you can try old favourites Marks & Spencer or BHS, both of which have a good cotton range to suit the climate. Prices can be inflated compared to the UK so it may be worth stocking up in the sales. Carrefour and Lulu Hypermarkets have good lingerie sections, as do Woolworths, Splash, Next, Mango (all in City Centre) and Sana Stores in Wadi Al Kabir, Ruwi. The Mutrah

Souk and Ruwi High Street are also good places to find affordable underwear and nightwear if you're not particular about colours or cotton content.

She's got a secret

Lingerie		
BHS	Beh Sabco Centre	24 562 456
Carrefour	Muscat City Centre	24 558 140
High Lady	Al Wadi Centre	24 567 134
Inner Lines	Muscat City Centre	24 558 228
Lulu Hypermarket	Ruwi	24 811 449
Mango	Muscat City Centre	24 558 244
Marks & Spencer	Markaz Al Bahja	24 536 035
Next	Muscat City Centre	24 558 801
Sana Fashions	Wadi Al Kabir	24 810 289
Splash	Muscat City Centre	24 558 981
Women's Secret	Muscat City Centre	24 558 452
Woolworths	Muscat City Centre	24 558 131

Luggage & Leather

There is a lane off Ruwi High Street that specialises in budget suitcases and bags, where you'll be able to find anything you want in any colour or size. As you walk along the street, the traders somehow manage to hear what you are looking for, so by the time you reach the end they'll come right out and say 'small, black, air cabin bag madam?'.

Upmarket luggage is sold in Khimji's Stores, Capital Stores, Salam Stores and Salman Stores; all of these shops also stock a range of leather items apart from luggage. Carrefour and the Sultan Centre have a good selection of functional bags and suitcases, similar to those you might find in the souk. Copies of designer handbags can be found in some shops and these make good presents although some are of better quality than others.

Shopping

Lingerie • Luggage & Leather

If you're looking for a leather jacket, you can try the men's clothing stores in Al Qurm and City Centre. Non-branded leather jackets from Pakistan are also found in the small souk in the Capital Commercial Centre (Al Qurm).

Luggage & Leather		
Capital Store	Head Office	24 561 888
Carrefour	Muscat City Centre	24 558 140
Khimji's Megastore	Ruwi	24 558 140
Muscat Trading	Ruwi High Street	24 831 440
Salam Studio & Stores LLC	Nr Al Qurm R/A	24 564 071
Salman Stores	CCC	24 560 135
	Ruwi (1)	24 707 620
	Ruwi (2)	24 795 881
	Al-Araimi	24 566 286
	Seeb	24 422 213
	Salalah	23 293 146
	Al Qurm	24 567 666
Sultan Centre	Al Qurm	24 567 666
Wala Trading	Ruwi	24 703 488

Maternity Clothes

Whilst Oman doesn't have a huge choice for fashion conscious mums-to-be, a few of the big name stores have some maternity clothes within their ranges. These include Marks & Spencer, Next and Woolworths. For those with some design flair and the urge to try something a bit different, head down to your local tailors where can make anything you request, in any size and any shape!

Maternity		
Marks & Spencer	Markaz Al Bahja	24 536 035
Next	Muscat City Centre	24 558 801
Woolworths	Muscat City Centre	24 558 131

Medicine

Other options → General Medical Care [p.78]

Pharmacies (or chemists) are found all over Oman. They are indicated on shop signs by a green cross or what looks like a snake wrapped around a glass. Many drugs that you need a prescription for in other parts of the world can be bought over the counter here, without a visit to the doctor. Pharmacists are willing to listen to your symptoms and suggest a remedy, but will not prescribe antibiotics. They can also recommend a cheaper alternative of the same drug. If you want to buy a specific medicine that you know from your home

country it is a good idea to take the empty packaging with you if you have it. The medicine you use may not be available here, but the pharmacist may be able to offer a suitable alternative. Remember to check the expiry date of the medicine before buying it.

Pharmacies also carry beauty products, sunscreen lotions, baby care items, and perfumes, and they usually give a set discount on these items. They have regular opening hours, usually 09:00 to 13:00 and 16:00 to 20:00. A list of pharmacies on 24-hour duty can be found in daily newspapers, on 90.4 FM radio and the English Evening News on Oman TV. The following pharmacies are open 24 hours a day: Scientific Pharmacy in Al Qurm and Ruwi, Al Hashar Pharmacy in Ruwi, and Muscat Pharmacy in Ruwi and Al Sarooj.

If you need simple medication for fever, sore throat or muscle pain, try the larger supermarkets like Sultan Centre and Carrefour.

Medicine		
Al Hashar Pharmacy	Ruwi	24 702 850
Abu Al Dahab Clinic & Pharmacy	New Salalah	23 291 303
Muscat Pharmacy	Al Sarooj	24 695 536
P.44	Muscat City Centre	24 558 704
P.191	Ruwi	24 702 542
Scientific Pharmacy	Al Qurm	24 566 601
	Ruwi	24 566 601

Mobile Telephones

Other options → Telephone [p.75]

A mobile phone (often known as GSM in Oman) is an essential accessory for almost every Oman resident. Most shopping areas and malls have at least one outlet selling a range of models. There are some stores which specialise in mobile phones and personal communication devices, but all the major electronic stores sell mobiles, as do Carrefour supermarkets.

Mobile Telephones		
Carrefour	Muscat City Centre	24 558 140
Lucky Phone	CCC	24 566 704

Music, DVDs & Videos

There are no megastores selling music or movies in Oman, but there are many smaller shops within shopping centres that stock current releases on CD,

Maternity Clothes • Music, DVDs & Videos

Shopping

DVD and video. Try New Age Music (24 568 858) in the Sabco Commercial Centre. Carrefour and Sultan Centre also carry a limited selection.

You'll find the latest offerings by international musicians, as well as a good range of Arabic, Bollywood and classical music, on CD and cassette. When new music is released it tends to sell out quickly. Some shop owners might be able to order certain titles for you; alternatively you can order online if you're prepared to pay the postage (try www.amazon.com).

Censorship is alive and well and there may be some films that you can't get in Oman; or films that you can get but that have been 'cut'. Items ordered over the internet will usually be held at the post office until you are present to oversee the search. If something is offensive, it will be confiscated or censored.

Of course there are the usual pirated DVDs and VCDs doing the rounds – just remember that the chances are high you'll get a poor quality copy.

Music, DVDs & Videos

Carrefour	Muscat City Centre	24 558 140
New Age Music	Sabco Centre	24 568 858
Sultan Centre	Al Qurm	24 567 666

Musical Instruments

Other options → Music Lessons [p.223]
Music, DVDs & Videos [p.168]

Musicians will find it hard to get what they want in Oman as there are a limited number of shops that sell musical instruments. The widest range can be found in the Musiq Souq in the Al Wadi Centre (Al Qurm), and Tunes on the Al Khuwayr service road, who also offer music lessons. ElectroCity in the Al-Araimi complex has drum kits and Yamaha pianos. Sheet music is not widely available and you might want to order it online or buy some on your next trip abroad.

Musical Instruments

ElectroCity	Al-Araimi complex	24 568 806
Musiq Souq	Al Wadi Centre	24 562 237
Tunes	Majan House	24 698 775

Outdoor Goods

Other options → Camping [p.194]
Hardware & DIY [p.163]

Oman is a perfect location for outdoor activities, and weekend breaks in a wadi or in the desert are popular. There are numerous places to pitch your

tent, surrounded by the splendour of Oman's varied and rugged landscape. The mild temperatures and low humidity make the winter months of November to March the best time for camping, picnics, diving, kite surfing, climbing, trekking, spelunking, or just sitting on your porch with a sundowner. However, even in the summer, outdoor activities can be pleasant if you go to the mountains or further south to Salalah during the 'khareef' (monsoon season). An evening at the beach in summer can also be great fun although the humidity can be exhausting. Omanis often sit around singing and chilling out until the early hours and they love barbecuing fresh seafood.

Most of the supermarkets carry basic equipment to enjoy the great outdoors such as coolboxes, barbecue stands, folding chairs and tables, gas stoves, tents and even portable toilets and showers. You can get a good range of equipment, especially considering the generally excellent weather conditions for camping in this region, but if you are looking for particularly specialised items, you might need to bring them from home or order them online. Carrefour and Sultan Centre are the best places to kit yourself out cheaply. Ruwi High Street and the Mutrah Souk are good for plastic mats. However, if your idea of enjoying the outdoor life is limited to your patio or garden, take a trip to the City Plaza or Ruwi High Street for plastic chairs and tables.

Outdoor Goods

Carrefour	Muscat City Centre	24 558 140
Home Centre	City Plaza	24 698 988
Sultan Centre	Nr Al Harthy Complex	24 567 666

Party Accessories

Big formal parties or theme nights are not as popular in Oman as garden parties and casual barbecues are much more common. Supermarkets and stationery shops often stock basic party needs. Toys R Us, in Markaz Al Bahja, has a good kids' party selection (24 540 360). While there are no independent party organisers in Oman, the larger hotels might be able to help you plan a special event.

Fancy Dress/Costumes

If you are invited to a fancy dress party, and you want a proper costume but can't sew, your best bet is to go straight to a tailor as there are no specialist costume shops. Explaining your design to them could be an amusing experience as it will be

Shopping

Musical Instruments · Party Accessories

something different from the usual dresses that they sew. Allow plenty of time before the party to try it on and get it refitted.

Perfumes & Cosmetics

Other options → Souks [p.182]

Many of the raw materials used in perfumes (such as jasmine, frankincense and musk) originate in the Middle East region, and this is reflected in the vibrant array of perfumes available in Oman. Small bottles of perfume essence (available at souks and special perfume shops) are excellent buys – put even the slightest drop of these pure perfumes on a scarf and the scent will last for days. The souks have hundreds of different fragrances and you might find it difficult to choose just one! If you don't like strong perfume, avoid 'oudh', or make sure you smell it before applying it as it is an acquired taste.

In shopping malls and duty free shops you'll find all the latest international fragrances as well as stronger Arabic perfumes in extravagant bottles. Amouage, 'The World's Most Valuable Perfume', is made in Oman and is sold here for about half the international price. You can visit the Amouage perfume factory in Rusayl, past Seeb, to discover the secrets that go into this opulent fragrance.

Maathir Perfumes in Al-Araimi Complex has a good range of perfumes as well as some interesting solid perfumes – great for packing in your suitcase without having to worry about glass bottles breaking. Al Ajmal, which has many branches (including one in the Al-Araimi Complex) specialises in reasonably priced Arabic perfumes (RO 5 – RO 10).

Many perfume shops also sell diluted fragrance in white plastic spray bottles – these are used for refreshing furniture, carpets and curtains and only cost a couple of rials. The effect in your house is subtler than incense.

All luxury brands of cosmetics (and some lesser brands) are widely available in Oman. They are not always cheaper

Frankincense

Trade in frankincense resin once made the southern region of Dhofar one of the wealthiest in the world. It is estimated that around the second century AD, over 3,000 tons of incense were traded each year between southern Arabia and Egypt, Greece and Rome. According to the Bible, the three kings presented gifts of frankincense and myrrh to the baby Jesus, and at the time these were considered more valuable than gold. Incense production is a serious industry in Dhofar and entire alleys in the Salalah souk are devoted to incense shops.

than you would find them at home, so shopping at Duty Free shops, on your way in or out of the country, may be your best bet. City Centre has branches of The Body Shop and MAC where you can buy international make up and cosmetics.

Incense

Oman is home to the world's finest frankincense. 'Luban' (frankincense in resin form) is a good purchase and the fragrance lasts for a long time. Oudh is made from flakes of perfumed wood, and it has a very strong smell. Burning a small piece of oudh in an incense burner gives off a strong fragrance – it is expensive, but you only need to burn a small amount. You'll need to buy the small blocks of charcoal, which are available in all incense shops, supermarkets, corner shops and souks.

Amouage

Perfumes & Cosmetics

Ajmal	Al-Araimi Complex	24 562 359
Amouage P.153	Muscat City Centre	24 558 581
Amouage Factory	Rusayl	24 540 757
Body Shop	Muscat City Centre	24 558 237
Capital Stores P.171	Markaz Al Bahja	24 545 532
Maathir Perfumes	Al-Araimi Complex	24 562 585
MAC	Muscat City Centre	24 558 842

Second-Hand Items

Other options → Books [p.156]
Cars [p.29]
Furnishing Accommodation [p.70]

Churches and charity groups will take your unwanted clothes, toys and appliances as donations for people in need. The Catholic Church

OBJECTS D' ART

in Ruwi operates a charity shop, which is worth a visit for its abundant selection of nearly new clothing and home furnishings. If you want to make a few rials out of the stuff you no longer need, you can put a notice up on supermarket noticeboards or book a classified ad in one of the local newspapers.

There is a row of shops behind the Polyglot Institute at the Wadi Adai Roundabout that sell second-hand furniture. They offer a delivery and assembly service for any large items that you buy.

Shoes

Other options → Beach Wear [p.155]
Clothes [p.160]
Sporting Goods [p.172]

From knee-high boots to plastic flip-flops, you'll be able to find the shoes you need in Muscat. Most sizes are available; just be sure to specify to the sales assistant whether you mean UK or US size.

For trainers and running shoes, sports shops are the best places. Here you'll be able to get professional advice on fit and support. Shoe City (branches in City Plaza and City Centre) has a wide range of shoes for men, women and children. You'll find good quality leather shoes in various outlets in City Centre and in World Shoes in the Al Khamis Plaza (Al Qurm).

Unfortunately the range of shoes in other areas of Oman (outside of Muscat) is not as good.

Shoes

Clarks Shoes	Al Khamis Plaza	24 560 992
Milano	Muscat City Centre	24 545 834
Nine West	Muscat City Centre	24 558 312
Orange	Muscat City Centre	24 558 148
Shoe City	City Plaza	24 601 002
	Muscat City Centre	24 558 342
World Shoes	Al Qurm	24 565 259

Strutt your stuff in Milano!

Sporting Goods

Other options → Outdoor Goods [p.169]

Muscat has plenty of good general sports shops all over the city which stock a range of equipment and clothing, including one in most shopping malls. Most shops sell racquets, balls and exercise equipment, although they may be slightly higher priced than you can find elsewhere.

With Oman's proximity and affinity to the sea, a variety of water sports are well catered for by shops in Muscat. Diving and snorkelling equipment is easy to find, with specialist shops at the Oman Dive Centre (near Qantab), at Rusayl Shopping Centre (on the way to Nizwa), and at ScubaTec in the Al Wadi Centre (Al Qurm).

Oman Trekking Explorer

A booklet and individual cards detailing amazing walks through the spectacular scenery of Oman. The easy-to-follow maps correspond to waypoints that are actually painted on the ground to aid navigation. With information on planning your trek, tips on what to take and safety guidelines, let the Oman Trekking Explorer be your trusty guide to this beautiful country.

Other marine equipment can also be found in the dive stores as well as places such as Sidab where there are a number of marine stores and at Marina Bander Al-Rowdha.

Other specialist sports are not so well catered for, and most people end up having to bring their own equipment from home or mail ordering from Europe or North America. Cavers or climbers might not be so lucky, but for some outdoor sports enthusiasts it is worth your while taking a trip to Dubai. There is still not a massive selection, but there are three or four stores selling quality kitesurfing equipment, more selling windsurfing gear, three good stores selling quality brands of road and mountain bikes such as Scott, Giant and Trek, and there is a Coleman outdoor store.

Sporting Goods

Al Shaali Marine	Sidab	24 740 991
Muscat Sports	Al-Araimi Complex	24 564 364
	Markaz Al Bahja	24 537 708
	Ruwi	24 790 241
Oman Dive Centre	Nr Qantab	99 340 096
Sports For All	Sabco Centre	24 560 086
ScubaTec	Al Wadi Centre	24 562 322
Sun & Sand Sports	Muscat City Centre P.186	24 540 355
Supa Sportsman	Nr Hamriya RA	24 833 192
Water World Marine	Sidab	24 737 438

Tailoring

Other options → Arabian Souvenirs [p.154]
Clothes [p.160]
Textiles [p.173]

While having an outfit made to order in Europe is a luxury that few can afford, it is a cheap and easy way to get custom made clothes in Oman. The many fabric shops sell such a vibrant range of material that you'll be spoilt for choice, but once you've made your selection you can then take the next step of choosing a tailor. There are many tailors in Oman, some good and some not so good, and to find a good one it's best to go by word of mouth recommendation. In Muscat, tailors are mostly located in little shops in the back streets of Ruwi, the Mutrah Souk, or in shopping areas like the Al Wadi Centre or the Al Khuwayr Souk.

The process of going to the tailor (if it's your first time) is an interesting experience that may test your patience in the beginning. The best results come from bringing a picture or an original garment for the tailor to copy, or the shop might have a few magazines for you to browse through. Sometimes the language barrier can be problematic, but that's where the power of pictures comes in handy!

When you are trying a tailor for the first time, order just one garment so you can check the quality of the work. Confirm the price before you leave the shop, and make sure you are clear about what extras the price includes (such as lining, zips or buttons) – feel free to negotiate if you feel the price you are given is too high. Always try the garment on when you pick it up so that you can have alterations made if necessary. Any alterations will usually be made free of charge.

Tailoring

Assarain Textiles	Ruwi	24 830 149
Mutrah Tailoring House	Nr Post Office	24 701 960
Raymond Shop	Ruwi	24 561 142

Textiles

Other options → Arabian Souvenirs [p.154]
Tailoring [p.173]

Textile shops in Oman are excellent and you can buy just about any fabric in any colour. Pure cotton can sometimes be difficult to find, since it isn't that popular among Arab customers. Even the smallest towns have fabric shops, selling material by the yard. The shop assistants can advise you how much fabric you need for the garment you have in mind.

In Muscat you'll find textile shops in all the major malls and on Ruwi High Street. In Ruwi you can buy cheap saris that make interesting curtains and tablecloths. The Al Khamis Plaza in Qurm has two stores (Abu Hani and Instyle) that stock a huge range of silk and linen, and a basement store selling printed Indian cushions and bedspreads at reasonable prices. Abu Hani sells a range of printed cotton for those making bedding and quilts.

Textiles

Abu Fahmy Textiles	Ruwi	24 750 414
Abu Hani	Al Khamis Plaza	24 571 609
Beauty Textile	Ruwi	24 782 194
Gulab Bhai Dwarkadas & Co LLC	Nr Mutrah Souk	24 712 409
Instyle	Al Khamis Plaza	24 563 242
Silky Textiles	Ruwi	24 793 730

Places to Shop

The following section on places to shop has been split into two. It covers shopping malls or centres, and their main outlets, and the main shopping streets or areas in the region.

Shopping Malls

Most shopping malls in Oman are spacious, always air-conditioned, and smell deliciously of incense. They serve as places for residents to relax over a cup of coffee, meet friends, or shop of course! Occasionally shopping malls host special events such as children's entertainment and art exhibitions.

City Centre and Markaz Al Bahja are currently the biggest malls in Oman. Several shopping centres are clustered together in Qurm, so 'shop-hopping' is easy. Popular malls frequently have raffles during Eid in order to increase customer flow – the grand prize for the lucky few is usually a car.

Outside Muscat there are no large shopping malls. Salalah has a few large department stores and other towns make do with small shops.

Most malls have at least one coffee shop. City Centre and Markaz Al Bahja have large food courts, as well as children's play areas and ample free parking. The following are the most popular shopping centres in Oman.

Shopping Malls – Main

Al-Araimi Complex

| Location ➜ Commercial Area · Al Qurm | 24 566 180 |
| Web/email ➜ alaraimi@omantel.net.om | Map Ref ➜ 8-D4 |

This bright and spacious complex boasts over 70 shops and is one of the more upmarket centres in the Al Qurm shopping area. The first floor is mainly devoted to sophisticated clothes shops, while the basement holds many electronics and computer shops, appliance stores, a sports shop and an Oman Mobile shop. In addition to electronics and some household appliances, ElectroCity stocks cameras (by Canon) and musical instruments, including Yamaha pianos and Zildjian drum kits.

The big parking lot is nearly always full as it is one of the last free parking areas in the Al Qurm shopping area.

Al-Araimi Complex

Books, Cards & Gifts

Basement book stall
Gulf Shells
Majid
New Gift Centre
Smart Kids Toys

Clothes & Textiles

Giordano
H. FLo
Hang Ten
L'Artisan
Levi's
MS
Nafaf
Nice Lady
Perfect Woman Fashions
Raymond Shop
Scarlet Plus Size
Sheetal
Silk Island Trading
Trendz
Urban Costumes

Department Stores

Salman Stores

Electronics

Bosch
ElectroCity
LG Electrical
OHI Electronics

Eyewear

Anne Optician
Modern Capital Optical
Yateem

Food

Al Shabab
Golden Gate Café

Furniture & Household

Marina

Jewellery & Gold

Al Felaij Watches
Al Raid Jewellery
Dgal
Golden Pearl Jewellery
My Jewellery

Music & Videos

Millenium Music

Perfumes & Cosmetics

Ajmal Intl
Arabian Oud
House of Aoud Amber & Perfume
Maathir Perfumes
Riyam Cosmetics

Services

Bin Jadid Exchange
Fotomagic
National Bank of Oman
Oman Mobile
Photocentre
Xerox Colour Photocopying
Youth Telephone Centre

Shoes

Al Qurum Shoes
Pretty Fit/ Bata

Sporting Goods

Muscat Sports
The Athlete's Foot

Muscat City Centre

Location ➜ As Seeb
Web/email ➜ www.majidalfuttaim.com

24 558 888
Map Ref ➜ 3-D2

This is currently the busiest, biggest and most modern mall in Oman. Not even its location, past Seeb Airport, deters people who come from far and wide to shop here. At weekends the huge parking lot is heaving with cars and you'll be lucky to find an empty space.

The main shop in City Centre is the French hypermarket, Carrefour. It is a great first stop for people setting up home in Oman – you can buy all the things you need for a new house, like brooms, mops, ironing boards, towels, pots and cooking utensils. On the food side, you can buy delicious French breads and pastries as well as other French products. Carrefour is open from 09:00 until midnight and is busiest at weekends and during Ramadan, when there are instore promotions.

If a mega shopping trip around this gigantic mall leaves you feeling peckish, the L-shaped food court has the usual fast food places, as well as Arabic, Indian, Italian and Chinese cuisine, Baskin Robbins and Subway. The eating area has separate sections for families and non-smokers. Next to the food court there is a Magic Planet amusement centre for children, and a strategically placed toy shop.

There is a coffee shop at each end of the mall – one Starbucks and one Costa Coffee – great for resting weary legs and watching the world go by.

Other shops in the mall sell fashion, shoes, jewellery and even special items such as Omani halwa, chocolate covered dates and local handicrafts.

The mall is open from 10:00 (except for Carrefour, which opens an hour earlier) to 22:00. None of the shops close for lunch.

Books, Cards & Gifts

Carlton Cards
Crystal Gallery
Patchi

Clothes & Textiles

Abdullah Hussain Khunji
Accessori mr
Al Washia
Alyashmac
Claire's
Domani
Gasoline
Ibn Al Naamani
Mango
Mona Lisa
Monsoon
Next
Pierre Cardin
Promod
Splash/Lifestyle
Terranova
Vidrio

Department Stores

Splash
Woolworths

Eyewear

Grand Opticals
Solo Sole
Yateem Optician

Food

Anoosh (chocolate covered dates)
Baskin Robbins
ChicKing
Chili's
Costa Coffee
Hardee's
KFC
Magic Wok
McDonald's
Omani Halwa
Santino's
Shamiana
Starbucks Coffee
Subway

Hypermarket

Carrefour

Jewellery & Watches

Al Felaij Jewellers
Al Felaij Watches
Alukkas
Damas
Himat
Hour Choice
Mont Blanc
Swatch
The Watch House

Kids Stuff

Adams
Early Learning Centre
Magic Planet
Millenium Games
Monsoon
Mothercare
Pumpkin Patch
The Baby Shop
The Toy Store
Woolworth's

Lingerie

Inner Lines
Triumph
Women's Secret

Medicine

Muscat Pharmacy

Perfumes & Cosmetics

Amouage
Arabian Oud
Areej
House of Aoud, Amber & Perfumes
MAC
Mikyojy
The Body Shop

Shoes & Bags

Colange
Milano
Misako
Nine West
Orange
Pretty Fit

Sporting Goods

Adidas
Sun and Sand Sports

Services

ATMs (Bank Muscat, Oman Arab Bank, National Bank of Oman, HSBC)
Foto Magic
Kwik Kleen
Lakhoos Money Exchange
Nokia
Oman Mobile
Travellers World

Shopping

Shopping Malls – Main

Markaz Al Bahja

Location → Nr City Centre · As Seeb
Web/email → markazalbahja.com

24 541 952
Map Ref → 2-D4

This enormous new shopping mall is still quite quiet, probably because of its out-of-town location towards Seeb. It is well worth a shopping trip – the mall is spacious and relaxing and there is plenty of free underground parking.

The main attractions are Marks & Spencer and Toys R Us, both of which are on the top floor. ID Design (the Danish furniture chain) is also here, and it has a corner coffee shop offering delicious crepes and pastries. In Shop & Shop you can find quality kitchen gadgets, office accessories and mugs, all priced at RO 10 or under. There are a few clothes shops but these cater more to Arabic tastes and specialise in abayas and dishdashas.

The food court is huge, but is limited to just a few fast food outlets including an Indian fast food shop and Glacier Express, where you can get icecream and Belgian waffles. There is a Baskin Robbins on the ground floor, next to a perfume shop.

Of all the malls in Muscat, Markaz Al Bahja has the most to offer in terms of family entertainment. The basement has an eight-lane bowling alley, complete with billiards and Internet café. There is a four-screen cinema, a small supermarket and a bakery with a coffee shop. Next to the food court, on the top floor, there is a games centre and amusement park, complete with mini rollercoaster and bumper boats in a huge tank of water.

M & S in Markaz

Books, Cards & Gifts

Computer Book Shop
La Bonita

Clothes & Textiles

Al Lubahna
Asdaf
Baqa Fashion
Black Net Abayas
Elle
Fancy World
Fulla Fashions
Ibn Al Naamani
Laura
Lujaina Fashions
National Fanar
Perfect Woman Fashion
Stones

Department Stores

Marks & Spencer
Mohd. Sharief Stores

Eyewear

Al Jamil Optical

Furniture & Household

Bodum
Bombay
ID Design
Shop and Shop
Zone

Jewellery & Watches

Golden Pearl Jewellery
Haider Stores
Muscat Watch Center
Rado Tissot

Medicine

Muscat Pharmacy

Shoes

Shoe Palace International

Kids Stuff

Toys R Us

Music & Videos

Film and Audio World

Perfumes & Cosmetics

Ajmal
Al Faisal
Capital Store

Sporting Goods

Muscat Sports

Services

Bank Muscat
Capital Skin Care Centre
Happy Saloon (barber)
Snowhite (dry cleaning/laundry)
Yazin Mobil (mobile phones)

MAB...
why Dubai?!

Located in Al Hail by Al Mawaleh Roundabout
Markaz Al Bahja P.O. Box 54,
P.C. 113 Muscat - Sultanate of Oman.
Tel: 24540200 Fax: 24541950
Email: johnjose@albahja.com
or oasis@albahja.com
Website: www.markazalbahja.com
Open: Sat-thurs: 10am - 10pm
& Fri: 2pm - 10pm

MARKAZ AL BAHJA

مركز البهجة

With an ever growing number of fabulous stores, & everything you need under one roof, you'll have no reason to shop in Dubai. Our outlets include:

D Design, Zone Denmark, Bodum, Bombay, Shop & Shop, Marks & Spencer, Toys R Us, Al Fair, Al Bahja Cinema, Fantasia (entertainment world for kids), City Bowling, Muscat Bakery Markets, Snow White Laundry, Rado Tissot, Muscat Pharmacy, Golden Pearl Jewellery, La Bonita, Muscat Watch Center, Al Jamil Optical, Ajmal International, Mohd Sharief Stores, Nazim Jewellery, Perfect Woman Fashions, Black Net Abayas, Baqa Fashion, Al Faisal Co, Ibn Al Naamani, Baskin Robins, Haider Stores, Yazzen Fashion, Capital Stores, Muscat Sports, United Resource Ent, Yazzen GSM, Happy Saloon, Fancy World, Mood Cafe, The Bazaar (Traditional Souq), Abu Hani Al Rawahi, Capital Skin Care Center, Laura Kids, Fulla Fashions, Stones, Al Lubahna, Asdaf National, Lujaina Fashions, Wally's Burgers, Coral Express, Chicking, Glacier Express & Bank Muscat.

Sabco Commercial Centre

Location ➜ Way 651 · Al Qurm
Web/email ➜ www.sabcogroup.com

| 24 566 701
Map Ref ➜ 8-D4

Even though is was the first true shopping mall in Oman, Sabco is still one of the best and remains very popular with locals and expats alike. It is a very relaxing mall, with gardens and a waterfall in the centre and plenty of wooden benches. The famous Amouage perfume is sold exclusively in their shop, Oman Perfumery, at the entrance. The authentically decorated souk, found in the corner, is an Aladdin's cave of old Omani silver, local handicrafts, souvenirs and pashmina shawls from India. Bargaining is allowed, making the prices competitive with Mutrah souk.

Sabco is also home to some upmarket shops like Godiva, Cerruti, Raymond Weil and Philippe Charriol. Creatures Pet Shop is the only one in Al Qurm and stocks everything that your pet needs. There is a busy coffee shop in the lobby, and an HSBC ATM. Raffles are often held and the grand prize is usually a luxury car.

Sabco Commercial Centre

Clothes & Textiles
Cerruti
Elle
Jazz
Moustach
Sayidaty
Shakeela Hamad Mohd
Tahani

Eyewear
Al Gazal Opticians

Furniture & Household
Al Raid
Antique Furniture Rugs
Carpets & Handicrafts
Rana Abdulrahim

Food
Godiva Chocolates

Jewellery & Gold
Jewellery Corner

Al Felaij Jewellers
Al Qurum Jewellers
Future Jewellery
Silver Jewel Box

Medicine
Muscat Pharmacy

Perfumes & Cosmetics
Amouage Oman Perfumery
Capital Store
Muscat Pharmacy Perfumes
The Body Shop

Shoes & Bags
Al Khamis
Gardini
Nine West

Sporting Goods
Sports For All

Jewellery & Watches
Al Felaij Watches

Le Carat
Muscat Watch Centre
Philippe Charriol
Raymond Weil
Watches

Electronics
Jazeera Electronics
Modern Electronics House
Samsung

Music & Videos
New Age Music
Video Centre

Books, Cards & Gifts
Al Batra Bookshop
Carlton Cards
The Flower Shop

Services
Abu Mehad Money Exchange
Foto Magic
Muscat Beauty Salon
Snowhite Laundry

Shopping Malls – Other

Al Harthy Complex

Location → Opp main shopping centre · Al Qurm
Web/email → ahcmpx@omantel.net.om

24 564 481
Map Ref → 11-E1

This stand-alone building looks either like a giant space rocket or a futuristic mosque. The mall is an impressive landmark, especially when the lattice roof and the blue dome are lit up at night. It is located opposite the Al Qurm commercial area, right beside the bustling Sultan Centre, and is one of the calmer malls in terms of shopping and parking. It is popular for the internet café and Muscat Pizza on the ground floor, and Kargeen Caffé on the first floor.

Within the mall, you'll find a shop run by the Association for the Welfare of Handicapped Children where you can buy cheap accessories, cosmetics and T-shirts – you can shop as much as you like, it's all in the name of charity!

The Gallery carries paintings by Omani artists, while Cards Store has a fair selection of greetings cards, toys and souvenir T-shirts. Fresh and dried flowers can be ordered from Caravans, and the Modern Technical Computer Centre sells Apple computers and accessories. The first floor is almost entirely made up of shops for women and young girls, including the biggest branch of Muscat Pharmacy Perfumes and Cosmetics.

The complex also provides a good range of services, such as a post office, a key cutting kiosk a barber and a few tailors. The Oman Association for Consumer Protection has an office on one of the upper floors, and it is worth paying them a visit if you feel you've been the victim of shoddy service or a bad deal.

Kids are kept busy in the small amusement park in the basement, with kiddie rides and a ferris wheel that reaches the ground floor.

Other outlets include: Patchi, Ajmal Perfumes, Al Mira Mobil Phones, Happy Salon (for children), Horia Ibra Shoes, Muscat Pharmacy, Muscat Apollo Photoshop, North Oasis Tailoring, The Unique Corner (cigarettes and newspapers), Al Felaij Jewelers, Italian Jewellery, Aman, Steps, Health & Beauty Natural Herbs Centre, Qurum Textiles, Oman Trading, Rahela Trading, Oman Perfumes Centre, Abu Ayat, Al Sulaiman Jewellers, Gift Store.

Al Khamis Plaza

Location → Nr Safeer Supermarket· Al Qurm
Web/email → na

24 562 791
Map Ref → 8-D4

Al Khamis Plaza in Al Qurm is medium-sized and spread over three floors. The top floor is a shoe shopper's heaven. There is a branch of Clarks, and a World Shoes where you can buy brands like Sebago, Caterpillar and Dockers, as well as Arabic-style sandals for men and women.

Although Al Khamis is not as spacious as newer malls it has some notable shops, including a couple of textile shops with an amazing stock of Indian silk, men's shops with suits from Pierre Cardin and Lanvin, and the elaborate and exclusive Mouawad Jewellery. The fountain next to the pleasant Café de Lotus provides the continuous, soothing sound of running water. Parking is free, but sometimes it is difficult to find an empty space.

Capital Commercial Centre (CCC)

Location → Way 667 · Al Qurm
Web/email → cccqurum@omantel.net.om

24 563 672
Map Ref → 8-D4

From the outside, CCC resembles a sprawling Omani fort, complete with flags and enormous, carved wooden doors guarding the Al Fair supermarket and the shopping centre inside. Its outside walls enclose a gigantic parking lot bordered by small shops and food outlets, including Bollywood Chaat, Pizza Hut,

Capital Commercial Centre (CCC)

McDonald's, Baskin Robbins and Nando's Flame-Grilled Chicken. CCC has recently seen a surge in customer traffic due to the opening of Second Cup, a local branch of the Canadian chain of coffee shops serving gourmet coffee and tea, as well as lovely desserts and sandwiches in modern, ultra-comfortable surroundings. Locals and expatriates gather here to meet friends or read the newspapers.

Just at the left side of the main entrance is a small souk where you can pick up a wide range of leather goods, trinkets and Omani handicrafts. Al Fair supermarket occupies one wing of CCC and is popular with expatriates for its western food products (including pork). The checkout counters sell stamps, and just past them is a small area selling inexpensive clothes, lingerie and camping gear. Just outside Al Fair you'll find an ATM (for Oman International Bank) and a semi-permanent car exhibition.

The other half of CCC is a shopping centre with the usual range of jewellery, phone, carpet and perfume shops. If you look up you'll see the beautiful stained glass roof, which lets plenty of natural light in. There is a small amusement park for kids, a key cutter, and an internet café.

CCC has three health stores under one roof. The Health Shop carries multivitamins, protein drinks, Scholl foot products, a limited selection of orthopaedic cushions and pillows and personal health diagnostic equipment (such as blood pressure monitors). Island Natural Herbs has a wall of dried bark and herbs, guarded by two old Omani men who can presumably concoct anything for what ails you, as well as 'natural' slimming products for women. Those who are serious about increasing their body mass will surely be delighted at the huge plastic jars of food supplements sold in Sport One.

The opening hours of the CCC are from 08:30 to 21:00, but individual shop opening times may vary.

City Plaza

Location → Nr Al Khuwayr R/A · MSQ | 24 698 988
Web/email → www.landmarkgroupco.com | Map Ref → 7-D2

City Plaza is an enormous, two-storey building with very high ceilings and is more a department store than a shopping mall. It is easily accessible from the Al Khuwayr Roundabout and very popular with all residents, especially those with children. The open plan format includes clothes shops for children and adults (Baby Shop and Splash), a toy

department, accessories section, Lifestyle, Shoe City and Sports 4 All. The mall offers a free gift-wrapping service. There is also a small, unguarded play area, under the escalators, for younger kids.

Home Centre, on the first floor, carries a huge variety of household and decorative items, artificial flowers and plants; you can even find wooden items and furniture from Malaysia and India that are vaguely ethnic/colonial in style, as well as affordable leather couches. Tucked away in the corner behind the bedroom suites is a branch of Kargeen Caffé, a quiet and comfortable place to rest while indulging in one of their delicious mixed fruit juices.

City Plaza doesn't close for lunch and is open from 10:00 to 22:00 (Saturday to Thursday), and 14:00 to 22:00 on Fridays. The parking is sufficient on ordinary days but becomes a nightmare during the sales season. You will usually find a few men in the parking lot, looking to make a few extra baisas by washing your car while you shop. You can politely decline if your car doesn't need washing.

Jawharat A'Shati Complex

Location → Nr InterContinental Htl · Shati Al Qurm | 24 692 113
Web/email → jasco@omantel.net.om | Map Ref → 8-A4

This complex attracts visitors from all over the city for its lively atmosphere and beachfront location. Shops are arranged on both sides of a carpark that is a bit too small to cope with the crowds at weekends. Lunchtime and weekday evenings are more relaxed.

Shop till you drop!

The centre is home to several restaurants, nearly all of which have open areas that are great for watching the beautiful sunset over the sea.

You'll find some unusual items on sale here – hand-rolled cigars, Turkish icecream, chocolate covered dates, Italian coffee, and Omani handicrafts, among others. A browse around the Oman Heritage Gallery is like spending time in a museum, and you can buy some beautiful, traditional Omani crafts, all of which are handmade by Omani artists. Nails, Muscat's only salon devoted purely to pampering your hands and feet, is hidden behind red and pink glass walls on the first floor.

Oops

Are you a shopaholic and think you could add your expertise to this book? If so, let us know your credentials and maybe you could be shopping till you drop for the 3rd edition of the Oman Explorer. If you fancy yourself as the next Imelda Marcos or Victoria Beckham then give us a shout at Info@Explorer-Publishing.com!

The main attraction in this complex is food. The Sushi Night buffet on Thursdays, at the Sheraton Qurum Resort, is always popular, the O Sole Mio Italian restaurant at the carpark entrance is highly regarded, and D'Arcy's Kitchen serves hearty international food from breakfast to dinner and is popular with expats. And if your life is empty without your huge cup of cappuccino, you have the choice of Starbucks or Costa Coffee.

On a practical level, there's a post office, a barber and a brokerage house on the top floor of the right hand building, and a car rental agency in the opposite building. An ATM (Oman Arab Bank) is located outside the Casa del Habano cigar shop.

> *Other outlets include: Armani Jeans, Kwik Kleen, Megastar (CDs and DVDs), a flower shop, Muscat Pharmacy, Muscat Pharmacy Perfumes & Cosmetics, Tahani Co., Beauty Centre, Jazz, Card Store, Light Moon for Herbals, Persian Carpet Bazaar, Al Batra Booksop, Foto Magic and European Jewellery.*

Khimji's Megastore

Location → Ruwi Street · Ruwi	24 796 161
Web/email → krmega@omantel.net.om	Map Ref → 12-D2

Khimji's Megastore is so exclusive that you can only enter its Al Qurm branch if the guard buzzes you in. Quite understandable, as this compact, chrome and marble store houses a virtual who's who of well known brand names like Chanel, Jaeger, Paco Rabanne, Samsonite, OshKosh and Cross, to name a few. The watch department has some of the world's finest timepieces, including Rolex and Cartier. There is also a branch in Ruwi.

Souk Al Khuwayr

Location → · Al Khuwayr	na
Web/email → na	Map Ref → 7-B3

Located right in the centre of Al Khuwayr, this is not a souk in the traditional sense, but rather a collection of small, individual shops in a huge block. They provide a range of goods and services including tailors, furniture makers, second-hand electrical shops, hardware shops, one-rial shops, launderettes, a bakery, a pharmacy and a few coffee shops. Cheap household items and fabrics are the main draws, although you can get films developed here and buy stationery too. There is also a fruit and vegetable market, operated by the government, where you can get good fresh produce for a fraction of supermarket prices.

Zakher Shopping Mall

Location → Way 3341 · Al Khuwayr	24 482 047
Web/email → zakki@omantel.net.om	Map Ref → 7-D2

This small shopping centre houses an Al Fair supermarket in one half, while the other half is a simple, two-storey area with about ten shops. It has the usual selection of shops found in other malls, but (surprisingly) no coffee shop. The mall (apart from Al Fair) caters mostly to Arabs but expats or tourists may want to go there to look for dishdasha or Arabic art. You can buy Bang & Olufsen and G. Hanz audio and video equipment at the Photocentre on the ground floor.

> *Other shops include: Body Shop, Hallmark Cards Store, Ajmal Perfumes, Emerald Jewellery, Snow Star Sweets and Gifts, Optic Bazaar, My Fashion, Muscat Pharmacy (with perfumes and cosmetics section), a CD/video store and a full colour copy centre. There is also an ATM of the National Bank of Oman at the entrance.*

Streets/Areas to Shop

Nizwa

Location → SW of Muscat	na
Web/email → na	Map Ref →

Nizwa is a great place for souvenir shopping. This atmospheric, historical town is an hour and a half drive from Muscat, and once you are there it is easy to get around. The drive is scenic, with impressive desert mountains all along the way. After a visit to the fort you can sample the shopping that Nizwa has to offer, particularly the souk. The people of Nizwa call themselves the 'real Omanis' and pride themselves on being friendly and helpful. The pace of life is much slower here and a day trip is a relaxing break from Muscat's hustle and bustle.

Ruwi Souk Street

Location ➜ Left at Ruwi R/A, then 1st right · Ruwi	na
Web/email ➜ na	Map Ref ➜ 12-D3

This very long, two-lane street that starts at the Al Hamriya Roundabout is more famously known as Ruwi High Street. This is the place to go for anything from toilet seats to diamond rings, from state of the art hi-fi systems to Delsey luggage and every thing else in between.

While most of the shops cater to low and middle income families, expats of all nationalities come here for the excellent and inexpensive picture framing shops and tailors, and to buy textiles, appliances and gold. Shops are generally open from 09:00 to 13:00 and from 16:30 to 21:00.

There are various textile shops, electronics stores and jewellers along the main road, with many official dealerships for international brands of watches, cameras and white goods. Bargaining is encouraged, and if you can out barter the shopkeeper then you should walk away with a good deal.

There are several smaller roads branching off the high street, and these are home to speciality shops and occasional temporary markets. Honda Road, for example, is devoted to building and construction materials. Smaller shopping areas down the side roads are full of fake designer jeans, Tintin T-shirts and tacky gifts that have made this area famous.

There are plenty of tiny cafés in the main street, although they offer mostly battered Indian snacks along with masala tea, coffee or fresh coconut juice. You'll also find some small but excellent restaurants serving Filipina, Chinese, Indian, Sri Lankan, Arabic and Turkish cuisine.

Salalah

Location ➜ Dhofar Region	na
Web/email ➜ na	Map Ref ➜ 1-E3

Located in the south of the country, Salalah is Oman's second biggest city but it retains the feel of a small village. It doesn't have the range or the variety of shops that Muscat does. For the dedicated shopper though, there are still some decent places to go bargain hunting, especially for local handicrafts such as perfume, incense, oils and incense burners. No one seems to know the exact location of things here so you may have to ask a few people and be prepared to get lost – eventually you'll find what you're looking for.

There are no shopping malls as such, but there are streets lined with shops selling clothes, textiles, groceries, appliances, stationery and more. Al Haffa Street is a long street with many small shops selling mostly women's clothes and accessories. This is where Dhofari women buy brightly coloured lengths of cotton-mix fabric (imported from Thailand) to make the traditional Salalah dresses ('thobe Dhofari'). These are basically a big square with a hole cut in the middle for the neck and the back longer than the front to create a train; they make comfortable house dresses for the summer. Dhofar City Centre has a little bit of everything under one roof, but sells mainly clothes and accessories for the whole family.

> ### Dressing Down
>
> *Don't underestimate the underlying modesty that exists in any Islamic country – while Muscat may be open and modern, you should still respect the core values and wear appropriate clothing. Smaller cities, like Salalah, are more conservative and women should wear long sleeved, loose clothing so as not to offend. Locals are friendly, but as a general rule men should approach men, and women should approach women.*

Salalah's semi-tropical climate has given rise to an agricultural industry that supplies Oman with fresh fruits and vegetables such as bananas, coconuts, tomatoes, and beans. Locally grown fresh produce is cheap and bountiful. Look out for the small stalls set up along the beaches or back streets where you can buy finger-sized sweet bananas straight off the trees and drink milk right out of the coconut.

Souks

Other options ➜ Bargaining [p.152]

Souk is the Arabic word for a market or a place where all kinds of goods are bought, sold or exchanged. Traditionally, dhows from the Far East, Africa, Ceylon and India would discharge their cargo and the goods would be bargained over in the souks adjacent to the docks. Over the years, the items on sale have changed dramatically, from spices, silk and perfume, to include electronic goods and the latest consumer trends. However, the atmosphere of a bustling market with noisy bargaining and friendly rivalry for customers still remains. Souks are lively, colourful and full of people from all walks of life – well worth a visit, even if you're not buying!

Oman's souks are some of the most fascinating in the Arab world, having retained the traditional way of doing business that has been lost in many places. Apart from the obvious commercial purpose they serve, they also provide a focal point for social interaction. In the interior, Bedouins come in from the desert, and villagers from the mountains, to meet other tribes or catch up on the latest news.

Every important town in Oman has at least one souk. The biggest and most famous souks are in Mutrah, Nizwa, Sinaw and Salalah. A women only souk is held in Ibra every Wednesday morning. In addition to the permanent souks, pre-Eid markets known as 'habta' souks spring up overnight in places like Fanja, Samayil, Suroor, Nafa'a and Nizwa. These open-air souks attract large crowds looking for everything from livestock to perfume and clothing to toys at bargain prices.

Visiting the souk is a fascinating experience at anytime, but it is probably best to go in the early morning or late afternoon when it is cooler. Souks usually start business at 07:00 (except for Mutrah souk, which starts later at 09:30). They then break for midday prayers at 12:30 or 13:00 and reopen from 16:30 to 19:00 every day except Friday, when they only open in the afternoon. Thursdays and Fridays are busiest as this is the weekend for most people. For the visitor, this is the best time to witness the souk in full throttle and take an active part in it.

Al Dhalam Market

Location → Nr Al Lawatiya Mosque · Mutrah | na
Web/email → na   Map Ref → na

Al Dhalam (darkness) Market in Mutrah extends from the Al Lawatiya Mosque to Khour Bimba – an area where sunlight doesn't reach the narrow twisting lanes, leaving them in semi darkness. The market was built from mud and roofed with palm leaves, and shoppers used lamps to find their way. It was considered an excellent barometer of Omani social and economic activity as locals from all walks of life came here to buy fruits, vegetables, dates, textiles and jewellery, particularly during the Eid seasons.

This small market has been renovated and now has paved alleys to keep feet dust free. The Al Lawatiya quarter was previously closed to foreigners, non-Lawati Muslims included! However, visitors who are appropriately clothed are now free to wander around, although you should leave your camera and video camera behind.

Gold Souk (Salalah)

Location → Al Salam St · Salalah | na
Web/email → na   Map Ref → 1-E3

People unfamiliar with Arabic gold may think it looks of poorer quality but the reverse is usually true. Most of the gold sold in this region is 24 carat, and is often softer and of better quality than gold bought elsewhere in the world. However, the gold is very yellow and the designs of the jewellery are definitely on the gaudy side. A visit to the Salalah Gold Souk may give you an opportunity to see young Dhofari girls choosing their wedding gold. You can shop around for a traditional Dhofari design, or design your own piece of you want a simpler, more modern look. This souk should not be confused with the gold souk in Souk Al Haffa – the Salalah Gold Souk is situated in the Salalah Centre (after Pizza Hut, turn right 50 metres before the traffic lights).

Mutrah Fish & Vegetable Market

Location → Nr Port· Mutrah | na
Web/email → na   Map Ref → 10-A3

The fish market, located at the Mutrah end of the Corniche, is one of the few places left in Muscat where you can still witness the true hustle and bustle of an Arabic market. Smelly and muddy with fish guts aplenty... it is an unforgettable experience (better for those who aren't too squeamish), and the best place to get fresh seafood at low prices. To get the best catches of the day you'll need to get there early – from 06:30 the small fishing boats are dragged up the beach next to the market to unload their catches. There seems to be at least one of every type of fish in the Indian Ocean on display, such as octopus, prawns, tuna, hammour, kingfish, and bream. Sadly, some brightly coloured reef fish also get caught in the nets, and some are so fresh out of the sea that they are still gasping. Once you've wandered round the stalls and selected your fish, you can get it cleaned and gutted in the area to the left rear of the market – it is fascinating to watch and the service only costs a few baisas.

There is also a very good fruit and vegetable market on the left side of the fish market. The wide variety of locally grown and imported produce is quite cheap, considering the huge quantities you go home with. At the entrance to the vegetable market is a row of meat shops, selling fresh cuts of beef, mutton and camel.

Fresh fruit and veg

Mutrah Souk

Location → Mutrah Corniche · Mutrah | na
Web/email → na   Map Ref → 10-A3

One of the most interesting souks in the Gulf, this warren-like covered market is still a source of many Omani families' daily household needs, as well as a hotspot for tourists looking for souvenirs. The main entrance is on Mutrah Corniche but there are many small streets in the village behind the Corniche that lead into the souk. There is paid parking all along both sides of the Corniche Road from the Fish Roundabout.

The main thoroughfare of the souk carries mainly household goods, shoes, and ready-made garments. Further inside, enjoy the mixed smells of frankincense, perfume oils, fresh jasmine and spices. When you get tired, you can stop at the juice bar before tackling the next section of the souk.

The real excitement of visiting Mutrah Souk is in exploring the side streets. The layout is confusing but keep walking and you will usually end up either at the Corniche or the main thoroughfare. A wander down any of the small side alleys and you'll usually discover a selection of tiny shops full of

dusty Omani silver, stalls of gleaming white dishdashas and embroidered kumahs, brightly coloured cloth and multicoloured head scarves. You'll also find Omani pots, paintings, hookah pipes, framed khanjars, leatherwork and incense, as well as casual clothes and household objects. There are plenty of bargains and no price is fixed.

Most shops in the souk are open from 09:30 to 13:00 and 16:30 to 19:00 daily, but are closed on Friday mornings. The only time the souk is closed for business is during the Eid holiday.

All that glitters...

Nizwa Souk

Location → Town Centre · Nizwa | na
Web/email → na   Map Ref →1-B2

Very near to the fort and mosque, and in the centre of the town, the renovated Nizwa souk lies hidden behind high, imposing, sand-coloured walls. Enter through one of the enormous carved wooden doors and you'll find a small 'village' of traditionally designed buildings, each labelled for the different products they carry (Silver Souk, Fish Souk, Meat Souk, etc). Although these buildings are all clean and well lit, the place remains full of atmosphere and traders conduct business as they have done for centuries. The new souks are well laid out and if visited in the early morning, are vibrant with local colour and full of life.

In the silver and craft souk, you'll find a mixture of old and new craft items made locally, such as Bahla pottery, old wooden chests, silverwork from the different regions of Oman, antique rifles, and frankincense as well as modern imports from India. You can watch silversmiths hammering intricate patterns into the hilts of khanjars. The shop owners are not at all intrusive and they sit drinking their coffee while you browse. Many antique silver dealers in Muscat come here to find things for their store and, although prices are rising with the level of tourism, with hard bargaining you can sometimes get a better price than in Muscat.

Nizwa souk hosts a lively animal market early each Friday morning where cows, goats and sheep are auctioned in the Goat Souk. This is an open-air market located close to the entrance on the left-hand side. The souk is worth a visit, especially just before the religious holidays, when farmers sell their livestock for the festivities. It often spills onto the enormous parking lot outside the souk walls where owners unload cattle from trucks and sell bales of hay to feed the animals.

Sinaw Souk

Location → Crossroads of Rte 33 & Rte 27 | na
Web/email → na   Map Ref →1-C2

Sinaw is a surprisingly busy outpost town set between the Wahiba Sands and the edge of the Empty Quarter, about a two-hour drive from Muscat. Bedouins gather here to do business or to socialise. The souk is located in a square in the middle of the town, behind mud coloured walls and through green metal doors decorated with a symbol of a car.

Camels, goats and young cattle are auctioned off around the outside walls. The camels are hobbled to keep them from running away, which probably explains their disdainful expressions and stubborn tempers! Loading the animals into trucks is a tricky business. Camels, in particular, can deliver knockout kicks and need at least six men to push them in.

Fruits and vegetables are sold in the central covered area. Bedouin women in their metallic face masks ('burqa') happily trade next to men (quite unusual in Islamic countries) and will joke with you as you try on one of their masks. Around the covered area are small shops selling jewellery and household necessities. You can watch old

silver being melted to fashion new jewellery, although gold is also popular.

Before Eid, many come to sell livestock or old silver to raise the money to buy little luxuries, so these are the times you can find some real treasures. It is a good place to find increasingly rare and old Bedouin silverwork, especially in the weeks approaching Eid. Sinaw souk is best visited early in the morning on weekends. The souk is closed on days designated as Eid public holidays.

Making perfect scents

Souk Al Hafah

Location → Al Hafah · 3 km west of Salalah | na
Web/email → na   Map Ref →1-E3

This souk is located in the coconut groves of the Al Hafah area of Salalah and is the best place in Oman to buy frankincense and incense powders. There are dozens of buckets on display, each with different qualities and compositions of perfumes. You can ask a local what the differences are, or just buy the one you like most. The smells are generally much stronger than in Muscat and a little goes a long way. Frankincense is poured into a bag and weighed, while incense comes in little silver or copper pots. Remember to buy some charcoal for burning the incense and some brightly painted clay Dhofari burners to put them in.

You can also buy textiles, gold and silver, Indian and Arabic dresses, and some traditional souvenirs. Local coffee shops serve Omani and Middle Eastern snacks such as hummus and mishkak (Omani style barbecue).

Shopping

Souks

Activities

EXPLORER

Activities

Table of Contents

Activities

Highlights...

Camping [p.194]

Once in a while there's nothing better than escaping the town or city and heading off to the wilderness to spend a night under canvas. Oman has many areas of outstanding natural beauty, and as long as campers respect any nearby residents and the environment, there are few restrictions to simply pitching your tent and enjoying getting back to nature. A trip into the 'outback' can often be combined with a spot of wadi or dune bashing in a 4 WD – see [p.212]

Diving [p.200]

With 1,700 kilometres of coastline, year-round warm seas and excellent underwater visibility, Oman is a key destination for divers of all abilities. Colourful coral reefs and an amazing array of marine creatures are just waiting to be discovered. Snorkellers will find countless secluded coves and beaches to explore, while Scuba divers will be spoilt for choice by the variety of dive sites available. A popular option is to travel north to Mussandam, where divers can experience the dramatic undersea cliffs in this 'Norway of the Middle East.'

Oman is a land of opportunity when it comes to both outdoor and indoor sports and activities. The rugged mountains, gently rolling seas, riveting Wadis, and roaming desert sands provide plenty of scope for outdoor pursuits and the warm winters offer the perfect environment for them. Typical winter pastimes can be anything from camping on any of the beautiful beaches, collecting shells, and swimming in pristine seas one weekend, to tackling the dunes of Wahiba Sands in a 4 WD and sand skiing the next. Even the heat of the summer doesn't stop some sports enthusiasts sailing the Gulf or hitting the greens regardless of the 48°C temperature. Those who remain in Oman during the summer can survive the extreme heat by venturing into the mountains for cooler climates or to Salalah for refreshing rains, heading to an air-conditioned gym, or partaking in one of the many courses offered around Muscat.

Oops

Did we miss your mountaineering club, or forget to give your shisha society a shout? If you participate in an activity and think that our readers would like to know about it, just send us some details to Info@Explorer-Publishing.com and we'll make sure you feature in next year's edition.

As in many countries, word of mouth is one of the best ways to get details and information about your favourite pastime. An assortment of sports and activities are available in Oman so it's well worth the hunt around. However if you don't find the conker club that you so desperately want to join then why not start your own – and then tell us about it! We are always looking for new activities to add to our guidebook, so if you belong to any club, organisation, or group; official or unofficial, we'd love to hear from you. Check out the Reader Profile Survey on our website (www.Explorer-Publishing.com) and give us your comments and details.

Aerobics

Other options → Aqua Aerobics [p.190]
Dance Classes [p.219]
Sports & Leisure Facilities [p.216]

Aerobics is an excellent way to keep fit throughout the year, no matter what the temperature is outside. Classes are available in most of the hotels and health clubs and you can choose from different disciplines and timings to suit you. Costs per class range from RO 1.5 – 2.5 (for members) and RO 2.5 – 3.5 (for non-members).

Amusement Centres

Other options → Amusement Parks [p.190]

Foton World Fantasia

Location → Markaz Al Bahja · As Seeb	24 537 061
Web/email → na	Map Ref → 2-D4

Situated on the top floor of the Markaz Al Bahja shopping centre, this is the newest addition to kids entertainment in Muscat. Run by Foton, specialists in 'Edutainment' for children, this centre offers a climbing wall, games, bumper boats and Oman's first roller coaster. At the time of writing, there are plans to increase the number of attractions and rides on offer.

Magic Planet

Location → City Centre · As Seeb	24 558 888
Web/email → na	Map Ref → 3-D2

This amusement centre is popular with kids of all ages. It has a small carousel, a mini train and bumper cars, as the main attractions. It is located next to the food court. RO 30 gets you an unlimited ride pass, or you can buy tokens for 200 baisas each. Magic Planet has a party zone area that can be booked for private parties.

Sindbad's Wonder Centre

Location → Al Harthy Complex · Al Qurm	24 794 677
Web/email → sindbad1@omantel.net.om	Map Ref → 11-E1

There are a host of fairground rides to amuse young children, up to age eight. You can bring your own food or get Sindbad's to cater in the separate dining area. Children will love the carousel, bumper cars, magic carpet train ride and spinning teacups. Parents can relax while the kids wear themselves out. There are a few Sindbad parks around but if you have younger children head down to the one behind Al Fair supermarket, which is especially built for children under the age of five years.

Aerobics · Amusement Centres

Activities

Amusement Parks

Other options → Amusement Centres [p.189]

Marah Land (City of Joy)

Location → Qurm National Park · Al Qurm | 24 562 215
Web/email → na   Map Ref → 8-D4

The park contains a large boating lake and fountain aptly named, 'Waterfall Hill'. Thrilling rides include the Space Gun, Flume Ride, Ferris Wheel, Bumper Cars, the Giant Wheel, Horror Ride, Roller Coaster, as well as less excitingly named games for children. A place with complete family entertainment in mind and includes a variety of food outlets offering both Arab & Continental fare.

Cost: Adults & children above 5 years 300 baisas, children 4 years and below are free. Purchase a package for RO 1 that includes 11 free games.

Aqua Aerobics

Other options → Aerobics [p.189]

Aqua Aerobics is an excellent activity for most ages, body shapes, and medical conditions. Water allows smooth movements and protection for joints while providing a good cardiovascular workout and strength training. Many of the local health clubs offer Aqua Aerobics, see the Health Club table [p.217] for more information.

Archery

Muscat Diving and Adventure Centre

Location → Nr Radisson Hotel · Al Khuwayr | 24 485 663
Web/email → www.holiday-in-oman.com   Map Ref → 7-B3

Even if you happen to be more Fryer Tuck than Robin Hood, the fully trained and friendly instructors will put you through your paces and show you just how much fun it can be trying to shoot an arrow straight. Lessons last for two hours. Prices start from RO 15 for adults (a minimum group of four is required) and RO 10 for children (must be ten years or over). A family of four (consisting of two adults and two children) will only cost RO 40.

Basketball

Courts for this fun American sport can be found at the Oman Basketball Association (24 793 802). The Omani Basketball Federation (www.asia-basket.com) is an active association and sub-committee for competitions. See their website for more details.

Boat & Yacht Charters

Other options → Coastal Cruises [p.143]
Dhow Charters [p.198]
Dinner Cruises [p.255]

Arabian Sea Safaris

Location → Htl InterContinental · Shati Al Qurm | 24 693 223
Web/email → www.arabianseasafaris.com   Map Ref → 8-A4

Arabian Sea Safaris has two boats available for charters – one 28 footer with an open deck and shaded area, and one 60 foot air-conditioned yacht with three cabins, a saloon, galley kitchen and deck area. Each boat is available for local trips around the Muscat coastline and is chartered with an experienced crew. The boats are fully equipped with first aid and safety equipment.

Prices for charter range from RO 80 for a half-day trip on the open boat to RO 150 for a full-day (six hours), for a maximum of six passengers. Prices for the yacht are RO 175 for a half day and RO 280 for a full day, for a maximum of ten passengers.

Capital Area Yacht Club (CAYC)

Location → Sidab | 24 737 712
Web/email → na   Map Ref → 13-E3

The Capital Area Yacht Club provides a beautiful location to moor your boat. They also offer charters, diving trips, a scenic beach and a restaurant to relax in. Boats are dry-docked and the cost of storing your boat depends on its size. There is also a garage for servicing your boat, should you require the service. A social membership to the club costs RO 120 for a family or RO 80 for individuals.

Marina Bander Al-Rowdha

Location → Marina Bander Al-Rowdha · Sidab | 24 737 288
Web/email → www.marinaoman.com   Map Ref → 13-E4

Set in a beautiful location surrounded by mountains, the Marina Bander Al-Rowdha has some of the most amazing views of the Omani coast. You can charter boats or take advantage of their Sunset Dhow Cruise, enjoy one of their

Work Hard
Play Harder

POCARI SWEAT

• Non Carbonated • Contains balanced amount of electrolytes • Low in calories
• Enriched with Vitamin C • Natural Mild Taste • Easily absorbed by body

The Ideal Health Drink

dolphin cruises or channel your energy into a deep sea fishing trip. Whatever you decide to do, head back to the Marina's restaurant by the pool afterwards for excellent food and fabulous views.

Marina life

Sea Tourism Co

Location → MSQ		24 602 949
Web/email → na		Map Ref → na

Sea Tourism has two double-decked motor boats that can be chartered for trips as short as three hours or as long as four days or more. Each cruise is prepared individually, whether for sightseeing, a business lunch, a romantic sunset dinner or a weekend break. Relax on deck and enjoy the beautiful coastline and clear blue waters, or picnic at one of the many remote beaches. Windsurfing, water skiing or diving can also be arranged. Both boats are fully equipped, have experienced crew and safety equipment.

Bowling

City Bowling Centre

Location → Markaz Al Bahja · As Seeb		24 541 277
Web/email → na		Map Ref → 2-D4

Whether you enjoy bowling, snooker, billiards or video games, the City Bowling Centre is a one-stop shop for fun and games! This new bowling alley houses 8 lanes, boasts a very active league, and organises bowling tournaments and social parties. They also have a junior club of about 25 members. The alley provides a variety of activities for birthday parties, corporate events

or serious bowlers. Don't worry about hunger either, within the alley is a Cyber Café to take care of your appetite. Fees for bowling range from 800 baisas to RO 2, depending on age and the day. If you want to avoid the crowds and work on your game, come during the week in the afternoons. Special discounts may be arranged for social events.

Sheraton Oman Hotel

Location → Sheraton Oman Hotel · Ruwi	24 799 899
Web/email → www.starwoodhotels.com	Map Ref → 12-E2

The Sheraton bowling alley is always busy. It has six fully automatic lanes where four leagues are played every week – three in the evening and one in the morning. The Bowling Centre has recently been refurbished and regular amenities renewed, like new shoes and balls. The first game costs RO 1.2 and each subsequent game only RO 1. Special attention is paid to children at the Sheraton and this extends to the Bowling Centre as well. It organises special get-togethers for children from the age of four onwards, with a special menu, lightweight balls and a kiddies' bumper to encourage the children to bowl. The Bowling Bar serves a good variety of snacks and drinks. In addition to the set menu, special menus can be tailormade for groups or special occasions.

Camel Rides

Other options → Camel Racing [p.129]

A visit to this part of the world is hardly complete unless you've been up close and personal with the 'ship of the desert', the camel. Many tour operators incorporate a short camel ride on their desert safaris. Alternatively, for a unique adventure, try a camel ride into the spectacular sand dunes. Your guide will lead you to a Bedouin camp, where you can enjoy a rest and some refreshments. Don't forget to take your camera, so you can remember this unique experience long after the aches subside!

Muscat Diving and Adventure Centre

Location → Nr. Radisson Hotel · Al Khuwayr	24 485 663
Web/email → www.holiday-in-oman.com	Map Ref → 7-B3

Organising two main tours along eco-tourism lines, the centre operates with Bedouin families of the Northern Region Sands (Wahiba) in Sharqiya, as well as expeditions in the Rub Al Khali in Dhofar. Camel trips or 'safaris' can vary in length from a

short daily ride to a 14-day camel safari across the sands. This is one of the country's most authentic tours and allows visitors access to Bedouin life with the opportunity of stopping overnight at a real Bedu campsite.

Camping

Other options → Campsites [p.28]
Outdoor Goods [p.169]
Wadi & Dune Bashing [p.212]

Camping is one of the best ways to explore Oman's varied landscape. Many expats pack their 4 WDs with camping gear and food supplies and set out for a whole weekend, particularly during the winter months when you can sleep under the stars. You can set up your tent wherever the mood takes you, as long as it is not too close to the villages.

For most campers, basic equipment will be enough for a successful trip. The following items are usually necessary:

- Tent
- Lightweight sleeping bag (or light blankets and sheets)
- Thin mattress (or air bed)
- Torches and spare batteries
- Cool box for food
- Water (always take too much)
- Camping stove, or BBQ and charcoal if preferred
- Firewood and matches
- Insect repellent and antihistamine cream
- First aid kit (including any personal medication)
- Sun protection (hats, sunglasses, sunscreen)
- Warm clothing for cooler evenings
- Spade
- Toilet rolls
- Rubbish bags (ensure you leave nothing behind!)
- Navigation equipment (maps, compass, Global Positioning System (GPS))

There are many wadis within two to three hours drive from Muscat, some of the more popular sites are along the coastal road from Quriyat to Sur, such as Wadi Shabs and Wadi Tiwi. South-east, down the coast beyond Quriyat and after Dibab, are a number of beaches between rocky outcrops. The most popular is Mokallah (also known as White Beach), where the snorkelling is excellent. Those who prefer the desert have the whole of the Wahiba Sands (Ramal Al Wahaybah) to cross, all the way to the coast.

You can camp in the Arabian Oryx Sanctuary in Jaaluni, more than six hours drive from Muscat. Facilities are very basic and you should check their website in advance to get a better idea of what is available (www.oryxoman.com).

Oman also has plenty of official camping grounds with full amenities. For RO 3 per person (including breakfast) and RO 4 per tent, you can make use of the Oman Dive Centre's site and watersports facilities (www.diveoman.com.om or call 99 340 096). To watch the nesting turtles at Ras Al Hadd, you can camp inside the Turtle Beach Resort (25 540 068) and enjoy life's little luxuries such as meals, showers, toilets and experienced guides. Costs start at RO 3 per adult and RO 1 per child. You can also camp outside the grounds, but there are no facilities (and you aren't allowed to cook).

On the more luxurious side, several tour operators have established their own permanent or rolling campsites in the Wahiba Sands, equipped with air-conditioned huts and refrigerators. Apart from the camping, you'll also get an Omani barbecue under the stars, as well as the opportunity to try dune bashing and camel riding.

Al Areesh Resort

| Location → Nr Ibra · Wahiba Sands | 99 317 107 |
| Web/email → na | Map Ref → 1-C1 |

The campsite at the Al Areesh Resort in the Wahiba Sands allows you to get away from it all in a peaceful 'back to nature' environment while still enjoying a good level of luxury – for camping at least! There are twelve tents with camp-style beds, making for a comfortable standard of accommodation. Meals are prepared on site and cooked over open fires.

Al Raha Tourism Camp

| Location → Nr Ibra · Wahiba Sands | 99 343 851 |
| Web/email → alrahatou@hotmail.com | Map Ref → na |

This desert camp in the Wahiba Sands offers visitors a chance to sample the Bedouin lifestyle (albeit a tourist-friendly version) and experience exciting activities such as dune buggy driving, dune bashing trips in 4 WD vehicles, sand boarding and skiing, as well as the ubiquitous camel rides. Accommodation is in clean but basic barasti huts, and meals are mostly buffets served in the traditional open courtyard which is

Camping

Activities

also the venue for live music and entertainment. Guests will find that a night of warm hospitality beneath the bright clear stars is an unforgettable experience.

Empty Quarter Tours

Location ➔ Various locations | 99 387 654
Web/email ➔ www.emptyquartertours.com   Map Ref ➔ na

Operating at the Nahar Farm in Ibra, 30 minutes from the famous Wahiba Sands, the camp provides comfortable facilities in a Bedouin setting. Accommodation is in fixed barasti (palm frond) shelters with modern conveniences including clean showers, toilets and a swimming pool surrounded by palm trees. Delicious Omani meals are served in a date palm garden or under the stars in dining areas fitted out with authentic Arabian carpets and cushions. Traditional performances by Omani dancers and musicians can be arranged. Empty Quarter Tours also offer camping at a 'Back to Nature' 1,000 Nights Camp in the Wahiba Sands.

Rugged Good Book

Many of Oman's most beautiful spots can only be reached in a 4 WD. So load up your vehicle with tents and supplies and head off into the rocky mountains, desolate dunes and winding wadis to explore. Oh, and don't forget to take the Oman Off-Road Explorer – it's the essential guide to roughing it like a pro! Available late 2005.

Turtle Beach Resort

Location ➔ Nr Ras Al Hadd · Sur | 25 540 068
Web/email ➔ www.surtoursonline.com   Map Ref ➔ na

A few kilometres from Ras Al Hadd, the Turtle Beach Resort offers no-nonsense accommodation and facilities, as well as varied activities, all at reasonable prices. Guest rooms consists of 22 traditional barasti huts, which are small and basic but perfect for rolling out of bed straight onto the beach. There's also a large restaurant/dining area built in the shape of an old boat. The big draw though is the resort's programme of activities, including turtle watching at Ras Al Jinz, dolphin and birdwatching around Ras Al Hadd, snorkelling and diving trips, and dhow cruises aboard their own vessel.

Canoeing

Other options ➔ Outdoor Goods [p.169]

There may not be any rivers or lakes for canoeing in Oman, but its coast is fantastic for serious enthusiasts. The coastline is characterised by many inlets and sheltered bays, some of which are big enough for groups. Many of the inlets guide you to isolated beaches, which make great picnic spots.

Canoeing is a great way to access hidden places of natural beauty that you wouldn't normally see. It is also a good way to appreciate the abundant bird and marine life of the country. Many hotels and adventure centres hire out sea kayaks, or you can bring your own.

Adventurous canoeists can visit Mussandam in sea-touring canoes – here you'll see some spectacular rocky coastlines with fjord-like inlets and towering cliffs (some as high as 1,000m).

Muscat Diving and Adventure Centre

Location ➔ Nr Radisson Hotel · Al Khuwayr | 24 485 663
Web/email ➔ www.holiday-in-oman.com   Map Ref ➔ 7-B3

If you are going to take to the waters then you might as well do it in a kayak. Explore the 1,700 kms of rugged Omani coastline, and stop at any of the small fishing villages in between, in a single or double sea kayak. Families can enjoy the marine life in one of the centre's glass bottomed canoes.

The price for a half-day kayaking session is RO 20 per person (minimum of four people); or RO 40 per person (minimum of two people). To rent a kayak only, it will cost you RO 15 per person. A credit card deposit is required.

Canyoning

Other options ➔ Hiking [p.205]

Interesting topography makes canyoning particularly popular in Oman. This is not a sport for the timid and can often be challenging and treacherous. It involves using various techniques, walking, abseiling, swimming and scrambling, to ascend or descend a canyon. There are some awesome treks in the country including Wadi Shab, Snake Canyon, Wadi Hajir, Wadi Haylayn and Wadi Qashah, each with its own individual challenge and beauty. Dress lightly and always expect to get wet. There are risks associated with scrambling or abseiling down uneven and slippery surfaces. It is advisable to go as part of a group and ensure you

Canoeing · Canyoning

Activities

have at least basic knowledge of first aid. Although canyoning is an activity more commonly enjoyed by experienced groups, some tour companies do offer adventurous treks, see Activity Tours [p.142].

Caving

The caving network in the Hajar Mountains of Oman is extensive and much of it has yet to be explored and mapped. The area includes what is believed to be the second largest cave system in the world. The most famous cave in Oman, and the most stunning in terms of size, is the Majlis Al Jinn Cave. Entering this cave is not for the faint-hearted as it starts with a 180m free abseil from the entrance in the roof.

Caving in Oman varies from the fairly safe to the extremely dangerous. Even with an experienced leader, it is not for the casual tourist or the poorly equipped. It is important to understand the dangers of going underground. Make sure you take plenty of water and basic first aid equipment.

Oman offers some of the most hair-raising cave exploration in the world and should only be attempted by experienced, fit cavers, preferably accompanied by someone who has traversed the caves before.

Many caves in Oman are actually underground wadis. Do not attempt any cave exploration if there is any chance of rain, or if there have been any recent rains in the area. Flash floods can rise in a matter of minutes, leading to disaster.

A popular cave for the less intrepid (although this certainly must not be considered by unaccompanied amateurs) is Hoti Cave, which comprises an underground cavern and subterranean lake system. Hoti Cave is a 2.7 km tunnel that runs from north to south through the Hajar Mountains near Al Hamra on the south-western side of the mountain range, not far from Nizwa. There are many offshoots to the main tunnel, but so far, experienced cavers have charted only approximately five kilometres. Do not attempt to wander from the main path

Caving Safety

If you are going caving, do not forget the basic equipment. You will need the following:

- *Two heavy-duty flashlights (replace the batteries before your trip and ensure the torches are in perfect working order)*
- *Extra batteries and bulbs*
- *Climbing helmet*
- *Plenty of water and high-carbohydrate snacks*
- *Good hiking boots and light-weight clothing that is suitable for climbing*

There are two entries to Hoti Cave – the Al Fallah entrance, accessed through a large gaping hole below a cliff overhang, or the Al Hota entrance, which is strictly for experienced cavers. The latter entry must not be undertaken without ropes, safety equipment and a guide, as it involves fairly perilous scrambles down slippery rock faces. Within the Hoti Cave is the subterranean lake that is home to unusual species of aquatic animals, such as blind fish that sense their way around the lake with feelers. The main lake within the cave system is around 800m long, but do not swim in the waters as you will disturb the delicate ecosystem.

The main chamber of Hoti Cave is around the size of the Al Bustan Palace Hotel's ballroom and contains some magnificent cave formations, stalactites, stalagmites, and beautifully coloured columns that have evolved over millions of years.

There are plans to open this cave up by building a small train line from a car park to the Al Fallah entrance of the cave, possibly even a small way inside. The illumination of the interior is also being considered although full details of the project are currently unknown, as are estimated dates of completion. This will obviously change caving in this area as they plan to limit access for cavers to the top entrance only. Also, trips going right through the cave will not be allowed, so cavers that enter at the Al Hota entrance will have to turn around and exit from there as well.

One of the largest sinkholes in the world, Teyq Cave, is located between Taqa and Mirbat. The two wadis in the sinkhole keep it topped up with water when it rains. Sultan Qaboos University houses a very active Earth Sciences Department, and this is a good source of further information on the Teyq sinkhole (www.squ.edu.om).

Muscat Diving and Adventure Centre		
Location → Nr Radisson Hotel · Al Khuwayr		24 485 663
Web/email → www.holiday-in-oman.com		Map Ref → 7-B3

Try caving with the skilled guides and instructors of the Muscat Diving and Adventure Centre. Recently added to their list of hot spot destinations is the second biggest cave in the world, Majlis Al Jinn. The breathtaking abseil in and out of the 180 metre deep chamber is not to be missed. There is a compulsory training session that you will have to attend before any excursion, to ensure familiarity with certain skills and techniques and to assess your level of confidence and control of the equipment. Prices start at RO 160 per person.

Caving

Activities

Climbing

First-time climbers in Oman need to get used to the nature of the rock – most climbs are on fairly soft and brittle limestone that is not always fully reliable. Rock that looks strong can easily flake and become detached when pulled too hard, so climbing in Oman is often more subtle than athletic, requiring balance and patience. The friction though is superb, and invites delicate moves using pressure and counter pressure.

Apart from the quality of the rock, Oman's hot climate is a limiting factor and during the summer months (May – September) the temperatures can reach 50°C. For the dedicated climber it is possible to climb through the summer, if you pick your crag carefully. North-facing crags are usually in the shade in the afternoon. The usual climbing equipment will normally be sufficient, but you will have to bring your own gear as there are no dedicated shops in Oman selling it. The Muscat Diving and Adventure Centre (listed below) can supply you with equipment and also guide you to the best climbs.

Proud to be a Trekkie

If your boots were made for walking, that's just what you should do... but not without a copy of the Oman Trekking Explorer in your pocket. This handy guide features a no-fuss booklet and a series of detailed route cards (with easy to follow maps and tips for each route) that will really take you places! Lara Croft or Indiana Jones outfits are optional...

Muscat Diving and Adventure Centre

Location → Nr Radisson Hotel · Al Khuwayr	24 485 663
Web/email → www.holiday-in-oman.com	Map Ref → 7-B3

MDAC have qualified instructors to introduce you to climbing and show you a more adventurous side to Oman (there is a maximum of ten people allowed per instructor). Alternatively, the centre can offer purely logistical support for experienced climbers on longer trips. Apart from climbing, the centre also offers activities such as caving, kayaking and trekking. Classes are offered on an individual or group basis. All equipment is provided, and the cost is RO 22 per person (there must be a minimum of three people).

Cricket

With the numbers of expats living in Oman from cricket loving nations, as well as an increasing number of Omanis entering the sport, there are plenty of chances to get yourself into a match. As well as currently 60 teams registered with the Oman Cricket Association, many organisations have their own cricket teams for inter company competitions and the sport is becoming more popular in schools. The Oman team are also the current holders of the Gulf Cup Cricket title after beating Bahrain in the final.

Oman Cricket Association

Location → Nr Haffa House Hotel · Ruwi	99 314 348
Web/email → na	Map Ref → 12-C2

The Oman Cricket Association has been actively organising league tournaments since 1979. There are currently 60 teams, divided into eight divisions. Every team must register with the association to play in the league. The cricket season begins in September and lasts until March, with tournaments beginning some time in April. If you are interested in playing please contact Madhu Sampat or Jesrani.

Cycling

Other options → Mountain Biking [p.208]
Sporting Goods [p.172]

Oman has tremendous scope for cycling, with many routes that run both along the beautiful coastline and through the rugged hills and mountains. Cycling is a great way to get to know Muscat too – you can ride along the corniche at Mutrah, weave through old Muscat, and scale the roads through the spectacular rocky mountains to Al Bustan and Qantab.

Riding in traffic requires care, as in any country, but even more so in the Middle East. Drivers are not very sympathetic towards cyclists and don't allow enough room and time for them. Caution has to be exercised when in busy areas of town, especially at junctions and roundabouts. On the plus side, road surfaces are decent and punctures are a rarity. Joining a cycling club will quickly introduce you to the routes and safety issues of cycling in and around Muscat.

Most of the main roads in the city have a hard shoulder, which provides a fairly safe lane for cyclists. Although bikes are not allowed in most of Muscat's parks, there are some nice rides through the quieter, residential, and pleasant green areas of the city.

Muscat Cycling Club

Location ➜ Ruwi | 99 324 594
Web/email ➜ na | Map Ref ➜ na

This group meets regularly for weekend rides. It welcomes both road and off-road cyclists, so whether you prefer speeding down the highway or bumping your way over rocks, they will happily accommodate you. They welcome new members and are active socially as well.

Dhow Charters

Other options ➜ Boat & Yacht Charters [p.190]
Coastal Cruises [p.143]
Dinner Cruises [p.255]

Al Marsa Travel & Tourism Co.

Location ➜ East Coast · UAE | +971- 6 544 1232
Web/email ➜ www.musandamdiving.com | Map Ref ➜ 1-A2

Al Marsa has two purpose-built dhows that are suitable for divers and tourists. You can relax on the sundeck for a day trip and discover fishing villages or you can go on an overnight voyage and explore fjords. Prices start at Dhs.370 for divers and Dhs.300 for non-divers.

Khasab Dhow Charters

Location ➜ Dibba Fishmarket/Port · UAE | +971-4 266 9950
Web/email ➜ www.khasab.tours.com | Map Ref ➜ 1-A2

Large independent groups can charter a dhow from the fishermen at Dibba to travel up the coast of the Mussandam. Be prepared to bargain hard to get a better price – knowing a bit of Arabic will probably smooth things along. Expect to pay about RO 250 per day for a dhow large enough to take 20 to 25 people.

It's advisable to take camping equipment and arrange for the dhow to stop along the coast for the night, although it is possible to sleep on board. Camping is only possible in certain areas. In the daytime you can go ashore, visit the villages or walk in the mountains. You'll need to take your own food and water as nothing is supplied except ice

lockers that are suitable for storing supplies. Conditions on board are pretty basic.

The waters are crystal clear and, although weather can seriously reduce visibility, turtles and dolphins can be seen from the boat. It's also ideal for diving, but hire everything before reaching Dibba. Try the Sandy Beach Motel, UAE for equipment hire. Alternatively, spend the days swimming, snorkelling and lazing, and for an extra RO 80 hire a speedboat for the day.

Musandam Sea Adventure Tourism

Location ➜ Khasab · Mussandam | 26 730 069
Web/email ➜ www.musandam-sea-adventures.com | Map Ref ➜ 1-A2

With its dramatic fjords, the Mussandam area is often referred to as 'the Norway of the Middle East'. Take a dhow cruise and experience the rocky topography, mountains jutting up out of pristine waters, and remote villages, stopping afterwards at Telegraph Island for a leisurely picnic. Dhow cruises can be various lengths, from half a day to three days, and costs range from RO 15 – 110 per person. Musandam Sea Adventure takes care of transportation, food, and lodging and creates a comfortable, but adventurous, tour.

Sail away into the sunset

Dhow Charters

Activities

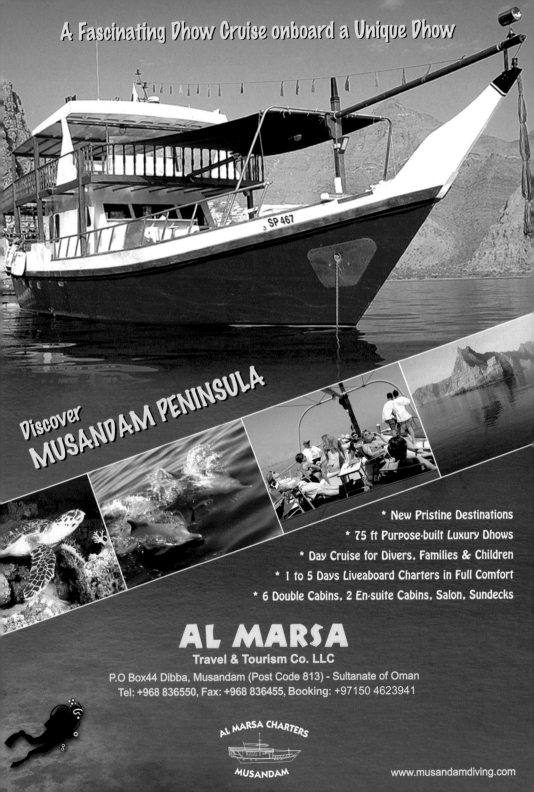

Diving

Other options → Snorkelling [p.211]
Underwater Explorer (Oman)

If you are fortunate enough to find yourself in Oman, year-round diving is one of the most breathtaking pleasures. Oman has a long coastline with a variety of underwater treasures. Marine life abounds, with coral reefs and shipwrecks providing a multitude of dwellings for sea creatures. The quantities and varieties of sea life, in a quiet atmosphere, will amaze any diver. While you're underwater it won't be other divers you bump into, but sea turtles, cuttlefish, stingrays, moray eels – the list is endless. Oman offers a truly exceptional environment for both novice and advanced divers. Those who prefer extra adventure will find cave diving a unique experience. Please be aware that all divers must have a diving permit from the ROP to dive in the waters off Oman. Most divers obtain the permit through the club or diving centre they are diving through.

Night dives are very popular, and provide the opportunity to see many nocturnal marine creatures that you wouldn't normally see. The phosphorescence in Oman's waters is much more visible after dark. This green-blue substance, released by plankton as a result of chemical reactions from their vigorous movements, makes for an amazing underwater display.

If you have never dived before, don't worry, there are plenty of centres that can provide training in PADI or BSAC, depending on your preference. PADI provides a shorter Open Water Certification, especially beneficial for those on holiday or who want to begin sea diving without too much delay. PADI also provides advanced diver training if you decide you'd like to pursue more diving opportunities. BSAC training is more extensive and, if you have the time, is especially good for the novice diver who wants to learn the finer points.

There are numerous dive sites in Oman. Below is a list of a few of the more popular ones, keep in mind that each site is extensive and you could spend years exploring every nook and cranny!

Fahal Island – Located in Muscat's Al Qurm region. This island has around ten dive sites and is especially good in a variety of weather conditions. Diving depth is from three to 42 metres. Should you happen to chose a particularly windy day, there is usually at least one area of the island that will offer perfect diving conditions. Around Fahal Island are isolated reefs, a swim-through cave, and artificial reef balls. The most notable fish in this area are angelfish, trigger fish and large broom-tail. Also look out for diamond-shaped stingrays (who enjoy backflipping out of the water), honeycomb eels and a few friendly sharks. You'll also find a large variety of coral types growing around the island. There is some good snorkelling on the western side of the island, if you'd like to take a break from diving.

Bander Khayran – Located near Muscat, about 20 – 30 minutes by boat or 40 minutes by 4 WD. This area is a small fjord system littered with inlets. The diving depth here ranges between one and 30 metres. It is known for diverse and beautiful corals and marine life attracted to coral reefs. Some of the corals you will see here are table, bush, boulder, brain, hedgehog, cauliflower, and pore corals; many often intermixed and in a variety of colours.

Al-Munassir Naval Shipwreck – Located near Bander Khayran. In April 2003 the Royal Navy of Oman purposely and successfully sank this naval ship to create an artificial reef in Omani waters. The ship is located approximately 30 metres underwater and spans a length of 84 metres, all canons and guns were removed from the ship before the sinking. The rooms in the ship were opened up for divers to easily pass through. Passing through the ship's engine, dining and other rooms creates an excellent environment for divers to learn orientation. It is also a great site to watch marine life adapt and emerge within the vessel.

> ### Underwater Explorer
> While Oman is a diver's paradise, neighbouring UAE shouldn't be overlooked. The UAE Underwater Explorer is the ultimate companion to help make the most of the spectacular submarine scenery. With meticulously detailed dive-sites, maps with GPS coordinates, and shipwreck histories and illustrations, this book will become as indispensable to divers as a mask and fins.

Daymaniyat Islands – A nature reserve made up of nine islands and named numerically from D1 to D9. They span approximately 20 kilometres from Seeb to Barka. Diving depth of the islands ranges from one to 30 metres. The Oman government designated the islands and surrounding coral reefs as a national nature reserve, and access is controlled. With an extensive coral reef and abundant sea life, the Daymaniyats are well known as a magnificent diving area amongst divers in Oman.

Life's a beach!

Blu Zone Diving

Location → Marina Bander Al-Rowdha · Sidab | 24 737 293
Web/email → www.bluzonediving.com   Map Ref → 13-E4

Blu Zone is a family run PADI five star dive centre with experienced instructors and comprehensive guides. Diving courses are offered from beginner to instructor level and, for those wanting to practise a particular skill, specific classes are offered including wreck dives and navigation. The Bubblemaker course is available for children eight years and older. All classes are offered in a number of different languages.

Capital Area Yacht Club (CAYC)

Location → Sidab | 24 737 712
Web/email → na   Map Ref → 13-E3

CAYC Divers offer a variety of activities including day and night diving, snorkelling and wreck dives. The centre offers BSAC courses. Members can dive at any time, but guests can dive at weekends only.

Moonlight Dive Centre

Location → Shati Al Qurm | 99 317 700
Web/email → na   Map Ref → 7-D1

This centre, situated on the public beach next to the Grand Hyatt Muscat, offers diving and watersports. There is an impressive list of activities including PADI dives, dolphin watching, sunset cruises and fishing trips. They also offer equipment rental and repair. For something a bit more relaxing there are boat trips along the coast to secluded bays, or snorkelling in some of the best waters in the Middle East. The centre can also arrange hotel accommodation and land tours.

Muscat Diving and Adventure Centre

Location → Nr Radisson Hotel · Al Khuwayr | 24 485 663
Web/email → www.holiday-in-oman.com   Map Ref → 7-B3

Catering to all of your water sporting needs, the Muscat Diving and Adventure Centre makes the very most of the vast beauty and abundance of fascinating sea life that Oman has to offer. Experienced and proficient instructors are on hand to teach beginners, or organise trips for the more experienced diver.

Oman Dive Centre

Location → Bandar Al Jissah · Al Bustan | 99 340 096
Web/email → www.diveoman.com.om   Map Ref → 15-E3

Popularly known as ODC, this centre offers five star PADI training facilities. It is set in the picturesque bay of Bandar Al Jissah, which is sheltered and a perfect spot for snorkellers and novices to practise before venturing into the ocean. Activities include day and night diving, snorkelling, underwater photography, wreck diving and first aid courses. Diving and snorkelling day trips to the Daymaniyat Islands and the Quriyat wreck can also be arranged.

Oman Dive Centre

Fishing

Other options → Boat & Yacht Charters [p.190]

Coastal Fishing

The Sultanate of Oman boasts some of the best surf fishing in the world. The coastline from Al Khaluf down to Salalah is home to a variety of species belonging to the warm waters of the Indian Ocean. Fishing along these coastal coves is seasonal due to the severe weather conditions caused by the monsoon.

Depending on the fishing area chosen, the species available include blue fish, travaly, shark, black bream, rays, grouper and spotted grunter. Sizes of species caught vary quite considerably – blue fish will range from five to 20 pounds, and ray and shark anywhere between ten and 200.

Light tackle and heavy tackle combos are a must for fishing these waters. All the various species tend to take turns in feeding during the day and night. Ensure your secondary tackle supplies are plentiful as you will often experience toothy beasts taking your bait.

Fishing the coastline of Oman beyond Al Khaluf can be taxing on both vehicles and supplies. This is not an average jaunt down to the beach with rod in hand. Most people do not transport their boats by road, but rather keep them moored in a harbour. The villagers along the coastline of Oman are very friendly and always happy to help (do remember you are in a Muslim country so respect their traditions and religious beliefs). Maps of the Oman coastline are available and it will be very helpful to have one on your first few trips.

Sitting on the dock of the bay...

Big Game Fishing

For big game fishing, the season from October to April is the most productive. The rest of the year tends to be slow, as the fish move further south avoiding the higher waters in summer. The true Indian Ocean meets the Gulf of Oman off the point of Ras Al Hadd. Different water colours and surface textures can be clearly seen when fishing this area.

The most common species of big game fish found during the high season is the yellowfin tuna, a tricky fish to hook and sometimes caught in weights exceeding 100lb. Although much larger specimens are available to offshore anglers fishing the Oman waters, these are usually only caught south of Muscat or much further out than the average fisherman cares to venture. On rare occasions yellowfin tuna close to the 250lb mark have been caught within five to ten km of the Muscat town coast.

Sailfish seem to be dominant in the waters off Muscat during the months of September and

October. It is believed that they migrate through on their way to the Arabian Gulf for breeding. They are often caught close to shore and vary in weight from 60 – 110lb.

Mai Mai/dolphin fish are found in abundance from the end of July to September. Travelling in schools, these fish make for some fast, light-tackle action. The size averages around the 15lb mark, but occasionally you might land something in the 35 – 45lb range.

Black marlin, on occasion, travel into the coastal waters off Muscat. However, to date, there has been only one confirmed capture and weigh-in recorded, a whopping 400lb+. There are reports that marlin are in greater abundance off the coastal area of Ras Al Hadd, confirmed by the local commercial fisheries who estimate an average of six to ten marlin a day brought in by their boats. The season is typically from November to April.

Along its length, the Oman coastline is met by underwater mountain ranges and drop-offs that go down to 300 metres (and more) in some areas. Due to the deep water ridges rising up into the warm coastal shallows, an abundance of game species are found feeding on the bait fish, that in turn thrive on the nutrients brought up from the depths – an excellent example of the natural food chain.

Arabian Sea Safaris

Location → Htl InterContinental · Shati Al Qurm   24 693 223
Web/email → www.arabianseasafaris.com   Map Ref → 8-A4

The team at Arabian Sea Safaris is dedicated to providing the ultimate in memorable fishing trips. They will happily take you to explore Oman's unspoilt waters by fishing, swimming, diving or snorkelling among beautiful exotic fish and breathtaking coral reefs. You can start your excursion with a swim with dolphins and end it with a leisurely stroll along a fabulous stretch of deserted beach.

Sidab Sea Tours

Location → Al Bustan   24 737 885
Web/email → sidabseatours@hotmail.com   Map Ref → 15-A1

With a local skipper who knows these waters like the back of his hand, you're almost guaranteed a good catch with Sidab Sea Tours, although it is never guaranteed! They organise half or full-day professional game-fishing excursions, with barracuda, tuna, marlin and sailfish as the intended targets. You can also try traditional handline fishing 'Omani style'. Whatever bait you choose, all tackle and equipment is provided and soft drinks are available on board. Sidab Sea Tours also run dolphin watching tours and coastal cruises.

Football

Like most places in the world, you don't have to travel far to see a game of football in Oman. Villages in the countryside usually have a group knocking a ball around on the local sand and rock pitch – see if you can join in. Also, there are often groups kicking about on the beaches, particularly the InterContinental beach strip.

There is a semi-professional football league in Oman with teams such as the Oman Club, Sidab and Quriyat participating. A maximum of two expatriate players are allowed to join each of these clubs, so the majority of expat football fans usually play in the weekly social soccer games at the grounds of the Oman Club. The main teams include Loan Service, Deuch PDO, Aerworks, British PDO, Royal Flight and the Sultan Qaboos University Squad.

Unfortunately, all of the above teams only accept players from within their own organisations, making it quite difficult for newcomers to get into the game. Alternatively you can always start a team of your own, either via your company or group of friends. Then if it turns into a regular event you can give Explorer a shout and we'll give you a shout out in the next edition of the Oman Explorer.

Half time in the hills!

For children, the schools arrange the football scene. The PSSL schools soccer league has five age categories, ranging from under-nines to under-19s. The students play from September to December, with the Irishman's cup for the under-13s a fitting climax to the season. The Al Sahwa school and PDO Elementary usually fare well in the youngest age group, while the American British Academy and Indian School Wadi Kabir tend to dominate the under-11s. The ABA is also strong in the under-13 sector, along with The Indian School Muscat. For the under-15 sides, Muscat Private School, British School and ISM are competitive participants. In the older category, Royal Guard and Sultan School tend to be the dominant forces.

Golf

Golf in Oman has a healthy band of supporters who play on 'brown' (sand) courses, nearly all of which are concentrated around Muscat. There is currently a lack of green courses, but this is all set to change. The Sultanate is poised to get its first green golf course, which will be situated behind the Seeb Novotel. To be named the Muscat Golf and Country Club, the unique 18-hole tournament-grade course has been designed by top golf course designer, David Thomas, to challenge the best golfers in the world. The construction of Oman's first green golf course is hoped to boost the country's tourism sector, as well as put the Sultanate on the world golfing map.

Even so, there are already several tournaments throughout the year, such as the Oman Ladies' Open Championship, the Men's Oman National Championship, and the Ras Al Ghala Trophy.

Those who have never played golf in the Middle East should be warned that the game here can be more physically demanding than elsewhere in the world – even acclimatised golfers avoid playing in the heat of the day during the summer months. While the cool breezes of winter bring lower temperatures, it is always wise to carry plenty of drinking water and wear a sun hat.

Al Maha Golf Course	
Location ➜ Oman Automobile Club · As Seeb	24 522 177
Web/email ➜ Atul@ohigroup.com	Map Ref ➜ 5-A4

The club has two distinct seasons – the summer season, which starts in April and ends in September, and the winter season, starting in October and ending in March. Due to the intense

Activities

Football · Golf

heat in the summer months, only 9 holes are normally played and summer competitions are also scheduled accordingly. The 18-hole season is played in winter when the temperatures drop. The club attracts a wide range of sponsors each year and is always looking for more competition golfers. Coaching is available for beginners throughout the year.

Costs: *Annual membership – RO 95 (individual) RO 125 (family) Visitors – RO 5 (RO 2 with a member)*

Ghallah Wentworth Golf Club

Location ➜ Nr Seeb Airport · As Seeb	24 591 248
Web/email ➜ na	Map Ref ➜ 6-C4

This is a fair challenge for any level of player. The club has a driving range built on concrete tee boxes and a few sets of clubs for hire. Players should bring their own Astroturf mats for teeing off. There are two separate golf seasons, winter (18 hole) and summer (nine hole), with competitions organised accordingly throughout the year. Lessons are available upon request.

Marco Polo Garden Course

Location ➜ Crowne Plaza Resort · Salalah	23 235 333
Web/email ➜ www.crowneplaza.com	Map Ref ➜ 1-E3

Due to open in April 2005, this grass course includes a driving range, putting green and training area. In between the coconut groves, an unusual nine-hole par three course is available. Golf Clubs and a professional golf instructor will be available on request.

Hashing

Other options ➜ Pubs [p.264]
Running [p.210]

Sometimes described as drinking clubs with a running problem, the Hash House Harriers form a worldwide family of social running clubs. The aim of running in this setup is not to win, but to merely be there and to take part. The first hash club was formed in Kuala Lumpur in 1938, and it is now the largest running organisation in the world, with members in over 1,600 chapters in 180 countries.

Hashing consists of running, jogging or walking around varied courses, often cross-country, laid out by a couple of *hares*. It's a fun way to keep fit and meet new people, as clubs are very sociable and the running is not competitive.

Jebel Hash House Harriers

Location ➜ Various locations	24 521 395
Web/email ➜ www.omanshash.com	Map Ref ➜ na

Founded in 1985, the Jebel Hash is a social, non-competitive running club that is part of the worldwide Hash House Harriers family. There are always two trails to follow – one for those wishing to walk and one that is a bit longer for the more energetic. A social gathering follows each run, so be prepared. The Jebel Hash runs take place anywhere within Muscat and its surroundings. Apart from meeting new people, it's a great way of seeing some places you might otherwise miss.

Muscat Hash House Harriers

Location ➜ Various locations	24 333 062
Web/email ➜ igronl@omantel.net.om	Map Ref ➜ na

Traditionally known as the Muscat Hash, this group meets every Saturday evening, with times varying with the changing times of dusk. There is a RO 1 fee for each meeting, these are organised in various locations around Muscat depending on where the hare has set the run. Celebrations for various international holidays are always lively!

Hiking

Other options ➜ Canyoning [p.195]
Outdoor Goods [p.169]

The hiking in Oman is excellent, whether you go on a casual walk on the beach or ascend one of the country's highest peaks (such as Jebel Shams).

The formation of mountains here has left some inspiring gorges, wadis, peaks, ridges and plateaus. The terrain is heavily eroded and shattered due to the harsh climate, but there are many excellent routes. These range from short easy walks leading to spectacular viewpoints, to longer treks up higher peaks over difficult terrain.

Many of the paths follow ancient Bedouin and Shihuh trails through the mountains. These are still used today as the only means of access to some of the more remote inhabited settlements. The terrain is incredible and one can only wonder at the skills of the hardy mountain people who pioneered these routes.

The main mountain area, shared in part with the United Arab Emirates, is the Al Hajar Range, which splits into the Northern, Eastern and Western Hajar.

Hashing · Hiking

Activities

In the south, near Salalah, are the Dhofar Mountains, with the highest point at Jebel Samhan. In the Al Hajar, the highest peak is Jebel Shams at just over 3,000 metres (in Arabic, 'Jebel' is mountain and 'Shams' means sun). Many of the mountains here are 2,000 metres and higher, providing excellent walking and fabulous views. The spectacular 'Grand Canyon of Oman' is also in this area and an energetic, but very beautiful, walk around the rim of the canyon is well worth the effort.

There are many documented treks in Oman that are rated according to difficulty. But it doesn't matter how proficient your hiking skills are, Muscat is full of easily accessible local walks that you can do on your own or as part of a group, taking full advantage of Oman's location and beautiful scenery.

If you prefer to venture further afield, Jebel Shams has numerous hikes. One of the shorter, less rigorous hikes (at four hours) is the Balcony Walk at Jebel Shams Plateau. Incredible canyon views and a trek through an abandoned village will delight all those with the energy to take part. Adventure trekkers looking for a more strenuous experience will be inspired by the Al Hawb to Jebel Shams summit. This hike requires good climbing abilities and an overnight camp. It may take up to 12 hours to reach the summit and the trek is a 20-hour round trip, depending on the descent path chosen. But the views at the top are the ultimate reward for all that hard work!

Be sure on any hike, short or long, that you consider the weather conditions in Oman. Always carry plenty of water and snacks, check your routes before you set out on any trek, notify a friend as to your whereabouts, and wear light boots and appropriate clothing. Take a compass or GPS and check the customs and conditions of the area before taking any long trips. Be warned, no mountain rescue services exist, therefore anyone venturing out into mountains should be reasonably experienced, or be with some one who knows the area. As long as you are properly prepared, your trek will be an outstanding experience leaving you with nothing but fond memories and perhaps sore feet.

Donkey Trekking

Location ➜ Various locations	**99 348 440**
Web/email ➜ na	Map Ref ➜ na

Trekking trips are run on Oman's newly established hiking trails in the spectacular Hajar Mountains, with donkeys to carry the luggage, enabling you to be free to enjoy the views. Hikes take you to remote areas of the mountains near the village of Misfat Al A'briyeen where you can sleep under the stars, eat traditional food and get into the local culture. Trips can be custom designed for the requirement of individual groups, call Ahmed or Reinhard for more details.

Muscat Diving and Adventure Centre

Location ➜ Nr Radisson Hotel · Al Khuwayr	**24 485 663**
Web/email ➜ www.holiday-in-oman.com	Map Ref ➜ 7-B3

Because of the varied topography, your trekking adventure can be as easy or as hard as you want. Whether you decide on little more than a brisk walk through a pleasant wadi or a struggle amongst the harsh desert rock, the centre has a number of different routes to choose from.

The cost is RO 16 per person for a half-day hike (minimum of four people).

Horse Riding

Other options ➜ Polo [p.209]

Al Hashmy Riding School

Location ➜ El Hail, Nr Airport · As Seeb	**24 545 823**
Web/email ➜ na	Map Ref ➜ na

This is a privately owned, well-established stable that provides pleasure rides on the beach, as well as riding and competitive jumping lessons. The riding school and stables have been Federation inspected as grade one. The school has four instructors who offer lessons to children, over age six, through to adults. Al Hashmy also offers special pony club courses and stable management classes, and issues certificates for completion of courses.

Qurm Equestrian School

Location ➜ Qurm Park · Al Qurm	**99 339 222**
Web/email ➜ na	Map Ref ➜ 8-D4

Located in the beautiful Qurm Park, Qurm Equestrian School is open all hours and teaches beginners to advanced riders. The school offers beach rides, carriage rides, riding lessons and carriage rental for weddings or special events. There are five instructors who provide one-hour lessons in riding, competitive riding and jumping. There are also four donkeys for smaller children to ride.

Ice Hockey

Other options → Ice Skating [p.207]

Muscat Oryx Hockey

Location → Ice Skating Centre · Al Khuwayr	24 489 492
Web/email → mikefern@omantel.net.om	Map Ref → 7-B2

This ice hockey club has different teams for various ages and levels of play, from beginners to advanced, and from teenagers to adults. New members are always welcome. Practice nights are on Tuesday evenings, beginning at 16:30 for juniors. You must provide your own equipment. The rink is only a third of the regulation size, so only practices are held here. However, the teams participate in tournaments in the UAE. The season starts in September and ends in May.

Ice Skating

Other options → Ice Hockey [p.207]

Figure Skating School

Location → Ice Skating Centre · Al Khuwayr	24 489 492
Web/email → mikefern@omantel.net.om	Map Ref → 7-B2

If you've ice skated in the past and spent the whole time tottering around the rink or clinging onto the side bar, it might be time to get professional help! Ice skating classes are available privately or in groups, in courses of six lessons (group students also get six free practice sessions). On the seventh week a test is taken, leading to the proficiency badge.

Prices per course are RO 30 (Pre-Alpha to Delta) and RO 33 (Freestyle 1 and above). Private lessons are RO 6 each for half an hour (this doesn't include practice sessions).

Ice Skating Centre

Location → Nr Zawawi Mosque · Al Khuwayr	24 489 492
Web/email → mikefern@omantel.net.om	Map Ref → 7-B2

Ice skating is the perfect cool leisure activity for the hot summer months, and the Ice Skating Centre will gladly accommodate requests for professional training for beginners and competitors alike. Group and private lessons are available. Figure skating and hockey competitions are also held at the centre.

Jet Skiing

Other options → Beach Clubs [p.217]

This is becoming a more popular pastime along the coast of Muscat. Much of Oman's coastline is open and accessible. Be wary of fishermen and swimmers – in the past, jet skiers have been prosecuted for accidents. For safety, it is a good idea to remain 500 metres from the shore. Most hotels and resorts rent jet skis for about RO 7-10 per half hour.

Karting

Oman Automobile Club (OAC)

Location → Oman Automobile Club · As Seeb	24 510 239
Web/email → www.omanautoclub.com	Map Ref → 5-A4

The OAC is said to have one of the best international standard tracks in the Middle East. The club conducts classes and competitions for all age groups and proficiencies, and meet for practice sessions on alternate Fridays. The race season begins in September and ends in May. You can bring your own kart or rent one from the centre. It is possible to reserve the track and karts for private functions and gatherings.

Kitesurfing

Other options → Beaches [p.132]

Kitesurfing is one of the fastest growing extreme watersports, not only in Oman, but in the region as a whole. With plenty of uncrowded beaches and often superb wind conditions, kitesurfing is definitely on the up and up in the popularity stakes. The sport involves using large kites to power you across the water, and a wakeboard to hold the edge and keep you afloat.

Currently you'll find a small group of kitesurfing enthusiasts gathering on Thursday and Friday afternoons at Azaiba Beach. Azaiba Beach is

Climb Every Mountain

We've trekked all over Oman, armed with nothing but fresh water supplies and a notepad, to bring you this handy guide to the art of trekking. It contains an info-packed booklet and some rather nifty route cards that will help you keep your bearings while out in the rough. It's as invaluable to any trek fan as a comfortable pair of hiking boots.

relatively quiet and sandy, offering perfect kitesurfing conditions when winds exceed ten knots. Be careful of the occasional car or group of people wandering across the beach, especially in the early evenings. During summer, the hardcore kitesurfers escape the relatively light conditions of Muscat and head for the east coast, where the winds are often 15 – 30 knots.

At present, there are no kitesurfing schools or shops in Oman, but if you have a chat to any of the regulars they will be able to offer advice about where to buy equipment and how to get started.

Martial Arts

Black Stallion Karate Do

Location ➜ Al Falaj Hotel Muscat · Ruwi	24 702 311
Web/email ➜ jonju@omantel.net.om	Map Ref ➜ 12-C1

Black Stallion Karate Do offers a variety of martial arts classes for children and adults. Options include karate, taekwondo kicks, aikido, judo, mun-chako, kendo sticks, Philippine arnis and gymnastics. Classes range in cost from RO 15 for children and RO 20 for adults, per month. Whatever your level of skill or fitness, these classes can help increase both your physical prowess and mental well-being.

Oman Karate-do Centre

Location ➜ Al Khuwayr	24 482 941
Web/email ➜ na	Map Ref ➜ 7-D2

The Oman Karate-do Centre provides martial arts for all levels, as well as yoga classes and women's self defence courses. Special courses are offered for ages ten and below, and any age over ten at beginner, intermediate and advanced levels. Courses and diplomas given are from Japan and England and are recognised worldwide. The Centre has several locations where you can take courses.

Moto-Cross

Other options ➜ Motorcycling [p.208]
Quad Bikes [p.209]

Oman Automobile Club

Location ➜ As Seeb	24 510 239
Web/email ➜ www.omanautoclub.com	Map Ref ➜ 5-A4

The Oman Automobile Club (OAC) operates under the umbrella of the Oman Automobile Association (OAA) and offers many activities, including motocross. It has a one-kilometre sandy moto-cross track complete with hills, jumps, twists and turns. It is a terrific track for learning on, or for sharpening your skills. The OAC hosts a number of rallies throughout the year. The track is excellent, but you need to provide your own bikes and equipment. The club contains an area to store bikes, for a fee.

Motorcycling

Other options ➜ Moto-Cross [p.208]

Harley Davidson Owners' Group (Muscat Chapter)

Location ➜ Nr Zakher Hall	24 489 428
Web/email ➜ www.geocites.com/hd_oman	Map Ref ➜ 7-D2

Following the official opening of the Harley Davidson Showroom in 1998, the Muscat Chapter of the Harley Owners Group commenced its activities. The Harley Davidson Owners' Group (HOG), which includes expats and Omanis, coordinates its meetings at the 'HOG Pen' (HOG coffee shop) in the Harley Davidson showroom. The club arranges regular meetings, activities, rides and events for Harley Davidson enthusiasts and their families. Rides are held on Tuesday evenings, Friday mornings and an overnight ride is organised at least once a month. For more information call in at the Harley Davidson showroom. For a background on the group, visit www.hogmuscat.com.

Mountain Biking

Other options ➜ Cycling [p.197]

Oman has some great mountain biking routes, with no end of off-road tracks winding their way through the mountains, wadis and along the coast.

The Bawshar Dunes close to Muscat offer some great rides, as do Sayh Ad Dhabi or the route from the InterContinental to the desalination plant.

Activities

Martial Arts · Mountain Biking

Riding in the mountains is adventurous and generally rocky, technical and challenging. There are many tracks to follow and the terrain is on a par with the classic trail areas of Utah and Arizona in the USA.

Those who are just getting into mountain biking should start on the tracks in the gentler hilly areas. For hardcore mountain bikers there is a good range of topography, from highly technical rocky trails to mountain routes – which can take hours to climb and minutes to descend! Be prepared and sensible – the sun is strong, you'll need far more water than you think and it's very easy to get lost or to have an accident. Contact the cycling clubs for more information or to get together with other mountain bikers.

Polo

Other options → Horse Riding [p.206]

Royal Cavalry

Location → As Seeb	**24 420 444**
Web/email → na	Map Ref → 1-B1

During winter, the Royal Cavalry hosts various competitions that are open to the general public, at no charge. The season runs from October to March, when the weather is a little bit kinder – the spring and summer months are too hot for competition.

The events are mainly polo matches but also sometimes dressage, coach and carriage driving, and horse racing. All competitions involve professional riders. Tent pegging, a sport that involves the rider picking up rings on a short stick whilst riding at a gallop, is also practised.

The events are generally held on alternate Sundays, starting mid-afternoon.

Quad Bikes

Other options → Moto-Cross [p.208]

The rough terrain and dunes of Oman's remote areas attract all kinds of motor sports enthusiasts. If you're into motorbikes, quads or dune buggies, and you have your own, it's possible to take yourself and a few friends for a fun day out – you don't run the risk of bumping into anyone else and you can explore at will.

The Bawshar Sands, just outside Muscat, are a great place to fly your bike or quad off a dune. If you don't have your own quad, you can rent one at many of the hotels and beach resorts. Unlike dune buggies, quad bikes have no roll cages and therefore extra care should be taken. Where possible get training, and get hold of safety equipment, to make the most of your thrills-and-spills adventure.

Rollerblading & Roller Skating

Other options → Beaches [p.132]
Parks [p.133]

An exciting sport, great fun and great exercise, it's best to be well protected since falls can be hard – especially on the head, wrists and knees. Though it's not very common in Oman at the moment, its popularity is picking up and the good winter weather is ideal for rollerblading.

A good spot for rollerblading at night is the Embassies area, since it is fairly quiet and the surface is smooth. Muscat's parks have long, wide walkways, although these often have interlocking tiles that make blading more difficult.

Rugby

Muscat Rugby Football Club

Location → Al Khuwayr	**24 604 890**
Web/email → www.muscatrugbyclub.com	Map Ref → 7-D4

Located next to the American British Academy, the Muscat Rugby Club is both a sporting facility and social centre. Weekly practice sessions take place every Monday from 19:00 – 20:30 at the club pitch. The club currently has over 100 members, all enjoying free use of the facilities and free flights to away games for playing members. The club takes part in the Arabian Gulf Rugby League and several other tournaments, including the Bahrain 10s and

Polo · Rugby

Activities

the Dubai 7s. A mini-rugby session for ages seven to 16 takes place on Wednesdays.

Running

Other options → Hashing [p.205]

Muscat Road Runners

Location → Various locations	99 250 870
Web/email → muscatroadrunners.com	Map Ref → na

Muscat Road Runners meet twice a week and run competitively every Tuesday. A designated race organiser is responsible for timekeeping and results. Social runs take place every Sunday, with a member of the group hosting a run and providing refreshments afterwards. Summer runs tend to be short (usually not longer than five kilometres) due to the temperatures. Winter runs are longer, culminating in the half marathon in late February.

Oman Athletics Association

Location → Ruwi	24 797 233
Web/email → omanaa@omantel.net.om	Map Ref → na

The OAA's main role is to train the national Omani team in track and field events, preparing them for National and International competitions. The organisation also arranges local competitions in all activities from running to marathons and these are open to everyone. There are categories for adults and children, and medals are awarded for first, second and third positions. The OAA maintains a list of contacts for all sporting activities, so give them a call if you would like to details about a particular interest.

Sailing

Other options → Boat & Yacht Charters [p.190]

Sailing off the coast of Oman is a wonderful experience – especially in winter when the temperatures are perfect for watersports. Don't relegate this sport to colder times though, since summer sailing is a great escape from the scorching heat inland.

Unfortunately, much of the club sailing in and around Muscat is closed to outsiders and the facilities are limited to employees of particular companies (although there is an Oman Laser Association and opportunities to sail in regattas and races at the PDO Club). This is certainly a sport where word of mouth is the best way to get information.

There are many companies who will take you out for a pleasure or fishing cruise, either for a couple of hours or for a full day. There are also companies from whom you can charter your own boat – whether you take it for a single day or several weeks is up to you.

Marina Bander Al-Rowdha

Location → Marina Bander Al-Rowdha · Sidab	24 737 288
Web/email → www.marinaoman.com	Map Ref → 13-E4

There are regular regattas held in the waters of Oman. Contact Marina Bander Al-Rowdha for more details.

Oman Laser Association

Location → Mina Al Fahal (PDO)	99 732 035
Web/email → na	Map Ref → na

The OLA has been in Oman for almost 20 years, promoting the interests of laser sailing and small boat sailing in general. They organise around ten competitions annually. The races are competitive yet friendly affairs, where the more experienced sailors readily share tips and techniques with others. Most races are held at the RAH Recreation Club, with occasional events in Sawadi Resort or the Marina Bandar Al-Rowdha. There are occasionally co-organised events that include instruction for beginners as well as organised races, in order to expand the Omani laser fleet.

Sand Boarding/Skiing

Other options → Tour Operators [p.141]

Head out to any area of the desert in the interior of Oman, find yourself some big dunes and feel the rush of the wind as you take a fast ride down the sandy slopes. It is an easy sport to learn, it doesn't hurt when you fall in the soft sand, and you'll feel a real sense of achievement when you master it and glide to the bottom. Most people tend to use snowboards, but you'll even find the odd skier taking to the sandy slopes. Standard snowboards or skis can be used.

The best places for sand boarding and skiing are the biggest dunes such as those in the Wahiba Sands area or the massive dunes of the Empty Quarter, in the south-west of the country. Many tour companies and camps provide equipment and direction.

Snorkelling

Other options → Diving [p.200]

A mask and snorkel are all you need for an awesome view of Oman's coast. The quantity and variety of underwater sea creatures are incredible, and the seas are pristine. You have an excellent opportunity to view much of the marine life simply by snorkelling. Most hotels or dive centres will rent out equipment. Costs vary greatly so shop around.

Paradise found

Softball

Muscat Softball League	
Location → As Seeb	99 337 593
Web/email → www.liezel.8m.com	Map Ref → 5-A4

The Muscat Softball League organises all softball games and tournaments in Oman. There are two divisions (A and B). There are women's, men's and mixed leagues within the divisions. The leagues play every second Thursday afternoon, and on Saturday and Sunday nights. There are two seasons, one from September to mid-December and one from January to April. The MSL also sends teams to participate in one international tournament each year. All games are played on the fields at the Oman Automobile Association (OAC), which is equipped with changing rooms and a children's play area. Hot food is available.

Squash

Other options → Sports & Leisure Facilities [p.216]

Squash is a popular sport in Muscat and there are excellent facilities all over the capital. Many of the health clubs have squash courts and often informal leagues run at the various clubs. For information on reserving a court or becoming involved in a league, contact one of Muscat's hotel health clubs.

Surfing

Other options → Beaches [p.132]
Kitesurfing [p.207]

So the mere mention of Oman may not inspire images of Hawaii style waves and surfer dudes, but you'd be surprised how popular the sport is here. After all you have everything you need to make for a good days surfing. The eastern side of Masirah Island is one of the better surfing spots and can easily be reached by ferry from Sana and the mainland, and then a short drive. Check for ferry times as these change with the tide. Depending on what time of year you happen to be visiting expect waves to average four to six feet.

Although it might not compare with the world's greatest surf spots, Oman is certainly one of the better places to surf in the Gulf because part of its coast is on the Indian Ocean. As a result, groups of surfers from other gulf countries (such as the UAE) make regular trips to Oman. While there are currently no major surf clubs in Oman, the Dubai surfers' group has an excellent website that gives information on surfing in the UAE, the Arabian Gulf and in Oman (www.surfersofdubai.com).

Swimming

Other options → Beaches [p.132]
Sports & Leisure Facilities [p.216]

Most hotels have swimming pools that are open for public use. Day charges range from RO 2.5 to RO 8, but expect to pay a bit more at the weekends (and keep in mind that the beach clubs tend to be more expensive). Swimming lessons are widely available and prices of these will vary.

Swimming off the beaches is possible, whether at a public beach or hotel beach club. Remember to be modest in your choice of swimwear and only wear it on the beach.

The tides and currents here can be surprisingly strong – do not underestimate them, especially in areas of the coast with which you are not familiar. With this in mind, take due care when swimming on quiet beaches. For your own safety it is better to choose somewhere with a few people around.

Jellyfish can be a problem in the summer, both in the water and when washed up on the beach. All are capable of stinging, but one particular variety, the box jellyfish, can be lethal. Stone fish and sea snakes are also venomous, but tend to keep well away from more populated areas.

Tennis

Other options → Sports & Leisure Facilities [p.216]

Tennis is a popular game in Oman, with courts available for use by the public, in hotels, or in private organisations, solely for their members. Many hotels have floodlit courts to allow play in the evenings, when temperatures are a bit lower. Prices for hiring courts vary between about RO 3 and RO 6.

The Oman Tennis Association organises the national Omani team for tournaments at home and abroad. They also organise a variety of annual local tournaments. These are mainly held at hotels and are usually for a mixture of standards, but include some for professionals only.

Coaching is available at the hotels by a variety of freelance coaches and again, prices vary. Expect to pay between RO 8 and RO 15 for an hour's private coaching.

Wimbledon here I come

Triathlon

Training for and participation in Triathlons is popular here, which is surprising considering the extreme heat. Enthusiasts of this sport enjoy a tough challenge and Oman certainly provides! Hash House Harrier clubs are good sources of information regarding triathlon schedules. Alternatively, events are usually well advertised at hotels and in local newspapers.

Wadi & Dune Bashing

Other options → Camping [p.194]
Desert Driving Courses [p.219]
Tour Operators [p.141]

With vast areas of virtually untouched wilderness in Oman, wadi and dune bashing are enjoyed by many of its residents. Most off-road journeys are on existing tracks, to protect the environment from any damage – the sandy dunes and rocky wadis support a surprising variety of flora and fauna that exist in a delicate balance.

Dune bashing, or desert driving, is one of the toughest challenges for both car and driver – it's also a great deal of fun once you've mastered it. The golden rule is never to go alone – if you are new to this activity then go with someone who is experienced. Driving on sand requires very different skills to road driving. Very close to Muscat are the Bawshar Dunes – although this is a small area there are numerous criss-cross tracks through the sand, providing and easy introduction to this challenging sport.

> **All Work and No Play...**
>
> *Makes you a very dull expat! Make the most of your weekends by heading out of the city to explore some of Oman's abundant natural beauty. Get your hands on a copy of the Oman Off-Road Explorer – it's full of maps, tips and trips, and is the groundbreaking guide to breaking new ground. It will be available in all good bookshops in late 2005.*

When you're ready for more serious stuff, head for the Wahiba Sands (just over two hours from Muscat) for endless stretches of undulating desert, or try the Empty Quarter, which is spectacular in its seclusion, remoteness and the impressive size of the dunes.

Useful equipment to take with you includes shovels, strong tow ropes, a pressure gauge, foot pump or compressor, matting or planks of wood, a

Views of Jebel Shams

full tool kit for the car, a spare tyre in good condition, a car jack (with an extra piece of wood to stop it sinking in the sand), extra petrol, and plenty of water for both cars and passengers.

If you don't think your driving skills are up to scratch, you could try dune bashing through any of the major tour companies (see Tour Operators [p.141]). All offer a range of desert and mountain safaris.

Driving in the wadis is usually more straightforward. Wadis are (usually dry) gullies, carved through the rock by rushing floodwaters, following the course of seasonal rivers. The main safety precaution to take when wadi bashing is to keep your eyes open for developing thunder storms – the wadis can fill up rapidly and you will need to make your way to higher ground pretty quickly to avoid flash floods.

It is always advisable to go off-road with at least two vehicles. If anything goes wrong, you'll be glad of an extra pair of hands and a tow. Although requiring less skill than in the desert, when you drive in the mountains and wadis you still need to use your common sense and forward planning (you need to think ahead about choice of gears for the hills and river crossings).

The Hajar Mountains offer spectacular drives amid rugged mountain scenery. You'll pass remote mountain villages and freshwater rock pools as the rough tracks take you to incredible views up to 3,000 metres above sea level.

The better known wadis are often over visited, especially by tour companies, not necessarily because they are the best but because they are the easiest to get to. If you are more adventurous and are prepared to travel further, you can find some amazing, almost untouched places.

For further information and tips for driving off-road, check out the *Oman Off-Road Explorer*. This fabulous new book, due to be released towards the end of 2005, features detailed routes, stunning satellite imagery, information on outdoor activities, striking photos and a useful off-road directory.

Well-Being

For some, it takes little more than the soothing sound of the sea to relax mind and body. Mental and physical well-being is within easy reach in Oman. Whether you choose to set the tone of your day with a morning yoga session, or you want to fix your weight, skin or hair, there are a number of centres that can help.

Beauty Salons

Other options → Hairdressers [p.81]
Perfumes & Cosmetics [p.170]

Beauty salons in Oman offer various treatments. We have included some of the more popular salons. The hotels have their own in-house styling salons which are available for the general public as well as guests. One of the more unique opportunities is the traditional practice of painting henna on hands and feet, especially for weddings or special occasions. It is still a very popular beauty treatment and the intricate brown patterns fade after two to three weeks. Salons that offer henna are identified by the pictures of patterned hands or feet displayed on their shops.

DIVA

| Location → MSQ | 24 693 011 |
| Web/email → na | Map Ref → 7-E3 |

DIVA is one of the most established salons in Oman. It is located just outside Madinat As Sultan Qaboos, and offers a wide range of treatments and therapies to suit all requirements. All the stylists are trained to the highest standards and offer the latest cutting and colouring techniques. Complementing the busy and popular hair salon is a serene and relaxed beauty treatment area. Booking is essential.

Hana's Hair & Skincare Centre

| Location → MSQ | 24 698 138 |
| Web/email → maftrdg@omantel.net.om | Map Ref → 7-E2 |

Hana's offers traditional beauty treatments as well as extended services such as a skin care clinic, semi-permanent makeup and various hair treatments. There is also a slimming centre with a focus on weight loss, spot area reductions and figure corrections without harsh diets or gruelling exercise. Hana's has an area specifically for men, with similar services available.

Lucy's Beauty Salon

| Location → Al Asfoor Plaza · Al Qurm | 24 571 757 |
| Web/email → Lucysalon2003@yahoo.com | Map Ref → 8-D4 |

Lucy's is a quaint salon with experienced and capable staff. Nail and beauty treatments are available in a comfortable environment and the salon is centrally located, so you can finish off your shopping or stop for a quick coffee before starting your treatment. Call ahead for an appointment or just drop in.

Muscat Beauty Salon

Location → Sabco Centre · Al Qurm | 24 562 541
Web/email → na | Map Ref → 8-D4

The international and experienced team at this top hair and beauty salon is on hand to give you the very latest in-style cuts, colour and highlights. Beauticians specialise in non-surgical facelifts, Decleor facials, body massage, luxury manicures and pedicures, acrylic nails and much more.

Raz Hair & Beauty Studio

Location → MSQ | 24 692 219
Web/email → na | Map Ref → 8-D4

Raz Hair & Beauty Studio boasts a thoroughly proficient and trained team of international staff offering a full range of beauty and hair services. You'll find Guinot facial treatments and home care products plus exceptionally good nail extensions, as well as the more routine salon treatments. The hair studio is a L'Oreal appointed centre and the

Take a tranquil time out at the Chedi Muscat

full range of Kerastase home use products are available for purchase as well. Hair extensions, hair pieces and wigs are available to order.

Health Spas

Other options → Massage [p.215]
Sports & Leisure Facilities [p.216]

Ayana Slim Spa

Location → Al Sarooj Plaza · Shati Al Qurm | 24 693 435
Web/email → na | Map Ref → 7-E1

Look good, feel good has been taken to a whole new level at the Ayana Slim Spa, where you can not only enter a slimming programme but also treat yourself to some beauty pampering. The Balinese-inspired décor, the cascading water features and soothing music all transport you into a state of tranquility where you can indulge in personalised spa treatments for the mind, body and soul (not forgetting hair!). Treatments from the Institute of Biologique Recherché care for every skin type and condition, while the slimming programmes are executed by an expert team of professional aestheticians and therapists, using state of the art endermology, ultrasound and electrolypolisis machines.

Spa, The

Location → Chedi Muscat, The · Al Ghubbrah | 24 498 035
Web/email → www.ghmhotels.com | Map Ref → 6-D2

Specialising in Balinese therapies, this luxurious spa is a serene haven of relaxation where you can spend the day getting massaged, scrubbed, conditioned and polished. Treatments are available either individually or as part of a spa package. Bookings are essential.

Massage

Other options → Health Spas [p.215]
Reflexology/Massage Therapy Table [p.82]
Sports & Leisure Facilities [p.216]

A massage is one of the best ways to pamper your body. Whether it is a regular weekly treat, or more of an occasional indulgence, it is a sure-fire way to relax body and mind. Health clubs and spas offer a variety of techniques to soothe your aches and pains. The cost for a full body massage ranges from about RO 10 to RO 30 for one hour.

Health Spas · Massage

Activities

Reiki

Reiki (pronounced Ray-Key) is a hands on healing art developed in the early 1900s by Mikao Usui, in Japan. The word Reiki comes from the Japanese words Rei and Ki, meaning universal life energy, and is used to describe both the energy and the Usui system of using it. The technique is based on the belief that energy can be channelled into a patient by means of touch, and converted into 'universal life force energy', which has a healing effect. Like meditation, Reiki can emotionally cleanse, physically invigorate and leave you more focused. You can learn the art of Reiki to practice on yourself or others, directly or remotely.

Reiki by Shyamal

Location ➜ Various locations	92 175 475
Web/email ➜ na	Map Ref ➜ na

Sometimes it's hard to keep up with the stresses of everyday life, and when Reiki master Shyamal Rao returned to India, Oman's stressed-out residents went into near panic. But there is nothing to worry about, as his capable daughter has taken over the Reiki reins. Using holistic positive energy therapy, a session will ease your aches and pains and invigorate your mind and body.

Sports & Leisure Facilities

Oman's health and beach clubs are one-stop fitness and leisure shops. They are mainly located in hotels and membership includes access to beach facilities, the hotel health club and various sporting activities. You can expect to find specialised instructors for everything from aerobics to salsa, and swimming to tennis. Many health clubs have separate facilities for men and women, as well as 'ladies only' times. Shop around at the various clubs to see what timings and facilities are best suited to you. Refer to the Club Membership Rates & Facilities table below for full details on the various clubs in Muscat, including their membership rates and amenities offered.

Club Membership Rates & Facilities

Beach Clubs – Muscat				
Al Bustan	Beach and Country Club	Al Bustan Palace InterContinental Muscat	15-A1	24 799 666
Qurm Heights	Cliff Club	Crowne Plaza	8-C3	24 560 100
Shati Al Qurm	Club Olympus Fitness Centre	Grand Hyatt Muscat	7-D1	24 641 155
	Palm Beach Club	Hotel InterContinental Muscat	8-A4	24 600 500
	Sheraton Resort Health Club	Sheraton Qurum Resort	8-A4	24 605 945

Health Clubs – Muscat				
Al Khuwayr	Fontana Health Club	Radisson SAS Muscat	7-B3	24 487 777
	Sur Fitness	Holiday Inn Muscat	7-A2	24 487 123
Al Qurm	Horizon Fitness Centre	Moosa Abdul Rahman Complex	11-C1	24 571 337
Ruwi	Al Falaj Health Club	Al Falaj Hotel Muscat	12-C1	24 702 311
	Sheraton Health Club	Sheraton Oman Hotel	12-E2	24 799 899
Shati Al Qurm	Future Health Club	Opp Shati Cinema	7-E1	24 600 030

Beach/Health Clubs – Out of Muscat				
Salalah	Health Club	Crowne Plaza Resort Salalah	1-E3	23 235 333
	Hilton Fitness Centre	Hilton Salalah	1-E3	23 211 234
Sohar	Health Club	Sohar Beach Hotel	1-B2	26 841 111

Beach Clubs

Other options ➔ Beaches [p.132]
Health Clubs [p.217]

Beach clubs offer a similar range of facilities to health clubs but with the added bonus of beach access. They are very popular with families at weekends, and you can swim, play sports or just lounge in the sun in a peaceful environment. Most include some excellent food and beverage outlets, so people tend to stay for the day. Generally, beach clubs require you to be a member before you can use their facilities, although many also have day guest rates.

For listings of rates and facilities at Muscat's beach clubs, see the table below.

Health Clubs

Other options ➔ Beach Clubs [p.217]

Most health clubs offer workout facilities such as machines and weights, plus classes in various disciplines such as aerobics or yoga. Some also have swimming pools and tennis or squash courts. Many beach clubs offer good sports and gym facilities, so these are worth considering if you want the added bonus of beach access. The Ras Al Hamra Club offers a wide variety of activities for PDO employees. Sometimes members are allowed to sign in guests for particular occasions.

Remember that when using the changing rooms of your health club, some people may feel uncomfortable if you do not use the private cubicles. Respect the modesty that prevails in any Islamic country, and always remain as covered up as possible.

For listings of Muscat's main health clubs, see the Health & Beach Club Table below.

Expand Your Horizons

Whether you want to star in a play, paint in beautiful watercolours, learn how to play a musical instrument, or delve into the fascinating world of birds or plants, Oman has plenty of options for those who wish to expand their horizons. It's a

Membership Rates				Gym						Activity				Relaxation			
Individual	Couple	Family	Children	Treadmills	Exercise bikes	Step machines	Rowing machines	Free weights	Resistance machines	Tennis courts	Swimming Pool	Squash courts	Aerobics/Dance Exercise	Massage	Sauna	Jacuzzi	Steam room
275	395	485	85	2	2	4	1	✔	✔	4FL	✔	–	✔	✔	✔	✔	–
215	330	430	50	4	4	2	2	✔	✔	2FL	✔	2	✔	✔	✔	–	✔
280	390	409	75	4	1	2	1	✔	✔	3FL	✔	–	✔	✔	✔	✔	✔
350	480	570	90	7	7	2	3	✔	✔	6FL	✔	2	✔	✔	✔	✔	✔
260	360	430	70	2	1	1	1	✔	✔	–	✔	–	–	–	–	–	✔
220	320	380	60	2	3	2	–	✔	✔	–	✔	–	✔	✔	✔	–	✔
185	315	395	40	4	3	1	1	✔	✔	1FL	✔	–	✔	✔	–	–	✔
240	340	460	50	8	5	3	–	✔	✔	–	✔	–	✔	✔	✔	✔	✔
230	300	400	50	8	4	4	1	✔	✔	1FL	✔	1	✔	✔	✔	✔	✔
150	180	300	50	9	6	2	3	✔	✔	2FL	✔	–	✔	✔	✔	✔	✔
195	290	440		–	–	–	–	✔	✔	–	–	–	✔	✔	✔	✔	✔
200	300	500	–	3	2	1	–	✔	✔	2FL	✔	1	–	–	✔	✔	✔
200	250	300	–	2	2	1	1	✔	✔	2FL	✔	–	✔	✔	✔	–	–
125	175	65	2	2	3	1	–	✔	✔	1FL	✔	–	–	–	✔	✔	–

Activities

Beach Clubs · Health Clubs

great way to keep busy, meet new friends and get more settled into life as an expatriate.

Art Classes

Other options → Art Galleries [p.122]
Art Supplies [p.155]

Daat Art Centre

Location → Way 2235 House 1756 · Al Qurm | 24 568 049
Web/email → daatart@omantel.net.om | Map Ref → 8-D4

The centre provides art classes for all levels of artist, in drawing, painting and oil painting. Classes cost around RO 20 per four lessons (each lesson is two hours).

Omani Society for Fine Arts, The

Location → Nr Al Sarooj R/A · Mutrah | 24 694 969
Web/email → www.omanartsociety.net | Map Ref → 7-A2

The Omani Society for Fine Arts was established in 1993, to encourage fine art and photography in the country. The group organises a number of activities and initiatives to support artists in Oman, and participates in various international exhibitions and events.

Hurry Potter!

Birdwatching Groups

Other options → Birdwatching [p.128]
Environmental Groups [p.220]

Oman Bird Group

Location → Various locations | 24 695 498
Web/email → ianmair@gto.net.om | Map Ref → na

Oman is an extremely interesting country for the bird watcher. Because it sits at the junction of three bio-geographical areas, the keen observer can see Palaearctic and African species, and others from further east. The Oman Bird Group has been in existence since 1986. Its aims are to encourage bird study in Oman and to coordinate all bird records, these are kept on a computerised database. Although the group does not organise trips or hold regular meetings, active bird watchers are welcomed and given advice on interesting sites and locations.

Bridge

Muscat Bridge League

Location → Ruwi Hotel · Ruwi | 99 354 467
Web/email → mukherji@omantel.net.om | Map Ref → 12-D2

Dedicated Bridge players in Oman have been organising weekly bridge sessions for the last 20 years. Attendance ranges from six to ten tables and the game is played over 22 – 24 boards. A sponsored full-day session is held once a month.

The game is friendly, with varying degrees of competence, and visiting players are always welcome. There is a nominal table charge. In an effort to popularise the game further, Muscat Bridge League is planning to hold sessions to familiarise and teach the game to those interested.

Muscat Ladies Bridge Club

Location → Crowne Plaza · Al Qurm | 24 600 306
Web/email → na | Map Ref → 8-C2

The Muscat Ladies Bridge Club plays duplicate bridge twice a week, on Sunday and Wednesday mornings (08:45 – 12:45), at the Crowne Plaza Hotel. A nominal fee is charged but this includes refreshments. Annual Membership is RO 6 per person. For the more competitive players, there are two tournaments a year. For more information call the above number or 99 471 014.

Activities

Art Classes · Bridge

Clubs & Associations

Other options → Scouts & Guides [p.224]

Futurekids	
Location → Nr Al-Araimi Complex · Al Qurm	24 567 699
Web/email → www.futurekids.com	Map Ref → 8-D4

At Futurekids, learning to use computers is lots of fun. Children are given personal attention and all the encouragement they need to master essential computer technology. The company has been at the forefront of computer training for the last ten years and has helped over a million children become expert users. The company also runs its programme in various schools across Oman. There are also summer camps offered for children – great fun and educational.

Futurekids is a recognised centre for IT examinations by the United Kingdom RSA Examinations Board and has the equivalent US accreditation. Contact the above number, email fukids@gto.net.om or visit the website.

Oman Automobile Club	
Location → Nr Al Maaridh St · As Seeb	24 510 239
Web/email → na	Map Ref → 5-A4

Hidden away in the picturesque dunes outside Muscat, and host to a variety of sporting events, is the OAC. This club also serves as a venue for a multitude of activities and leisure pursuits. You can play softball, ride motorbikes or go-karts, play golf, or participate in hobbies such as remote control cars and helicopters.

Annual club membership costs RO 90 for individuals and RO 125 for families.

Cookery Classes

Several of the premier hotels in Muscat offer gourmet nights. These special evenings provide food lovers the opportunity to create mouth-watering treats with a renowned chef. Picking, tasting and sampling is unavoidable at these nights, but the real treat comes right at the end when the feast is laid out for all to enjoy. Most chefs allow you to walk away with their recipes in hand, ready to create your own in-home fine dining. For information on these events contact the food and beverage

departments of the major hotels, they are often held during promotions so it is also worth checking the local newspaper. The InterContinental has regular cookery classes on the last Saturday of every month, call 24 487 777 to book a place. The Radisson SAS (24 600 500) will hold cookery seminars on request if the size of the party is sufficient.

Dance Classes

Other options → Music Lessons [p.223]

Scottish Dancing	
Location → Various locations	24 675 721
Web/email → na	Map Ref →na

Scottish dancing fans will be very welcome at this Muscat-based group. Steps and formations are taught for both the easier dances and some more challenging ones. All are welcome, even if you've never danced before.

Classes are taught at the British School, ABA and TAISM schools. There is a demonstration team that performs throughout the year at various Muscat events, plus at all the Caledonian Society's social functions. Call any of the schools mentioned to obtain practice times and current contact details.

Desert Driving Courses

Other options → Wadi & Dune Bashing [p.212]

National Training Institute	
Location → MSQ	24 605 273
Web/email → na	Map Ref → 7-E2

If you'd like to learn how to put your 4 WD through its paces off-road, or you need to get expert advice on desert, wadi or mountain driving, consider taking a course in off-road driving. You will learn the theoretical side of off-road driving, followed by plenty of hands-on experience in the vehicles. After the course you should have a better idea of how to control skids, brake safely on sandy or rocky surfaces, and drive in the dunes. The instructors also offer advice on safety precautions, emergency procedures and what to do when things go wrong. They also offer a two-day defensive driving course to help you cope with the roads and other drivers in Oman.

Clubs & Associations · Desert Driving Courses

Activities

Drama Groups

Muscat Amateur Theatre

Location → Htl InterContinental
Web/email → kezar157@hotmail.com

24 562 511
Map Ref → 8-A4

The group was formed in 1980 and members of Muscat Amateur Theatre have so far presented 37 plays at the InterContinental, by a variety of playwrights, ranging from Neil Simon to Shakespeare. They have also had the pleasure of performing plays in a variety of Muscat's other beautiful hotels.

Environmental Groups

Oman is fortunate to have some beautiful environmental assets, so environmental protection issues will always be a priority of the government. There are currently three nature reserves where there is the facility for controlled tourism – the Daymaniyat Islands, the Ras Al Jinz turtle reserve and the Arabian Oryx Sanctuary. To visit these fascinating reserves, you will need to get a permit from the Directorate General of Nature Protectorates. Visits to the Arabian Oryx Sanctuary can only be arranged through approved tour companies (see [p.141]).

In addition to the government's efforts in promoting protection of the environment, there are also several interest groups and environmental organisations that are represented in Oman. Oman is a member of the International Whaling Commission (IWC), and although it is not yet a signatory to CITES (Convention on International Trade in Endangered Species), it follows the guidelines laid down by CITES, such as stopping trade in endangered species.

On a more everyday level, there are increasing numbers of bottle/can recycling points around Muscat. These are sponsored by various local companies, and are located mainly near shopping centres.

Historical Association of Oman

Location → Mutrah
Web/email → www. hao.org.om

24 563 074
Map Ref → 8-E3

The Historical Association of Oman was founded in 1972, with the main aim of collecting artefacts for a museum. The club provides lectures and field trips on subjects including archaeology, geology and

natural history, by local and visiting lecturers. Exchange visits with similar groups in the GCC states are also regularly organised. At present, there are approximately 150 members of various ages and from all walks of life. Meetings are held mainly at the PDO Oil and Gas Exhibition Centre and programmes are circulated to members on a monthly basis, with no additional fee for participating in lectures or trips.

Annual membership costs RO 20 per family, RO 10 for individuals and RO 5 for students.

Oman Whale & Dolphin Research Group

Location → Various locations
Web/email → www.whalecoastoman.com

24 696 912
Map Ref → na

This is a group of interested volunteer scientists who work together to collect and distribute facts about Oman's dolphins and whales. They are independent researchers whose work is recognised and approved by local Ministries. They work closely with the Oman Natural History Museum, the Ministry of Agriculture and Fisheries, and the Raysut Marine Laboratory. The group's primary activities include emergency rescue services for whales and dolphins, maintenance of a database of sightings and strandings, and cooperation with local tour operators to promote responsible whale and dolphin-watching activities. If you are interested in volunteering or just want to find out more about local whales and dolphins, give them a call.

> **Hi There Neighbour!**
>
> Did you know that the glitzy, glamorous city of Dubai is just a short drive from Muscat? And did you know that Dubai is packed with hundreds of star-rated restaurants, luxurious hotels, buzzing nightspots and glorious beaches? And did you know that the Dubai Explorer is the ultimate guidebook to this amazing, progressive city? Well now you know!

Planetarium – PDO Oil Exhibition Centre

Location → Mina Al Fahal (PDO)
Web/email → Marwan.Shwaiki@pdo.co.om

24 675 542
Map Ref → 9-A2

Stargazers across Oman can marvel at the twinkly dome of the PDO Planetarium, which opened in 2000. Since then, seven different features have been presented, three of which have been locally produced. Shows are in English and Arabic, and

Turtle watching at Ras Al Jinz

are all free of charge. The Planetarium also hosts guest lecturers, conferences, and workshops. They arrange special social gatherings when astronomical events occur.

First Aid

Medic First Aid

| Location → Various locations | 24 450 464 |
| Web/email → skinny@omantel.net.om | Map Ref → na |

This international organisation provides first aid training in 82 different countries, including Oman. After successful completion of a 12-hour course, candidates will be awarded a certificate that is valid for three years. The course combines knowledge and practical skills in basic first aid techniques and CPR. Two course formats are available – Basic First Aid with CPR (adult) and Paediatric First Aid with CPR (adult, child and infant). Either course can be carried out in your home, or at a convenient location, with timings to suit you.

Oman Dive Centre

| Location → Bandar Al Jissah · Al Bustan | 9 340 096 |
| Web/email → www.diveoman.com.om | Map Ref → 15-E3 |

The Oman Dive Centre offers a general introductory first aid course aptly called the Emergency First Responder. This course is suitable for everyone, not just divers, and can be taught either at the dive centre, or at a location of your choice.

Kids' Museums

Other options → Museums – City [p.125]

Children's Museum

| Location → Nr Qurm Nature Reserve · Al Qurm | 24 605 368 |
| Web/email → na | Map Ref → 8-C4 |

The Children's Museum is a delightful place for young children to play and gain knowledge at the same time. The building is filled with numerous activities to foster inquisitiveness and inspiration, as well as feed hungry minds and fuel imagination. Children will love it and parents will be thrilled to see their kids having fun while they learn. The facility encourages school groups to benefit from these educational opportunities and charges a minimal entrance fee.

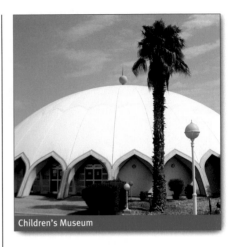

Children's Museum

Language Schools

Other options → Learning Arabic [p.86]
Basic Arabic [p.14]

British Council

| Location → MSQ | 24 681 000 |
| Web/email → www.britishcouncil.org | Map Ref → 7-D2 |

The British Council in Oman offers a variety of services, with the main focus on education. The Teaching Centres in Muscat and Seeb provide English courses for adults and young learners, IELTS preparation courses, teacher training courses and special courses for contract clients. The Council's Education Information Centre has a wide selection of information for anyone considering further education and training in Britain. Contact the Examinations staff in Muscat for queries concerning British exams, copies of rules and regulations and syllabus details.

Omani French Language Centre

| Location → MSQ | 24 697 579 |
| Web/email → csomct@omantel.net.om | Map Ref → 7-D2 |

This centre offers tuition in French at all levels, and they provide an official diploma from the French Ministry of Education. Spanish and German language classes are also available. Their highly qualified instructors teach courses for beginner, intermediate and advanced students. Courses are run mainly in the evenings, although there are some morning

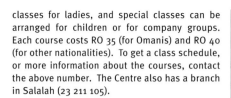

classes for ladies, and special classes can be arranged for children or for company groups. Each course costs RO 35 (for Omanis) and RO 40 (for other nationalities). To get a class schedule, or more information about the courses, contact the above number. The Centre also has a branch in Salalah (23 211 105).

Polyglot Institute Oman	
Location → Nr Wadi Adai R/A · Al Wutayyah	24 835 777
Web/email → na	Map Ref → 12-B3

The Polyglot Institute Oman LLC was established in 1975, and offers courses in commercial subjects, translation services, management seminars and training, computer tuition and national vocational qualifications, as well as English and Arabic language courses. Before they commence, all programmes are approved by the Ministry of Social Affairs, Labour and Vocational Training. All Polyglot staff have qualifications and experience relevant to their own teaching subject, and English language teachers are all native speakers. The institute has branches in Ruwi and in Al Surror Street, Al Hail (next to Omantel).

Libraries

Other options → Books [p.156]
Second-Hand Items [p.170]

Biblioteque Française	
Location → French Embassy · Shati Al Qurm	24 681 874
Web/email → na	Map Ref → 7-B1

This is a lending library and information resource for French language books and videos. Biblioteque Française carries a wide selection of fiction and non-fiction literature by French and foreign authors, as well as magazines, French videos and children's books. Books are lent for a two-week period.

Oman Chamber of Commerce & Industry	
Location → CDB · Ruwi	24 707 674
Web/email → www.chamberoman.com	Map Ref → 12-E2

This small library has a range of books available for reference only. Most are in Arabic, but there is a small collection of English language books on business or trade-related subjects, such as economics, accounting, management and finance.

Public Technical Library	
Location → Mina Al Fahal (PDO)	24 673 111
Web/email → na	Map Ref → 8-E3

The library contains over 14,500 volumes, with a balanced split between Arabic and English. The subjects covered are mainly in the areas of science and technology. However, there are also materials covering topics in the humanities and social sciences, such as environmental issues and Omani history. You'll also find general encyclopaedias, language resources, dictionaries and atlases. A collection of videos is being developed.

US Information Service Resource Center	
Location → American Embassy · Shati Al Qurm	24 698 989
Web/email → na	Map Ref → 7-C1

This highly informative reference library specialises in US policy, legislation, trade data and social and cultural issues. In addition, the IRC offers access to the internet and computer databases to students and researchers. There is also a reading section – the IRC carries around 20 periodicals in hard copy, including Time, Newsweek, Life, Fortune and The Herald Tribune. Full text versions of more than 200 journals and magazines are available. There are many books on American states, literature, art, social history and science, as well as information on Oman.

Music Lessons

Other options → Dance Classes [p.219]
Music, DVDs & Videos [p.168]
Singing [p.224]

Associated Board of the Royal Schools of Music	
Location → Mutrah	99 440 441
Web/email → cantamus@omantel.net.om	Map Ref → na

The Associated Board of the Royal Schools of Music was established in 1889, initially as an agreement between the Royal Academy of Music and the Royal College of Music. The board acts as an examining body for local music examinations and aims to improve the standard of musical education. It offers a scheme of examinations suitable for candidates at different stages of ability in all orchestral instruments, as well as in keyboard and in theory of music. The board maintains a database of music teachers in Oman.

Libraries · Music Lessons

Activities

Daat Art Centre

Location → Way 2235 House 1756 · Al Qurm | 24 568 049
Web/email → daatart@omantel.net.om | Map Ref → 8-D4

The Daat Art Centre teaches basic musical skills for children – classes cover listening, singing, playing (the recorder), moving and creating. These classes are taught in various age groups and are suitable for children aged between three and seven years.

Adults can take piano lessons at the centre – lessons are taught on an individual basis and there is one half-hour lesson per week. Having access to a practice piano is essential. The monthly charge for piano lessons is RO 24.

Melody Music Centre

Location → Way 1952 · Darsayt | 24 782 834
Web/email → na | Map Ref → 9-C3

Melody Music Centre was initially started in the mid 90s. Since then, the centre has obtained recognition from the Associated Board of the Royal Schools of Music, UK (ABRSM- UK), to teach both a theoretical and practical syllabus. Examinations take place for different grades, ranging from Preparatory Grade One to Grade Eight levels. They also offer classes in piano, keyboard, guitar, drums, conga drums, violin, arnatic vocal and classical dance (Bharatanatyam).

Time to chime!

Scouts & Guides

Other options → Clubs & Associations [p.219]

Although there is a group called the Oman National Organization for Scouts and Guides (you can get more information about them at www.arabscout.com), they only have Omani boys and girls as their members. Indian School Muscat offers Scouts as one of their extramural activities, but only for pupils of the school. There are currently no UK or US Scouts groups operating, although there is an Oman branch of British Guides in Foreign Countries (see details below). For more information on Scouts and Guides abroad, and on starting up your own group, see www.scoutbase.org.uk or www.bgifc.org.uk.

British Guides in Foreign Countries

Location → Shati Al Qurm | 24 677 333
Web/email → johnmmalcolm@hotmail.com | Map Ref → na

British Guides in Foreign Countries is a division of the United Kingdom Guide Association, which caters for girls wishing to continue their Guiding while living overseas. The groups are open to all nationalities, but there is sometimes a waiting list and priority is given to girls who have been members in their own country. All of the packs base their programme on the British system to provide continuity.

Singing

Other options → Music Lessons [p.223]

Muscat Singers

Location → British School Muscat · MSQ | 99 473 709
Web/email → kateclarkeoman@hotmail.com | Map Ref → 8-E1

One of the longest established choirs in Muscat, this group welcomes new singers from all backgrounds and nationalities. The choir covers a broad spectrum of music ranging from classical and light opera through to folk and jazz. Much of the singing is in parts and there is always a need for new members of all singing styles. The ability to read music is not essential but previous experience of choral singing is an advantage. The minimum age is 15 years, but there is no upper limit! The choir meets on Saturday evenings (starting from 19:30) at the British School Muscat.

Scouts & Guides · Singing

Activities

Social Groups

Other options → Clubs & Associations [p.219]
Support Groups [p.84]

American Women's Group

Location → Various locations | na
Web/email → awgmuscat@yahoo.com | Map Ref → na

AWG is an international women's social organisation, serving the women of Muscat for 30 years, with almost 1,000 members representing over 45 nationalities. Monthly meetings are held on the second Sunday of every month from September to May. Meetings are held in local hotels and each one features a short programme, announcements of interest to the members, sign-up sheets for the various activities, and the opportunity to meet and talk with other women. For membership details and information please contact the Membership Chair by email.

Caledonian Society of Oman

Location → Various locations | 99 207 593
Web/email → na | Map Ref → na

This philanthropic society tries to promote the spirit and culture of Scotland in Oman.

A nominal annual subscription charge pays for a monthly newsletter and discounted entry to all the society's functions. In addition to the St Andrew's Ball and the Burn's Supper, the society organises highland gatherings, two annual ceilidhs, Scottish folk evenings, there are also practice sessions for Scottish country dancing. There is no specific meeting place and social events are advertised in the newsletter, call the above number after 3pm.

Royal Omani Amateur Radio Society (ROARS)

Location → MSQ | 24 600 407
Web/email → roars@omantel.net.om | Map Ref → 11-A1

The Royal Omani Amateur Radio Society was founded in 1972 and membership currently stands at 155 people. The society offers courses to obtain radio licences, on Sunday and Tuesday evenings, but for Omanis only. Anyone may join who has a current licence from their home country, for a fee of RO 15 per year. Seminars, trips and social gatherings are scheduled several times a year and are open to all members.

Women's Guild in Oman

Location → Various locations | 24 516 433
Web/email → na | Map Ref → na

The purpose of the Women's Guild is to offer fellowship, raise funds for charities, and provide an opportunity for women to meet and enjoy a varied programme of speakers and events. Membership is open to women of all ages and nationalities. The Women's Guild has an excellent reputation in Oman for distributing funds to charities in the country.

Summer Camps & Courses

Futurekids

Location → Nr Al-Araimi Complex · Al Qurm | 24 567 699
Web/email → www.futurekids.com | Map Ref → 8-D4

Futurekids offers an opportunity for your children to expand their knowledge of computers and become more skilled in utilising software programs. There are courses and summer camp sessions in word processing, desktop publishing, and website design. Summer Camp courses are designed for children aged five to 17, depending on the topic.

Greenery in the city

Social Groups · Summer Camp & Courses

Activities

Going Out

EXPLORER

Going Out

Highlights...

Highly Recommended

With so much choice, it can be tricky to track down the very best of Oman's eateries. The scores below each review should give you a clue to what's hot and what's not, but we've distinguished the places that deserve a real thumbs-up by giving them just that – a thumbs-up symbol next to their name. These are the places that really tickled our tastebuds, and we're sure they'll tickle yours too – bon appetit!

Enjoy the View	
Club Safari Rooftop Grill	254
Marina Café	259
Mumtaz Mahal	246
Uptown	263

Cheap Chow	
Curry House	246
Karachi Darbar	252
Palayok Restaurant	244
Woodlands	247

High-Class Hangouts	
Al Marjan	244
Med, The	254
Restaurant, The	250
Señor Pico	250

Romantic	
Al Marjan	244
Blue Marlin	254
Med, The	250
O Sole Mio	250

Omani Experience	
Al Madinat	236
Bin Ateeq	252
Omani Hut	252
Seblat Al Bustan	252

Family Friendly	
Chili's	232
Golden Spoon	246
Kargeen Caffé	238
Silk Route	244

Alfresco Favourites	
Club Safari Rooftop Grill	254
Come Prima	249
Kargeen Caffé	238
Olivos Coffee Shop	240

Off the Beaten Track	
China Mood	240
Kargeen Caffé	238
Omani Hut	252
Seblat Al Bustan	252

Table of Contents

Going Out

Oman offers a wide variety of dining experiences and while the majority of visitors to Salalah, Nizwa, Sohar, Sur and other areas outside Muscat tend to dine in their hotel, interesting independent Arabic restaurants can be found if you take the time to explore. This section, however, concentrates on places to discover in Muscat as the majority of visitors and expats use the capital to explore their culinary tastes and find a surprising variety of restaurants, bars and cafés here. It might not be Dubai but with the drive of tourism in Oman the nightlife is constantly improving and whatever your scene you should find something to suit most appetites and budgets. The following section has been divided into two; restaurants are listed under Eating Out [p.229], while cafés, bars, pubs, nightclubs and 'cultural' entertainment such as theatre, cinema and comedy clubs, are under On the Town [p.261].

Eating Out

Oman's multi-cultural heritage and population is reflected through the variety of international cuisines on offer. From Arabic to Mediterranean, Polynesian to Zanzibarian and everything in between, there really is something to suit every taste... and budget.

Eating out is a time honoured Arabic pastime as it is allows friends and family to exchange news and gossip and argue the merits of any thing from a foreign leader to the latest mobile phone. Most restaurants open early in the evening, around 19:00, but generally don't get busy until around 21:00. Lunchtimes can vary between 12:00 and 15:00 so check before you arrive. Many places are very popular with locals and expats alike, so it's advisable to book a table if you wish to dine at the weekend, especially if going as a group.

A large number of Oman's restaurants are situated in hotels, especially in Muscat, but there are also many independent restaurants throughout the town, some of which are licensed. (If you want to have a tipple with your meal, check for the Alcohol Available icon in individual reviews). While the licensed restaurants are popular for obvious reasons, it is worth remembering that there are a vast number of excellent independent restaurants around town that shouldn't be ignored just because they are teetotal!

Generally the more upmarket restaurants offer one or two types of cuisine, while the smaller outlets will often entice you with a variety of cuisines, for example, an Indian restaurant may also serve Thai and Chinese food. In addition, many places promote theme nights with different styles of cooking, such as seafood, Italian or sushi. Many restaurants also have weekly buffet nights when you can eat, and sometimes drink, as much as you like for a great value, all-inclusive price. Good news for your wallet, but bad news for your waistband!

Drinks

Other options → **Alcohol [p.152]**

Despite Oman being an Islamic country, it has a relatively liberal attitude towards the consumption of alcohol by non-Muslims. Alcohol is available in restaurants and bars, which are generally in hotels that have the appropriate licence. However, drinking alcohol in these establishments can be an expensive pastime – nearly double what you are probably used to paying.

Non-Muslims can also apply for an alcohol permit, which allows them to purchase alcohol from a liquor store. However, don't expect to find a huge selection in your local off-licence. The price of wine can be triple over here, but spirits are cheaper.

Local bottled water is produced either in Oman or the neighbouring Emirates and is of high quality, even compared to premium imported brands. Instead of paying extortionate amounts for a international label, try the local water, which is around 200 baisas for a 1.5 litre bottle.

Hygiene

Don't be fooled by the unhygienic appearance of some of the informal dining outlets you see here – they are usually not as bad as they look. Then again, some of them are, so you have to use your judgement. The local authorities are clamping down on hygiene so many places have improved standards and started to follow procedures and guidelines as laid out by the municipality.

Tax & Service Charges

On bills there will be an extra 8 – 10% service charge, a municipality tax of 5% and a tourism tax of 4%. Sometimes the service charge and tourism tax will be grouped together. The service charge cannot be withheld due to poor service.

Eating Out • Tax & Service Charges

Going Out

The amount of tax and service charge should be shown clearly at the bottom of each page on your menu. If it is not, it is already included. If tax is extra it can sometimes be referred to next to a price as +, ie RO 5 +.

Tipping

Tipping is up to you. If you do wish to tip, around 10% of the bill is normal, although most people tend to leave the small notes from their change, particularly in cafés.

Independent Reviews

We undertake independent reviews of all restaurants that we include in the book. Our reporters have visited all the following outlets and the views expressed are their own. The aim is to give a clear, realistic and, as far as possible, unbiased view which we are allowed to print!

Ratings

Rating restaurants is always a highly subjective business. We ask our reviewers to summarise their experiences (see the bottom of each entry) in terms of Food, Service, Venue, and Value. They were asked to consider their restaurant compared to other venues in that category, and in the same price range. In other words, you may notice that a local café has the same summary rating as a premium gourmet restaurant. This is not to say that they are equal to one other. Instead, this is a way of comparing restaurants that are similarly styled and priced to each other. We hope this will help you to make informed choices regardless of your taste or budget.

Each rating is out of five – one dot means poor, two and a half means acceptable and five means fab:

Food●●●○○Serv●●○○○Venue●●●●●Value●●●●○

Venues scheduled to open late 2004 received 'na' ratings (not available), as a review could not be carried out:

Food – na   Service – na   Venue – na   Value – na

Restaurant Listing Structure

With over 100 listed outlets serving food and drink in Muscat, the choice of outlets is reasonable considering the size of the city. Listed alphabetically by commonly known style of cuisine, this section hopes to add to the variety of your dining experience in Muscat by giving as much information as possible on the outlets. For an 'at a glance' clarification of this listing, refer to the index at the beginning of this section.

In order to categorise the restaurants by cuisine we have placed restaurants that serve varying cuisines or styles either under their prominent cuisine, or under International [p.247] if the mix is truly varied. In addition, as we have listed the restaurants by cuisine and not theme we have also included Explorer Top Picks [p.234] that highlight selling points such as alfresco restaurants or romantic haunts.

If, however you are looking for a restaurant in a particular hotel then flip to the index at the back of the book, look up the hotel and you will find all the outlets listed with their relevant page numbers.

When selecting an establishment there are a number of factors that will affect your choice. If you want to enjoy a drink with your meal then look out for the Alcohol Available icon but bear in mind that the hotel restaurants may be a little more expensive that the independent venues. Also don't forget that there also exists a wide variety of non-licensed establishments that offer delicious Arabic fare for excellent value.

Finally, in order to avoid any confusion concerning a particular restaurant's listing, as a rule, any non-English names will retain their prefix (ie Al, Le, La and El) in their alphabetical placement, while English names are listed by actual titles, ignoring prefixes such as 'The'. Bon appetit!

For information on door policies and dress code, refer to Bars in On the Town [p.261].

Privilege Cards

Everyone loves a bargain, and Oman's restaurants certainly aren't short of delectable discounts. Privilege cards are designed to encourage customers to return as often as possible to their favourite dining establishments by offering a discount on meals and sometimes beverages. Some schemes have additional member advantages such as reduced rates on accommodation in hotels or reward vouchers (which can even be for a night's stay in the particular hotel).

Many hotels offer privilege cards so it is worth investigating, especially if a couple of your favourite restaurants are in the same hotel.

WHERE TIME STANDS STILL

You'll never notice the passage of time in Kargeen –
the coffee shop with a difference. Where you can
relax in an ambience that calms the soul and feeds
the spirit... not to mention your appetite.

Savour our wholesome daily special soups,
sandwiches, traditional Arabic dishes, salads and
pastries. Food that has been prepared with all the
loving care you'd expect from a home kitchen.

**Relax and savour the moment. A moment in time
that stands still... at Kargeen.**

KARGEEN caffè

Al Harthy Complex (Branch)	Madinat Qaboos (Main Branch)	City Plaza (Branch)
+ 968 24 560 531	**+ 968 24 692 269**	+ 968 24 694 048
Open 8:30am to 2:00pm	**+ 968 24 692 110**	Open 10:00am to 10:00pm
4:30pm to 10:00pm	**Open 8:30am to 1:00am**	

Office Tel + 968 24 699 055, Fax + 968 24 699 522   Open 8:00am to 1:00pm and 4:30pm to 7:30pm

Reservations Zubair + 968 99 338 322 / Manoj + 968 99 818 338

web www.kargeencaffe.com   **e-mail** info@kargeencaffe.com

Icons – Quick Reference

The price guides are calculated as the cost of a starter, main course and dessert for one person. It includes taxes, but not drinks. The RO 5 icon means that an average meal would cost RO 5 (give or take).

Quick Reference Explorer Icons

 Explorer Recommended!

 Average price ± RO 2.5
(3 courses per person, including Tax & Service)

 No Credit Cards Accepted

 Live Band

 Alcohol Available

 Have a Happy Hour

 Will Deliver

 Kids Welcome

 Reservations Recommended

 Dress Smartly

 Outside Terrace

 Vegetarian Dishes

Restaurants

American

Chili's

Location → Muscat City Centre · As Seeb
Web/email → www.chilis.com

24 545 815
Map Ref → 3-D2

Chili's has a great menu, a fun atmosphere and helpful and amiable staff. The menu caters to all tastes, even including a number of 'guiltless' and 'low carb' recipes for those counting the calories. The burgers are good, the lunchtime soup 'n salad combos popular, but to really get your tastebuds going, try the steak and fish dishes. Children are welcome and given crayons and a separate menu to keep them happy. As the only sit-down restaurant in City Centre, it is a great place for some respite away from the bustle of the food court.

Food●●●●○ Serv●●●●○ Venue●●●○○ Value●●●●○

Tea with a view

Arabic/Lebanese

Other options → **Omani [p.252]**
Persian [p.253]

Al Barouk

Location → Beach Hotel · Shati Al Qurm
Web/email → www.omanbeachhotel.com

24 604 799
Map Ref → 8-A4

If you're looking for Lebanese food in Shati Al Qurm then Al Barouk is a good option. Alfresco dining is available, the best spot being by the hotel pool where you can relax, take in the view and enjoy some shisha. The interior is simple yet thoughtfully decorated and the atmosphere conducive to a relaxed meal, with the gentle tunes of the Lebanese musician and singer who play several nights a week. The menu includes all the Lebanese favourites as well as a few extras and while it might not be fine dining it is excellent value. If you want good Arabic food in a relaxed atmosphere then this is a worthy choice.

Food●●●●○ Serv●●●○○ Venue●●●○○ Value●●●●○

Did your waiter stick his thumb in your thermidor? Or was the waitress slower than an indecisive snail? If your dining experience was less than you expected, then log on to www.EatOutSpeakOut.com and let us – and the rest of the web-surfing world – know all about it. Sloppy staff – you have been warned!

www.*EatOutSpeakOut*.com

AL BUSTAN PALACE
InterContinental.
MUSCAT

THE WONDERS OF OMAN.

THE SPLENDOUR OF THE PALACE.

Oman, a country of dramatic mountains, breathtaking dunes and historic forts, a rare geology of rock, sand and wadi with some of the world's most spectacular underwater life. Discover the mystique of the oldest of nations and the newest of destinations.

2003 CONDÉ NAST TRAVELER MAGAZINE READERS CHOICE AWARD FOR BEST MIDDLE EASTERN HOTEL

For further information contact us:
P.O. Box 1998, Postal Code 114, Muttrah, Sultanate of Oman, Tel: (968) 24 799 666, Fax: (968) 24 799 600

www.al-bustan.intercontinental.com · albustan@interconti.com

Explorer Area Top Picks

Barka

Omani Hut	Omani	252

Al Bustan

Al Khiran Terrace	Buffet	238
Al Marjan	French	244
Atrium Tea Lounge	Afternoon Tea	260
China Mood	Chinese	240
Seblat Al Bustan	Omani	252
Beach Pavilion	Seafood	254

Al Ghubbrah

Chedi Poolside	International	248
Restaurant, The	Mediterranean	251
Lobby Lounge, The	Cafés	258

Al Khuwayr

Olivos Coffee Shop	Buffet	240
Alauddin Restaurant	Indian	245
Golden Spoon	Indian	246
Bin Ateeq	Omani	252
Cellar, The	General Bars	265

Al Qurm

Automatic	Arabic/Lebanese	236

Come Prima	Italian	249
Nando's	Portuguese	253
Silk Route	Chinese	244
Mumtaz Mahal	Indian	246

Al Wutayyah

Passage to India	Indian	247
Curry House	Indian	246

Ghala

Barrio Fiesta	General Bars	262
Khaboura Café	International	248

Madinat As Sultan Qaboos

Al Madinat	Arabic/Lebanese	236
Kargeen Caffé P.235	Arabic/Lebanese	238
Pavo Real	Mexican	251

Ruwi

Mongolian Barbecue	Mongolian	251
Golden Oryx	Chinese	242
Palayok Restaurant	Filipino	244
Woodlands	Indian	247
Tokyo Taro	Japanese	250
Green Mountain	International	248

Oliver	General Bars	263

Shati Al Qurm

Tuscany	Italian	250
Med, The	Mediterranean	250
Club Safari Rooftop	Steakhouses	254
Club Safari	General Bars	263
Mado Café	Cafés	258
Mokha Café	Buffet	240
O Sole Mio	Italian	250
Señor Pico	Mexican	251
Café de Muscat	Cafés	256
Majlis Al Shams	Cafés	259
Green Cedar	Arabic/Lebanese	238
Trader Vic's	Polynesian	253
Le Mermaid	Cafés	258
Sirj Tea Lounge	Afternoon Tea	260
Trader Vic's	Cocktail Lounges	262
Lounge, The	Nightclubs	265
Al Ghazal Pub	Pubs	264
Copacabana	Nightclubs	265

Sidab

Blue Marlin	Seafood	254

Explorer Category Top Picks

Arabic/Lebanese

Automatic	Al Qurm	236
Al Madinat	MSQ	236
Fish Village	Al Khuwayr	238
Kargeen Caffé	MSQ P.235	238

Buffet

Al Khiran Terrace	Al Bustan	238
Olivos Coffee Shop	Al Khuwayr	240
Mokha Café	Shati Al Qurm	240

Chinese

Golden Oryx	Ruwi	242
Silk Route	Al Qurm	244
China Mood	Al Bustan	240

Indian

Woodlands	Ruwi	247
Passage to India	Al Wutayyah	247
Alauddin	Al Khuwayr	245
Mumtaz Mahal	Al Qurm	246
Curry House	Al Wutayyah	246

International

Chedi Poolside	Al Ghubbrah	248

Khaboura Café	Ghala	248

Italian

Tuscany	Shati Al Qurm	250
Come Prima	Qurm Heights	249
O Sole Mio	Shati Al Qurm	250

Mediterranean

Med, The	Shati Al Qurm	250
Restaurant, The	Al Ghubbrah	251

Mexican

Señor Pico	Shati Al Qurm	251
Pavo Real	MSQ	251

Mongolian

Mongolian Barbecue	Ruwi	251

Omani

Seblat Al Bustan	Al Bustan	252
Omani Hut	Barka	252
Bin Ateeq	Al Khuwayr	252

Portuguese

Nando's	Al Qurm	253

Blue Marlin	Sidab	254
Beach Pavilion	Al Bustan	254

Steakhouses

Rooftop Grill	Shati Al Qurm	254

Cafés & Coffee Shops

Mado Café	Shati Al Qurm	258
Majlis Al Shams	Shati Al Qurm	259
Café de Muscat	Shati Al Qurm	256
Kargeen Caffé	MSQ P.235	258
Lobby Lounge, The	Al Ghubbrah	258

General Bars

Club Safari	Shati Al Qurm	263

Pubs

Al Ghazal Pub	Shati Al Qurm	264

Nightclubs

Lounge, The	Shati Al Qurm	265
Copacabana	Shati Al Qurm	265

Seafood

Explorer Area Top Picks · Explorer Category Top Picks

Going Out

234

2005 OMAN EXPLORER

Enjoy your meal with one of the best views in Muscat.

No other restaurants in Muscat can offer you a view like ours. With our superb cliff-top location, all of our restaurants have outdoor terraces overlooking the Gulf of Oman. It means you can eat outdoors and admire the view at the same time - whether you're having breakfast on your private terrace, lunch at our English pub or dinner at our Italian or Persian restaurants. And thankfully the view is something that will always be on the menu.

CROWNE PLAZA®

MUSCAT

Or... Relax at our tropical beach resort right here in the Gulf.

Long sandy beaches, clear blue sea, coconut groves and year-round temperatures of just 30°C. If this sounds like your ideal beach holiday you may be surprised to find that it's available right here on your doorstep - in Salalah. This is Oman's very own Indian Ocean hideaway. In fact our climate is so unique to the Gulf, we even have monsoon rains and lush green hills during the summer! So if you're looking for a taste of the tropics, give us a call today at the Crowne Plaza Resort Salalah.

CROWNE PLAZA®

SALALAH

www.crowneplaza.com

For hotel reservations book online to benefit from our 'Lowest Internet Rate Guarantee' or call toll-free in Oman on: 800 777999
From all other countries in the Middle East call Dubai on: tel: +971 4 3311732* or fax: +971 4 3311629* *(*International call charge will apply)*

To contact the hotels directly for restaurant reservations:
Crowne Plaza Muscat, tel: +968 24560100, fax: +968 24560650 or e-mail: cpmuscat@cpmuscat.com
Crowne Plaza Resort Salalah, tel: +968 23235333, fax: +968 23235137 or e-mail: cpsll@omantel.net.om

A fine way to end an Arabic meal...

Al Deyar

Location → Nr Cinema · Shati Al Qurm | 24 603 553
Web/email → na   Map Ref → 7-E1

If you're planning a trip to Shati Cinema, check out this newly renovated restaurant and you can dissect the film along with some Arabic delectables and interesting décor. Bizarre sculpted concrete on the walls and suspended mats on the ceiling give the place a kind of surreal stage appearance, and the fact that the till sits perched upon a fish tank is somewhat novel. The great thing about this restaurant is there is ample outside seating – perfect for shisha and enjoying the nearby sea breeze.

Expect to wait some time for your shawarma, grilled meats and salads as it can get very busy in the evenings.

Food●●●●○Serv●●●○○Venue●●●○○Value●●●●○

Al Madinat

Location → MSQ Centre · MSQ | 24 696 515
Web/email → na   Map Ref → 7-E2

Sitting adjacent to the ever-popular Kargeen Caffé this corner of the Madinat As Sultan Qaboos Centre is always buzzing with people and comes alive at night with candles and fairy lights. Sit yourself down on comfortable majlis cushions inside or enjoy the fresh air under the trees outside. Friendly staff offer you a selection of sandwiches, salads,

Arabic/Lebanese

Going Out

pastries and fresh juices, and the Arabic meze is great to share with friends.

Food●●●●○Serv●●●●○Venue●●●●○Value●●●●○

Arabic Oven

Location → CBD, HSBC Junction · Ruwi | 24 797 276
Web/email → na   Map Ref → 12-D2

Located in the heart of the CBD area and convenient for local office workers, Arabic Oven is a nice change from the usual sandwich at your workstation. The giant water feature on the wall makes for tranquil background noise while you enjoy biryanis, curries, shawarmas, or pay-per-plate buffet salads. If you want a healthier option (in other words not drowning in dressing) then the salads from the main menu are great low-fat, carb-free lunch options. For those who couldn't care less about carbs the home baked Omani bread with hummus or moutabel is delicious.

Food●●●●○Serv●●●○○Venue●●●○○Value●●●●○

Arabic Coffee Shops

While we have highlighted some of the preferred Arabic restaurants there is also a wide variety of independent outlets across Oman worth checking out. However don't be deterred by their names – you will find a vast number of Arabic restaurants which are self-titled as 'coffee shops'. While Arabic coffee is certainly on the menu many of these outlets will also have delicious fruit juices, shawarmas, falafel and other traditional dishes.

Automatic

Location → Nr Sabco Centre · Al Qurm | 24 561 500
Web/email → na   Map Ref → 8-D4

If you've made it to the Middle East then you have to indulge in the food culture – fresh juices, meze and large portions for very reasonable prices. Automatic has established itself as a standard of choice with locals and expats. The waiters are efficient and the food quick to your table. Four daily specials will test larger appetites, while the range of traditional starters, salads, grilled meats and locally caught seafood dishes and Friday brunch should be enough to satisfy everyone's tastes. A must!

Other locations: Al Khuwayr (24 487 200), As Seeb (24 424 343)
Food●●●●○Serv●●●●○Venue●●●○○Value●●●●○

A Fine Hotel
with the
Finest Facilities.

At InterContinental Muscat we strive to make sure we offer you optimum service, whether you choose to dine at any of our 'Award Winning' restaurants or use our state-of-the-art recreational or banquet facilities. We guarantee to satisfy your needs and create a memorable experience in one of Oman's finest hotels.

For more information call Tel.: 24600500 Box office Ext. 8707, or log on to www.muscatoman@intercontinental.com

INTERCONTINENTAL.
MUSCAT

P.O. Box 398, PC 114, Muttrah, Sultanate of Oman. E-mail: muscat@interconti.com

Fish Village

Location → Nr Automatic · Al Khuwayr
Web/email → na

24 480 918
Map Ref → 8-D4

  5

With a somewhat ambiguous name you may be forgiven for not realising this is an Arabic restaurant, but the shisha and shawarma give it away. Located opposite the Radisson SAS hotel, Fish Village looks out over the Taimer mosque and beyond towards 'White Mountain' and is worth a visit for the spectacular view if nothing else. The outside seating area is large and merges with the other restaurants on either side. Just make sure you go with a clean palate so as to fully enjoy the spicy squid, shish tawook or a sizzling tajin.

Food●●●●○ Serv●●●○○ Venue●●●○○ Value●●●●●

Green Cedar

Location → Nr Al Sarooj Centre · Shati Al Qurm
Web/email → na

24 602 844
Map Ref → 7-E1

5

This might be a 'drive-through' café nestled between Al Fair Supermarket and the petrol station but the food is good enough to savour. There are a small number of tables outside if you wish to linger a little longer to fully appreciate your traditional snack. You'll find the usual shawarma-stand favourites like chicken or mutton sandwiches wrapped up with spicy sauce in local bread. The real jewel, however, is the falafels, which are particularly tasty with lots of tahina sauce and crunchy vegetables. If you're lucky you may even come across a french fry in your sandwich – a local delicacy!

Food●●●●○ Serv●●●○○ Venue●●●○○ Value●●●●○

Jenin

Location → Nr Ramada Htl · Shati Al Qurm
Web/email → na

24 696 049
Map Ref → 7-C2

5

Head upstairs to enjoy this bright, airy and spacious restaurant serving a traditional selection of Arabic dishes. You can opt to sit at the more formal tables or lounge on the sofas and armchairs at a lower table, gazing out at the jebels through traditional Arabian windows. Choose from a selection of kebabs and grills accompanied by Arabic salads, all at a reasonable price.

Food●●●○○ Serv●●●○○ Venue●●○○○ Value●●●○○

Kargeen Caffé

Location → MSQ Centre · MSQ
Web/email → www.kargeencaffe.com

24 561 575
Map Ref → 7-E2

5

Quirky ornaments and furniture, that could easily be part of someone's home, adorn the tented area that makes up this quaint café. The menu comprises hearty soups, salads and Arabic tasters, as well as burgers, pizzas and steaks for mains. Those with any space left for dessert can choose from a range of cakes, deserts and fruity cocktails. This outdoor spot is a delightfully unusual way to enjoy a leisurely coffee-and-cake session or a complete meal within a great setting.

Other Locations: City Plaza (24 694 048), Al Harthy Complex (24 560 531)

Food●●●●○ Serv●●●○○ Venue●●●●○ Value●●●●○

Buffet

Other options → **Friday Brunch [p.261]**

Al Khiran Terrace

Location → Al Bustan Palace · Al Bustan
Web/email → albustan@albustanpalace.com

24 799 666
Map Ref → 15-A1

15

A large, open and bright space with fantastic views of the garden and the beautiful bay is only the beginning. This is perhaps one of the friendliest restaurants in Oman; combine that with some of the most mouth-watering themed buffets and you have yourself a culinary treat. There is also an Italian a la carte menu available every night for those who prefer more restrained dining. The staff area more than attentive and will ensure your evening is one to remember.

Food●●●●○ Serv●●●●○ Venue●●●●○ Value●●●●○

Kargeen Caffé

Buffet

Going Out

Beautiful Cities, Beautiful Sights

From Dubai's dreamy deserts to Geneva's joie de vivre, our photography books have captured the beauty of some of the world's most captivating cities. Whether you buy one as a gift or as a souvenir for your own coffee table, these books are packed with images that you'll want to view again and again.

Jean's Grill

Location → Sultan Centre · Al Qurm
Web/email → na

24 567 666
Map Ref → 11-D1

 5

Located within the Sultan Centre supermarket, Jean's Grill seems an unlikely destination for lunch or dinner. However, what used to be a simple snacky buffet has since been revamped into an exciting international spread.

> **Crystal Clear...**
>
> *Isn't it annoying when you ask for a bottle of mineral water and are cleverly served the most expensive one on the menu? Be aware, the imported brands may be much dearer but the Omani water is just as good. So don't be shy – specify! Or pay the price.*

Start with your choice of soups and salads, through to pasta, curries, grilled meats, fish and even braised duck. Tuck into pastries from around the world, unlimited soft drinks, tea and coffee and all for a very reasonable set price. The perfect pit stop after a mammoth shopping excursion!

Food●●●○○Serv●●●○○Venue●●●○○Value●●●●○

Mokha Café

Location → Grand Hyatt Muscat · Shati Al Qurm
Web/email → www.muscat.hyatt.com

24 641 234
Map Ref → 7-D1

15

Sharing its enormous domed ceiling and elegant surroundings with the lobby of the hotel, the Mokha café lacks identity, but benefits from the hotel's terrace, overlooking the gardens and sea. The café offers an extensive buffet of international cuisine ranging from sushi and salads to meat and seafood, cooked fresh for discerning individuals, with a good array of vegetarian options available. Staff are attentive, service is good and as this café caters for children, it is an ideal venue for Friday brunch.

Food●●●●○Serv●●●○○Venue●●●●○Value●●●○○

Olivos Coffee Shop

Location → Radisson SAS Muscat · Al Khuwayr
Web/email → Muscat.Info@RadissonSAS.com

24 487 777
Map Ref → 7-B3

 10

More of a restaurant than a coffee shop; Olivos overlooks the hotel's swimming pool and gardens, a nice enough setting if dining alfresco. During the evenings they lay on buffet theme nights (although

a la carte is also available and there is always a wide range of international dishes on offer). With great service in a relaxed atmosphere, Olivos is a good value for money restaurant and an ideal location for a relaxed dinner with friends.

Food●●●●○Serv●●●●○Venue●●●●○Value●●●●○

Chinese

Other options → **Far Eastern [p.244]**

China Mood

Location → Al Bustan Palace · Al Bustan
Web/email → albustan@albustanpalace.com

24 799 666
Map Ref → 15-A1

 20

Acknowledged locally as one of the finest Chinese restaurants in Muscat, China Mood excels on many levels. For a start, the atmosphere is decadent and the staff ensure that your plate is consistently filled with delectable treats in fabulous colours, tastes and textures. The meats are tender and juicy and the vegetables perfectly cooked and free from the usual overuse of oil. China Mood is a fantastic place to enjoy a Far Eastern meal, if you can secure a reservation!

Food●●●●○Serv●●●●○Venue●●●●○Value●●●●○

Great food at China Mood

China Town

Location → CCC Complex · Al Qurm
Web/email → www.goldenspoon.com

24 567 974
Map Ref → 8-D4

 5

As soon as you arrive at this restaurant, with its Chinese decorated façade, it's easy to guess that the dinner awaiting you inside is going to be nothing less than splendid. Much-loved and well-

Chinese

Going Out

The perfect place to
begin the adventure
that is Oman.
Awaiting your arrival...

Rugged mountain cliffs rise from coral seas, majestic sand dunes extend to endless stretches of unspoilt beaches and deep green palm groves fill mountain valleys. Scuba diving, game fishing, wadi bashing, desert skiing and visits to fortress towns are just some of the experiences awaiting you. Situated in the heart of the city, the Radisson SAS Hotel, Muscat offers outstanding levels of service and comfort in 156 tastefully designed and well-appointed bedrooms, suites and Business Class rooms. Leisure facilities include an outdoor swimming pool set in beautifully landscaped gardens, a fully equipped gym, massage, sauna, steam rooms and a complimentary shuttle service to beach facilities. Dining and entertainment at the hotel suit every mood. Five banqueting and function rooms adapt to host from 10 to 210 guests.

Radisson SAS Hotel
P.O. Box 939, P.C. 133, Muscat, Sultanate of Oman
Tel: +968 24487 777, Fax: +968 24487 774

www.radissonsas.com

HOTELS & RESORTS

known dishes are available and for those watching their waistline, expect fabulous fare without having to unbutton your trousers. A takeaway and delivery service is also available, but for those dining in, the food is presented in a fuss-free manner by friendly and courteous staff in a serene setting.

Food ●●●●○ Serv ●●●●○ Venue ●●●○○ Value ●●●○○

Chinese Garden

Location → Nr Centre Ice Rink · Al Khuwayr **24 605 414**
Web/email → na   Map Ref → 7-B2

Though a tad garish in design this eatery is the epitome of cheap and cheerful Chinese cuisine. Attached to Oman's only ice rink in Al Khuwayr, the small interior supplies tasty and satisfying food in a 'no frills, no big bills' manner. The atmosphere is friendly and the service is quick. This is a great venue for a laid-back supper but beware, you can just about make out the low, rumbling vibrations coming from the ice rink generators.

Dubai Explorer

With reviews of over 300 restaurants, cafés and bars, the Dubai Explorer is the perfect companion for anyone taking their tastebuds on a tour of this cosmopolitan city. From cheap and cheerful to five-star finery, this insider's guide will help you make the most of delicious Dubai!

Food ●●○○○ Serv ●●●○○ Venue ●●○○○ Value ●●○○○

Chinese Palace

Location → Opp Sheraton Oman Htl · Ruwi **24 812 223**
Web/email → joldway@omantel.net.om   Map Ref → 12-E2

Most famous for its delicious RO 1 office lunch boxes, but the Chinese Palace is larger than life inside the restaurant. Private dining rooms seem popular in the evenings, juxtaposing the fact that you can be the only customer dining here at lunchtime. All the Chinese classics appear on the menu, with a good selection for the vegetarian diner too. Service is quick and the portions are large. Be prepared to make your own noise, as it can be eerily quiet!

Food ●●●○○ Serv ●●●●○ Venue ●●●●○ Value ●●●●○

Golden Dragon

Location → MSQ Centre · MSQ **24 697 374**
Web/email → na   Map Ref → 7-E2

This attractive, spacious, upmarket Chinese restaurant is located in a quiet part of the MSQ shopping centre, and has an extensive menu covering both Chinese and Thai dishes. Recommended are the interesting specialities, such as the Dragon Boat consisting of a range of starters served on a miniature wooden boat, as well as the sizzling dishes from the Chinese oven. The Golden Dragon is the place to go for good value, fine Chinese cuisine served by friendly, experienced staff.

Food ●●●●○ Serv ●●●●○ Venue ●●●●○ Value ●●●●○

Golden Oryx

Location → Opp Bank of Muscat · Ruwi **24 702 266**
Web/email → goryx@omantel.net.om   Map Ref → 12-D1

The Golden Oryx is a Chinese-Thai restaurant set in the heart of the CBD. As this can be a bit of a drive, its popularity is a credit to the chefs. The décor is sumptuous and the service impeccable, right down to the free water throughout your meal. The Chinese Crispy Duck, in plum or barbecue sauce, is a particular favourite, and the Chicken Satay starters, served with loads of crunchy, decadently rich sauce, are not to be missed!

Food ●●●●○ Serv ●●●●○ Venue ●●●●○ Value ●●●●○

Golden Oryx

Chinese

Going Out

For a journey to the Orient, travel to the Golden Oryx !

Chinese, Thai and Mongolian Cuisine to stir your senses. Great food, authentic cuisine and a splendid ambience. Come, discover the exotic flavours of the Orient.

Silk Route

Location → Nr Sabco Centre · Al Qurm
Web/email → www.witowell.com/silkroute

24 561 741
Map Ref → 8-D4

 100

Did your waiter stick his thumb in your thermidor? Or was the waitress slower than an indecisive snail? If your dining experience was less than you expected, then log on to www.EatOutSpeakOut.com and let us – and the rest of the web-surfing world – know all about it. Sloppy staff – you have been warned!

Silk Route is not the cheapest Chinese restaurant in Muscat, but it is one of the best. With loyal clients in both the local and expat communities, you can expect it to be busy in the evenings, particularly on weekends, so book in advance. Choose from a varied menu of Chinese, Cantonese and Szechwan cuisines, including delicious dim sum and a particularly good Crispy Aromatic Duck. Service is friendly and helpful and the atmosphere is warm and welcoming.

Great for families too.●

Food●●●●○ Serv●●●●○ Venue●●●●○ Value●●●●○

Far Eastern

Other options → **Chinese [p.240]**
Filipino [p.244]
Japanese [p.250]
Mongolian [p.251]
Polynesian [p.253]

Far Eastern Restaurant

Location → Sheraton Qurum Resort · Shati Al Qurm
Web/email → sheraton@omantel.net.om

24 605 945
Map Ref → 8-A4

 100

Even though it's located at the Sheraton resort on Qurm Beach, this restaurant just misses out on a seaview. Fortunately this doesn't affect its popularity – it's usually busy with happy diners. Choose your meal from a selection of Chinese and Thai dishes and all the takeaway classics including lemon chicken and seafood noodles. Typical Oriental puddings round off your meal perfectly without being too rich. Service is prompt between courses and the atmosphere is relaxing and peaceful, however it is supposedly very busy on Thursdays for Sushi Night.●

Food●●●○○ Serv●●●●○ Venue●●●○○ Value●●●○○

Filipino

Other options → **Far Eastern [p.244]**

Palayok Restaurant

Location → Nr Ruwi R/A, Opp OCC · Ruwi
Web/email → na

24 797 290
Map Ref → 12-D2

 50

Palayok is tucked away in Ruwi, but once you manage to find it, the hunt will be worth it! The slightly dull exterior opens up into a bright, cheery interior. Mr Marlon will make you feel at home and is happy to make menu recommendations. Fresh vegetables, fish and meat are selected and perfectly combined with spices and sauces to create some of the best Asian dishes in Muscat. Whether you decide to eat in or make use of the home delivery, add it to your must-try list!●

Food●●●●○ Serv●●●●○ Venue●●●○○ Value●●●●○

French

Al Marjan

Location → Al Bustan Palace · Al Bustan
Web/email → albustan@albustanpalace.com

24 799 666
Map Ref → 15-A1

 200

Often cited as the best restaurant in Muscat with several awards to prove it, Al Marjan certainly delivers the goods. A modern European menu, with samplings from the Continent's finest cuisines, ensures that all will be pleased. A live harpist soothes the soul and provides calm relief as you plough through one of Oman's better and most extensive wine lists. Al Murjan is a fitting signature restaurant to what is undoubtedly one of the Gulf's finest hotels.●

Food●●●●○ Serv●●●●○ Venue●●●●○ Value●●●●○

Who's turn is it to do the washing up?

Going Out

Far Eastern · French

Ban the Bland

You didn't come all this way just to have the same old fodder you can get at home, so next time you're out, forgo the fish 'n' chips and pizza and take your tastebuds on a trip round the world. You're in the birth region of Middle Eastern cooking, which is delicious and not too spicy – a good start for those unaccustomed to 'foreign' cuisine. Once you've mastered hummus, falafel, khouzi and kibbeh, you can move on to the dishes of the Far East – the exotic spices used in Thai, Chinese and Japanese cooking will take your appreciation of taste to new heights. Finally, up the stakes by trying the many flavours of the Subcontinent – Indian and Pakistani food is rich and sometimes fiery hot, but once you've learnt to appreciate the masterful blend of spices, you can pat yourself on the back, for you are now a certified culinary tourist!

Greek

Bellapais

Location → Al Rusayl Centre · Rusayl | 24 521 100
Web/email → na   Map Ref → 3-D4

    10

This unpretentious gem of a restaurant is well worth the 40 km drive from downtown! Don't be put off by the décor – the quality of food surpasses all initial impressions. A carnivore's dream serving authentic mousaka, baked lamb, steaks and seafood with all the charm of a traditional Greek tavern. Try the meze to start – an ideal introduction to your journey through Grecian gastronomy. Bellapais comes alive at lunchtimes, is quieter in the evenings and no one ever leaves hungry!◉

Food●●●●○Serv●●●●○Venue●●○○○Value●●●○

Indian

Other options → **Pakistani [p.252]**

Al Aktham

Location → Nr Oman Int Bank · Al Khuwayr | 24 603 292
Web/email → na   Map Ref → 7-C2

    5

Behind a rather rundown exterior hides a surprisingly large restaurant with an even larger menu. Choose from Arabian, Indian, Chinese and Filipino dishes or if you are not in the mood for something Eastern there are Continental dishes to

tickle your tastebuds. The restaurant contains private screened rooms for those entertaining. No matter what you choose, you are sure to have an excellent value meal served by polite and friendly staff. For lunch or dinner the Al Aktham is a hidden gem.◉

Food●●○○○Serv●●●○○Venue●●●○○Value●●●●○

Alauddin Restaurant

Location → Khalil Bldng · Al Khuwayr | 24 600 667
Web/email → na   Map Ref → 7-D2

   5

You'll be hard pushed to find someone living in Muscat who hasn't eaten at, or had a takeaway from, Alauddin. It is deservedly an old favourite. However don't expect the décor to knock your socks off and because this place is not licensed people don't come for a wild night. However, they do come for a gastronomic overload with the excellent Indian, superb Arabic, mouth-watering Chinese and tasty Continental cuisine, all served to deliciously high standards. An absolute must.◉

Food●●●●○Serv●●●●○Venue●●●○○Value●●●●○

Bollywood Chaat

Location → CCC · Al Qurm | 24 565 653
Web/email → khimjis@omantel.net.om   Map Ref → 8-D4

 5

A Bollywood Film themed vegetarian menu, of many light meals and snacks, all set in a bright and jolly fast food/takeaway style venue. Try the heart shaped potato cutlets (Kajol Cutlet) or the sweet and sticky dumplings (Moon Moon Gulab Jamun), two dishes not to be missed. The fact that this menu is very reasonably priced makes every dish that little bit more special. Service is prompt and cheery with staff willing to help explain the ingredients of the dishes on offer.◉

Food●●●○○Serv●●●○○Venue●●●○○Value●●●○○

Copper Chimney

Location → CBD Area · Ruwi | 24 706 420
Web/email → na   Map Ref → 12-D2

  10

Behind the impressive copper door of the Copper Chimney lies an even more impressive interior and a fabulously impressive kitchen. The high, arching ceiling, complete with huge hanging copper lamps,

Greek · Indian

Going Out

gives an airy, spacious feel. Once you have ordered your meal from a mouth-watering selection of dishes you can watch it being cooked in the great clay oven in the kitchen that opens on to the restaurant. For impressive Indian food in an impressive setting, look no further than the Copper Chimney.

Food⬤⬤⬤⬤○ Serv⬤⬤⬤○○ Venue⬤⬤⬤⬤○ Value⬤⬤⬤○○

Curry House

Location ➜ Nr Al Wutayyah RA · Al Wutayyah
Web/email ➜ na

| 24 564 033
Map Ref ➜ 12-A2

Eating with your fingers always tastes better! Located near the Al Watayyah Roundabout, the Curry House has some of the best service you'll find in Oman, as well as a delicious and cheap buffet with a mouth-watering a la carte selection of authentic Northern Indian cuisine. Many of the curries are served in 'karahi'; lovely copper bowls imported from India and the suggested accompaniment is a beautifully fragrant vegetable pilau (you don't have to eat with your fingers of course!) Cheap and very cheerful.

Food⬤⬤⬤⬤○ Serv⬤⬤⬤⬤○ Venue⬤⬤⬤○○ Value⬤⬤⬤⬤○

Golden Spoon

Location ➜ Nr Zawabi Mosque · Al Khuwayr
Web/email ➜ na

| 24 478 215
Map Ref ➜ 7-B2

This is a popular casual spot for good, inexpensive Chinese or Indian food. The décor is dark, but comfortable, and friendly smiles from the attentive staff more than compensates for any interior misgivings. The menu is varied and includes excellent specials of the day. Portions are generous and the food is flavourful. The sweet & sour soup makes you want to make a meal of it, but don't – save room for tasty entrées such as the Jade Chicken.

Other locations: As Seeb (24 424 214)

Food⬤⬤⬤⬤○ Serv⬤⬤⬤⬤○ Venue⬤⬤⬤○○ Value⬤⬤⬤○○

Grill House

Location ➜ Nr City Plaza · Al Khuwayr
Web/email ➜ na

| 24 603 660
Map Ref ➜ 7-D2

It's all new at the Grill House, a stone's throw from the Al Khuwayr Roundabout near Madinat Qaboos, and easy to find thanks to its large sign out front.

The service is fast and always accompanied by a smile, while the menu is varied and great value. The well-prepared dishes of Chinese, Indian or Thai will satisfy the healthiest of appetites. The Grill House has been refurbished and reorganised, and this revamped Asian restaurant will leave nothing but a pleasant taste in your mouth.

Other locations: As Seeb (24 541 502)

Food⬤⬤⬤⬤○ Serv⬤⬤⬤⬤○ Venue⬤⬤⬤○○ Value⬤⬤⬤⬤○

Khyber

Location ➜ CBD Area · Mutrah
Web/email ➜ khyberrest@omantel.net.om

| 24 781 901
Map Ref ➜ 12-D2

Situated near the Central Bank of Oman in Ruwi's busy CBD area, this licensed restaurant, with two bars and separate dining areas, serves an extensive range of Indian and Chinese food. The Executive Lunch Special consists of veg and non-veg dishes, rice, naan and dessert – all for RO 2.5 (eat in) or RO 2 (takeaway). Other specialities include delicious Indian sweets and home-made frozen and fried ice cream. The restaurant boasts a mobile tandoori oven for outside catering events.

Food⬤⬤⬤○○ Serv⬤⬤⬤○○ Venue⬤⬤⬤○○ Value⬤⬤⬤○○

Mumtaz Mahal

Location ➜ Above Qurm National Park · Al Qurm
Web/email ➜ mmtzrest@omantel.net.om

| 24 605 907
Map Ref ➜ 8-C4

Mumtaz Mahal is one of the most interesting dining experiences to be had in Muscat. Costumed waiters scurry past with baskets of poppadoms and dips (the date chutney is superb), while the

Mumtaz Mahal

traditional Indian band plays in the centre of the room. The atmosphere is lively and relaxed. Vegetarians will be very happy here – lots of paneer and spicy vegetables – while meat lovers will be equally impressed with the selection of curried fish and meat.

Food●●●●○Serv●●●●○Venue●●●●○Value●●●●○

Passage to India

Location ➜ Nr Hatat House · Al Wutayyah | 24 568 480
Web/email ➜ na | Map Ref ➜ 12-B3

Ruwi's finest, located around the back of Hatat House, is a truly special place to enjoy your food. For most of the evening traditional Indian music plays very quietly in the background, but periodically dancers in exquisite costumes perform beautifully synchronised, regional dances. A dinner at Passage to India is more than just an average meal out – the combination of a relaxing ambience, efficient service, exciting food and good value makes it an exceptional venue.

Food●●●●○Serv●●●●●Venue●●●●○Value●●●●○

Prince's Restaurant

Location ➜ Nr Zawawi Mosque · Al Khuwayr | 24 602 213
Web/email ➜ na | Map Ref ➜ 7-B2

Despite the gloomy interior, Prince's Restaurant serves up a wide and delicious range of Indian, Mugali, Chinese, Continental and Tandoori dishes at an appealing price. The décor is eclectic but the interior is comfortable and the service quiet and efficient. The kitchen aromas entice you to try the Indian specialities, such as the tandoori from the clay oven, which are delicious and filling. You can feast on delicious food from the world's most interesting culinary regions, at a very low price.

Food●●○○○Serv●●○○○Venue●●○○○Value●●●●○

Spicy Village

Location ➜ Rusayl Commercial Complex · Rusayl | 24 510 120
Web/email ➜ na | Map Ref ➜ 3-D4

One of two Spicy Village outlets in Muscat, this branch in Rusayl serves authentic Indian and Chinese cuisine. It may lack atmosphere and a licence to serve alcohol, but its no-frills approach

offers customers generous portions of good Asian food at very reasonable prices. Unfortunately, 'no-frills' extends to the décor, atmosphere and ambience, but for cheap fare, this is the place.

Other locations: Ruwi (24 700 175)

Food●●●○○Serv●●●○○Venue●●○○○Value●●●●○

Woodlands

Location ➜ Nr Europcar Bld, CBD area · Ruwi | 24 700 192
Web/email ➜ na | Map Ref ➜ 12-D2

The good thing about this place is that it hits all the right spots – service with a smile, fabulously large portions of delicious south Indian cuisine and an easy-on-your-wallet bill to top it all off. If you're stuck as to what to choose, allow one of the friendly waiters to talk you through the menu and for the faint hearted, watch out for those brutal south Indian chillies and spices. This is a good place for an easy night out.

Other locations: Salalah Airport (23 204 280)

Food●●●●○Serv●●●●○Venue●●●●○Value●●●●○

International

Other options ➜ **Buffet [p.238]**

Al Daleh Restaurant

Location ➜ National Hospitality Institute · Ruwi | 24 813 141
Web/email ➜ www.nhioman.com | Map Ref ➜

There are a couple of things that make this place an ideal choice for lunch. Firstly, they serve big portions at small prices, and secondly, you get the chance to experience the gastronomic talents of up and coming chefs. As friendly as the wait staff are, they aren't completely on top of their game, but you'll still leave full to bursting and very happy. Wednesday's lunch buffet is only RO 2 and the regular fast-track two-course lunch is only RO 1.5.

Food●●●○○Serv●●●○○Venue●○○○○Value●●●●○

Al Falaj Coffee shop

Location ➜ Al Falaj Hotel Muscat · Ruwi | 24 702 311
Web/email ➜ www.omanhotels.com | Map Ref ➜ 12-C1

This coffee shop makes a suitable place for an intimate lunch and is perfect if you happen to be working in the busy business district of Muscat.

Overlooking the hotel's swimming pool, you can sit, relax and tuck into the small lunch buffet or choose from a variety of seafood and Indian fare from the a la carte menu. Not much of an atmosphere here but good friendly service makes it a popular stop for the locals, which is a recommendation in itself.

Food ●●●○○ Serv ●●○○○ Venue ●●○○○ Value ●●○○○

Al Nouras

Location → Ramada Qurum Beach Htl · Shati Al Qurm
Web/email → www.ramadamuscat.com

24 603 555
Map Ref → 7-C2

Hungry but not entirely sure what you want? Then head down to the Ramada Hotel and sit yourself down in the Al Nouras dining area. Indian, Arabic, Chinese and Continental – it's all here. The diversity of the menu is impressive, but like so many other places that try to be everything, overall quality and taste leaves a bit to be desired. Sit on the terrace and you'll be tucking into your meal overlooking the car park and some of Muscat's flashiest cars.

Food ●●●○○ Serv ●●●○○ Venue ●●●○○ Value ●●●○○

Chedi Poolside Cabana, The

Location → Chedi Muscat · Al Ghubbrah
Web/email → www.ghmhotels.com

24 498 035
Map Ref → 6-D2

This is one of those places you're unlikely to find unless someone has told you to look for it – and it's worth looking for. The Beach Cabana is a tranquil and intimate place to enjoy a cool evening breeze and a choice of set menus. A small number of tables ensures efficient service. The flavour is Mediterranean with an emphasis on seafood, served with the usual Chedi finesse and finished with their wickedly decadent puddings. Not cheap, but worth it!

Food ●●●●○ Serv ●●●●○ Venue ●●●●○ Value ●●●●○

Four Corners, The

Location → Haffa House Hotel · Ruwi
Web/email → www.haffahouse.com

24 707 207
Map Ref → 12-C2

The style of food is Arabian buffet, with a hint of Indian influence. The buffet is simple so don't worry about being spoilt for choice, but what is on offer is all tasty. There is an a la carte menu but it's the favourably priced buffet that draws the punters in. It certainly makes for good value, but the ambience and setting is more business than pleasure.

Food ●●●○○ Serv ●●●●○ Venue ●●●○○ Value ●●●●○

Green Mountain

Location → Sheraton Oman Hotel · Ruwi
Web/email → www.starwoodhotels.com

24 799 899
Map Ref → 12-E2

Located in the Sheraton Hotel, Ruwi, a formal exterior (reminiscent of a 1970s Dallas skyscraper) makes way for a relaxed, all you can eat buffet venue – with an a la carte menu also available. An international buffet through the week makes way for a seafood extravaganza on Wednesdays – highly recommended! Vegetarians will be pleased with the healthy variety of dishes on offer and the sweet toothed are also pleasantly catered for with some awesome sweets and puddings.

Food ●●●●○ Serv ●●●●○ Venue ●●●○○ Value ●●●●○

Khaboura Café

Location → Majan Hotel · Ghala
Web/email → www.majanhotel.com

24 592 900
Map Ref → 6-E4

Despite plugging its 24-hour service, Khaboura Café appears to close at 01:00 or whenever it's empty enough to warrant not staying open. This is a European-style café, fairly plain but clean and welcoming. The range of food is good; Arabic, Asian, Chinese and Continental cuisine with prices starting at RO 1 to RO 5 – very reasonable for good grub. The café is not licensed but serves a good selection of juices and coffees.

Food ●●●○○ Serv ●●●○○ Venue ●●●●○ Value ●●●●○

Marjan Poolside Restaurant

Location → Grand Hyatt Muscat · Shati Al Qurm
Web/email → www.muscat.hyatt.com

24 641 234
Map Ref → 7-D1

Marjan Poolside is situated in the beautifully landscaped garden of the hotel's interior courtyard, at the side of the beach, overlooking the Arabian Gulf. The treat here is the fact that you get to choose your fish, the cooking method (steamed in a banana leaf, grilled or fried) and then pick your sauces and

International

Going Out

side dishes, before tucking in and enjoying every last morsel. This is a great place for either a romantic meal or a rowdy dinner with pals.⭘

Food●●●●○Serv●●●○○Venue●●●○○Value●●●○○

Palm Beach Restaurant

Location → Htl InterContinental · Shati Al Qurm | **24 600 500**
Web/email → www.interconti.com | Map Ref → 8-A4

  10

Simple food at a poolside setting, the service here is prompt and friendly. The desserts are well presented and delicious but all in all the menu is fairly limited and quite pricey, especially for what you get. The snacks aren't too bad and certainly convenient for those hanging out by the pool for lengthy periods. It's also quite a cool hangout later in the day. Please note that a fee is charged for use of the pool facilities.⭘

Food●●●○○Serv●●○○○Venue●●○○○Value●●○○○

Something for everyone

Tropicana

Location → Crowne Plaza · Qurm Heights | **24 560 100**
Web/email → www.crowneplaza.com | Map Ref → 8-C3

 5

Located at the poolside of the Crowne Plaza Hotel in Al Qurm, Tropicana hosts an international menu ranging from Oriental, Indian and Mediterranean classics to the good old American burger. Decorated tastefully, this restaurant features a loaded lunch buffet of intercontinental

dishes and is well frequented during the afternoon hours. The appetising dishes arrive in generous proportions, accompanied by excellent service and a reasonable price tag. The poolside location offers a pleasant view, and outside seating is available.⭘

Food●●●○○Serv●●●●○Venue●●●○○Value●●●○○

Italian

Other options → **Mediterranean [p.250]**
Pizzerias [p.253]

Come Prima

Location → Crowne Plaza · Qurm Heights | **24 560 100**
Web/email → www.crowneplaza.com | Map Ref → 8-C3

    15

Inside or outside, this establishment has the best views in town. Top that with garlic bread like it should be – hot, fresh, and very, very moreish – a traditional Italian menu with home-made pasta, pizza, meat and seafood dishes and you have yourself the makings of an excellent night out. Food is served at a relaxed pace, allowing time for chats. Maybe not the trendiest restaurant in town, so come here to enjoy the food and your friends – not to be seen!⭘

Food●●●●○Serv●●●●○Venue●●●●○Value●●●●○

> ### Dress Up
>
> *Muscat seems to have an unspoken (smart) dress code on the social scene. You could, perhaps, get away with shorts in some of the pubs and hotels. However, it is recommended that you check out the dress code beforehand (particularly for nightclubs) in order to avoid the embarrassment of being refused entry because of your dodgy attire!*

La Mamma

Location → Sheraton Oman Hotel · Ruwi | **24 799 899**
Web/email → www.starwoodhotels.com | Map Ref → 12-E2

    15

Casual Italian dining in the heart of the busy business district of Oman is what stands La Mama head and shoulders above the rest. Quaint red and white chequered curtains, endless strands of hanging garlic and an abundance of olive oil may seem garish, but works to complete the traditional Italian theme. The menu is composed largely of simple but delicious Italian fare including classic

Italian

Going Out

antipasti, a variety of pastas and a selection of main courses. Friendly and attentive wait staff complete the evening.

Food ●●●○○ Serv ●●●●○ Venue ●●●○○ Value ●●●○○

O Sole Mio

Location → Jawharat A'Shati Complex · Shati Al Qurm | **24 601 343**
Web/email → jasco@omantel.net.om | Map Ref → 8-A4

 100

This award-winning restaurant – with its lively atmosphere, musical entertainment and delicious Italian food – is ideal for a candlelit dinner for two or an informal dinner with friends. The menu is extensive, portion sizes ample and presentation acceptable. The grilled food options are ideal for dieters. Staff are attentive and the service is fast and efficient. O Sole Mio's popularity stems from its prime location and its ability to deliver good food at reasonable prices. Advisable to book in advance. ⊕

Food ●●●○○ Serv ●●●●○ Venue ●●●○○ Value ●●●●○

Tuscany

Location → Grand Hyatt Muscat · Shati Al Qurm | **24 641 234**
Web/email → www.muscat.hyatt.com | Map Ref → 7-D1

 150

Tuscany is the essence of all things authentically Italian. The restaurant comes complete with Romanesque pillars and a fountain ordains the centre. The food is superb with an extensive menu of all your classic Italian dishes, but if your favourite happens to be missing from the menu, just ask the chef! The service is impeccable. The restaurant strikes a perfect balance between formal dining and a relaxed atmosphere. Tuscany is always busy, so be sure to reserve a table. ⊕

Food ●●●●○ Serv ●●●●○ Venue ●●●●○ Value ●●●●○

Japanese

Other options → Far Eastern [p.244]

Tokyo Taro

Location → Al Falaj Hotel Muscat · Ruwi | **24 702 311**
Web/email → www.omanhotels.com | Map Ref → 12-C1

150

This place is vibrant with the smells and sounds of the preparation of authentic Japanese food. Meat, vegetables and seafood sizzle at the teppanyaki

bar and the green tea is on tap. All of this in a serenely authentic setting. If you are in a group, book one of the private dining rooms and enjoy your meal sitting at a traditional Japanese banquet table. Dining here is more than a tantalising eating experience – it is a night out of Japanese fun.

Food ●●●●○ Serv ●●●●○ Venue ●●●●○ Value ●●●●○

Mediterranean

Other options → Italian [p.249]

Med, The

Location → Oasis By The Sea · Shati Al Qurm | **24 602 757**
Web/email → www.chamberoman.com | Map Ref → 8-A4

150

Enter through the sumptuous velvet curtains to discover a real gem of a venue. The luxurious décor and perfect lighting set the scene for a night of gastronomic decadence. Seafood lovers will be spoilt for choice. Superb food and contemporary elegance usually reserved for five-star hotels, feel right at home here. The Med's edge is the fresh ingredients, caught locally, with the culinary flair of international expertise. Service is very friendly, if a little too fast. A dining experience not to be missed. ⊕

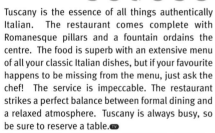

Abu Dhabi Explorer

Muscat – tick. Dubai – tick. Make Abu Dhabi next on your list of GCC cities to explore. As the capital city of the UAE, it's full of culture and tradition. It's also absolutely packed with shops, restaurants, and plenty of fun lovin' expats. So go forth; and let the Abu Dhabi & Al Ain Explorer be your guide...

Food ●●●●○ Serv ●●●●○ Venue ●●●●○ Value ●●●●○

Musandam Café & Terrace

Location → Htl InterContinental · Shati Al Qurm | **24 600 500**
Web/email → www.interconti.com | Map Ref → 8-A4

      100

Great for breakfast or brunch, but less so for dinner during off-season, this is your typical hotel buffet. Fresh fish and salads, roast meats, an egg station and live pancake making make this an ideal venue for a hungry family. Children can get their faces painted and run around to their heart's content while you fill up at the buffet. ⊕

Food ●●●○○ Serv ●●●○○ Venue ●●●○○ Value ●●●○○

Restaurant, The

Location ➜ Chedi Muscat, The · Al Ghubbrah
Web/email ➜ www.ghmhotels.com

24 524 400
Map Ref ➜ 6-D2

      20

The Restaurant boasts a fusion of contemporary Arabic and Far Eastern décor, aptly reflecting its menu. Choose from sushi, tajin dishes, fish or curries from one of the open kitchens, but leave room for the puddings and cakes – the best you will ever taste in Muscat, be careful! Prices are high, especially for alcohol, but the wine list is extensive. Afterwards, take a stroll around the tranquil gardens or along the beach and enjoy your coffee alfresco.

Food●●●○○Serv●●○○○Venue●●●●●Value●●●○○

Mexican

Pavo Real

Location ➜ MSQ Centre · MSQ
Web/email ➜ pavoreal@omantel.net.om

24 602 603
Map Ref ➜ 7-E2

   15

Muscat is perhaps the last place in the world you'd expect to find a slice of real Mexico, but that's

Pavo Real

exactly what you get walking through the doors of Pavo Real, from staff uniforms and the Mexican paraphernalia, to the chef and his delightfully authentic menu. Don't eat too much of the complimentary taco chips and salsa because you'll need room for the fabulous food and must-have Margaritas (non-alcoholic also available). Awesome ambience, friendly wait staff, fabulous food and fun live music, all the ingredients for a great night out!

Food●●●●○Serv●●●●○Venue●●●●○Value●●●●○

Señor Pico

Location ➜ Htl InterContinental · Shati Al Qurm
Web/email ➜ www.interconti.com

24 600 500
Map Ref ➜ 8-A4

     15

Nestled in the lower back corner of the InterContinental Hotel is this Latin American delight. Quaint, nicely decorated in cool Aztec style and conducive to conversation before 10:00pm. But don't be fooled, this is one of the most hopping and happening restaurants in Muscat. The cuisine is Mexican – fajitas, enchiladas, and the most fantastic must-try nachos. You will also find an excellent selection of succulent Latin grills. The food is well presented and appetising. Complement your meal with the best Margarita in Muscat.

Food●●●●○Serv●●●●○Venue●●●●○Value●●●○○

Mongolian

Other options ➜ **Far Eastern [p.244]**

Mongolian Barbecue

Location ➜ Golden Oryx · Ruwi
Web/email ➜ goryx@omantel.net.om

24 706 128
Map Ref ➜ 12-D1

 15

At first glance the menu seems limited, but after your choice of soup or starter (the latter at additional cost), you join the queue, are presented with a large bowl and create your own meal, which you can watch being cooked. If you manage, somehow, to keep each portion small enough, you can return again and again, sampling all combinations of meat, vegetables and delicious sauces. A relaxed venue with reasonably priced, potentially excellent food (depending on your own culinary combining).

Food●●●●○Serv●●●●●Venue●●●●○Value●●●●○

Going Out

Mexican

Omani

Other options → **Arabic/Lebanese [p.232]**

Bin Ateeq

Location → Nr Shell filling station · Al Khuwayr | 24 478 225
Web/email → binateeq@omantel.net.om   Map Ref →

🪧 🚐 👤 📞 🚭 5

One of the friendliest and most welcoming restaurants in Muscat, Bin Ateeq offers Omani food at its best. The takeaway queue is testament to its popularity with locals. The cane-clad walls are reminiscent of a jungle hut, but huts with air conditioning units and televisions in every private dining room. Simply spiced meat, chicken and fish, all still on the bone, and mountains of fried fluffy rice are brought to you on your majlis cushion. Prepare to get messy! 🆑

Food ●●●○○ Serv ●●●●○ Venue ●●●○○ Value ●●●●○

> ### Oops
>
> *Did we miss your favourite French brasserie? Or overlook an Omani culinary gem? If there's an eatery that you think deserves a mention then drop us a line to Info@Explorer-Publishing.com and we'll make sure it features in the next edition.*

Ofair Public Foods

Location → Nr Shell · Al Khuwayr | 24 693 965
Web/email → na   Map Ref → 7-A2

🍸 5

You may have to squat on traditional cushions to enjoy your authentic Omani dishes, but go in a group and at least you get to do it in the privacy of your own (small) room. Just remember that if you visit for the authentic atmosphere (if you ignore the TV) you need to respect local customs and women should cover their arms and legs. The food is pretty basic but for the price you can definitely fill a hole, not only in your stomach but in your cultural experiences. 🆑

Food ●●●●○ Serv ●●●○○ Venue ●●●●○ Value ●●●●○

Omani Hut

Location → Al Sawadi Beach Resort · Barka | 26 795 545
Web/email → www.alsawadibeach.com   Map Ref → na

  10

Set in a traditional Omani majlis, this restaurant is in a great location – sitting on a beautiful unspoilt beach – and makes for a fabulous place to come and enjoy the legendary Omani shuwa. The staff are welcoming and very friendly and the enthusiastic belly dancer adds a certain spark to your evening's entertainment. The more than reasonable prices ensure that Omani Hut is an ideal venue, perfect for an intimate dinner or a casual get-together with a group of friends. 🆑

Food ●●●●○ Serv ●●●●○ Venue ●●●●○ Value ●●●●○

Seblat Al Bustan

Location → Al Bustan Palace · Al Bustan | 24 796 666
Web/email → www.al-bustan.intercontinental.com   Map Ref → 15-A1

 10

Dine in Bedouin tents, under the stars and among the swaying palms in the hotel's grounds while you tuck into tasty Omani food. Traditional music and folk dancing, bread making, henna and handicrafts make this more of a cultural experience than just a meal. And since you've come this far into the culture, be sure to taste the shuwa, Oman's local dish. Finish the evening with traditional coffee and dates. A shuttle bus takes you to the tented village from the hotel entrance. Every Wednesday night in season (September to May) from 19:30 to 23:00. 🆑

Food ●●●●○ Serv ●●●●○ Venue ●●●●○ Value ●●●●○

> ### Dress Up
>
> *Muscat seems to have an unspoken (smart) dress code on the social scene. You could, perhaps, get away with shorts in some of the pubs and hotels. However, it is recommended that you check out the dress code beforehand (particularly for nightclubs) in order to avoid the embarrassment of being refused entry because of your dodgy attire!*

Pakistani

Other options → **Indian [p.245]**

Karachi Darbar

Location → Next to Zawawi Mosque · Al Khuwayr | 24 604 360
Web/email → www.goldenspoongroup.com   Map Ref → 7-B2

    5

This is a fantastic fast food joint and perfect if your lunch hour consists of grabbing something fast and tasty and little else. A good sign is its popularity with the local community, particularly later in the day and around dinnertime. Expect a limited menu of curries and grill dishes, but everything here is delicious, especially the spicy tandoori chicken which is to die for. Great value for money for casual dining, and definitely one to try.●

Food ●●●○○ Serv ●●●●○ Venue ●●●○○ Value ●●●●○

Persian

Other options → **Arabic/Lebanese [p.232]**

Shiraz

Location → Crowne Plaza · Qurm Heights
Web/email → www.cpmuscat.com

24 560 100
Map Ref → 8-C3

 10

Shiraz offers a hearty menu of Iranian favourites in a lovely venue. A mock tented ceiling and open bread baking area lend authenticity to a plush, if somewhat uniform, indoor setting. Take along a huge appetite for generous, delicious complementary appetisers of cheese, salad and freshly baked Arabic bread. Starters and desserts are a particular treat for the tastebuds. Main courses, sadly, are a little bit on the bland side by comparison. Terrace dining, in cooler months, with stretching views of the coastline and mountain backdrop, will no doubt delight daytime and evening diners alike.●

Food ●●●●○ Serv ●●●○○ Venue ●●●●○ Value ●●●●○

Persian Splendour at Shiraz

Pizzerias

Other options → **Italian [p.249]**

Everyone loves a slice of pizza now and again and thankfully you can satisfy your craving in a variety of outlets around Muscat. The following table lists places where you'll find great pizza – obviously you can get a pizza at most Italian restaurants also, but those listed below are some of the best (marked with an 'R' on the table). Of course, the takeaway pizzas are pretty good too, and we've listed our favourites below (marked with a 'T').

Pizzerias		
O Sole Mio (R)	Jawharat A'Shati Complex	24 601 343
Papa John's Pizza (T/R) (T)	Lulu Hypermarket	24 503 333
	Airport, As Seeb	24 519 468
Pizza Hut (T/R)	Airport Station	24 521 122
	Al Khod	24 542 951
	Shati Al Qurm	24 563 798
	Prisunic Delco	24 566 533
	MSQ	24 693 564
	Al Khuwayr	24 483 563
Pizza Muscat (T)	Al Khuwayr	24 483 393
	Al Harthy Complex	24 565 618
	Ruwi	24 817 715
Santino's Pizza (T)	Muscat City Centre	24 558 698
Tuscany (R)	Grand Hyatt	24 641 234

Polynesian

Other options → **Far Eastern [p.244]**

Trader Vic's

Location → Htl InterContinental · Shati Al Qurm
Web/email → www.interconti.com

24 698 028
Map Ref → 8-A4

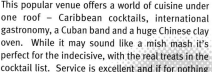 **15**

This popular venue offers a world of cuisine under one roof – Caribbean cocktails, international gastronomy, a Cuban band and a huge Chinese clay oven. While it may sound like a mish mash it's perfect for the indecisive, with the real treats in the cocktail list. Service is excellent and if for nothing else, this is one of the only places to do a good Irish Coffee. Dining here does not come cheap, but for a good night out or special occasion, it's worth it.●

Food ●●●●○ Serv ●●●●○ Venue ●●●○○ Value ●●○○

Portuguese

Nando's

Location → Beh CCC · Al Qurm
Web/email → www.nandos.com

24 561 818
Map Ref → 8-D4

 5

There is something great about this place – tasty and nutritious food served quickly. Alternative starters, main meals to eat with your hands, or the legendary Chicken Espetada, will have your appetite nicely satisfied. The speciality of this restaurant is their marinated chicken, which is then butterfly grilled on a naked flame. A warm greeting at the door, rustic décor, you can see your food being cooked and reasonable prices – you just can't go wrong!

Food ●●●●○ Serv ●●●●○ Venue ●●●○○ Value ●●●●●

Chicken on the run

Seafood

Beach Pavilion

Location → Al Bustan Palace · Al Bustan
Web/email → albustan@albustanpalace.com

24 567 825
Map Ref → 15-A1

The seashore location of the Beach Pavilion makes this a delightful place to enjoy a light lunch, watch the waves crash onto the shore as you tuck into good food. Home-baked rolls supplement smallish portions and the staff are only too happy to adjust a dish to suit your needs. Service is slow at weekends and holidays – in fact, you will be lucky to get a table at these times without booking first, it's that popular!

Food ●●●●○ Serv ●●●○○ Venue ●●●●○ Value ●●●○○

Blue Marlin

Location → Marina Bander Al-Rowdha · Sidab
Web/email → www.marinaoman.com

24 737 288
Map Ref → 13-E4

A haven of tranquility, intimacy and serenity, the Blue Marlin Restaurant at the Marina is one of

the most picturesque locations in Muscat. Modern European cuisine is fantastically prepared and presented, surpassed only by the service. The menu offers a good selection of seafood with a fabulous twist, as well as some unusual variations on non-fish dishes. This is one of the few restaurants where as much care is taken with the presentation as with the food itself. A lunchtime favourite, under utilised as an dinner destination.

Food ●●●●○ Serv ●●●●○ Venue ●●●●○ Value ●●●●○

Steakhouses

Club Safari Rooftop Grill

Location → Grand Hyatt Muscat · Shati Al Qurm
Web/email → www.muscat.hyatt.com

24 641 234
Map Ref → 7-D1

Spectacularly set overlooking the pool, with a backdrop of the sea. As the name suggests, this is a grill house serving dishes such as steaks and lobster. Fresh salads and assorted accompaniments to the meal are also included, as are soups to start and desserts to finish. The price includes beer, wine and other selected beverages, making this a great spot for a party night out. The all-inclusive set menu starts at RO 15.

Food ●●●●○ Serv ●●●●○ Venue ●●●●○ Value ●●●●○

Vegetarian

Vegetarians should be pleasantly surprised by the range and variety of cuisine available in restaurants in Muscat. Arabic food, although dominated by meat in main courses, offers a staggering range of meze, most of which is vegetarian, and the general affection for fresh vegetables provides enough variety to satisfy even the most ravenous diner. Also, due to the large number of Indians who are vegetarian by religion, many Indian

Going Out   Portuguese · Vegetarian

restaurants offer so many styles of cooking and such a range of tasty dishes, that Indian cuisine is hard to beat.

In other restaurants, most outlets now offer at least one or two veggie dishes. Highlights include some excellent Italian, Mexican, Far Eastern and International restaurants all over the city, as well as cafés, often a good choice for inventive and delicious vegetarian dishes.

A word of warning – if you are a strict veggie, confirm that your meal is completely meat free. Some restaurants cook their 'vegetarian' selection with animal fat or on the same grill as the meat dishes. Also, in some places you may need to check the ingredients of seemingly vegetarian items.

Dinner Cruises

Other options ➜ Boat & Yacht Charters [p.190]
Dhow Charters [p.198]

Arabian Sea Safaris

Location ➜ Various locations
Web/email ➜ www.arabianseasafaris.com

24 693 223
Map Ref ➜ 7-D1

As part of their range of sea tours, Arabian Sea Safaris offer dinner cruises along the coast from Marina Bander Al-Rowdha, with fresh sea air, stunning views of Muscat and excellently prepared food. The menu is mainly seafood based, grilled or barbecued, but caters to most tastes. Trips usually go out twice a week during the cooler months but custom trips can also be arranged on request if your party is big enough. For more information contact Grand Hyatt.

Sea Tourism Co.

Location ➜ Various locations
Web/email ➜ na

24 602 949
Map Ref ➜ na

Sea Tourism has two luxury motor boats available for charter either for a simple two hour trip or a dinner cruise. All cruises are custom designed so can be made to suit your exact requirements. Business lunches, romantic sunset dinners or a trip to a remote beach for picnic can all be arranged. Watersports are also available on trips.

Cafés & Coffee Shops

Other options ➜ Afternoon Tea [p.260]

Muscat has a relatively thriving café scene, due in part to the split shifts with long lunch breaks the generally relaxed and laid back attitude of residents. The numerous cafés around the city vary from those that will serve you a three-course meal, to those that will serve you a doughnut or sandwich to accompany your cup of coffee. Whether you go for a relaxed business lunch, a lazy evening hangout or just a good cup of coffee and a dose of people watching, café culture is one of the best ways to pass the time. The major international coffee house chains are all represented, with branches of Costa Coffee, Second Cup and Starbucks in various locations across Muscat.

Costa Coffee alfresco!

Al Mas Brasserie

Location ➜ Bowshar Hotel Deluxe · Al Ghubbrah
Web/email ➜ www.bowsharhotel.com

24 501 105
Map Ref ➜ 6-E2

The Al Mas Brasserie is located in the Bowshar Hotel just north of the Ghubbrah/Bawsher Roundabout. The sleek hotel décor sets the pace for this fabulous little café. Open most hours, this is more of a restaurant than quick coffee stop, and its menu is bursting with tempting Indian, Chinese and Arabic cuisine. Those wanting just a quick coffee stop can choose from the small menu of snacks and quick bites. The staff are friendly and convivial and the prices surprisingly reasonable.

Food ●●●●○ Serv ●●●●○ Venue ●●●○○ Value ●●●●○

Going Out   Dinner Cruises · Cafés & Coffee Shops

Because one is never enough...

Al Radha Bistro

Location → Best Western Hotel · Shati Al Qurm | **24 692 121**
Web/email → www.bestwestern.com | Map Ref → 7-D1

5

Just off the hotel lobby, the tiny Al Radha Bistro is conveniently located for breakfast, lunch or a light evening meal. The interior is a jazzy fusion of east meets west, with its painted mirror walls in Egyptian patterns. The same can be said of the menu, which, alongside the standard international hotel fare of pasta and sandwiches has Middle-Eastern treats such as koftah, kibbeh and shawarma. Al Radha offers a flavour of the Middle East in a western-style café.

Food●●●○○Serv●●○○○Venue●●●○○Value●●●●○

Café de Muscat

Location → Oasis By The Sea · Shati Al Qurm | **24 602 757**
Web/email → na | Map Ref → 8-A4

Despite the arrival of global café brands close by, Café de Muscat remains a great place to visit in one of the best locations of any café here in the city. Sit out on the large terrace under the shade of barasti palms for beautiful views along Al Qurm Beach. The menu includes quality café fare alongside tasty Continental and Indian dishes, and portions are generous. Service is relaxed, perfectly fitting the pleasant surroundings and agreeable atmosphere.

Food●●●●○Serv●●●●○Venue●●●●●Value●●●○○

Café Glacier

Location → CCC · Al Qurm | **24 560 974**
Web/email → cccqurum@omantel.net.om | Map Ref → 8-D4

This spacious café serves as a welcome shopping centre pit stop and has long been a favourite of families and weary shoppers. Well-presented dishes and generous portions satisfy a hungry crowd. Free popcorn will appeal to the kids, and high chairs are available for toddlers. As well as serving Rombouts coffee, there are herbal teas, fruit smoothies and a menu that includes breakfasts, pasta, salads, soups, sandwiches and pancakes, all served by friendly and efficient wait staff.

Other locations: Zakher Mall, Al Khuwayr, 24 694 245.
Food●●●○○Serv●●●○○Venue●●●○○Value●●●●○

Café Samaharam

Location → Haffa House Hotel · Ruwi | **24 707 207**
Web/email → www.haffahouse.com | Map Ref → 12-C2

Far enough away from the bustling centre of Muscat's CBD to be relatively peaceful, Samaharam is still a convenient retreat for a lunch break from the office, a leisurely informal evening meal or a relaxing shisha for those in the area. Food is simple but tasty, quick to arrive, and the grills, pasta, sandwiches and fruit juices all make for filling fare. After your meal indulge in a headily pungent shisha, or sniff at the one being smoked near you.

Food●●●●○Serv●●●●○Venue●●●●●Value●●●●○

D'Arcy's Kitchen

Location → Jawharat A'Shati Complex · Shati Al Qurm | **24 600 234**
Web/email → jasco@omantel.net.om | Map Ref → 8-A4

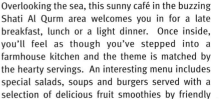

Overlooking the sea, this sunny café in the buzzing Shati Al Qurm area welcomes you in for a late breakfast, lunch or a light dinner. Once inside, you'll feel as though you've stepped into a farmhouse kitchen and the theme is matched by the hearty servings. An interesting menu includes special salads, soups and burgers served with a selection of delicious fruit smoothies by friendly staff. Whether for a light meal or just a coffee, D'Arcy's welcomes you in.

Food●●●●○Serv●●●●○Venue●●●●○Value●●●●○

Chat. Laugh. Drink. Enjoy.

Conveniently located at Capital Commercial Centre, Qurum, Second Cup offers a wide variety of premium beverages and delicious pastries, decadent cakes and sandwiches. Open from 7.30 am to 12 midnight everyday.

The Ultimate Coffee Experience
CCC Qurum Tel: 24566616
Drive-thru facility available

SECOND CUP
COFFEE CO.

ADINC

D'Arcy's Kitchen

Golden Gate Café

Location → Al-Araimi Complex · Al Qurm
Web/email → alaraimi@omantel.net.com

24 571 644
Map Ref → 8-D4

 15

Nothing fancy at the Golden Gate Café, but don't let that stop you from trying it out. Food comes quickly and is relatively inexpensive and the venue is a good getaway from the hustle and bustle of the busy shopping district of Al Qurm. Located downstairs in the Al-Araimi Complex, a fairly wide selection of quick meals will refuel the die-hard shopper. The soup, served inside a massive crusty roll, is recommended. Service has to be beckoned but comes with a smile.

Food●●●○○Serv●●●●○Venue●●●○○Value●●●●○

Kargeen Caffé

Location → MSQ Centre · MSQ
Web/email → www.kargeencaffe.com

24 561 575
Map Ref → 7-E2

 5

Please see Kargeen Caffé review under Arabic/Lebanese [p.232].

Food●●●●○Serv●●●○○Venue●●●●○Value●●●●○

Le Mermaid

Location → Nr Grand Hyatt Hotel · Shati Al Qurm
Web/email → alhamidint@hotmail.com

24 602 327
Map Ref → 7-D1

 5

In the shadow of the Grand Hyatt stands one of the coolest cafés in Muscat. With a large outside seating area and great sea views, majlis tents and shisha, this popular café has people buzzing all over town. Dishing up a wide range of seafood, grills and snacks, Le Mermaid is a hidden treasure. Indulge in a refreshing fruit cocktail or choose from the range of coffees and local hot drinks.

Food●●●○○Serv●●●○○Venue●●●●○Value●●●●○

Lobby Lounge, The

Location → Chedi Muscat, The · Al Ghubbrah
Web/email → www.ghmhotels.com

24 498 035
Map Ref → 6-D2

 5

Another aspect to the tranquil haven that is the Chedi Hotel. Situated just beyond the Majlis area at the entrance, the Lobby Lounge is an intimate arrangement of comfy seating areas in a brightly sunlit room. At night, the guests spill outside to bag one of the much sought after tables around the giant gas fires in heavy black planters. Perfect for an after dinner drink or sundowners, but you will need to hover about to claim one – people don't give them up easily!

Food●●●○○Serv●●●○○Venue●●●●○Value●●●○○

Kargeen Caffé

Mado Café

Location → Oasis By The Sea · Shati Al Qurm
Web/email → na

24 602 442
Map Ref → 8-A4

 5

Mado is the newest entrant on Muscat's café scene, with an unusual and exotic slant on the typical café menu. Furnished with a choice of seating outside

Cafés & Coffee Shops

Going Out

and inside, and some interesting décor, its biggest selling point is the signature ice cream and a mouth-watering range of Turkish delicacies (both sweet and savoury). Turkish breakfasts and the more substantial lunch and dinner options are also worth a taste, as is the strong, dark, authentic Turkish coffee. Definitely deserves a visit.

Food●●●●○ Serv●●●○○ Venue●●●●○ Value●●●●○

Must do Mado!

Majlis Al Shams

Location ➔ Htl InterContinental · Shati Al Qurm   **24 600 500**
Web/email ➔ www.interconti.com   Map Ref ➔ 8-A4

A relaxing long light lunch or an indulgent coffee and cake session are on offer at this café in the InterContinental Hotel. The coffee shop offers a range of freshly prepared sandwiches, freshly squeezed juices, a selection of teas and coffees, and a delectable variety of cakes and pastries. Situated in the hotel lobby, the place is surprisingly peaceful and intimate despite its grand surroundings. The service is extremely friendly, and coupled with the comfortable sofas and chairs an afternoon here easily slips away.

Food●●●●○ Serv●●●●○ Venue●●●○○ Value●●●●○

Marina Café

Location ➔ Below Crowne Plaza Htl · Al Qurm   **24 567 825**
Web/email ➔ na   Map Ref ➔ 8-B3

This is a great little place, newly built on the beachfront in Al Qurm. The curved walls of the

contemporary architecture lead you into the cool and comfortable café, or up to the next floor where you can dine alfresco. Serving a range of seafood and salads, snacks and juices, the Marina is popular with both locals and expats. Service is slow but portions are big and worth waiting for.

Food●●●●○ Serv●●●○○ Venue●●●●● Value●●●○○

Icecream Cafés

Tropical Juices and Ice Cream

Location ➔ Nr Sur Centre · Al Khuwayr   **24 482 476**
Web/email ➔ na   Map Ref ➔ 7-A1

Tall glasses of freshly squeezed juices made from various fruits, home made icecream, milkshakes and sundaes that melt in your mouth – a trip to this juice and icecream bar is a treat for your tastebuds. This is an ideal after-dinner hangout, frequented by families, couples and groups of friends.

Other locations: CCC, Al Qurm 24 560 473, Opp Kamat, Ruwi 24 799 884, Seeb Commercial Complex, Seeb 24 424 204

Food●●●●○ Serv●●●●○ Venue●●●●○ Value●●●●●

Shisha Cafés

Other options ➔ **Arabic/Lebanese [p.232]
Omani [p.252]**

Shisha cafés are common throughout the Middle East, offering relaxing surroundings and the chance to smoke a shisha pipe (aka 'hubbly bubbly' or 'narghile') in a variety of aromatic flavours. They are traditionally the preserve of local men who meet to play backgammon and gossip with friends. However, the cafés are popular with locals and visitors alike, especially in the cooler winter evenings. Most outlets offer a basic menu, generally Arabic cuisine plus coffees, teas and fresh fruit juices. If you want to puff in the comfort of your own home you can buy one from some of the larger supermarkets or at Mutrah Souk, where you can also buy flavoured tobacco and coals to go with it. Despite the obvious health risk, it's an activity you should try at least once!

Too much pepper in your prawn balls... and the muscle bound chef looks like he wouldn't take criticism lightly? Smile politely, go home, and log on to Eat Out Speak Out. Rant and rave to your heart's content! We'll not only publish your comments, we will also pass them on to the chef – anonymously of course...

Going Out

Icecream Cafés · Shisha Cafés

Shisha Cafés

Al Barouk	Beach Hotel
Al Deyar	Nr Al Shati Plaza Cinema
Al Madinat	MSQ Centre
Automatic	Nr Sabco Centre, Al Qurm
Fish Village	Al Khuwayr
Kargeen Caffé [P.235]	MSQ Centre
Layali Al Hilmya	Nr Zakher Mall
Le Mermaid	Nr Grand Hyatt Htl
Marjan Poolside	Grand Hyatt Muscat
Seblat Al Bustan	Al Bustan Palace InterConti

Afternoon Tea

Other options → Cafés & Coffee Shops [p.255]

Atrium Tea Lounge

Location → Al Bustan Palace · Al Bustan | 24 799 666
Web/email → www.al-bustan.intercontinental.com Map Ref → 15-A1

There is, perhaps, no better way to take in the splendour of the palatial Al Bustan Palace than in the Atrium Café. Relax under the magnificent dome while enjoying a coffee, one of their delicious cakes or pastries, or a traditional afternoon tea. The friendly service, plush surroundings and gentle music provided by their pianist or harpist makes it easy to linger in the lap of luxury and get away from it all, for a while at least.

Food●●●●○ Serv●●●●○ Venue●●●●○ Value●●●●○

Sirj Tea Lounge

Location → Grand Hyatt Muscat · Shati Al Qurm | 24 641 234
Web/email → www.muscat.hyatt.com Map Ref → 7-D1

Comfortably furnished in typical Arabian style, the Sirj Tea Lounge offers you the choice between tented or open areas in which to relax. Traditional English afternoon tea consists of finger sandwiches, home-made scones with clotted cream and jam, and a large slice of the cake of your choice. There is a good selection of fresh juices to choose from and you may be lucky enough to catch a rendition from the resident pianist while you sip away your afternoon.

Food●●●●○ Serv●●●○○ Venue●●●●○ Value●●●○○

Internet Cafés

Other options → Internet [p.77]

Internet cafés or shops can be found in most areas of Oman, generally in shopping centres but also in small shops. Not surprisingly, Muscat has more internet cafés than the rest of Oman, especially in Ruwi. Prices range from 400 to 700 baisas per hour, with different rates during evenings and at weekends. Many places allow you to pay per quarter of an hour. Shop around to find a café that suits your needs – not all have broadband, printers, scanners or webcams. The best value shop is Mamoon Internet Services in Al Khuwayr (692 369). They have the cheapest rates and the best service and equipment. First Internet Café in CCC Shopping Centre (Al Qurm) is the most expensive at 700 baisas per hour (no broadband).

Food on the Go

Bakeries

In addition to bread, Arabic bakeries offer a wonderful range of pastries, biscuits and Lebanese sweets. Look out for 'borek' (flat pastries, baked or fried with spinach or cheese) or the biscuits filled with ground dates. All are delicious, and must be tried at least once. Omani Halwa is a sticky sweet made from sugar, ghee (clarified butter), rosewater and saffron, made in huge batches and served in little dishes with a spoon.

Fruit Juices Etc.

Other options → Cafés & Coffee Shops [p.255]

Fresh juices are widely available, either from shawarma stands, juice shops, 'coffee shops' or cafés. They are delicious, healthy and cheap, and made on the spot from fresh fruits such as mango, banana, kiwi, strawberry and pineapple (have the mixed fruit cocktail if you can't decide). Fresh lemon mint juice is also very popular (ask for no sugar if you prefer), and the local milk is called 'laban' (a heavy, salty buttermilk that doesn't go well in tea or coffee but best drunk on its own). Arabic mint tea is available, but probably not drunk as widely as in other parts of the Arab world; however, Arabic coffee (thick, silty and strong) is extremely popular and will have you buzzing on a caffeine high for days!

Afternoon Tea · Fruit Juices Etc.

Going Out

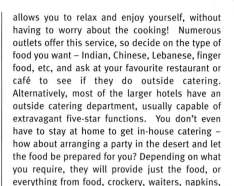

Shawarma

Other options → **Arabic/Lebanese [p.232]**

Sidewalk stands throughout the city sell 'shawarma', rolled pita bread filled with lamb or chicken carved from a rotating spit, and plenty of salad. Costing about 300 baisas each, these are inexpensive, well worth trying, and offer an excellent alternative fast food to the usual hamburger. The stands usually sell other dishes, such as 'falafel', or 'ta'amiya', (small savoury balls of deep-fried beans) or 'foul' (a paste made from fava beans).

While most shawarma stands offer virtually the same thing, slight differences make some stand out from the rest. People are often adamant that their particular favourite serves, for example, the best falafel in town. These can often be the first place you eat when you come to Oman, but make an effort to look around; every restaurant has its own way of doing things and you might find that the best is, surprisingly, the smallest, most low-key restaurant you happen on by chance.

Friday Brunch

Friday brunch is perfect for a lazy start or end to the weekend, especially once the really hot weather arrives. Popular with all sections of the community, it provides Thursday night revellers with a gentle awakening, and often much needed nourishment. For families, brunch is a very pleasant way to spend the day, especially since many venues organise a variety of fun activities for kids, allowing parents to relax and concentrate on the fine food and drinks on offer. Different brunches appeal to different crowds; some have fantastic buffets, others are in spectacular surroundings, and some offer amazing prices for all you can eat. It's good to shop around for the perfect brunch location since many of the 4 and 5 star hotels offer an incredibly enticing spread as well as use of their facilities (pool, gardens, beach access) as part of the deal. Ask around and find out who does what, where and for how much and make a day of it.

Parties at Home

Caterers

A popular and easy way to have a party, special occasion or business lunch, in-house catering allows you to relax and enjoy yourself, without having to worry about the cooking! Numerous outlets offer this service, so decide on the type of food you want – Indian, Chinese, Lebanese, finger food, etc, and ask at your favourite restaurant or café to see if they do outside catering. Alternatively, most of the larger hotels have an outside catering department, usually capable of extravagant five-star functions. You don't even have to stay at home to get in-house catering – how about arranging a party in the desert and let the food be prepared for you? Depending on what you require, they will provide just the food, or everything from food, crockery, waiters, napkins, to tables and chairs and often a clearing up service afterwards! Costs vary according to the number of people, dishes, services and so on. Check the Yellow Pages for contact details and look out for flyers.

On the Town

Muscat is a small capital city with a fairly high level of expatriates. Life is led at a relatively sedate pace – there's less chance of a wild night on the town here than in other cities in the region, such as Dubai. Places tend to wind down quite early, so if you're moving here for the nightlife, you've probably made a bad choice!

However, considering its size, Muscat has a reasonable variety of restaurants and bars. The following section covers cafés, bars, pubs and nightclubs as well as 'cultural' entertainment such as theatre and comedy. A lot of Muscat's social scene may appear a little exclusive to a newcomer, with cliques that seem to have limited memberships. However, once you're in, you're in and the expat community is in fact very friendly and welcoming. As there isn't a huge number of places to go out on the town, you will begin to see familiar faces time after time.

A lot of socialising takes place at people's houses, particularly after the bars and nightclubs have closed and especially during Ramadan. In addition, much of the nightlife centres on the hotels, which organise a variety of events throughout the year. Special nights are usually arranged about a month in advance, so it is a good idea to have your name added to their mailing lists to receive information on what is happening. They will usually email or fax details of their forthcoming events.

If a lively bar scene interests you, it's worth checking out some of the places listed in the

Going Out   Shawarma · Caterers

Restaurants section [p.232]. Some restaurants also function as a bar, and a few even have a dance floor so you can eat, drink and be merry!

Throughout the week, some of the bars and restaurants hold special nights and promotions to attract custom. Wednesdays and Thursdays tend to be the busiest nights out as, depending on what working week you follow, they are the start of the weekend. Most bars and nightclubs close between midnight and 01:00, especially those in hotels, with the occasional bar open until 03:00.

Bars

Other options → Nightclubs [p.264]

Muscat has a reasonable number of bars with a good variety of styles. Most are located in hotels and the 'in' places buzz with after-hours activity. In addition to the bars reviewed here, there are plenty of others (usually in the smaller hotels), which may not attract the regular crowd but are worth checking out if only to sample something a little different for the weekend.

Door Policy

Some of the 'cooler' hang outs implement a 'members only' policy, which allows them to control the clientele frequenting the place.

Even with the mix of nationalities that makes up the cultural melting pot of Oman there are sometimes instances of certain bars and nightclubs having a selective entry 'policy'. At quieter times, non-members may have no problem getting in, even if unaccompanied by a member. Basically, the management uses the rule to disallow entry if they don't like the look of you or your group, and they will point to their sign and say 'sorry'. Often large groups of men are refused entry, so breaking up your group of recruiting some friendly ladies is a worthwhile tactic. If you are refused entry then the best bet is to find somewhere else more accommodating as getting irate really won't get you anywhere.

Dress Code

Most bars have a reasonably relaxed attitude to their customers' dress sense. Some places, however, insist on no shorts or sandals, while others require at least a collared shirt and no jeans. Nightclubs generally have a dressier approach, so dress to impress. As Oman is well on its way to becoming a trendy tourist destination, the dress code will no doubt get stricter.

Specials

Some places hold occasional promotions with different themes and offers. These run alongside special nights, such as Ladies' Night, which are usually held weekly. For the promotions, you can find out what's coming up in the weekly and monthly entertainment publications and from the venues concerned. Special nights, such as the popular quiz nights, are mainly promoted in a bar or pub, and many attract quite a following. As a bonus, the (liquid) prizes are often quite good.

Cocktail Lounges

John Barry

Location → Grand Hyatt Muscat · Shati Al Qurm	24 641 234
Web/email → www.muscat.hyatt.com	Map Ref → 7-D1

A five-star piano bar designed to give the impression of being on board the ill-fated SS John Barry after it was sunk off the coast of Dhofar. Unique features include aquarium, nets, ropes, rusty rivets, sea chest tables and sailor boy waiters. This is a low-key, sophisticated, smart bar with a good range of cocktails (both alcoholic and non-alcoholic), spirits, beers, soft drinks and good house wine by the glass. Great for a pre-dinner drink or a quiet beer after work.

Food●●●○○ Serv●●●●○ Venue●●●○○ Value●●●●○

Trader Vic's

Location → Htl InterContinental · Shati Al Qurm	24 698 028
Hours → 12:00 – 14:30 19:00 – 01:00	
Web/email → www.interconti.com	Map Ref → 8-A4

Please see Trader Vic's review under Polynesian [p.253].

Food●●●●○ Serv●●●●○ Venue●●●○○ Value●●●○○

General Bars

Barrio Fiesta

Location → Majan Hotel · Ghala	24 592 900
Web/email → www.majanhotel.com	Map Ref → 6-E4

The space age 1970s theme bar, named after a famous village near Manila, has a resident Russian band playing a mixture of Arabic, Russian and European tunes that sometimes border on the cheesy side. It isn't really the best location for a girl's night out (despite the inordinate amount of men) but the brightly-lit stage and its players seem to be the real draw. A novelty experience.

Food●●●◐○ Serv●●●◐○ Venue●●●●○ Value●●●●○

spirits and wines at average hotel prices and providing you with an interesting selection of salty nibbles to keep you thirsty. Popular with local businessmen and hotel guests, this bar is great for a chilled out drink and conversation, appealing to a slightly older customer.

Food●●●○○ Serv●●●●○ Venue●●●●○ Value●●●◐○

Cellar, The

Location → Radisson SAS Muscat · Al Khuwayr
Web/email → info.muscat@radissonsas.com
24 487 777
Map Ref → 7-B3

Located below the efficiently run Radisson SAS is Muscat's only sports bar. The long bar entices, while food is provided by Olivos Coffee Shop, where the variety and taste is always excellent. Add to this the cocktail list and your night is made. But choose your night, as weekdays tend to be quiet unless there is a promoted sporting event or theme night on. A great place to start or end an evening.

Food●●●●○ Serv●●●◐○ Venue●●●◐○ Value●●●●○

Club Safari

Location → Grand Hyatt Muscat · Shati Al Qurm
Web/email → www.muscat.hyatt.com
24 641 234
Map Ref → 7-D1

Club Safari has really taken its jungle theme to heart with ethnic African décor galore. Faux animal skins, African masks and bamboo adorn the walls and ceiling creating an atmosphere that is a little over-the-top but appealing nonetheless. The Safari Pub, on the middle level of this three floor extravaganza, has a distinct party atmosphere and regulars range from sports fans who come for the multitude of TV screens to party princesses who strut their stuff and sip the (not cheap) exotic cocktails.

Food●●●◐○ Serv●●●●○ Venue●●●●◐ Value●●●◐○

Coral Bar

Location → Radisson SAS Muscat · Al Khuwayr
Web/email → www.radissonsas.com
24 487 777
Map Ref → 7-B3

It's hard not to notice the fabulous underwater themed murals that adorn the walls. This is a piano bar with live entertainment that changes every three months. The staff are very friendly, offering beers,

Le Pub

Location → Al Falaj Hotel Muscat · Ruwi
Web/email → www.omanhotels.com
24 702 311
Map Ref → 12-C1

Le Pub is situated on the eighth floor of the second oldest hotel in Muscat, next to the Japanese restaurant Tokyo Taro. It has spectacular views over the Ruwi area, especially at night, if you are lucky enough to get one of the two window booths. The bar is very quiet, frequented mainly by in-house guests and local men. In one corner, live entertainment is provided every night and if you're peckish, a menu of light snacks is available.

Food●●●○○ Serv●●●◐○ Venue●●●◐○ Value●●●◐○

Oliver

Location → Sheraton Oman Hotel · Ruwi
Web/email → www.starwoodhotels.com
24 799 899
Map Ref → 12-E2

Whether you are feeling homesick or just keen to while away the afternoon, Oliver makes a good attempt at recreating a traditional old English pub, complete dimly lit tables, alcove seating and English memorabilia dotted around the place. This quiet pub is ideal for catching up with a few mates or just getting away from it all. The service is friendly and the bartenders are only too happy to 'lend an ear', in the traditional sense.

Food●●●◐○ Serv●●●●○ Venue●●●◐○ Value●●●●○

Uptown

Location → Opp Golden Oryx · Ruwi
Web/email → na
24 706 020
Map Ref → 12-D1

A new addition to Muscat's nightlife scene, this is certainly a distinctive hangout. The décor is an unusual fusion of South-East Asian and European, but still in typical swanky bar style with dimly lit ambience, sofa and table seating. A large screen plays the latest sporting events in

one corner of the bar and the simple but moreish bar snacks will keep you ordering from the reasonably priced drinks menu. All the ingredients for a good night out.

Food●●●○○ Serv●●●●○ Venue●●●●○ Value●●●○○

Karaoke Bars

Pavo Real

Location ➔ MSQ Centre · MSQ
Web/email ➔ pavoreal@omantel.net.om

24 602 603
Map Ref ➔ 7-E2

Monday nights are for karaoke at this popular Mexican restaurant and bar. The singers are pretty good and some take it very seriously! Oddly, no dancing is allowed except by special licence. You must book a table, and your song, as the place gets full very quickly.

Omani Bars

Al Khaima

Location ➔ Majan Hotel · Ghala
Web/email ➔ www.majanhotel.com

24 592 900
Map Ref ➔ 6-E4

Whether this is a club or a pub remains open to debate, but what is clear is that this Arabic venue is exclusively male and seems in no hurry to change. The room resembles a small theatre; all seats and tables face the circular 'performance area' in the middle of the room. The band, two musicians and five ladies pump out Arabic tunes at near deafening volume to a limited audience. A place suited to large groups of males for a stag night.

Food●●○○○ Serv●○○○○ Venue●●●○○ Value●●●○○

Pubs

Al Ghazal Pub

Location ➔ Htl InterContinental · Shati Al Qurm
Web/email ➔ www.interconti.com

24 600 500
Map Ref ➔ 8-A4

Set within this five-star hotel, with a friendly atmosphere, a huge selection of beverages, delicious pub grub and live entertainment, the Al

Ghazal Pub is second to none in offering the traditional pub experience. Tables individually partitioned offer diners intimate areas to enjoy a variety of tasty snacks, sandwiches, juicy steaks and fish and chips. Good food, drink, service and reasonable prices ensure this pub is nearly always crowded with regulars.

Food●●●○○ Serv●●●○○ Venue●●●●○ Value●●●○○

Chambers, The

Location ➔ Majan Hotel · Ghala
Web/email ➔ na

24 592 900
Map Ref ➔ 6-E4

Chambers maybe small in size but it's huge in stature. Complete with pool table, large TV, and a few gaming machines thrown in for good measure, this bar is packed with regulars – mostly local and eastern European men. Refreshment offerings are limited – don't expect to find any draft beer here, but the rest of the beverage selection is very reasonably priced. The staff are friendly enough and the overall feeling here is of a working mans pub in the UK.

Food●●●○○ Serv●●●○○ Venue●●●○○ Value●●●○○

Club Bar

Location ➔ Ruwi Hotel · Ruwi
Web/email ➔ www.omanhotel.com

24 704 244
Map Ref ➔ 12-D2

Situated in the heart of the Ruwi business district, this is a small, no-frills hotel bar designed mainly to serve the many businessmen in the area. A friendly, low-lit bar decked out in standard British pub paraphernalia with the addition of a snooker room and quiet, efficient service. It starts off as an unassuming bar and ends when the lively Russian band gets started. A good menu supplements the drink options and cocktail choices.

Food●●●○○ Serv●●●○○ Venue●●●○○ Value●●●○○

Nightclubs

The nightclub scene in Muscat is limited, but the few places available are very busy, even on weekdays. The music is an eclectic mix of up beat Arabic dance music through to funky R&B and smooth soul. The club-savvy may be a little disappointed at the variety of venues but the plethora of people-watching opportunities make up for it!

Karaoke Bars · Omani Bars

Going Out

Though they are growing in number, there are still only a few nightclubs in Muscat but you'll come across quite a few bars that have a nightclub atmosphere and often a dance floor. Live entertainment is popular. Particularly worth a try are Club Safari, Uptown Bar, Duke's Bar and Pavo Real. See Bars, [p.262].

Copacabana

Location → Grand Hyatt Muscat · Shati Al Qurm | **24 641 234**
Web/email → www.muscat.hyatt.com | Map Ref → 7-D1

   10

One of the liveliest nightclubs in Muscat – especially if people-watching is high on your evening agenda. The music is an eclectic mix of the good, the bad and the ugly from anything spanning the last 15 years or so. Entry is largely aimed at couples but local men seem to dominate the dance floor. Service is friendly and efficient, with staff dressed in frilly rumba style outfits, wandering between giant fake palm trees and the long well-stocked bar. Noisy but nice!

Lounge, The

Location → Oasis By The Sea · Shati Al Qurm | **24 602 575**
Web/email → oasisbts@omantel.net.om | Map Ref → 8-A4

   5

Located inside the Oasis By The Sea restaurant, The Lounge takes up three full floors each with a different vibe. One of the most happening nightspots in Muscat, this place is always busy. The bouncers can be choosy with who they decide to let in, which can be frustrating, but smile sweetly and chance your luck. Great table service is available too.

Entertainment

Cinemas

A trip to the cinema is a popular pastime in Oman and movie lovers are reasonably well catered for, although showings are generally limited to the latest Bollywood, Arabic and Hollywood releases. There are two English language cinemas and a few smaller ones, primarily showing films in Hindi and Arabic. Cinema show times are printed (sometimes inaccurately) in a few of the local daily papers and release dates vary considerably. Films don't tend to hang around for long and are well attended so don't delay or you may miss your chance.

Cinemas			
Name	**Tel No.**	**Location**	**Languages**
Al Shatti Plaza Cinema	24 692 656	Shati Al Qurm	A, E
Al Bahja Cinema	24 540 856	Al Khawd	E
Al Nasr Cinema	24 831 809	Ruwi	H
Ruwi Cinema	24 780 380	Ruwi	E, H

Comedy

The regular comedy scene in Muscat is unfortunately limited. However, there are shows on an ad hoc basis. The Green Can Laughter Factory makes regular trips to Muscat and is very well received. Keep an eye on the local press or get your name on hotel mailing lists.

Concerts

Classical music concerts in Muscat are held every now and again but there are no regular long-term events. For information on what is coming up check local newspapers and magazines. Details are often only available about a month in advance of the event. The hotels, mainly the Hyatt Regency and the Al Bustan Palace Hotel, also arrange events, for example with the Royal Oman Symphony Orchestra performing. For pop/rock concerts, again there is no regular scene, although you can catch a few performances at PDO camp (Petroleum Development Oman), the British Ambassador's residence and the City Amphitheatre in Qurm Park (mostly showcasing Asian music). Listen out for details on Oman Radio

Theatre

Other options → **Drama Groups [p.220]**

Theatre in Muscat is limited, but there are occasional professional performances. One highlight is The British Airways Playhouse, which tours all over the world. Due to the constraints of travelling theatre, the cast is usually quite small (don't expect to see *Les Misérables*!). However, the quality of the performance is usually high. The amateur theatre companies always welcome new members, either on stage or behind the scenes. There are also the occasional murder mystery dinners where you're encouraged to display your thespian skills by being part of the performance.

Cinemas · Theatre

Going Out

BUY ME YOU GENIUS!

INSIDERS' CITY GUIDE

Dubai **9th** EDITION

EXPLORER

Bright lights, big city... buy the book!

The unrivalled insider guide to Dubai, and the best source of info for shopping, sleeping, eating, exploring and more. The Dubai Explorer is the ultimate lifestyle companion to help residents, tourists and visitors live this exciting city to the full.

Phone (971 4) 335 3520 • Fax (971 4) 335 3529
Info@Explorer-Publishing.com • www.Explorer-Publishing.com
Insider Guides • Photography Books • Activity Guidebooks • Commissioned Publications • Distribution

EXPLORER
Passionately Publishing

Maps

Maps

User's Guide

To further assist you in locating your destination, we have superimposed additional information, such as main roads, roundabouts and landmarks, on the maps. Many places listed throughout the book also have a map reference alongside, so you know precisely where you need to go (or what you need to tell the taxi driver).

The Muscat overview map (opposite) is at a scale of approximately 1:300,000 (1 cm = 1.3 km). The Oman map (Map 1) is 1:4,000,000, and all other maps are 1:20,000 (1 cm = 200 m).

Technical Info - Satellite Images

The maps in this section are based on rectified QuickBird satellite imagery taken in 2004.

The QuickBird satellite was launched in October 2001 and is operated by DigitalGlobe(tm), a private company based in Colorado (USA). Today, DigitalGlobe's QuickBird satellite provides the highest resolution (61 cm), largest swath width and largest onboard storage of any currently available or planned commercial satellite.

MAPS geosystems are the Digital Globe master resellers for the Middle East, West, Central and East Africa. They also provide a wide range of mapping services and systems. For more information, visit www.digitalglobe.com (QuickBird) and www.maps-geosystems.com (mapping services) or contact MAPS geosystems on (+971 0) 6 572 5411.

Online Maps

If you want to surf for maps online, a good starting point is www.map24.com. This site has detailed maps of countries throughout the Arabian Peninsular (as well as Europe and North America), and allows you to search by street name, hotel name, or by points of interest.

Oman Towns and Cities

The following is a list of the main towns and cities in Oman, which can be found on the Oman map (Map page 1).

Town/City	Map Ref
Ar Rustaq	1-B2
Buraimi	1-B3
Hayma	1-D2
Ibra	1-B1
Ibri	1-B2
Izki	1-B2
Jazirat Masirah	1-D1
Khasab	1-A2
Madha	1-A2
Muscat	1-B1
Muqsin	1-D3
Nizwa	1-B2
Quriyat	1-B1
Salalah	1-E3
Sohar	1-B2
Sur	1-B1

Muscat Area & Street Index

The following tables list the main areas and streets in and around Muscat, and where they can be found on the Muscat maps (Map pages 2 – 15).

Area	Map Ref
Al Bustan	15-A1
Al Ghubbrah	6-E3
Al Khurayis	2-A2
Al Khuwayr	7-C3
Al Mawalih	2-C4
Al Murtafa'ah	3-D4
Al Qurm	8-D3
Al Azaiba	6-B3
Ghala	6-C4
Hayl Al Awamir	2-C2
Madinat As Sultan Qaboos	7-E2, 11-A1
Muscat	10-D4
Mutrah	10-A4
Ruwi	12-D3

User's Guide

Maps

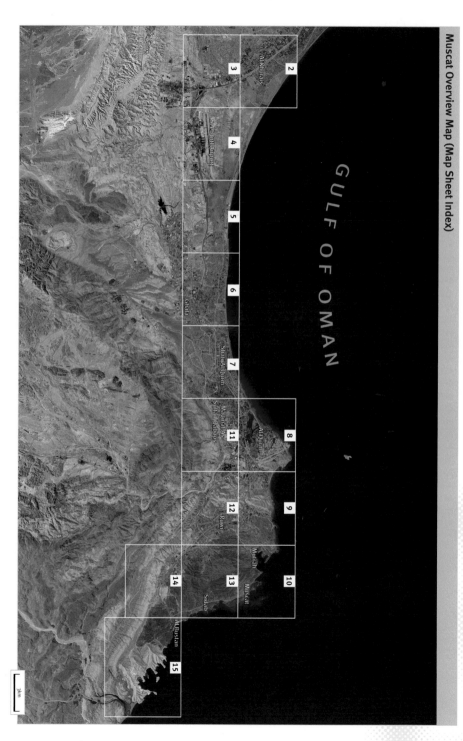

GULF OF OMAN

Street Name	Map Ref	Street Name	Map Ref
27 St	7-E3	Al Sadiyah St	10-D4
38 St	6-E3	Al Seeb Street	2-B2, 2-C4, 3-D1
39 St	7-C4	Al Wadi Al Kabir St	13-A3
40 St	6-E3	Al Wazarat St	7-B2
44 St	6-C3	Al Wilaj St	8-D4
45 St	7-B3	An Nahdah St	11-E1, 12-B2
46 St	5-E2, 6-A2	An Nur St	12-D2
47 St	7-B4	As Saruj St	7-D1
49 St	7-B4	As Sultan Qaboos St	4-B4, 5,A3,6-A3, 8-B4
68 St	5-D2	As Surur St	2-A1, 2-B2, 2-C4
99 St	4-D4, 5-D4	Bab Al Mathaib St	10-D4
A' Shati St	8-A4	Bait Al Falaj St	9-D4, 12-E2
Al Amrat Rd	12-B3	Darsayt St	9-D3
Al Bahri Rd	10-B3	Dawhat Al Adab St	7-A2
Al Baladiyah St	12-E3	Fuhud St	8-D3
Al Bashair St	7-D2	Ghala St	6-B4
Al Burj St	12-D1	Hayma St	8-D2
Al Bustan St	14-B2	Madinat As Sultan Qaboos St	7-E2, 11-A3
Al Fahl St	8-E2	Maydan Al Fath St	9-A4
Al Farahidi St	12-C2	Mutrah St	9-E4, 10-A4
Al Fursan St	12-D2	Muaskar Al Murtafah St	3-E4
Al Ghubbrah St	6-E4	Nizwa Rd	3-A3, 3-D3
Al Hayl Ash Shamaliyah St	2-A1, 2-C3	Qantab Rd	14-E3
Al Ilam St	8-B4, 11-B2	Ras Al Hamra St	8-E2
Al Inshirah St	7-E1	Ruwi Street	9-D4, 12-C1
Al Kharijiyah St	7-E1	Sayh Al Malih St	8-D4
Al Khurayis St	2-D3	Sidab St	13-E3
Al Kuliyah St	7-A3	Souk Al Khuwayr St	7-B3
Al Maaridh St	4-D4, 5-A3	Souk Ruwi St	12-D3
Al Mathar St	4-B4, 4-C4	Street 10	8-E4
Al Mina St	9-E3	Street 35	10-D4
Al Mujamma St	12-D1	Street 63	13-A4
Al Murtafa'ah St	3-D4	Way 2113	3-b1, 3-C1
Al Omran St	5-E4	Way 2811	8-A4
Al Qurm Heights Rd	8-D4, 9-A4, 9-C4	Way 2827	8-A4
Al Qurm St	8-C3	Way 5221	6-A4
Al Rowdah St	2-B1, 2-C2	Way 5007	6-B4
Al Rumaylah St	12-B2	Way 6529	13-A3

Map Legend

- **E** Embassy/Consulate
- **H** Hotel
- **M** Museum
- **S** Souk/Shopping Centre
- **+** Hospital
- **GHALA** Area Name
- **Darsayt** Town Name
- ▬ Motorway
- ▬ Main Road

Map page 1 is at a scale of 1:4,000,000 (1cm = 40km)
Map pages 2-15 are at a scale of 1:20,000 (1cm = 200m)

Map Legend

Maps

DIGITAL GLOBE™

C L E A R L Y   T H E   B E S T

61 cm QuickBird Imagery is the highest resolution satellite imagery available. We offer products and resorces to both existing GIS users and the entire next generation of mapping and multimedia applications.

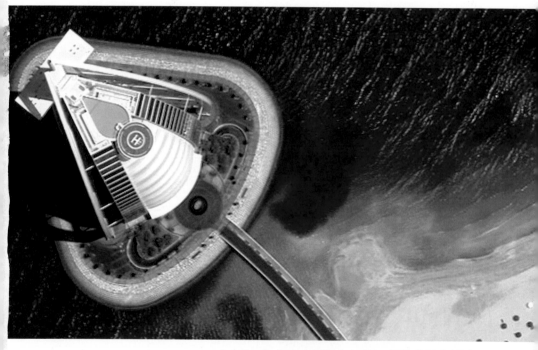

Burj Al Arab, Scale 1:2500, dated May 2003 © DigitalGlobe

MAPS geosystems

DigitalGlobe's Master Reseller serving the Middle East and East, Central and West Africa

MAPS (UAE), Corniche Plaza 1, P.O. Box 5232, Sharjah, UAE.
Tel : +971 6 5725411, Fax : +971 6 5724057
www.maps-geosystems.com

For further details, please contact quickbird@maps-geosystems.com

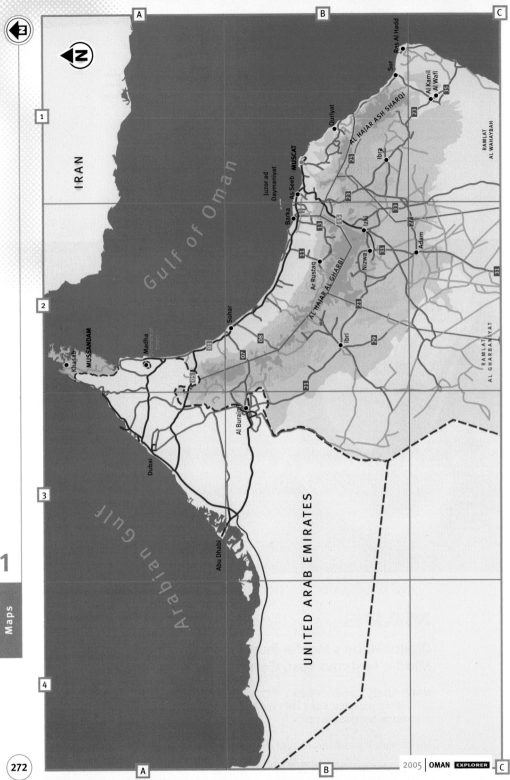

IRAN

Gulf of Oman

Arabian Gulf

UNITED ARAB EMIRATES

MUSSANDAM

RAMLAT AL WAHAYBAH

RAMLAT AL GHARBANIYAT

AL HAJAR ASH SHARQI

AL HAJAR AL GHARBI

Khasab
Madha
Sohar
Dubai
Abu Dhabi
Al Buraimi
Ibri
Nizwa
Izki
Adam
Ibra
Quriyat
MUSCAT
As Seeb
Barka
Ar Rustaq
Juzor ad Daymaniyat
Sur
Ras Al Hadd
Al Kamil
Al Wafi

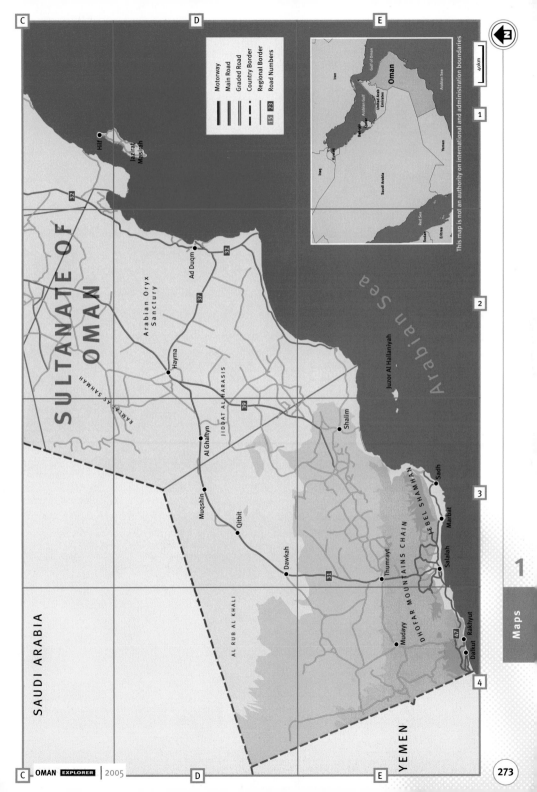

This map is not an authority on international and administration boundaries

Oman

Motorway
Main Road
Graded Road
Country Border
Regional Border
Road Numbers   15 23

SULTANATE OF OMAN

SAUDI ARABIA

YEMEN

Arabian Sea

Jazirat Masirah
Hilf

Ad Duqm

Arabian Oryx Sanctuary

RAMLAT AS SAHMAH

Hayma

JIDDAT AL HARASIS

Al Ghaftyn

Shalim

Muqshin

Qitbit

Dawkah

Juzor Al Hallaniyah

Sadh

JEBEL SHAMHAN

Marbat

Salalah

Thumrayt

DHOFAR MOUNTAINS CHAIN

AL RUB AL KHALI

Mudayy

Dalkut   Rakhyut

32

32

37

39

31

47

1

Maps

N

Imagery courtesy of MAPS geosystems – Master Reseller for *Digital Globe*

Ar Rowdah St

As Surur St

Al Hayl Ash Shamaliyah St

Al Basaateen St

As Seeb St

1

2

AL KHURAYIS

3

Hayl Al Awamir
Al Janubiyah

2

Maps

4

AL MAWALIH

Way 2113

GULF OF OMAN

HAYL AL AWAMIR

Hayl Al Awamir
Ash Shamaliyah

Ar Rowdah St

Al Khurays St

Al Seeb St

Markaz
Al Bahja

200m

2

Maps

MAPSgeosystems

Way 2113

Imagery courtesy of MAPS geosystems – Master Reseller for Digital Globe

1

2

Al Hayl Souk

Oman
Perfume
Factory

3   Nizwa Rd   Nizwa Rd

4

A   B   2005 | OMAN EXPLORER   C

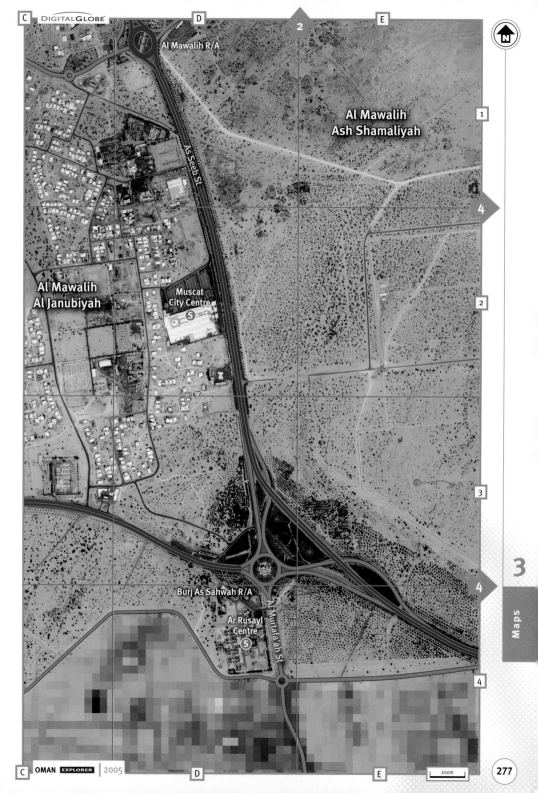

C   D   2   E

N

Al Mawalih R/A

1

Al Mawalih
Ash Shamaliyah

As Seeb St

4

Al Mawalih
Al Janubiyah

Muscat
City Centre
S

2

3

4

Burj As Sahwah R/A

Ar Rusayl
Centre
S

Al Murtafa ah St

3

Maps

4

Imagery courtesy of MAPS geosystems – Master Reseller for Digital Globe

As Seeb International Airport

As Sultan Qaboos St

Murtafa'at Al Matar

Al Matar St

4

Maps

C D E

1

5

2

3

As Sultan Qaboos St

Al Maaridh St

4

Maps

5

Al Matar R/A

Al Matar St

Oman Air

(H) Golden Tulip Seeb

Oman International
Exhibition Centre

99 St

N

GULF

Imagery courtesy of MAPS geosystems – Master Reseller for *Digital Globe*

1

Civil Aviation
Recreation Centre

4

2

As Sultan Qaboos St

3

Al Maaridh St

5

4

Oman Automobile
Club

Maps

4

99 St

A

Al Maha
Golf Course

B

2005 | OMAN EXPLORER

C

O F   O M A N

Police Beach Club

46 St

68 St

Al Maaridh St

99 St

Al Oman St

1

6

2

3

6

4

5

Maps

Imagery courtesy of *MAPS geosystems* – Master Reseller for *Digital Globe*

GULF OF

1

5

46 St

Hillat Awlad Kulayb

2

AL AZAIBA

Oman National Transport Co.

44 St

As Sultan Qaboos St

3

Al Udhaybah R/A

5

Ghala S

5007 Way

GHALA

4

Way 5221

Ghala St

H Holiday Inn Madinah

OMAN

Al Mansuriyah

The Chedi Muscat (H)

46 St

46 St

38 Street

40 Street

AL GHUBBRAH

Al Ghubbrah R/A

Hillat Al Badi

As Sultan Qaboos St

Al Ghubbrah St

As Sultan Qaboos Mosque

Royal Hospital

Ghallah Wentworth Golf Club

Majan Hotel (H)

Al Ghubbrah St

Muscat Private Hospital

200m

6

Maps

GULF OF OMAN

E UAE ·   E Iran   E
E Egypt   E
E France   E Qatar   E Saudi Arabia   Jordan
    E Kuwait

Ministry of Agriculture & Fisheries

Ministry of Civil Services

Ministry of Water & Electricity

Ministry of Labour

Ministry of Development

Ministry of Oil & Gas

Ministry of Post & Telegraph

Ministry of Health

Natural History Museum

Ministry of Interior

M

Al Wazarat St   Al Wazarat St

Al Khuwayr St

Holiday Inn
H   Ice Skating Centre

Souk Al Khuwair St

39 St

AL KHUWAYR

Dawhat Al Adab St

Al Kulliyah St

S

Souk Al Khuwayr

Al Kulliyah St

Bawshar R/A

H Radisson SAS Muscat   49 St

45 St

6

49 St

Way 4907

Way 4901

Janub Al Khuwayr

47 St

7

Maps

Imagery courtesy of MAPS geosystems – Master Reseller for *Digital Globe*

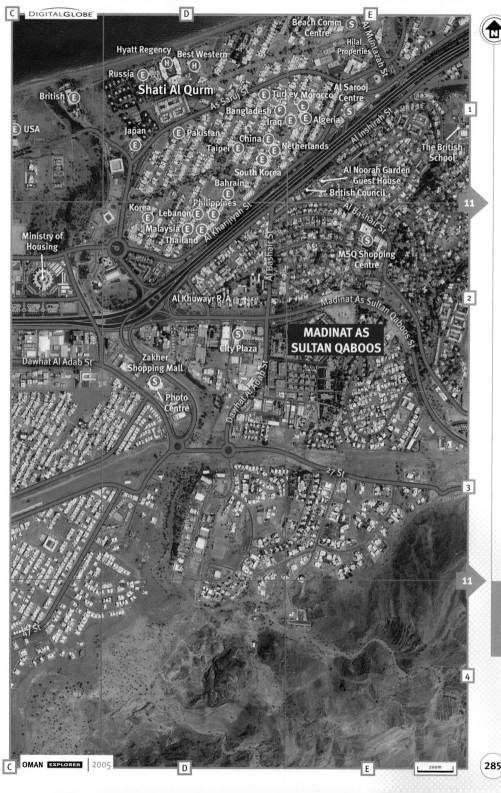

DIGITALGLOBE
N

Beach Comm (S)
Centre
Al Mumtazah St
Hilal (S)
Properties

Hyatt Regency
Best Western
Russia (E) (H) (H)
Al Sarooj
Shati Al Qurm Turkey Morocco Centre
British (E) As Saruj St (E) (S)
Bangladesh (F) Al Inshirah St 1
USA (E) (E) Iraq (E) Algeria
Japan (E) Pakistan China (E) (E) (E) The British
Taipei (E) (E) Netherlands School
(E) (E)
South Korea Al Noorah Garden
Bahrain Guest House
(E) British Council
Korea Philippines Al Bashair St 11
(E) Lebanon (E) (E)
Malaysia (E) (E)
Thailand Al Kharijiyah St MSQ Shopping
Centre

Al Bashair St

Ministry of
Housing
Al Khuwayr R/A Madinat As Sultan Qaboos St 2

MADINAT AS
SULTAN QABOOS
City Plaza (S)
Zakher
Dawhat Al Adab St Shopping Mall
(S)
Photo
Centre
27 St 3

47 St
11

7

Maps

4

Imagery courtesy of *MAPS geosystems* – Master Reseller for *Digital Globe*

1

2

Qurm Heights
Park

Holiday Villa
Hotel
Ⓗ

Ⓗ
Crowne Plaza

3

Marina Cafe

G U L F   O F   O M A N

8

Maps

Sheraton
Qurum Resort
Jawharat   Ministry of
A'Shati   Foreign Affairs   As Saruj   Children's
Ⓗ   Museum
Muscat
InterContinental   A'Shati St.   Ⓜ
4   Al Kharijiyah R/A   Intermediate
Oasis By   Teacher's College
The Sea
Way 2811
Ⓔ Egypt   Way 2827   Al Ilam St.
Ⓗ   As Sultan Qaboos St
Beach Hotel   Al Ilam St.
Ⓔ Tunisia

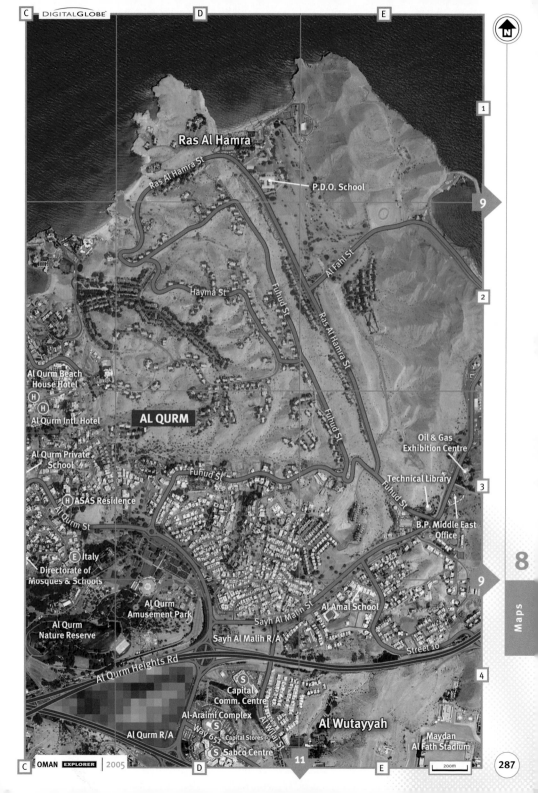

Ras Al Hamra

Ras Al Hamra St — P.D.O. School

Al Fahl St

Hayma St

Fuhud St

Ras Al Hamra St

Al Qurm Beach House Hotel

(H)
(H)
Al Qurm Intl. Hotel

AL QURM

Fuhud St

Fuhud St

Oil & Gas Exhibition Centre

Technical Library

Al Qurm Private School

Fuhud St

(H) ASAS Residence

Al Qurm St

B.P. Middle East Office

(E) Italy

Directorate of Mosques & Schools

Al Qurm Amusement Park

Al Amal School

Sayh Al Malih St

Al Qurm Nature Reserve

Sayh Al Malih R/A

Street 10

Al Qurm Heights Rd

Capital Comm. Centre

Al-Araimi Complex

Al Wutayyah

Maydan Al Fath Stadium

Al Qurm R/A

Way 6511

Capital Stores

(S) Sabco Centre

Al Wfal St

8

Maps

9

1
2
3
4
9
9

Imagery courtesy of *MAPS geosystems* – Master Reseller for *Digital Globe*

MAPSgeosystems

GULF OF

1

8

2

3

9

Maps

8

Al Qurm Heights Rd

Institute of
Health Sciences

Street 10

4

Khoulah
Hospital

Maydan Al Fath St

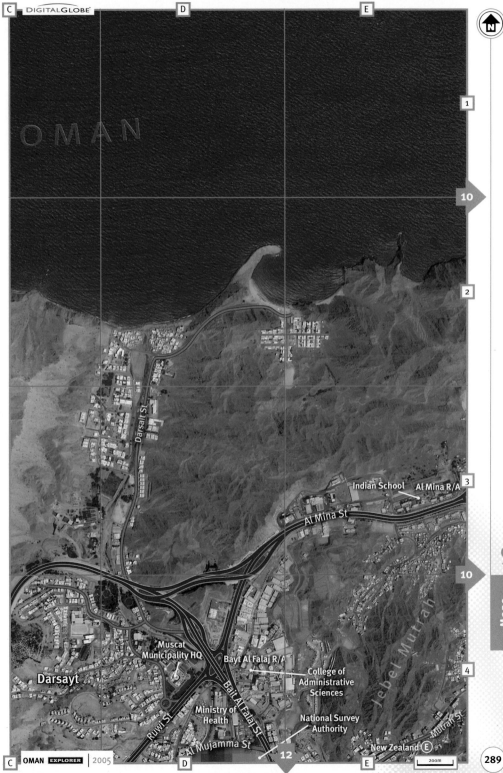

OMAN

1

10

2

Indian School Al Mina R/A 3

Al Mina St

9

Maps

10

Muscat Municipality HQ

Bayt Al Falaj R/A

College of Administrative Sciences

Darsayt

Jebel Mutrah

4

Ruwi St

Ministry of Health

Bait Al Falaj St

National Survey Authority

Al Mujamma St

12

New Zealand (E)

Mutrah St

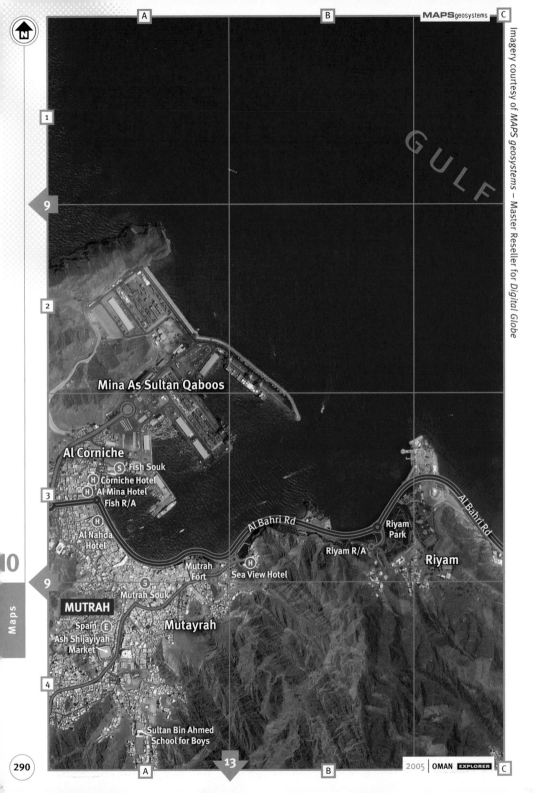

MAPSgeosystems

Imagery courtesy of MAPS geosystems – Master Reseller for Digital Globe

1

9

GULF

2

Mina As Sultan Qaboos

Al Corniche

(S) Fish Souk

(H) Corniche Hotel
(H) Al Mina Hotel
Fish R/A

3

(H) Al Nahda
Hotel

Al Bahri Rd

Riyam
Park

Al Bahri Rd

Riyam R/A

Riyam

Mutrah
Fort

(H) Sea View Hotel

9

(S) Mutrah Souk

MUTRAH

Spain (E)
Ash Shijayiyah
Market

Mutayrah

4

Sultan Bin Ahmed
School for Boys

10

Maps

13

2005 | OMAN EXPLORER

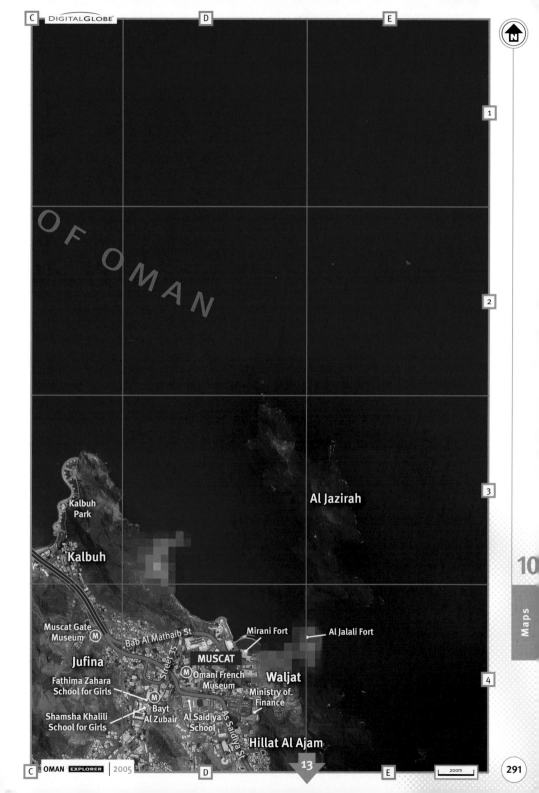

1

OF OMAN

2

3

Al Jazirah

Kalbuh
Park

Kalbuh

10

Maps

Muscat Gate
Museum Ⓜ

Jufina

Bab Al Mathaib St

Street 35

Mirani Fort

Al Jalali Fort

MUSCAT

Ⓜ Omani French
Museum

Fathima Zahara
School for Girls

Ⓜ Bayt
Al Zubair

Shamsha Khalili
School for Girls

Al Saidiya
School

As Saidiya St

Waljat

Ministry of
Finance

4

Hillat Al Ajam

Al Inshirah St

MADINAT AS SULTAN QABOOS

1

Ⓜ Oman Museum

7

Hidden Valley Golf Club

R.O.P. Hospital

2

Al Ilam St

Oman Newspaper House HQ

Madinat As Sultan Qaboos St

3

11

Maps

7

4

Imagery courtesy of MAPS geosystems – Master Reseller for Digital Globe

C D 7 E

N

Mercedes-Benz Showroom

Police Stadium

BMW Showroom

Madinat As Sultan Qaboos St

An Nahdah St

1

Al 'Ilam St

Switzerland E

S Al Harthy Commercial Centre

Muscat Private School

Al Wutayyah

12

2

3

11

Maps

12

4

N

9

Sharia & Law College

Maydan Al Fath St

Al Wutayyah R/A

1

Automobile Showrooms

11

E Mexico
E Chile

An Nahdah St

Ar Rumaylah St

2

Hillat Al Sud

Hatat House

Wadi Adai R/A

Al Amrat Rd

An Nahdah Hospital

3

12

Wadi Adai

11

Maps

4

Al Amrat Rd

9

Armed Forces Museum
M

Oman Hotel
H

Mutrah St.
Mutrah Hotel
H

Mutrah R/A

N

Ruwi St.

Al Mujamma St.

Al Falaj Hotel
H

1

Al Buri St.
As Sultan Shopping Centre
S

13

Al Buri R/A

White Nite Hotel
H

Bait Al Falaj St.

M
National Museum & Islamic Library
H

Norway
Denmark
E
E

An Nur St.

Finland
E

Central Business District

Haffa House Hotel
H

Chamber of Commerce
Sheraton Hotel
H

2

Al Farahidi St.

Ruwi St.

Austria
Canada
E

Al Jami St.

Ministry of Commerce & Industry

RUWI

Al Fursan St.

Ruwi Hotel
H

Oman Comm. Complex
S

Ruwi R/A

India
E

Al Raha Hotel
H

Ruwi St.

Souk Ruwi St.

Al Baladiyah St.

Makha Hotel
H

Al Fursan St.

3

12

An Nahdah St.

Germany
E

Al Hamriyah R/A

Maps

Al Hamriyah

Najiyah Bint Amer School

Al Waljah

4

200m

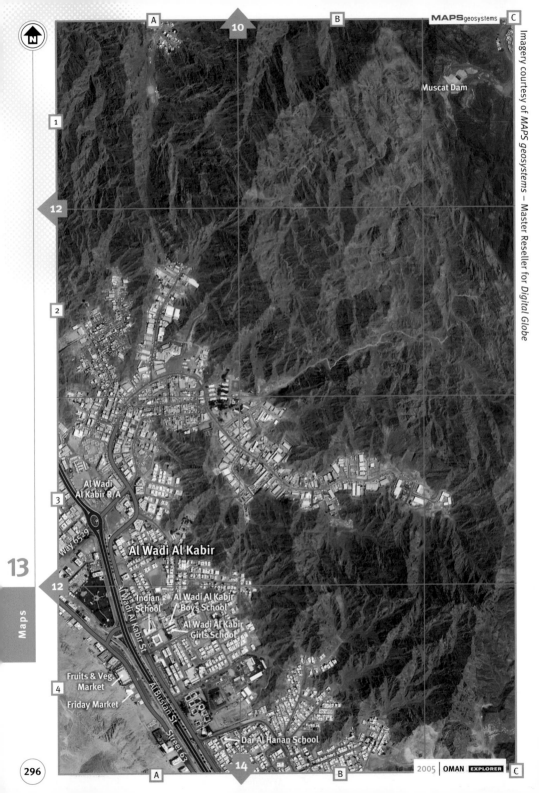

MAPSgeosystems

Imagery courtesy of MAPS geosystems – Master Reseller for Digital Globe

N

Muscat Dam

1

12

2

Al Wadi
Al Kabir R/A

3

Way 6529

Al Wadi Al Kabir

13

Maps

12

Indian
School

Al Wadi Al Kabir
Boys School

Al Wadi Al Kabir
Girls School

Wadi Al Kabir St

Fruits & Veg.
Market

4

Friday Market

Al Bustan St

Street 63

Dar Al Hanan School

2005 | **OMAN** EXPLORER

C

DIGITALGLOBE

Indian Temple

At Tawiyan

Sidab

Sidab St

Rashid Bin Nadhar
School

Sidab Sports Club

Haramel

Zubaida Elementary
School for Girls

Capital Area
Yacht Centre

Jebel Bardah

Sidab St

Marina Bander
Al-Rowdha

Marine Fisheries
& Science Centre

13

Maps

13

Al Bustan Sports Club

Al Wadi Al Kabir
Boys School

Al Nahda Modern
Private School

Ruwi Sports Club

Sri Lankan School

Street 62

Al Wadi Al Kabir St

Al Bustan St

1

2

3

4

14

Maps

Imagery courtesy of *MAPS geosystems* – Master Reseller for *Digital Globe*

C
D
E

Sidab St

13

N

1

15

Al Bustan St

2

Qantab Rd

3

14

15

Maps

4

C
D
E

200m

Imagery courtesy of MAPS geosystems – Master Reseller for *Digital Globe*

N

AL BUSTAN

1

Al Bustan R/A

Al Bustan Palace
Hotel

14

Qantab

Qantab Rd

2

Qantab Rd

3

15

14

Maps

4

To Yiti

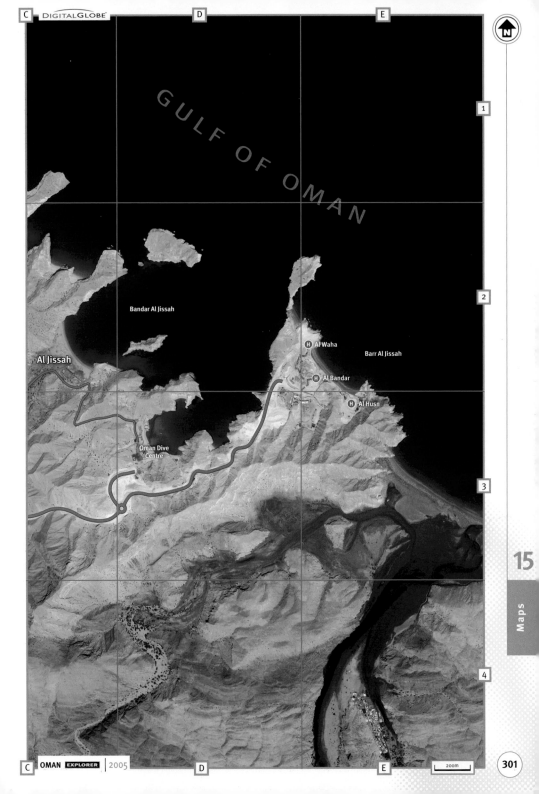

C   DIGITALGLOBE

D

E

N

GULF OF OMAN

1

2

Bandar Al Jissah

Al Jissah

H Al Waha

Barr Al Jissah

H Al Bandar

H Al Husn

Oman Dive
Centre

3

15

Maps

4

Index

EXPLORER

Index

Index

Index

EXPERIENCE OMAN

Historic Places

Thrilling Getaways

Underwater Adventures

Sun-Drenched Beaches

Exotic Souks

Experience Oman with Oman Air Holidays - the holiday division of Oman Air. As the national airline of Oman, no one knows Oman better than we do. With holiday options ranging from treks to the top of rugged mountains to thrilling dives into the sea, we offer you the very best of the beautiful Sultanate of Oman, sprawled with ancient forts, exotic souks, landscapes, colourful culture and pristine beaches. Experience Oman with a great value holiday package from Oman Air Holidays.

Exotic Destinations! OMAN AIR HOLIDAYS *Exciting Packages!*

For more information ask your travel agent or call Muscat: 968 24765129, Salalah: 968 23292777, Khasab: 968 26730487
Al Ain: 971 3 7669943, Abu Dhabi: 971 2 6266800, Dubai: 971 4 3521777, Sharjah: 971 6 5748212